The Scottish Gallovidian Encyclopaedia

The Scottish Gallovidian Encyclopedia,

or,

the original, antiquated, and natural curiosities
of the
South of Scotland;

containing

Sketches of eccentric characters and curious places, with explanations of singular words, terms, and phrases;

interspersed with poems, tales, anecdotes, &c. and various other strange matters;

the whole

illustrative of the ways of the peasantry, and manners of Caledonia;

drawn out and alphabetically arranged.

by

John Mactaggart
1824

The Grimsay Press

The Grimsay Press
an imprint of
Zeticula
57 St Vincent Crescent
Glasgow
G3 8NQ
Scotland

http://www.thegrimsaypress.co.uk
admin@thegrimsaypress.co.uk

First published in 1824
This edition Copyright © Zeticula 2008

First published in this edition 2008
ISBN-13   978-1-84530-051-7
ISBN-10   1 84530 051 3

TO

ALL HONEST AND WARM-HEARTED

GALLOVIDIANS,

THIS WORK IS DEDICATED,

BY

THEIR AFFECTIONATE FRIEND,

AND HUMBLE COUNTRYMAN,

THE AUTHOR.

INTRODUCTION.

A^S it has been fashionable with authors now a long time, to place before their books things called Introductions, I dare say then (to be something like those strange fellows in whose corps I am enlisted), one must appear before mine, though methinks they are not of much use on the whole, but resemble, in general, a methodist *dranting grace* before dinner.

O! that I could make mine seem like a lovely country lass, with fair yellow hair, red cheeks, and bosom divinely moulded; just like her who conducts strangers down a worthy farmer's *trance*, to where, in rural divan, are assembled a heavenly family.

But doubtful am I that it will turn out to be more like a "*rouch curr tyke*," seated in a comfortable manner on some foggy *tomack*, on his "*ain twa tashellie hurdies*," introducing, with many *bouchs* and *bow-wows*, a straggling club of ill-tongued *tinklers*, with their *cuddies*, their *hampers*, and their *ram-horns*, to a wild *clauchan*, situated in the "*loop*" of some wild moorland glen.

Be these things as they may, however, either as fancied, or, like the great English Lexicographer's "Two-and-forty pounder before the door of a swine-stye," I shall proceed as quietly as possible, though, most likely, in a rambling manner.

How, and when the notion of this production first struck my foolish brain, I am at a loss to say; I am inclined to imagine

b

that it is mostly the work of instinct; that the conception of it was created in my scull, when that thick scull itself was created, and afterwards expanded as it expanded; for, from my youngest days I have been a wanderer amid the wilds of nature, and keenly fond of every curious thing belonging to my native country; while Providence has surely been very kind to me in this respect, for casting my lot in a nation among a rare and singular class of mankind.

There is nothing I am prouder of than that I am a *Scotchman*, and, I may add, a *Scotch Peasant* too; for where on all the earth is there a country that can be compared to Scotland, in every noble thing that elevates a nation? and where is there a class of human beings to be found like her peasantry? they are not only an honour to the land they live in, but a credit to the whole world, though I, for one, add little to their glory.

The songs which have been produced by them, charm some of the inhabitants of every zone. Italian ditties, formed by the most tuneful bards of that country, are but like the " *Cheeps o' the Strowmouse*," to the mellow notes of the " *Mavis*," when compared to them; and when the lays of the land, like a " *boot*," sink so far beneath those of the glens of the north, those of no other department of the globe dare be sung in competition with them.

But the divine art of a Burns, or an Etterick Shepherd, is not by any means the only thing which upraises, or has upraised, the " *kintra-folks o' Auld Scotland*," they have it in their power to brag of producing learned men and philosophers; they have turned out Euclids and Socrates's. *Mungo Park*, too, the celebrated traveller, was a peasant; but, above all, they have the patriot *Wullie Wallace*, whom none but a Switzerland Tell can be put on the weigh-beam with; and, what is all this to their warm honest hearts, their tender feelings, their simple manners, and their strong independent minds? He would be a writer of pith, indeed, who could praise them too much, and one of matchless impudence who could revile them; they are, though, in need of neither, for they exist before the eyes of the world, and speak for themselves.

Yet for all, till of late, the Scotch peasantry have been allowed to remain on their dear rural mountains and dales, without being ever looked at almost by travellers, or said a word about by historians. It was not until they themselves found out the way of noting upon paper, that any thing respecting them has come to light; and their great modesty hath not allowed them even yet to say very much.

We have volumes on volumes, as many as would fill a *score* of *whurl-barrows,* all wrote respecting our *Kings, Queens,* and " *ither big fowk,*" yet hardly a word said about the " *people;*" nor is this neglect to be wondered at, when we consider what noise and stir these nobles made in the days of yore; no poor *penman chap* durst think or speak of any other creatures but them, when guns are a " *crackin aff at our lugs,*" and dirks a driving into " *briskets*" to the *hilt*; few are so bold as be so composed; as to tell old tales or sing a *bunch* " *o' hamely ballads.*"

So then, our works in the vernacular language of the olden time are but scanty; and suppose there had been more, suppose there had been yet extant the poems of fifty bards as old as " *Tom the Rhymer,* or *Barbour,*" still I am inclined to think that the lingo of those distant days, as spoken by the peasantry, could not be hunted out; the natives mostly of every nation, have generally at least two tongues they work with, the rustic and the polite, the one spoken by the grandees, the other by the commonalty; now, methinks, our old bards have all written in the former, for it is the same language with ancient English and German, in which we find their books wrote, and this was the court language of their day; for my own part, I doubt there has never been a genuine *rustic MS.* of an ancient date come before the world.

But true it is, there is no race of men stands less in need of historians to record their deeds and draw their manners than these I have been talking of; for, as they abide so close by the laws of nature, their variations are few, their artless simplicity admits of little change to take place, though learning may be a *boggle* for frighting away some of their *freets* and superstitious observances, yet these they do not in a hurry forget for all; for though some of them now may fail, for instance, to hold " *auld*

b 2

halloween," still they know well how it was wont to be held, and the same with every other concern of the time gone by. There are still many who see *fairies* yet, and believe in the tale of *warlocks, ghaists, wraiths,* and *witches,* and while there are such persons, and such there always will be in Scotland, nothing of ancient fun and fancy has a chance to be lost. And so long as old people delight to talk about themselves, and young ones listen, and so long as such goodly things as *forenichts* are kept up, it is likely that the most of what respects the " *kintrafowk"* will be known, when time is a very " *lyart-headed auld carle.*"

So I scamper along rather in the " *ram stam"* manner, and a beautiful introduction is doubtless a composing : fearless quite of criticism am I, and by no means sharkish inclined for fame ; this work, intended from the beginning a *present* to my native country, makes me no way afraid that it shall soon perish; it will be found in many a rustic library of the south of Scotland, scores of years after I am in the grave; it will be a book that will never create much noise, yet still it will not be in a hurry forgot; in that same " *bole"* with the " warks" of *Allan Cunning-ham, Burns, Nicholson, Peden's Prophecies,* and *Rutherford's Letters,* will it take its place. And though some, in looking it over, may laugh and wonder how any body of common sense would take time up writing and printing such *silly*-looking matters, still the more they consider the affair the less they will be inclined to wonder, and at last feel rather disposed to come over to my side of the question : for I have heard a good *Scotch tale* laughed at by Scotchmen, and ratherly ridiculed at the first and second reading, and an *English poem* praised at first glance to the skies, which, in a little time, changed hues like the chamelion, changed so that the darling poem was not spoke about at all, whereas the other was read and better read, until a lasting edition became printed on the heart.

Perhaps it may be thought that I am sporting myself at present at *vanity fair,* but I beg to say that I am quite serious; I am prophecying what experience tells me will come to pass, for little of this faulty book of mine was composed in the closet, in the musty library of cobwebs; no, it was gathered by my own eyes and ears, concocted in my own slender intellect while at my rural employment, and wrote down on scraps of paper as

I found it convenient, in the midst of the works of nature, in the open air, beneath the flaring sun, in a *quarry hole* perhaps. Sometimes again on a " *brae side*," and *ablins* whiles in a " *thick wud*," or on the back of a " *grey stane*;" the whole, therefore, has the smell, as it were, of Nature; her rudeness is about it, and when her *plaid* keeps the shoulders of any thing warm, that thing looks contented indeed.

No *Advocates' library* has been flung open to me—no *Auchenleck MS.* has been given to favor my researches—the whole is the doing of habit and memory—never having the opportunity to receive regular education—my learning has been all got by snatches—and good *hints* have been of service to me. And this I regret the less, for had I been a mighty scholar, books would have filled my brain; I could have discovered few *Nootka Sounds*, or places and things out of the common navigator's tract; and more so, there was little need that I should be deep read in the *Earse*, the ancient Scandinavian, and Norse languages, in order that I might hit the roots of the strange words I bring forward; (as the worthy Dr. Jamieson has bravely done, with the Scotch words found in books;) for if he pleases, he may give, if he can, the derivations of my words, caught as flying from the *Peasant's mouth*.

He may rummage the archives of yore to satisfy the throbbing heart of the inquirer. I will take the world as it stands, and see what I can find to please myself and other rustics:—some of the Doctor's words I have also put down to make mine more complete, and it will be found I am obliged to differ from him whiles with respect to their meanings. It is not one man nor ten that can compose a national dictionary; it takes much time, and many writers, to produce a standard, and it will also be found, it is to be hoped, that I *copy* nothing from him, nor any other.

I have none to thank for lending me a hand to perform the job— indeed, I asked none; the whole was composed without any knowing but myself that such a concern was on the " *stocks*," by keeping the thing dark I came on better; for none were afraid to talk with me on old matters, because they did not suspect I was " *takin notes*;" had they thought that, the " *auld wives*" and many others would have trembled for me, and keep'd their mouths sealed. As it was, it required me to use some craft in order to get at information I wanted; by putting questions direct nothing is obtained, but to talk in a careless manner about the subjects wanted, as if it was little matter about them, then every thing comes bolting out.

From those characters most famous for originality of mind, I received the things of greatest value; these are all mostly patriotic Gallovidians, and scorn to lose any of that darling legacy left them by their forefathers; they scorn to lisp English, but tell their honest tales in plain " *Braid Scotch.*"

For there are many classes of peasantry in Scotland, they are by no means all " *tarr'd wi' the same stick*," as the saying is. Their various situations and various tempers help to make the difference. Those of the *Lowthian* and *Berwickshires*, for instance, are quite different from those of *Yarrowdale* and *Galawater*, and just because the one is a level, fertile, ploughable tract, and the other a pastural land, of hills, of glens, and wild mountains. The natives of these latter pleasant places have their minds more poetically tinged than the former, being much more among the works of nature; and then, being in general shepherds, they have leisure to behold and admire her in every form, while the others are confined to the arts of agriculture, and are obliged to grovel in the earth without almost having time to look up at the sun even for a moment. In every way do peasants so differently situated differ from each other; and in nothing more than their language. The dung-cart hind has a stinking slang which he gilds his turnip ideas with, whereas the other plaids his rare fancy in pure simple words, which are at once pleasingly melancholy and beautiful.

Neither of these ranks of peasants though, whom I have been talking about, are the same with those of the South of Scotland; they occupy a place somewhere between them, and partake a little of what belongs to both. They are not exactly of the mountain nor of the plain, but of the hills, the hollows, the woods, and the waters between; their imaginations wallow not in putrid sludge, neither do they live with phantoms beyond the moon, and spirits of the blast; but with matters of a manly and strong substantiality.

When tracing the nature of their language, it is soon seen that they are rather of a Celtic and Saxon origin; the three letters "*och,*" which terminate many of their words, strike one at once, that old Gaul has been amongst them with a witness; and the various terms which have their roots in the Saxon and Teutonic, bespeak the Scandinavians having, too, "a finger in the pie." However, I doubt not but my natives of the South use many strange words, which neither Celt or Saxon ever mouthed—but tribes of more remote antiquity than any of them. Who knows but old "*Daddie Druid,*" who dipped so deeply into the works of nature, might have let a few of his rare secrets escape his temple *aneath the gnarl'd oak tree,* for there are few races of beings on the earth a match for them at mimicating the sounds into words, which Nature herself is heard to utter; not a sound she emits by any of her works, but they follow her to an astonishing closeness; and so a good part of their tongue is of an universal stamp, and might be understood by the inhabitants of almost every country.

Thus the word "*guldering,*" which we use to express the sound a turkey cock emits when in wrath, with his tail "*up-fan'd*" and "*bubble red,*" is much like "*glowglowter,*" used for the same purpose by the French and Germans.

But I must be thinking of coming to a conclusion, and the sooner I suspect that happens, the more I shall look like a wise man.

If any consider themselves hurt by the mention I may have made of them in the course of the work, their pardon I ask, for I am by no means of a surly temper; and though I sometimes bite my own tongue between my teeth, it is because I am not aware that it is in a place liable to be bitten; so if I have injured any one, it is because I was not aware of that either.

Those whom I have drawn as originals, as surely they are, will not rail against me, for originals care not what is said by any one respecting them; and as for the errors of the work, and many there are in it, let them rest on my own *broad back.* Works of this kind are always fuller of errors than any others; also, should any be displeased because I have not taken notice of some curiosity which was a favourite of their's, be it told, that I was either not of their way of thinking, or that I knew nothing about it.

If the concern ever comes to a *second edition*, a thing not to be expected, in this *century* at least, it may be made more complete by the mention of what has escaped notice—till then, it may remain as it is; and if I could hear the genuine opinion of one honest warm-hearted *rough countryman*, and that opinion favourable, then I would be beyond the grasp of the fangs of all the *critics* in the world—for his judgment is dictated by Nature, and when she is pleased, all is well.

I am pretty sure already, that there are some *" kintra-fowk"* it will not anger very much, and that they will let me share *" pot-luck"* with them, when I take my fishing rambles away by the wild moorland *" burns."*

Perhaps some may think I deal too much in *poetry*; I must tell those, that it is not to shew that I know a trifle about the art—for a *" trifle"* I only know, being *no poet.* But I am fonder always of something wild and out-of-the-way, than if it were humble and tame; that is to say, I admire the manners of the *" Foumart"* before those of *"Bawdrons;"* and a *"Brock"* more than a *" Lap dog."* So, God bless my friends, and Heaven ever smile on the natives of the South of Scotland; for a better race of beings is no where to be found between the sea and the sun.

Torrs,
February 12th, 1823.

THE
GALLOVIDIAN ENCYCLOPEDIA,

&c. &c.

A.

A'—All. But the natives of Galloway, and their neighbours of the South, take a larger *mouthfu'* of it than the other people of Scotland ; that is to say, they pronounce it broader, and can be known to belong to that district of the *Làn o' Cakes* by this little circumstance.

ABEE—Alone. *Let me abee, or let me bee* ; means, let me alone ; these phrases are much used by children, and wanton maidens ; the latter of whom desire their *Lads* often to *let them abee*—When the truth is, they would take it very ill were they obeyed.

ABEIGH—Aloof, shy, &c. *She keep'd hersell abeigh* ; means, she *fought shy*, that her affections were not easy to gain.

ABLINS—Perhaps, likely, may be, &c. Sometimes a word pronounced *able*, is used in its stead.

ABOK, or Yabok. A name for a *gabbing*, impudent, chatting child.

ABOON—Above. *The Lift aboon.* The Firmament above.

ABOON-BROE—Above water. It is said of those who can hardly keep themselves from sinking in the horrific pool of misery, that they can barely keep themselves *aboon-*

A

broe; broe, in this and all other cases, meaning, a *tap liquid* of some kind or other.

ABOUT THE BUSS—About the bush. A very old phrase, signifying, not downright, the way of a mean sculking coward. Thus we say of an honest man, that he never *gaes about the buss;* he never attempts to cheat, has no doublings to defraud; he makes *nae lang wund stories,* and *whaups i'the rape.* No, no; he drives right forward, through bush and brier.

In that good old Poem, the *Cherrie and the Slae,* written by Captain Alexander Montgomery, about 1590, and printed by Bob Walgrave, some seven years after, we meet with this phrase respecting the *Buss* very frequently; as in the 46th verse, when branding dread, danger, and despair, as cowards :

> " They are mair faschions, nor of Feck,
> " Zon fazards durst not for their neck,
>   " Clim' up the craig to us.

> " Frae we determined to dee,
> " Or else to clim Zon Cherrie Tree,
>   " They bade—About the Buss."—&c.

And in the 77th verse of the same Poem, it is said of Experience,

> " For Authors quha alleges us,
> " They wad na gae about the buss,
>   " To foster deidly feid, &c."

In no other author of the Captain's day, nor in any I have seen before him, is this phrase to be met with ; and as it is heard used at the present day ten times in Galloway, for once in any other part of Scotland, it may help to prove, that Montgomery was either a native of the country, or well acquainted with its language. It is said he was born in Germany, but that the greater part of his life he passed in Scotland, but where in Scotland, has been a question ; various towns and counties claim him. Tradition says he lived at Cummingstown, on the banks

of the Tarf—Galloway—now known by the name of
Cummstown; this seems very probable, for many reasons, but particularly from passages in his Poem, actually
pointing out the natural scenery of this seat of the Cum-
ming. In truth, his muse seems often to have heard the
roarin sough of the *Doachs o' Tongueland Water.*

ABREED—Abroad. Scatter it *abreed* to the *four wuns*
means, scatter it abroad, to the mercy of the winds.

ACKAVITY, ACKWAVITY, or ACKWA.—The chief of all
spirituous liquors, viz. Whisky, when taken to excess,
does not even make such a wreck of the human constitution as others do, such as rum and brandy, and when
taken in moderation, as it should be, there is none other
half so good. Far be it from me to hold up any thing
that may be thought allied to vice; and if whisky be so,
as many grave men think, I have little cause to eulogize
it, being no great bottle man : nature having given me a
frame of body that is a sworn foe to any fluid stronger
than *Adam's Wine.* However, as the majority of men are
moulded different, I will say, that a *dram o' gude ackwa*
and *cauller-water,* refreshes a fainting heart, in a sultry
simmer day; and the same quantity o' Farintosh, is quite
comfortable to take in a cauld wunter morning, while
even a *Tumbler or twa o' Toddy,* looks social on an evening. So I won't join with M'Neil and others, in saying
it is the *Scaith o' Scotlan.* I am more inclined to *side* with
Burns to a certain extent. Scotland may be very thankful
that it is her prevailing *drink* ; as a *drink,* like every other
nation, she must have; the English have their drowzy
brown stout, the Turks their opium, the South Sea Is-
landers their kava; but what brings on a quicker, or a
happier intoxication, than the pure *Mountain dew?* how
it exhilirates the soul, how it exposes the sons of men,
and shows them in their true colours, be they good, bad,
witty, or how; it tries their strength, as itself is tried by

specific gravity; letting it be known, the *beads they sink or swim*. The old song is at this of it:

> " A man whan he's sober is deils ill to ken,
> " Gude sooks than there's nae kenning o' him,
> " But prime him wi nappie than ye mae gae ben,
> " And learn what he is—for 'twill show bim."

Many have whisky to be a slow poison, which, perhaps, it may be, in a certain degree, particularly if any way adulterated.   A person told the celebrated Billy Marshall the *Tinkler*, once, that it was a *slaw pizion*— " It maun be deils slaw indeed. quoth the Gypsey Chief, for I hae tooted it owre in nogginfus now, for mair than a hunner year, and am tae fore yet hale and fear." He died when 120 years of age.

And once, a *Kirkcubrie carter*, having brought some coals to a certain very abstemious medical man, the doctor, according to the custom of the country, presented him with a *dram o' whisky* for by-payment.   The carter drank it off in a moment, making his *wee finger twirl* above the quickly emptied glass, in fine stile; when, quoth the Doctor, with some emphasis—" That's a nail in thy coffin, Sanders." " May be sae (replied the drunkard) I wish it were fu o' sic tackets."

ADDER-BEADS—Beads made by Adders. Such beads are common now in museums, and other repositories of rarities; they are mostly about the size of a hazle-nut, oval shaped, of an amber hue, but full of specks of other beautiful colours—The hole through them is about half an inch in diameter, and large enough to admit a child's little finger. That the Adders make them, is never doubted, but how, is as yet never exactly known; the country people say it is gone about this way. Seven old Adders, with manes on their backs, have a meeting in some snug heather bush, before the sun; with them is also a long small white one; operations are begun by the hairy reptiles, putting forth from their mouths a glutinous matter of a honey colour. The white Adder moulds this into a certain shape, forming the hole by creeping through it— and still as it creeps in-through and out-through the matter, the old ones keep salivating it—so the bead is constructed, and left to harden in the sun.

But (add the peasantry) it is impossible to stand any time, and behold them thus at work in their bead manu-factory—as at these times they are full of wrath and swiftness; so that if the observer be seen by them, he has little chance to get off alive.

For my own part, I much doubt if this operation of the viper hath ever yet been beheld by human eyes; the beads are found in the places where the Adders abound, and no where else; they are found too, in greater or less quantities, according as the serpents are for number; so every thing about them argues they are a production of the Adder, but for what purpose they form them none can tell; the subject, though, methinks, might be dipped deeper into by naturalists than it is. To illustrate it, however, a little farther, I may give the Poem of the

ADDER-BEAD.

Sawners Beiliebank a peeling
   Heathery scraws upon the moor,
To riggin tight his simple shieling
   The shiel whilk did his bairnies co'er.

Sol was beeking warm and brissling,
   In a heather buss hears he
Fuffing soun's—and meikle fissling,
   Sawners steps aside to see.

But—mercy on his auld grey beardy,
   Sic a sight he never saw;
A sight for whilk he was afeard, ay,
   While a day on him did daw.

Adders rough, and gruesome horrid,
   Casting on their amber-bead;
A white ane, wattled and bored,
   Gluey tongues did slake and feed.

Sawners at the knees did totter,
   Deil the tae the man cud gang;
Still he stood—his flesh did sotter,
   Sure was he they wad him stang.

Travellers hae aften stated
   That Indian bodies, ow're the sea,
Hae been like Sawners fascinated,
   Unfit frae rattlesnakes to flee.

Ay, he shook and swat and glowred,
   Blinkers winking no ava ;
Expecting just to be devoured,
   But faith, his Flauchter-spade did fa'.

This broke the charm—than Sawners held it,
   Down the moor wi speed he flew :
What spangs he made, how quick he wheeld it,
   Thinking the adders did pursue.

And that they wampuzd just ahin him,
   Gaining on him every spang ;
And that they'd soon be darting in him
   Mony a witterd poisonous stang.

Up the fell his son was climing,
   Wi' the nocket in his han' ;
He sees his father bounding, skimming,
   For what, he cudna understan.

" What's a' the hurry, father," cries he,
   " See ye the boggle o' the moor ?"
But the parent never spies he,
   Nor yet heard him, we are sure.

The boy, thus frightened wi' his father,
   Flang awa the mid-day chack ;
And down the brae, amang the heather,
   Followed him what he could crack.

At last the body, sairly scared,
   Got within his castle gate ;
He dash'd it too, and had it barred,
   Quaking at an unco rate.

" Gude preserve us, my dear Sawners,
   " What in a' the warl is wrang ;"
(Quo' the wife) than stan's and won'ers
   Wi' a wrinkled craig fu' lang.

He took himsell a skilt o' water,
   Pech'd and drauk, and pech'd again ;
Than tell'd his family a' the matter,
   How he was sae nearly slain.

At length his restless pulse mair queem grew,
  He'd tae bed and tak a nap ;
His kind Lucky glad did seem now,
  And wi' the cuiting him did hap.

Through the neighbours ran the story,
  Ilk ane trimmled that did hear ;
Aroun' the shielin, on the morrow,
  Shepherds armed did appear.

Some had whups and some had cudgells,
  A' had tykes wad worry fast ;
Some had meikle heather budjells,
  To blaze and throw the de'ils aghast.

An Irish lad frae county Derry,
  Brag'd that he'd do this and that ;
By St. Patrick, swore he merry,
  " Adders will not harm a Pat."

Sawners, laith to be the leader
  O' the daring armed squad,
Paddy choose to be its header,
  Let the sport be good or bad.

Soon aroun' the awfu centre
  Circled the crew wi' speed ;
Close beside it ane did venture,
  And beheld the Adder-bead.

He click'd it up, and in his bosom
  Clap'd the bonny freckled gem,
Crying—" It will deck my blossom,"
  Lovely flower o' sappie stem.

Whilk was Sawnies' bonny daughter,
  Wi' her merry een sae gleg ;
Lang the lad had wooing sought her,
  Nee'r refused him darling Meg.

Collies' thrang about were snuffing
  The awfu game cud no be seen ;
At length, out wampuxd three loud fuffing,
  Rough and strong wi' blazing ee'n.

Now an unco kauch and hurry
  Mang the bravoes did begin ;
Whups did smak and Collies' worry
  Down the moor did Paddy rin.

Was ere it thought the son of Erin
  Wad been the first to turn and flee,
But na matter, without fearin,
  Gallovidians stood the spree.

And o'ercam the hules completely,
  Adders killed they nine or ten ;
Clear'd the moor o' vermin neatly,
  Fire made them quickly sten.

He wha found the bead swunged monniest,
  A gallant handsome younker he ;
His sweetheart was amang the bonniest
  Maidens ever man did see.

By a ribbon he suspended
  Roun' her bonny neck wi' speed,
The what he frae the serpents rended,
  The amber shining Adder-bead.

Soon the blythesome pair war married,
  Pretty damsels did they breed ;
And the prettiest always weared
  The hinnie spreckled Adder-bead.

Sae whan we meet in Gallowa
  A fair-haird lass wi' cheeks fu' red,
We say she's bonny—ay, and braw,
  Weel wordy o' an Adder-bead.

God bless them a', exclaims the poet,
  May they lack o' lads ne'er dread,
And mony hae, and yet not know it,
  Title for an Adder-bead.

This is a very silly Poem, but given here merely because it treats of that mystic subject the Adder-bead.

ADDER O' BALDOON.—Amongst the many traditions of Galloway, appears one, entitled the *Adder o' Baldoon*, the foundation of which is, that a reptile of enormous size was killed about sixty years ago, on the fertile *howms* of Baldoon, near Wigtown ; it measured somewhere about eight or nine feet in length, and in thickness that of a man's arm. A shepherd traced it out one dewy morning, by the path it had left on the wet grass, and his dog having come up on it beyond a dyke, a dreadful conflict ensued between *Collie* and our *Boa Constrictor*; the strong *Tyke*, however, succeeded in worrying the huge monster, but not until the serpent had stung him so that he died next morning. The herd himself was so panic struck with the scene, that he was never like *himsell* again ; and died soon afterwards; poor fellow, he fancied that it was an

Hurchon that *Rover* had fallen in with at first—little did he expect it was an Adder, and one of such magnitude. Such seems to be nearly the true part of the tale. The stuffed skin of it is yet to be seen, I am told, in some gentleman's museum in that part of the Country. Warm imaginations have made a good deal of the tale though. They give it wings and claws, and finishes a dragon, which was as thick as a *corn sack fu'*; so the whole becomes good food for *bairnies* to take during a *Forenicht*.

ADDER'S AITH.—What follows is an Adder's Oath—

" I hae made a vow—and I'll keep it true,
" That I'll never stang man, through gude sheep's woo."

So it may well keep it, for it cannot break it. The Adder cannot pour its venom into a wound made by its fangs, through any thing woollen; the wool brushes away the virus; there is some invention in this *Aith*, ascribed to the viper. It is in vain to take the oath of a man, for instance, who is base, poisonous, and of a reptile nature, for he will break all oaths, and sting as before; but when he is sworn from harming any thing that is not in his power to harm, whether the oath be off or on; then all's well.

ADDER SLOUGHS.—The outer skins Adders moult at certain periods; whether annual or no is not yet discovered; they are very common on lands infested by those reptiles.

ADDER STANGS.—The peasantry in general think, that the tongue of the viper is its sting; as it comes nearer to their idea of a sting, from its similitude to that of insects; but it is two large projecting teeth in the upper jaw which do the devilry, called fangs; they are rooted in bags of poison, and when the serpent strikes them into any thing, they are pushed back on the same bags, which squeezes the venom out of the valves, to flow down the conducting teeth into the wound; though this be all

known to some, many argue in favour of the tongue; that
it has *witters* on it like a *fishhuik,* and as blue as the
main spring o' a watch.

ADIST.—The opposite of *ayout.* The one is on the nearest side of any thing, the other the reverse. An old
riddle respecting the *nettle* runs this way—

" Heg Beg adist the dyke—and Heg Beg ayout the dyke—
" Gif ye touch Heg Beg—Heg Beg—will gar ye byke."

AGGIE.—A name for Agnes.

AGLEE.—Not direct, off at a side; when the target is
missed at *shootings* by a marksman, he is said to have
shot aglee. Those, too, who follow what nature never
intended them to follow, are said to guide the genius
Aglee.

AHIN—Behind. The same with *Ahint.*

AIKS O' KIRKCONNEL.—A celebrated haunt for the fox
in Galloway.

AIN—Own. *Ainsell,* ownself.

AIR—Oar. Also for, early.

AIRNIN' CLAISE.—The art of smoothing clothes with a
warm iron.

AIRNS O' A PLEUCH.—Those implements of iron which
belong to a plough, and which have to be repaired frequently at *smiddies* during the ploughing season. What
a consequence ploughmen assume sometimes when they
meet at forges—giving directions to Vulcan how they want
their *airns set*—how the *couter* must hang to the *sock*—how
the *beam* and *head* agree—if land be *scanty* or *plenty,*
and what not—to plough as *ein as a die*—and put a *skin*
on the *furr* as *sleek as a salmon.*

AIRT—To encourage devilry. Thus we say of those who
puff up others to fight, that they are *airters* of the savage
broil; the word is never used in the other sense—to in-
cite to laudable actions—we never hear of any *airted on*

to read the bible for instance—but boys are said to airt on *tykes to collieshangie ilk ither.* This word *airt* is no way connected, in my opinion, with the other *airt,* which refers to the compass.

AIRT O' THE CLICKY.—When a pilgrim at any time gets bewildered, he poises his staff perpendicular on the way, then leaves it to itself, and on whatever direction it falls, that he pursues; and this little trait of superstition is termed the *Airt o' the Clicky*—the direction of the staff. And townsmen, when they mean to take a trip into the country for pleasure, and are quite careless to what part of it they wend their way, this they decide sometimes in the same way—the fallen stick determines the course to be pursued; and often as much amusement is found this way, as if the chart had been pricked out. But there are few buridan asses which will starve between bundles of hay, not knowing which to turn to—so those generally, who seek direction from the staff, mostly cause it to gravitate toward the place they have a secret inclination to go to. As in the *auld sang* of " Jock Burnie"—

> Ein on en' he pais'd his rung, then
> Watch'd the airt its head did fa',
> Whilk was east he lap and sung then,
> For there is dear bade—Meg Macraw.

AIRTS O' THE LIFT.—The points of the compass.

AISLERWARK.—Masonic work, with hewn stones.

AIZLETEETH.—The double teeth—the grinders.

ALECK—Alexander, the man's name, the same with Sawnders, Sawny, &c.

ALICREESH—Spanish licorice, made of the refuse of sugar. Is made up in black rolls, about a foot in length, and sold in the grocers' shops; it is much used in breweries; by people troubled with the cough, and by those who have been in the habit of chewing tobacco. This singular term I have given for it, as used by the greater part of the

natives of Scotland, comes from the ancient word *ali*, a
compound, and *creesh*, grease. Rustic lovers tell other
whiles, that they are as sweet as *Alicreesh*. In truth,
lovers are oft at a loss to find sweet enough comparisons
for their darlings: a fellow once would write a letter to
the dictation of a lover, and asking, " what he'd break off
with," the poor wretch, with the burning heart, replied—
" Say first, 'Tam'—" *and in big letters—' My dearest,
dearest Henniesuckle."*

ALLAN-HAWKS—A sea-fowl with very small wings, common to be met with on the shores of Britain; its colour is
black, all but on the breast, there it is white. I wonder
how Edwards, Willoughby, and others, who have treated
of British birds, have missed this one in their ornitholo-
gies. It is similar to the puffin in size, but it cannot fly;
often after storms they are found driven in dead upon
shores; whether it is that the storms so agitate the deep,
that they deprive them of food, and so they famish amid
the waves, or whether by diving on surfy shores they are
dashed against the rocks, is not yet known; nor can it be
conjectured how they come to have the name of *Allan-
Hawks.*

ALLAN KINNIGHAM, the poet—Allan Cunningham, Esq.
one of the truest poets, and best of men, Scotland has ever
given birth to. He was born and bred in Nithsdale, but
the greater part of his father's family are Gallovidians,
and lived long near the village of Killpatrick. His father
was gifted with the rare talent of a poet too, to a certain
degree, and wrote many good little things for a magazine,
which was published in Dumfries about sixty years ago,
by Jackson, printer there; he was an East Lothian man,
but the ancestors of the family are found to have belonged
to that third division of Ayrshire called Cunningham;
they had been there honest millers time out of mind, but
took up arms in defence of their dear country when Oliver

Cromwell invaded Scotland. The worthy subject of my
present little sketch, began to show symptoms of the
poet very early in life; he became extremely fond of
books, and listened always with a greedy ear to the tales
of other days; and the singing of wild ancient ballads,
the feeling old *cronoch* of these thrilled with extacy
through his heart; while the charming rural scenery on
the banks of the Nith quickened the whole, and winged
the imagination for soaring high in the poetic firmament.
As to receiving education at school, that was as scanty
with him as it ever was with either Burns or the Etterick
Shepherd. To men of strong genius, a school is not worth
a farthing, a school rather does them more harm than good,
unless the *dominic* allows them to learn whatever they
please according to their taste; but the moment they are
obliged to alter their course, from that time they are not
a guiding a right. For all, where find we a better scholar
than Burns, or one to match Cunningham; the memories of such men let nothing slip they have once grasped,
and they know more of a book by giving it a careless
glance, than others do by reading it three times through
with *double milled specks* on their noses.

Until our bard came to be about fifteen years of age he
wrote not on paper any of his little tender aspirations,
but from this time he began now and then to try his hand,
and a happy sight to him was a few verses in the corner
of a Dumfries newspaper; he even went so far as to try
to have an *insertion* in a London Magazine; while thus
the days of his boyhood glided away in song making, and
labouring at his trade of a mason, Mr. Robert Cromek
came into Galloway a legend gathering, and having soon
found out our wonderful young bard, they wandered together through all the fairy haunts and warlock glens of
the country; and having obtained a wallet-full of very
strange matter, Cromek set off with the *bag and the nails*
to London. Mr. Cunningham was invited to follow, and

aid the publication of the work, which was the " Nithsdale and Galloway song;" the whole of which almost is
the work of our poet; and there he truly shines a poet
indeed. What a quantity of pure poetry is in that book.
*The Mermaid o' Galloway—The Lord's Marie—She's
gane to dwall in Heaven—The Lass o' Preston Mill—
My ain Countrie,* and many other songs in it, are perfectly exquisite, the ancient-like mould in which they are
cast, their strong originality and feeling natural touches—
charm every Scotch mind, while the gentle melancholy
that tinges them all, finishes them off in a manner so
beautiful, that when we read them we neither think ourselves nor this earth, such gross things as they be, but we
have entered, or about to enter, some kind of elysium.
After the publication of that book, in which he shines so
gloriously, he became a constant writer in a London
newspaper; but something going wrong in the manage-
ment of this paper, he laid down his pen like a true philosopher, and stood by his trade of the hammer. But a
man of great merit, honesty, and industry, will be taken
by the hand, so our bard received a situation under the
celebrated sculptor, Mr. Chantry; and this situation he
yet holds, beloved by his master and by all who have
the pleasure of knowing him. For Mr. Cunningham is
not only a poet and an enthusiast about poets and poetry,
of the very first kind, but he is also a man extremely
cheerful in society, kind every where, and liberal to the
last degree; he is one of those few men who conduct
themselves in such a manner that we do not see any of
their faults; he is open and free, hides nothing, dashes on—
a Scotchman every inch; we see Caledonia in him; in
every look, in every move, he makes: he gives his native language its truest swing; the words flow from him
with the greatest ease, and with a manly pith. Sometime
ago Blackwood, the Edinburgh bookseller, would have
him to become a writer to his magazine; he did so, and

produced therein " Mark Maccrabbin, the Cameronian,"
a very able and singular production; but some misunder-
standing taking place between that bookseller and him,
he withdrew his valuable pen, and wrote for a London
magazine; the articles inserted there he has since taken
out and published in two volumes, the tales of which are
very wild, poetical and original.

Also lately he has published a drama, named " Sir Mar-
maduke Maxwell," full of passion and poetry; and a wild
legend, termed " Richard Faulder ;" these have been highly
praised, even the " great unknown"—the Laird of Ab-
botsford—hath publicly lauded both them and their
author. At present he is preparing two volumes of
Scotch songs for the press; and as far as I am aware has
dipped deeper into the nature and worth of these songs
than any writer hath yet done. Cunningham beats up
game in a country, different from that of either Burns
or Hogg; he is not such a mannerest as the first, nor such
a fairy man as the last; his melancholy is of a solemn,
sombre cast, not like Burns, flaming in the vortex of passion; nor like Hogg, dancing lightly and wildly round the
halos of the moon; he has a place between them—a
place untouched and unpolluted, for such a situation, a
religious cast of a rare kind was necessary, and this
Mr. Cunningham has in an eminent degree; it is a
poetical religion, felt by some of the covenanters when
they assemble on the wild *breekany brae*, beneath the blue
canopy on a Sabbath morning.

To conclude, though I may add to the biography of
him, that he has been married now to a worthy, pleasant woman these several years, from Galloway, and
they have a good many *bairnies*; that he himself is a strong,
hardy man, above six feet in height, swarthy visage, with
pleasant features, his eyes and eye-brows bespeak great
intellect; with all men of genius of the day he is intimate,
with Sir Walter Scott, Wordsworth, Wilkie, Irving, &c.

and that they all are pleased with the friendship of Cunningham.

So, therefore, be my thoughts briefly stated respecting this gifted individual. If I have said any thing wrong, I shall be sorry—if I have said too much in his favour, then I am happy—for to say too much to his praise is a thing impossible; he is a subject that would not disgrace the best, the strongest pen that ever was wielded, and he who thinks I am a flatterer knows nothing of the character of Mactaggart.

ALLAN CUNNINGHAM.

Yestreen in Fame's splendid ha'
     Was held a festival,
Apollo he was in the chair,
     Amid his votaries all.
When the claith was furl'd, the god he raise
     Within his fist a dram,
And sang " A bumper toast," my friends,
     'Tis Allan Cunningham.

Dear Allan, thus continued he,
     My Allan frae the Nith,
He is my charming bard for sang,
     His muse is pangd wi' pith.
Whan fancy's flood-gates he unlocks
     Forth gushes sic a dam,
As carries with it every heart,
     Rare Allan Cunningham.

He is na like some I cnd name,
     Wha wordy drive alang,
And clink awa for clinkings sake
     Thout feeling what is sang.
Mere Gomeralls, manufactory bards,
     Their sangs are all a sham,
They want the touch—the thrill—the glow,
     O' Allan Cunningham.

Bards maun be bred in rural world,
     There they maun be the child,
There wade in burns, and clamber hills,
     And listen stories wild.
See nature in a million forms,
     While she their noddles cram,
With what will burst upon a day
     Like Allan Cunningham.

Ay they maun doze on sunny braes,
  And happy dream awa,
Ay likewise ken what winter is,
  And his fell blasts o' sua;
While through the curious warle o' man,
  They dance about ram-stam,
And queer poetic secrets gain,
  Like Allan Cunningham.

And there's a jade that bards maun ken,
  Ay be acquainted deep,
Her name it Melancholy is,
  She baith can laugh and weep ;
Can clean owreset the senses a',
  She flings them in a dwam,
Her potent arm is brawly kend,
  By Allan Cunningham.

My heart was hurt wi' Scotlan's wae,
  About the loss o' Burns,
For wha cud stap their lugs ava,
  Whan sic a nation mourns;
I order'd Scotias Genius then,
  To forward bring her caum,
Sae in her mint she truely cast
  My Allan Cunningham.

Apollo ended, and the shouts
  Of joy that sounded there,
Tremendous were, the hall it shook
  With bravo! every where;
Then music rang, and seas of wine
  The glorious party swam,
And oft again the toast went round,
  To Allan Cunningham.

ALLICOMGREENZIE.—A little amusing game played by young girls at country schools. They form themselves into a circle, faces towards the centre; one goes round on the outside with a cap, saying, while so doing—

    " I got a letter from my love,
    " And by the way I drop'd it—I drop'd it."

Then she lets the cap fall behind some one, the which seeing, takes it up and runs after the other in order to catch her; but she eludes her as well as possible, by crossing the circle frequently, and the follower must exactly follow her steps; if she fails doing this, she must

B

stop, and stand in the circle, face out all the game afterwards; if she succeed in catching the one, the one caught
must so stand, and the other take up the cap and go round
as before.

ALLICOMPAIN.—Enula Campana, the medical plant; the
Elecampain of *materia medica*; truely the root is a useful
thing in medicine, but my famous "Yirbwives" which
shall afterwards be spoken of, think it an antidote almost
against every distemper that inflicts either body or mind;
so it is common in many rural gardens; beside it, is generally set a sun-dial, and the rustics are often seen wonder-
ing at the two wonders, a thing poetic to see. I have
heard two verses of an old song on this herb—

ALLICOMPAIN.

O! my pow again is free frae pain,
I am like mysell again,
For twall hours I hae lain
    Upon my Allicompain O!

Whan howstin made me unco' sair,
Whan my poor breast wad rack and rair,
I drank the broe—it haled me fair,
    The broe o' Allicompain O!

ALLOMTREE.—The elm tree. The juice of the bark of
this tree is extracted by boiling it, and applied to sprained
limbs.

AMAIST—Almost.

AMANG HANS—Amongst hands. Little jobs are sometimes done *amang hans*; that is to say, they are done without, in any shape retarding the large job.

AMATON.—A thin boney person—an *automaton*.

'AN—Used frequently for *than*—then.

AN—a. " I'll lae thee Jean for gude and a"—means, " I'll
leave thee Jean for good and all."

ANES-ERRAN—One errand, for the one purpose. I came
to see ye *anes-erran*; means, I had no other errand than
to come and see you.

An die—The man's name Andrew.

An'ro Gemmle—I cannot say, neither can I find any who can, whether this famous Andrew, this notable mendicant, or *Gaberlunzie-man*, was a native of any of the parishes of the South or no; be that as it may, however, sure it is, that he made them one of his favorite begging tracks, and was generally to be found in some " neuk o' Gallowa or anither."

He was a strong *tall Carle,* and had served in the army in the capacity of a dragoon; he was always called " The King of the Beggars," as well he might, for he not only begged himself, but had numbers of beggar wives who ran the country and begged for him; he supplied them with " mealpowks," appointing always on Monday mornings, when they " broke off" the " howf," they should meet at next Saturday night, and she who brought him the most meal, became his favorite sultanna for that time, turning off those who made small returns, and taking the *Powks* from them.

He was of a " *crazed nature,*" like every old soldier who hath seen much blood, and when any little thing curled his temper, he became a madman complete; he boasted of his prowess at the fireside game of " *dams,*" alias *drafts,* and whenever his antagonist was like to be too deep for him, he took the " *men*" of the " *brod*" and dashed them in the fire with a vengeance. He was very fond too of playing off little *jeux d'esprits* of his own formation. Once, as a priest was going to his church on the Sabbath day to hold forth, he espied An'ro on the road a little before him, seemingly in the most profound meditation, pondering deeply with " leaden eye that loves the ground," something lying in the way, and stepping seriously round it. The clergyman came up, and seeing the object of his wonderous gaze, said, " Well, An'ro, what's this that seems to be puzzling you so? for my part I see nothing but a horse-shoe on the road." " Dear me, returned the Gaberlunzie, with uplifted hands, what disna that lair do, I hae glowrd at that shoe now the best part o' hauf an hour, and deil take me gif I cud say whether it was a horse-shoe or a mare-shoe." This is Walter Scott's—Eddie Ochiltree—only he was not a " Bluegown."

ANKLET—The aukle.

ANORDINAR—Extraordinary.

ANTON—Name for the man's name Antony.

ANTRUM—The name in some parts of the country for that repast taken in the evening called *four hours*, anciently termed *e'enshanks*. This Antrum comes from the old French, a den or cave, now Antrum time is den time, then some animals go to their dens; the sun also is said to sink to his den or cave. Glass, in one of his songs, has lovers going out at *Antrum time* to court, and so forth.

ANYING or ANANYING—Owing.

APEN QUEYS—Young cows; those who have not had calves.

APLOCHS—Remnants of any thing. Some few years ago a field of corn could not be shorn, nor a meadow mowed, without parts of them being left in corners uncut, these were called *Aplochs;* they were left for the benefit of the warlock race, so as to keep their favour, but farmers have long ago defied all beings of the sort to do their worst; *Aplochs* now are vanished away.

APPETIE—Appetite. *Appetezed,* having an appetite.

ARDWELL—A ridge of rocks lying between two that are larger.

ARK o' THE CLUDS—or Noah's Ark. The various forms the clouds assume in different seasons, are very attractive to the eye of man; that one mentioned in scripture, which rose out of the sea like a man's hand, soon changed its shape. The famous Dean Swift thought he would be a clever fellow if he could tell what shape a cloud would be in when it set in the east, by seeing it rise in the west; ere they cross the canopy of heaven, they fling themselves into numberless figures, whiles they are one thing whiles another, and whiles " very like a whale," as Shakespeare says. But there is no conglomeration of the clouds, no figure they assume and hold by longer without changing, than this called the *ark*, or *Noah's ark*, a description of its appearance I shall attempt to give. In the winter season (for the *ark* is not common in any other), when the sky is clear and weather frosty, curious light grey clouds in the shape of ribs will oft arise from a point in the horizon, and stretch over the sky to its opposite on the other side; these cloudy ribs narrow in bulk towards the horizon, and are at the widest right over our heads, or in the zenith. " If great things can be compared to small," as Milton says, I would liken this figure of the clouds to the half of a cocoa-nut shell split lengthways, or a Norway yawl, in this form will it appear for a day together, and even longer; what is singular too we have no *half arks*, the one half never sinks beneath the horizon and leaves the other half above; we have the scene always in perfection, or we have it not at all; we have it as if it was calculated to appear in our latitude and longitude, and in no nations else; for it begins to form, comes to perfection, and vanishes away, all in our canopy; we may therefore say there are *arks* for every country.

When seen in frosty weather, as it generally is, *wather-wise fowk* prognosticate a thaw instantly, attended wi' an *awfu spate*, to the gnawing grief of the keen veteran curler, who cries out yonders the *curse that drowns the chanlestane, and cuts the head and feet frae bonspiels.* To be short, the *ark* is a great thaw sign, and brings commonly with it enough of water. It is from its appearing somewhat in the form of a boat, and from its being attended by a deluge, that it has been termed the *ark*.

ARSET—Backwards. Inclining to go astern ; the way of a swine.

ARSLINS—The same as above.

ASCHET.—The king of the trencher tribe. Some time ago they were made of pewter, a mixture metal of lead and tin, and took the lead as they do yet of all the other plates on the dresser, and stood on the loftiest *skelf* like so many shields. Ashets seem to have been the first things of *lame ware*, alias porcelain, that have been made, as about old camps, castles, &c., pieces of them are frequently dug up, and nothing else of earthen ware, if we except urns; and these specimens seem to say the *ashets* have been stamped and highly ornamented.

ASKS—Newts. Animals of the lizard species, they are always considered to have poison somewhere about their *hinnerliths*.

ASKLENT—Aslant. Out at a side.

ASS—Ashes.

ASSBACKET—Ashbucket.

ATA'—At all.

ATEEN—At evening. At night.

ATEN OUT O' PLY.—Some animals are said to be *aten out o' ply* when they are extremely lean in flesh, although they have been taking a great deal of food. Thus few gourmands are very fat, they eat themselves out of ply; that is to say, over-do themselves with eating. Crows in harvest are very light in body, because they have too much food; and in dead of winter, when it is not so, they are fat; eating much more than enough to satisfy nature is an abominable thing—far rather be a drunkard than a glutton, the latter is the most beastial of the two. To see a person sitting down to dinner, and clearing the table before him, is damnable; let such brutes be tossed out of the window.

ATESTRAE—Oatenstraw.

AUCHEN—A field, in the Saxon. Thus, *auchen flower*, field of flowers.

AUCHLATE—An old measure. Two were a peck; one, a stone of meal nearly; but these may be much more or less according to the craft of the measurer.

AULD—Old.

AULD BOY.—A name for the devil; or one with devilish habits is called an *Auld Boy*.

AULD EVER MORE IN A POWK.—The whole of the works of the olden time in a bag; when such would be the case, it is fancied that much stir and commotion would take place in the same bag. So when any one is driving on, and never looking behind, nor to the right or left, it is said he is then going on like *Auld ever more in a powk*.

AULD-FARRENT—Cunning beyond years.

AULD HUNTSMAN—A curious Song.

> O! heard ye o' the Auld Huntsman
>   Wha dee'd upon Bengairn,
> Tak pity on the Auld Huntsman,
>   And ay big up his cairn;
> For ance a day—we weel may say
>   A clever cheel was he,
> Nane was his match, the tod to catch,
>   In a' the moor countree.
>
> For wha cud rin wi' the Auld Huntsman?
>   Wha cud keep up wi' him?
> O! but he had a brisket wide,
>   And tight in lith and lim;
> How he cud scour out owre a moor,
>   And lae us a' ahiu,
> Whane're to blaw—we stood ava,
>   Than he wad faster rin.
>
> He keep'd ay the dogs in sight,
>   And airted on the chase,
> He maistly ay wan in tae death—
>   The glory o' the race;
> While far awa—a mile or twa,
>   Us followers wad hae been
> O'wrecome wi' heat, a' in a sweat,
>   Yet pechin after keen.

For him todlowrie gat na rest
  In bonny Gallowa,
Our geese and gaizlins met na scaith,
  Our cocks did crousely cra' ;
He tous'd the deil roun Criffle-screel,
  And owre the Cairnsmuirs three,
Down heuchs and craigs—and glens and hags,
  As fast as he cud flee.

Nae place but Casslemaddies yird,
  Defied the Auld Huntsman,
But there slee foxie laugh'd at him,
  And scorn'd his deepest plan ;
For in that keep fu' soun' he'd sleep,
  Tho' terriers roun sud yelp,
Ne'er start wad he—to whusk and flee,
  And owre the clints gae skelp.

But age cam on the Auld Huntsman,
  His marrow-banes ran dry,
The stitches and the rheumatiz,
  Wi' pain whiles made him cry ;
His tykes wore few, and warna true
  Moormen forsook him too,
His voice cud no make hauf a noise
  To start the talliehoo.

Than poverty beset him sair,
  Wi' his clauts o' cauld airn,
Sae his twa staves he taks ae day
  And hirples up Bengairn ;
He sat him down, and glower'd roun'
  On heach an' laich countree,
Afar awa by Barrlocka,
  And south by Barrcheskee.

Now sigh'd wi' grief the Auld Huntsman,
  Than back himsell he'd throw,
The merry scenes o' Auld Langsyne
  Now brought upon him woe ;
His fits, his faints—his sair complaints,
  Nae langer cud he dree,
Himsell he laid within his plaid,
  And wi' a groan did dee.

Neist day the shepherds on the hill,
  The Auld Huntsman they foun',
Wi' his auld hat drawn owre his e'en,
  Stiff streeket on the grun ;
Roun' him the nowt did snuff and rowt,
  Sad was the sight to see,
His corpse did crave, frae them a grave,
  Sae they in mools laid he.

Gane, gane, then is the Auld Huntsman
  To his lang hame he's gane,
He's buried on Bengairn sae hie,
  And on his wyme's a stane:
The tod slee boy may howl wi' joy,
  For his fell fae's awa;
And now and than for the Auld Huntsman
  A tear we may let fa'.

AULD MILLHAW. An old man of the name of Sproat. He lived at a place called Millha, in the parish of Borgue; and so his name became Auld Millha. He was a great railer against modern manners, and a praiser of the days of his youth. As a specimen of his mind, I give here the " Lamentations o' Auld Millha."

" Dear me, but fourscore years mak an unco odds o' the times, and that's about as lang as I can min' ought now. Mony an up and down in the warl has haen Auld Millha, and there's a queer something comes owre him whan he claps his auld bum down on the mossaik by the cheek o' the chaumer door, and begins to think awee and glowre back.——There's no a human cratur drawing the wun o' life now that I ken'd in my young days; they're a' i'the mools lang syne; the last ane wha I min' o' that waded about i'the burns wi me whan a boy, and neiv'd beardocks, was Wullie Coskery, and he's gane to his lang hame aboon hauf a dizzen year sin. Wullie was ay but a pieferin useless body a' the days o' him, and ken'd about little but how to mak beeskeps, and wattle saughcreels— than he wad hae glaiber'd about the splittin o' breers for the hale o' a lang forenicht i'the wunter time, without wearyin.——Wattie Bennoch was gane afore him. Wattie and me had mony a day o't thegether, but he was ane clever cheil, and as sharp as a preen. We gaed awa ance—it's langsinsyne now—wi a wheen nowt, tae South o' Englan, and as we war gaen by a bit on the road they ca'd (let me think), ay, they ca'd, now when it comes cross me, Templesorby, out came a meikle bill dog frae a tan- naree, and was beginning to fley our drove, when Wattie drew his gude hazle rung frae neath his çoat-tail, and hit him a whap wi't aneath the lug, till goth he gaed heels owre gowdy without a bough. But some o' the town-folks gat scent o't, and out they cam bizzin like bees, to ding Wattie and me to the deil. I laid on, and sae did he, till some o' us a' hech'd again. We gat out amang them tho' at last wi sair banes; but gin we hadna been a pair o' gye strang rouchtous, we wad hae lain like the thick-nosed collytyke that day.

" Dear me,' what an unco alteration there is now—that auld scrunted hawthorn there afore me, adist the dyke whare the flecket pyets charkin on, and me, are about an age, coming fast up or sliding down the figures 9 and the 0.——Folk are no now ava as the war langsyne; they're puir shilpet craturs the best o' them. I hae seen the day I wad hae pulled ony o'm aff their doups at the sweertree. Auld Millha laments to see them. I cud hae shorn ance too man. O! I cud hae sweeped it down, spread mysell laigh on the rigg, and gaen up the lan' scrieven. There warna mony i'the days cud hae kemped wi Auld Millha. My theebanes war then like milltimmers, and my fingers like dragtaes. O! I cud hae open'd out an awsome bris-ket; I was fit for baith sock and sythe; rid han'd, nae wark cam wrang to me.

" O! for the days again whan I was young. I kenna what the cheels about twenty are gude for now ava; they want the heart someway athegether; they canna take ae dram o' liquor now, without haeing as mony mimins and prieins to gang through as if they war a' born gentry. Langsyne I hae kend Tam Ma'min and me cowpin owre a dizzen bumpers o' strang Holland gin, rare smuggled stuff, down at the Brighousebay, in the wee while o' a forenicht, and never giein a kink either owret or aftert.

" It's a pity to see them, a pity faith—the warls fast degeneratin; banes now are as frush as the branches o' an auld daezd plaintree ; the folk hae nae intimmers, as they were wont to hae, ava.

" Wullawuns and its come to this o't—Hizzies gaen spangin and flaiperin about wi white muslin frocks on, wha in my younger days wad hae been glad o' a piece hame-made stuff, or drogget, and nae bonnet ava; whereas they hae bonnets now co'erd wi gumfloors ; and O it was bonny to see the yellow-haird lasses coming happin owre the kirkstyle on a simmer Sunday, wi that laugh o' luve they gaed in every look. Than they war sae healthy and rosey in thae days by what theyre now. There was never a lass but ane, I think, in my kennin, wha dee'd o' a wastin, and she was ane o' the name o' Tibbie Mitchell, a bastard bairn o' ane Girzy Mitchell's, wha wond in the Tannimaws. (The doctors said it was o' that she dee'd, tho' it was whusherd that it was wi takin owre heavy drinks o' the sap o' the savingtree—to keep a wee scraichin sinner frae seeing the light o' day). There was nae tea amang them in thae days—nane o' that vile spoutroch sae meikle sloated owre now-a-days—na, na, we had nae jabblin thing like scaud ava to sipple wi ; but milkporritch, sowings, and sic like glorious belly-timmer—famous swatroch, man ; noble stiveron.

" Whan we pang'd our pechans wi sic like, there war nae asthmas or cruchlins ever heard o'; we cud hae hunted the fox roun Cairnhattie, without a turn'd hair being seen on our heads, and putted a stane, fifty pun weight I dare say, near hauf a mile ; ane wad hae thought ——. The young lasses get nae men now sic as the are either, as they gat langsyne ; deil a hizzy, gin she had leuked ony think like marryin ava, but wad hae got somebody, or she wan to twenty ; but now they gae by thratty, and mony a ane bids fareweel to matrimony, and curses the men athegether, on the borders o' forty.——Sad wark, man— Hoch anee.

" Hechhowhum, granes auld Millha by the cheek o' the caumer-door; on the bink o' auld mossaik, and what's gaen to come o' the parish of Borgue; ava my gude auld native parish, the Browns and the Sproats are a weedin awa; they hae been a taking gye thrang o'late, to the lane kirk-yard down on the shore.

" A new set o' folk is coming about me athether now, wha talk about plowin and middinmakin; gin they be allow'd to come in amang us as they hae been, we'll be herried out o' house and ha in a crack, for they say they can afford sic rents for the lairds, and can manage a grun sae and sae. I dinna like them ava : I wuss they wad a gie wa the road they cam—awa by the Dinscore or Mochrum—and fash us douce bodies nae mair wi' their glaiberin nonsense——.

" I hae seen the days whan there war nae carts wi' wheels in a' the parish, nor harrows wi' airn teeth, but carrs and harrows wi' teeth o' whunroots, and yet we did full weel for a'; had ay rowth to eat and drink and smiok amang o' the best of things. —— Them wi' their thrashing-machines, airnpleuchs, and turnipbarrows, mere falderaloes, ripin up a' the bits o' green hoams, and forcing wheat to grow whar Providence never intended it, and a' for the lairds, the tennant bodies are never a babee the richer o't; awa wi' yer nice agriculture, yer game laws, and yer Madeira wines—Borgue disna lang for a sight o' them—Howt's no——.

" Awa wi' yer readin priest, yer Latin dominies, yer rooms spread wi' carpets, yer fallow fiels, and yer fenders; and let me hear a cheel skelpin a sermon affloof, anither learnin the bairns the rule o' three and plain arithmetic; the bare sleek yird I hae mony a time shook my shanks on—fiels to plow just as my father plow'd, and nae fenders to hinder the aizles frae spangin out, but lads and lasses, bare-fitted and bare-leged, wedged thick roun the bonny ingle——.

" Never turn, gentle Borgue, or thou'llt gang a' to the bumwhush; stick by the creed o' thy forefathers, never laugh at the gude auld law——.

" Dear me, but it makes my heart sair—to see things chynged and chyngin sae far frae their ancient wont. There's nae courtin gaen on now amang the burnbraes, the glens, and aneath the soughin hawthorns—na, na—the primrose, the bludifinger, and the crawtae grow unsqueez'd and unlooked at; the mavis and the yellow-nebed blackburd, let them sing now as they will, they are never heard. How't tow't, there be nae meetings now on a snug barn mow to pass a night. Burnies too maun a rin anither gate now frae what natur intended; lochs too are a' drained—wild-ducks hae nae wallees now to guddle in, ane can hardly get a bit dub for a chaunlestane rink——.

" Hech how, there's nae fun ava now amang the fowk; they're a' grown as serious as our auld minister wont to be at a sacrament; nae meetings at ithers ingles to sing sangs, and tell divertin tales; nae boggles now to be seen about Hell's-hole and the Ghaistcraft; nae witchwives about the clench, nor warlocks about the Shellin Hill o' Kirkaners. How't no—what's the folk guid for; the Dei'l has crossed their een with his club, or else Peggy Little, the gillwife, has broke some charm wi' her rowantree beetle or kirn-staff——.

" Fairies and brownies hae fled Borgue athegether now; even a donsy beggarbody, wi' a snug sheepskin-wallet and pikestaff, is now to be seen. The folk are a drownin themsells in trackpots and teabroe, fiykin wi' cups and saucers and peutrin about nothing; there's no a chiel worth a doit amang them—but some ane or twa, there be nane worth a tinkler's tip-pence——.

" O! for the days again whan I brew'd and sell'd yill at the Saughligget; thae war days, but they're gane now, and Borgue will ne'er see the like o' them——.

" But its foolish in me to lament and fret mysell sae about things ; short maun may be my time o' the warl now ; soon shall I be carried heels foremost out o' that auld biggin, and laid a gude Scotch ell aneath the mools o' the lane kirk-yard ; my family is a' there afore me, a' but ane, and he's awa by the Ingies. O that he was aside me now ; what tales wad I no tell him, and sing him scores o' auld sangs, that maun a' sink aneath the sod wi' auld Millha———.

" I'll lift tho', and gae wa intae auld chaumer—read a bit o' St. Luke's worthy sayings—tak a blaw o' the cuttypipe, and syne hirsle my body intae my ain auld warm croovie o' a bed———."

AULD MILL O' MOCHRUM.—There are few men in Scotland who are fond of hearing news and curious things, who have not heard of the *Auld mill o' Mochrum*; any person who seems to want something obviously, is said to be like this mill, for she has a want also, which art could scarcely supply, which is a back door ; now all mills should have a door of this kind, and because she cannot have one is, that her back is built against a blue solid rock. Also this mill is used to fling out the inquisitive ; thus, if a person be met on the road, and asked at " where going," to the " *auld mill o' Mochrum*" is frequently the reply ; so the *auld mill o' Mochrum* is used in the west the same as the *auld kirk o' Dinscore* in the east, and makes the forward blush. " Whar do ye live whau ahame," quoth a countryman in the Gallwaygate, Glasgow, to another whom he had just sold an horse, " Ken ye whar the *auld kirk o' Dinscore* is," was the reply—" *ay*," returned the other, " *wi than*," said the next. The poor farmer inquired about the said *auld kirk* till he was wearied out, and satisfied that he had been hoaxed of his horse.

AULD MORTALITY.—This was a man of the name of Thomas Paterson, and was born and bred, as I am told,

in the parish of Baulmagie, one of our Galloway parishes;
there are living yet many hundreds who personally knew
him, of the people of these parts; he was of this world
before my time of marking any thing; yet I am acquainted
with some of his relations, particularly with a lovely young
woman, Miss Paterson, his niece; whether he served a
regular apprenticeship to the stone-cutting or carving
trade, or took it up at his "own hand," as the saying is,
cannot now be known; but it would seem the latter way
is nearest the truth, as he never was very dexterous at the
art, his letters are always clumsy and ill-shaped; frequently
too, the words are divided when the margin of the stone
intrudes, and even some of his lines are interlined. The
honest "Kintrafowks" are at no loss to tell the "wark o'
Tamous Paterson" from that of another's, when they meet
with it in kirk-yards, whether it is on a "*Throuch* or a
head-stane."

He was a singular enough character, and well deserving
the attention of Sir Walter Scott's mighty genius, and, perhaps, there is not a finer piece of writing, fraught with every
thing beautiful and charming, in the many darling volumes
written by that wonderful author, as his description of Auld
Mortality, at the beginning of the "Tales of my Landlord;" the potent penman has given that detail of him
a melancholy poetic tinge, which causes the engraver to
touch our affections in a twinkling.

Then he has drawn him almost exactly to the truth;
the licence he has used with him is small; just as he says,
he wandered about the country amongst the kirk-yards,
with a little white shelty, cleaning and taking a parental
charge of the martyrs stones, viz. those martyrs of the
covenant whom Scotland stood by, and saw butchered by
a set of lawless and base courtiers, to her eternal disgrace!
wherever he found these stones, whether on wild moors or
lonely kirk-yards—the fogg he scoured neatly of them,
and renewed their inscriptions with his chisel.

But this engrossed only a small part of his trade, as he plied his tools to all who employed him, stopping at night in any decent farm-house that came in his way, for being of a religious turn of mind, he was made welcome almost every where, and kindly treated by the inmates, more particularly too by the Hillfowk, for the care he took in preserving the memories of their glorious brethren; he seldom carried a bag or wallet with him, as the writer of the famous tales says, wherein was his tools for working with; no, I am firmly told he had rarely, if ever, such a thing; but an old chisel in his pocket, and for a mallet to strike with, he used a " *Whunstane*" for common, picked up about where he intended to work; these stones are yet to be found in burial-grounds, hollowed out a good deal on one side, by striking the head of the carving implement; so to be minute—he often would weep when labouring on a martyr's stone, the cause of this may be understood, without it being told. And there was a stone in *Kirkandros* kirk-yard, in the south of the parish of Borgue, and is there yet, which he was often beat with to clean, the inscription so overpowering his feelings by conjuring up before him the following inhuman truth :—

"In the days of that infernal persecution of the innocent and independent *covenantors,* taylors had the clothes of both males and females to make among the common folks, there were no mantua-makers concerned with the rural natives in these times, and the women had a fashion of having pieces of lead about different points of their dresses, to make these points gravitate, in what was then considered the *bon* mode; so the sons of the ' thimble' were obliged to have always plenty of this metal about them, that they might go on with their trade, and supply their customers :

" One of these taylors fell unfortunately into the hands of a party of Grier o' Laggs men, as he was going to one of his houses to work, and these blood-suckers finding lead in the pockets of the poor fellow, they instantly charged him, that he was going to cast bullets with it.

In vain did the lad deny the charge, and still in vain did he implore them to mercy; then and there they bound a napkin on his eyes, and shot him through the heart. O! Hell, you contain no villains greater than these!

But let me cling close to my present subject :—Auld Mortality liked a dram by a time, like many another honest man, and often would have come to my grandfather's house at Conchieton, in the gloaming, pretty glorious; and one night, as he was wandering through Annandale, with his old shelty, he took too much of the " *Cratur*," which " doiter'd" him, and made him lose his way; and having wandered on until he and his companion became quite exhausted, he alighted off the back of his faithful comrade, for the last time, and betook himself to a quarry-hole for shelter, and there, with the fatigue and the " nappie," he fell asleep—no more to awake in this world—for a stormy night of sleet came on, and the cold froze the warm blood in the heart of Auld Mortality; but his memory shall not perish; it has got a famous *heazie* already; and should this unvarnished sketch of mine do any good to it, by way of a test, I shall always feel happy.

AULD STRENGTH—The strength of an old man.

AULD STRENGTHS.—Those strong places, in the days of yore, where parties of men kept themselves secure from their foes, such as caves, camps, castles, &c. What a number of these are in the south of Scotland, accounts of some of the most astonishing will appear by and by at their proper article.

AULD WARL FAIRY.—A human being not like this world, having a strange appearance; some of the sons of genius are so called; when in the country, they haunt out of the way *neuks* as *auld glens*; they are commonly strangely clad, with long hair and quick eyes.

AULD WIFE.—A man having much the nature of an old wife about him.

AUM—Allum.

AUMBRY.—A large oblong press or box, which stands on end in a nook of almost every country kitchen; it is generally divided into two apartments, a higher and a lower, with a broad folding-door to each; in the *heigh aumbry*, as the upper place is called, *faurls o' bread*, or oaten cakes, on their edges, lie closely packed together for daily use, also the *meal basie*, the feather *swooper*, and such things. In the *laigh aumbry*, or lower place, bacon, hams, and beef, which have *reestled* long enough in the smoke, barley for the broth, *woo' shears* for *clipping sheep, fining woo' kames*, and a variety of other articles, remain huddled together.

AUNTIE—Aunt.

AURR—The mark of a scar.

AURRIE O' KIRKS.—That space or area down the middle of churches, between the rows of seats; country people pay great attention to the manner in which strangers walk up and down the *aurrie*.

AUSTRAN CARLE—An old man of an austere manner..

AUX—Ask; inquire, &c.

AVA—At all.

AVAL.—When an animal lies down upon its back, in such a manner that it cannot bring its feet to bear up its body, so as to rise again, we say, that animal is *aval* Ewes with lamb are often in this state, and must be set on their feet by the shepherd's aid, if not, they soon be-

come a prey to the *corbies* and *hoodycraws*. In an old
Poem on Corbies, this verse appears—

> Whane'er they fin a ewe fa'en aval,
> Her trolly bags they do unravel,
> The hoodycraws and them will caval,
>   And worry owre her;
> The e'en out o' her pow they'll naval,
>   And sae devour her.

Men, too, whose affairs run wrong, when they cannot help
themselves, but by the help of man, are said to have *fa'en
aval*. There is a line in a Poem which hits lawyers
amongst the unfortunate—

> " Tho' they croak owre us, as owre avald sheep."

AVAL LAN.—Land which has once been broken up by the
plough ; land, as it were, laid down to be cropped ; this
word *aval*, as applied to land, seems to be quite connected with the other.

AVERIN—Talking carelessly.

AWMOUS.—An alms ; charity ; generally the *fu o' the gude
wife's han* of oatmeal *frae* out the *four-part dish* : old
greedy luckies in ill times—used only to cover their
knuckles, and so cheat many a *waefu' body*.

AWN'D—Owned. He never *awn'd* me ; he never owned
me; he never seemed to know me.

AWNS O' BEAR.—The beards of the grain barley ; there
are other kinds of grain which have beards or *awns*, but
this is the most common.

AWRIGE.—Those little ridges which are made by the plough,
and are so laid one by another, that they cover the seed
when they are harrowed down on it ; it is the angular
points, as it were, above the level of a ploughed ridge.

AWSE O' A MILLWHEEL.—Those boards fixed on the
periphery of a wheel, to receive the water after it leaves
the *trowse* for the purpose of moving machinery.

AWTEALS.—A small kind of teal, little larger than snipes.

AYONT.—Beyond ; there is a place talked of, called the
" back of beyont, where the mare foaled the fiddler."

B.

BAA—A word used in lulling a babe to rest. In the old song of *Rocking the cradle,* "hushie baa babie lye still" is a line much used; it is a very musical word, *baa*; I have heard nurses give it a melancholy cadence, that I have weeped to hear them. Beggar wives with infants at the breast know well the value of the word, and can twang it up on so many mournful keys, that it thrills a good *awmous* from the hardest heart.

BA—A ball, more commonly used for a soft ball than for one hard.

BABIE—A babe.

BABIECLOOTS—A babe's clothing.

BABBLES—What may be considered foolish nonsense, though they often turn out to be facts, and facts sometimes *babbles.* When we hear of a *bonny lassy,* or a virtuous lad going astray in the paths of rectitude, we exclaim *howts babbles,* though we believe in the truth of it at the same time. *Babbles* may therefore be said to be nonsense, yet admitting of doubts, to be truth.

BABBS—That vile *luce* or slimy matter a razor scrapes off the face in shaving.

BACH—An ejaculative word, expressive of disgust.

BACHLES—Old shoes; also the lumps of snow which adhere to shoes when walking among snow.

BACHRUNS—Excrement of oxen, dried in the summer sun; they are used, *viz. bachruns,* by poor people instead of peats for fuel ; and they even gather them off the autumn green fields for winter's use ; " mony a gude tale is tauld, and mony a cutty is made lunt owre the glead o' a *bachrun.*"

BACK-AND-BREESTED—In that Scottish game at cards called *Lent,* which is generally played at for money, when one of the gamblers *stands,* that is to say, will play, and is *lented,* which is, outplayed by those who *stood* and played also ; then, if this happen, and the *divide* too at the same time, this person is said to be—*back and breested.*

BACKCREELS—Baskets made of willows, formed to fit the human back—ere the invention of " wheel-barrows," these were used in cleaning byres, stables, what not.

BACK-DOOR-TROT—The diarrhœa ; those with the body in a lax state, are said to have the *back-door-trot.*

BACKEN—That space of time between harvest and winter—the back-end of the year as it were—many a farmer leaves pieces of work in spring and the summer, to be done in the *backen ;* but when that period arrives, they are still left undone, perhaps till the next *waurtime* : thus, bad jobs are put off till the last ; nor do these little procrastinations do much harm for all. Gallovidians love to be contented ; they are naturally so ; they dislike to be pushed and hurried, and to make the *warle a' faught.* They are never very rich in money, nor yet very poor ; have enough for the necessaries of life, even in a civilised state ; enough for the back and belly, and something of an overplus whiles to help one another in straits ; so, what more, ye philosophers, I would ask, is a wanting for the enjoyment of this world ?

BACKIEBURD—The bat ; these half mice — half birds, are fond of any thing white. On fine evenings, when they are bickering about, if a white cloth, or a " mutch" be put on the top of a long pole, they will gather round it, and rest themselves in the folds thereof.

BACK-LICK—A back-blow. Commonly these blows are the most severe of any.

BACK OUT OWRE—Backover.

BACKRANS—Backwards.

BACKSET—A setting-back of any thing, or a something that retards : thus, wet weather is a " backset" to the farmer in " the hay and harvest time."

BACKSIDE—One of the many names for the seat of honour.

BACKSPANG—Backspring; men not overly honest, too are said to " hae mony a *backspang* about them."

BACKSTANE—A large broad stone, placed behind those good peat fires which burn on hearths, not in grates. Such fires are common in the moor country; and it is no strange thing to see a wearied " herd," in the winter, taking a sleep sometimes on the *backstane*, as that stone is always thick enough to be a seat.

BAD—Did bid.

BADE—Stayed; did not shift.

BAE—The bleat of a fat sheep.

BAGGIE—A person with a big belly.

BAGGRELL—A young person, of awkward growth; big-bellied.

BAILLIE DAYS—Those days on which farmers laboured to their lairds, now partly done away with. *Bailly days* were mentioned in tacks, as so many days of *bailly harrowing*, so many of *baillie peating*, and on so: they were very troublesome days to farmers, and these *bailly works*, I may add, brought *kempin* to great perfection, for when the labourers of many farmers met, they behaved little better with other than when strange herds of oxen meet, goring and frothing about who to have the mastery—

BAINS—Bones.

> They wha buy beef, buy banes,
> And they wha buy lan, buy stanes.
>   OLD PROVERB.

BAIRNIES—Children.

BAIRNTIME—The time a woman takes to breed her family. Old wives mention always this bairntime with much reverence; indeed, it is generally the most eventful period of a female's life, not to be entered into rashly by them if they thought much; but young girls are so formed by nature, as neither to dread beginning with it, nor to think any thing of it—Give them a dear " man"—then all their woes are at an end.

BAIRNSPLAY—Any kind of game or sport more becoming children to play at it, than people grown up.

BAISSIE, or BAISHEN—A bason; a vessel for holding any thing, commonly meal.

BAITH—Both.

BAKEBOARD—A board to bake oatmeal cakes on.

BAKIES, or BAKED-PEATS—Peats baked with the hand; not cut with spades.

BALDERDASH—Nonsense—foolery.

SIR BALDERDASH.

Some twa'r three thousan' years ago,
　　Ane bastard-bairn somehow
Was got atween a curious pair,
　　A Gomerall and a Gow.

The barnie like a breckan thrave,
　　It never took a brash;
Twas fed on new kirned butter-milk,
　　And named Balderdash.

The bairnie soon became a man
　　O' mickle fame and cash,
For whilk his king did title him
　　The grand Sir Balderdash.

Amang the ladies then fu' gay
　　He made an unco flash,
And bonny Madam Clashmaclaver
　　Wan Sir Balderdash.

O! Madam was a blooming wench,
　　And gabbed night and day;
A tinkler's curse she did na care
　　What she did think or say.

Nae hizzie was a match for her
　In clauchan or in town ;
O ! but she liked weel to gab
　A dizzen fallows down.

Which pleased weel Sir Balderdash,
　And made him fondly flether ;
As she gae'd tongue, and he gae'd tongue,
　And baith gae'd tongue thegether.

And, strange to tell, they seldom ere
　Complained that they war weary ;
He to his bosom aft wad squeeze
　His sweet enchanting deary.

And saftly whusher in her lug
　That he wad never waver ;
But love, to this yirth's latest birl,
　His charming Clashmaclaver.

And, strange to tell, it never coold,
　They ay war pack wi' ither ;
E'en to this day they blythly look,
　And never seem to wither.

Her cheeks yet blush rosieways,
　Her breasts seem scarcely wore,
They look fu' fit yet to gie sook
　To bairnies mony a score.

Though mony a Gow and Gomerall,
　Though mony a Goaf and Glumf,
Though mony a Haverall they hae bred,
　And mony a famous Sumf.

Sae brave Sir Balder drives about,
　And looks fu' spruce and trig ;
The de'il a gouty tae has he,
　Nor belly curving big.

And no a hair upon his pow
　Seems yet akin to white ;
And a' the tusks ere had his jaws
　Can quick as ever bite.

Though nought but twa he ever had,
　Twa gruesome tusks to snack ;
Twa azle fangs—but clean unfit
　The nits o' sense to crack.

The fashions he o' every age
　Doth follow to an inch ;
By laws nonsensical he stands,
　And frae them wunna flinch.

In Parliment he whiles appears,
   And tells a lang wund story;
Sometimes he seems to be a Whig,
   At ither times a Tory.

And whiles he'll try a blunnerboar
   Wi' his queer whup to lash,
He misses him—the cracker backs,
   And nips Sir Balderdash.

Wi' soldiers he doth seldom ever
   Gae to fields to slash,
But pesters ay the warl o' saul,
   The blockhead Baulderdash.

Nor yet wi' sailors, mang the seas,
   Will he gae duck and swash;
He'd rather loll wi' fiddlers,
   The mighty Balderdash.

The poets he ca's a' his friends,
   And they wha deal in rhyme,
He gies a monthly pension to,
   And suppers mony a time.

And priests wha i' the pulpit rant,
   And caper on a tub,
At market-crosses, to attract
   The ragged hubblebub.

Thae be his cousin Germans a',
   In truth ilk worthy hash
In estimation high is held
   By big Sir Balderdash.

And baith himsell and the gude wife
   Hae written meikle trash;
O! mony a library is pang'd
   Wi' her and Balderdash.

For, no a day flees ow're their heads
   But volumes they do pen,
And still their plots and stories come
   Nae nearer to an en'.

That warl o' fancy they adore
   O' subjects ne'er rins out;
That spring, Castalian, whilk they quaff,
   Is an eternal spout.

But let us damn or praise them now,
   Or let us neither fash;
But leave Sir Wisdom to himsell
   To rule Sir Balderdash.

BALLOP—The shop door in a man's nether clothing; the same with " *Spare*," (which see).

BAMBOUZLED—Confounded, affronted, treated rudely.

BAMF—A fellow with broad feet.

BAMFIN—Tossing, tumbling, &c. Auld John M'Clellan, wha's now awa, *Bamfd*, in the Solway Frith, many a storm with his shell-wherry, according to his queer account. He wont to be " *bamfin aff the heads*" wi' *Collier Briggs* whiles, and they under close reefed *tapsails*. Seldom ever was he out any long voyage with his boat, but the " *wather bruik*" on him, or he got back: once going into Ramsay-bay, in the Isle of Man, the " *wather bruik*" on him, and " dog a bit," (as he told the story), there came a sea ow're the whurrie's quarters, and swept his hat and wig wi't; sae he had to spread his sea-coat, in the " *stern-sheets*," to keep out the sea, while he steered the " whurrie" into Ramsay, wi' a " *pirnie* on his pow."

John was an oddity, and told strange tales; when it happened he was telling one, and any thing made him lose the " thread," he always referred to the wife to set him right again, by inquiring at her, " Whar was I, Meg." Meg knew all his tales, the greater part of which were lies; but, by his telling them long, he came to think them truths.

John was a celebrated country fiddler in his day, and his tunes are very popular.—The life and character of this being, drawn fully out, would form a diverting book.

BANEFIRES—Bonfires; fires of joy.

BANS'MEN—Men who bind sheaves, and put those sheaves in " stooks," alias shocks, behind reapers. These men are commonly old steady men, who have seen many a *harrest*. They gather straws, and keep the boon, in order, when the gude man's back is at any time " turned."

BAN'STERS—The same as above.

BANG—A blow.

BANNOCKS—Round thick cakes, ornamented frequently with a hole in the centre: butter is often used in their composition; but if they can be got " *haurnd*," toasted on a " *kelpkill*," when the *kelp* is in fusion, then they have no need of butter. For more particulars, see the article— *Millbannock*.

BANTON-COCKS—A small species of cock, yet full of spirit; some say they are good fighters. An Irishman's opinion on them once was, that he did not doubt " but that there was as much game in *Banton-cocks* as there was in the " *Carrik smokers*," the first brood for the pit in his country. Little men, fond of fighting, are too termed *Banton-cocks*.

BAPS—Little rolls of loaf-bread.

BAREFIT—Barefoot; schoolboys, particularly in the country, strip off shoes and stockings, " whanere the harrows begin to trot," and put them not on again, till the *hinharrest time*; indeed, many of them are so hardy, as not to shod their feet the year round. I have seen them slide on ice barefit, and wade through snow to the knees; and I have followed their example for fun whiles myself, and found it not so cold as fancied: also, I have run barefit with them through " Rossen's o' Whuns, after burds."

BAR FOR BAR—The game of rhyme; Gallovidians are so fond of clink, that they have a game with it, and a strange one it is truely, when thought of: two or three, and sometimes more, amuse themselves with it, to *dinnle awa the time*, as they say. One of the players invents a line, the next that follows must give one to *clink* to it, and have a little sense also; a third follows, and on so: those who can hold out longest, and clink best, gain the game, and are allowed by all for that *heat* to have most of the poet in their composition.———

Although, like Hudibras—

> They who write in rhyme, still make
> The one verse for the other's sake;
> For, one for sense, and one for rhyme,
> They think sufficient for a time.

I may give a specimen of the game, as played by three players—

The first ——— O, Tam, I dearly lo'e a lass;
second ——— Is she a maid that has the brass?
third ——— Or is she o' the bonny class?
first ——— Weel, Jock, ye're but a cuddy ass,
second ——— And what's Tam but a stinking mass;
third ——— His sweetheart's breath smells worse than gass.
first ——— Why, Jock and you are just like glass,
second ——— Through us, ye think, the light doth pass,
third ——— And that we're fit to feed on grass.
first ——— Twa fools ye be, alas! alas!
second ——— But thou'rt a fool as such ne'er was,
third ——— And has a voice like music's bass.

So the third becomes the winner, and puts an end to the balderdash.

BARKEND WI' DIRT—Stiff with dirt; this from ship's sails, being sometimes " barkend red" in tan-pits, with the juice of oak-bark, to make them endure longer.

BARLEY—Parley; to treat, to have peace for a moment. This word is much used in rural games; " a barley" is often cried for the sake of momentary relief.

BARLIEFETTERER—An implement of many edges, used for taking the beard off the grain barley.

BARLIEHOOD—When one is angry, it is said to have on the *barliehood.*

BARM—Yeast; the froth which works ale. Yeast from malt-ale will not only work malt-ale, but all other ales; whereas, the barm from " *bragwort*" and " *trikleyill*" is useless.

BARMWHUN—A thick close branch of a whin, whereon barm is laid by thrifty *gudewives,* and hung carefully upon some *nag*; there will it keep good long, and answer for brewing with.

BARNIEWATER—What a number of original characters has this Galloway, at one time and another bred; it is a perfect nest for them, not two of the country folks being found any way similar to other; nature so sports herself in the formation of them, that she moulds no pair alike. In towns she casts thousands with one " *caum,*" but in a wild rural country, she uses a *new caum* at every *cast,* and what rude grotesque creatures she whiles will produce: one of these, to an eminent degree, was *Barniewater.*

He was of the name of Livingston, but was always named *Barniewater,* from a moor-farm, in the parish of Girthon, which he many a day was the tenant of. It was there where he made a considerable sum of money, and first presented his originality to the world. With this cash he purchased a little estate of the name of Grobdale, not far from the famous fountain of *Lochenbrack,* and there he died, a few years ago, a very old man. His hair hung down his back as white as a " *lintstraik,*" and his eyes looked out from beneath his hat, in that sly shrewd manner which bespeaks no common intellect.—He was naturally very fond of money, so that some went the length to say, " his greed made him lift mair than his ain whiles." I am inclined to doubt this—for it is always the case when a person gets rich in a place where no others can, that he is branded with the epithet of being dishonest; now, it is true that *Barniewater* scraped a good deal of cash out of one of the most barren sterile places that can well be fancied—where only rocks, *moss-hags, clints, garries, gall,* and heather were to be seen—in a place where no animal of farm-stock kind could live; even the goat had much ado to exist on it in the heart of summer; yet for all, what will industry and care not overcome. When he went to a market or fair, for instance, he eluded those roads whereon were fixed toll-bars—he paid for no whisky—he was at no expence—he was always plotting the best method of evading it ; so saved much in this little way, which many others did not——.

In coming to Kirkcudbright, he was always pestered with the Tongueland toll-bar, in his way ; but he left his horse before he came through it, and walked on foot to the town and back, though a walk of four miles, to save two-pence—and this he did to the last of his days ; old age could not alter his rigid economy. To behold him, mounted on his old shelty, was truely a laughable scene, the animal being always so lean—a perfect " *rickle o' banes*," and the saddle a goat-skin, by way of " *suggan*," with stirrups worn to mere skeletons in their way——.

Before he got a wife, he rummaged the whole country in order to find one : wherever he heard of a woman being in the matrimonial market, there was he, and there did he treat with themselves or their parents about striking a bargain, as if they had been brute animals. Love was never felt nor spoke about — he would have said, -" that he had the farm of Barniewater—his name was Livingston— *ablins*, they had heard o'him—he had a gude deal o' sillar, *sax or aught score o' gates*, and about as mony black-faced sheep, and of course he expected that the wife wad bring him something equivalent."

Thus went he on for a long time, and all the girls of Galloway became acquainted with him, yet he found few willing to treat with him about a match : at length, he brought one so near the point of closing, that he would allow her five minutes to make up her mind whether she should have him for a husband or not.———The short space of five minutes soon fled, and she agreed to wed *Barniewater* ; she brought him something like an equivalency too, and a " *sonsy*" daughter, as a " *luckpenny,*" in a short time after—.

This daughter, being bred in a wild moorland region, where few of her kind she ever met with, except her strange parents, the *lassie* became extremely wild, ran like a hare, and hid, if she had seen any human being approach the house——.

Her father was prevailed on by some person to send her to a boarding-school awhile, to get some education ; he took her to Dumfries, for that purpose, and had much ado in leaving her behind him : she clung by his coat-tails, and " *scraich'd* " out as if she had been a creature from the shores of Nootka Sound, or some such out-of-the-way place, and at night she set up a horrible howling. Next morning, betimes, she took to her " *scrapers,*" as the Irish phrase it, and skelped home in a crack, on the " light side of her foot," to *Barniewater*——.

She was troubled no more with a boarding-school, or indeed any other kind of school but that of nature, and has turned out to be one of the cleverest females, both in mind and body, as is in the country: she could ride the wildest young horse that ever " lap" *bare-backed*, with nothing on its head but a " *cowd* hair halter ;" this she would do not " *saddle to side,*" as women ride, but " *leg on every,*" as the men do : and for working amongst sheep, there was not a *herd* so good in her neighbourhood ; she would have brought the goats off *Cairnsmoor* too in grand stile, running up and down precipices as quick as them.——But whether she " *gather'd wide,*" as many thought her father did, it becomes not me to say. I have taken her father's part, that he was not in reality such a person as was suspected, and I shall stand by it, though report is flat against me, that the mark he knew his flocks by, was the mark of " *rounstowing,*" that is, cutting off the ears altogether— that he flung his *marches* open to his neighbours' sheep,

and when they came upon his land, he " *rounstow'd*" their
ears, which was doing away with all other marks, and so
getting them to become his property——.This character
made him be disliked by his neighbours, and there were
often serious broils between him and them. One of these
affairs, with a farmer of the name of Clark, came before
a court of justice, and can be found told at great length,
in the Dumfries newspapers of that time : the law went
against *Barniewater*, and he and his wife were put in gaol
some time about it——.

And my opinion is, that he was badly used in that concern. The affray took place on a Sunday afternoon, to be
sure, which was not a right thing : but this Clark met him
and his wife, taking a walk on that day, and insulted them
with tales of " *rounstowing*," which, no one could say was
actually true, which stuff roused *Barnie's* wrath, and he
and the wife gave the insolent fellow a laughable drub-
bing——.

Barniewater was a creature of patience, perseverance,
and good nature; he never keep'd company with those
whom he termed " *debush'd curses*," but sober plodding
souls, like himself, were his favourites. He had a custom,
as all moor-farmers have, of throwing the bones they pick,
over one of their shoulders to their dogs in waiting: he
was taking his dinner somewhere, and behind him on
the wall hang a looking-glass ; he threw a bone smack over
his shoulder, which sent the mirror to pieces. To pay
the damages, pleased him ill, but he had to cash out, much
against the inclination——.

Such was a very rare being—was one writing a novel,
he could be done some justice to ; whereas, in short
sketches of this kind, it is difficult to lay him so before
strangers, that they may behold him as he was. To know
a person well, one must hear him often speak—know how
his pulse beats on various occasions—and so get glimpses,

as it were, of the interior of the bosom—with some knowledge of what goes on in the pericranium.

BARNMAN'S-JIG—This is a dance which those persons have who thrash with the flail. The *swoople* on the end of the *hand-staff* being whirled round on the barn-floor by the *barnman;* every wheel he gives it, he leaps over it, and so produces a very singular dance, worth walking a mile to see, yet few of the *barriers* who do this dance in stile, are willing to perform before spectators. The girl who *kaves the corn* is the only one for common who is gratified with the sight. I once insisted on an Irishman, whom I was told was good at it, to let me see; but all I could insist availing nothing, he got angry, and exclaimed—" Hoch, by the frost, don't bother me—I won't give a spring at this time; you may as well whistle jigs to a mile-stone."

BARRIED—Thrashed; as with a flail.

BARRIES—Flannel belts, for wrapping round the bodies of infants.

BARROWTRAMS—The side bearers of a hand-barrow.

BARRS—Large hills, ridges, &c. What a number of *barr-hills* there are in Galloway; these were barriers in the days of yore—places of defence—places which divided the power of barons.

BARR's CAT—Perhaps Macvey Napier, Brewster, Miller, &c. have not an article in all their encyclopædias, like this one in mine, termed *Barr's Cat.* It was a very large monster of a *bawdrons,* that was known about the farm of Barr, in the parish of Pennigame, about sixty years ago: it was as large a cat as *Crumwhull's Gibb,* to be afterwards spoken of: the size of it became proverbial all over the country, and every thing larger than it should be, was said to be a *rouser,* like *Barr's Cat.*

BASH—A blow.

BASHFU'—Backward—modest.

D

BASKWATHER—Dry withering weather; the wind, when such prevails, blows out of the east and north-east, just as it blew on the Prophet Jonah, when it withered his gourd.

BATCH—A crew of blackguards, who keep each others company.

BATCHELORS'-BUTTONS—A beautiful red button-shaped flower.

BATT—A blow.

BATTLES O' STRAE—Bundles of straw, folded neatly, as it were, into themself. See *Wapps.*

BAUBEE—An half-penny.

BAUDMINNIE—An herb having the same qualities as the " *Savingtree,*" which see.

BAUDRONS—One of the cat's names.

BAULDIE—The name Archibald.

BAULDY CORSON—What an original character was Bauldy; sometimes called Serjeant Corson; he was a native of Galloway, and could boast of having not a little high born-blood in his veins—but, as Pope says,

" That ancient, but ignoble blood,
" Has creep'd through scoundrels ever since the flood."

For this our hero cared nothing; in learning and dissipation he passed his youth, and before he was twenty, enlisted into a regiment of militia, called the *Buccleughs,* in honour of that worthy Scottish family of Buccleugh. In it he did not long remain as a private, for his genteel address and bewitching manner, soon had him adorned with a sash, and furnished out as a serjeant; such a person as Bauldy soon caught the eye of his commander, the Duke, for though not a tall man, his figure as a soldier was great, and his natural talents of the first rate; he was advanced again to the high post of a recruiting serjeant, and sent with a party of good looking privates, into the towns and country places of Scotland, to enlist the unwary.

And never was there a character better cut out for his
station than he, and seldom ever was there need for
such characters as he, at that time, when all the continental world growled around us, threatening an invasion every day; he possessed as it were, every property
that can be supposed qualifications for the office; he
could give a damn with singular bravado ; he was a blackguard of great grace, and drank whisky after a most enticing manner. The *cock* of every company he was in ;
the head-man of every party. At fairs, and other public
gatherings, what fascinating speeches and harangues did
he not make at the *drum-head*; those who before had an
utter abhorrence of a military life, just leap'd at the *bounty;*
then he was as good at keeping his recruits' as he was at
enlisting them ; when any desertions took place, none were
found so capable of ferreting them out as the serjeant ;
if he was beat with finding them, they were bid *fareweel*
to cheerfully; when Bauldy, the sly hound, was let slip
on them, the game was almost sure to be caught ; he was
often obliged, in this service, to traverse the greater part
of the three kingdoms. What tales he had about catching
those run-aways, starting them, perhaps, out of some den
in the dark Cannongate of Auld Reekie, then following
in view over Berwick-upon-Tweed, and afterwards *het fit*
to London ; or if they had taken the westerly range it was
all one to the serjeant ; he'd cross *Stranegower;* post after
them through Green Erin, and hook them up in the devil's
own city, Dublin. But whisky and debauchery fairly
taking the upperhand of him, he was obliged to turn tail
on the regiment, retired into Galloway, and took to himself a *rib*. Still, however, his friend the Duke, could not
altogether lose sight of him, but got a birth for him in
the Customs, viz. that of a *Tide waiter's*. While in this
situation he played the devil with the smugglers all along
the shores of Solway Firth ; he discovered all their dens
for secreting contraband goods ; nothing could go beyond

his craft; he fairly *cowd the gowan,* as the saying is. On
hearing, once, of the arrival of a smuggling lugger at Port
Mary, away he posted, in order to learn what had become
of the cargo, but knowing this not to be altogether an easy
matter, he had recourse to the following stratagem.

Having put himself under a garb of disguise, he went
running with great haste into one of the smuggler's houses,
and cried out amongst a bevy of their wives who were assembled, " That the hale o' the Corbies o' the Custom-
house war within less than a mile o' the Burnfit, and that
if they did na set too instantly, and hide every thing better
than it was hidden, they wad fin' the haleware in a twinkling."

The which intimation created no small stir amongst
them, thinking the informant to be one of their well-wish-
ing neighbours; to better hiding they went, and Bauldy
stripp'd the coat and seemed to work the throngest. But
no one appearing to alarm, they concluded that the person who raised it, must have been mistaken, so they returned to their houses, satisfied that this was the case.

The Achan of the camp, however, slunk away from
them, and returned next day with a party, seized the
whole, to the utter astonishment of the smugglers in that
quarter.

Still, he took spirits to excess, was no very good husband, flashed away a small estate of land he fell heir to,
lost his government place, got quite reduced, retired into
the country, brought his scholarcraft into action, and
taught a small rustic school. Bauldy though was too
long in turning the dominie; his pupils were few, so he
was obliged, though sore against his will, to mow and sow
corn occasionally. After all, he was a fellow of great
abilities; could I look through man with the same eyes that
Bauldy used, I should think myself very clever indeed;
he knew the lineage too, of all the families of note in
Galloway; could follow them out like a squirrel along

every branch of the tree, and over and above, and double
all that; he had good stories to tell for ever; good old tales,
as many as would fill fifty numbers of any magazine now
published; and then he told them, in a dialect of which
he was a complete master, the Gallovidian; then he could
sing well; that old song " The Shepherds of Galloway,"
he could give a twang to, that made it quite charming;
he had numberless barrs and staves of song, but they in
general had so many threads of *blue* interwoven in their
frame, that I won't insult modesty by giving them. I may,
however, note down a few verses of a very singular Poem
he used frequently to recite, called " The Soldier's
Prayer:"

> Frae a' lang marches on rainy days,
> And frae a' stappages out o' our pays,
> And frae the washerwoman's bills, on the damned claise,
>   Gude Lord deliver us.
>
> Frae mountain guard whan the snaw rides deep,
> And frae standin sentry whan ithers sleep,
> And frae barrack beds, whar lice and bugs do creep,
>   Gude Lord deliver us.
>
> Frae a' bridewell cages and blackholes,
> And officers canes, wi' their halbert poles,
> And frae the nine-tail'd cat that opposes our souls,
>   Gude Lord deliver us.
>
> May a' officers wha make poor men stand,
> Tied up to the halbert, foot, thigh and hand,
> Die rotten in the p—x, and afterwards be d—n'd,
>   Gude Lord deliver us.

The following verse of the old song he sang in fine stile :

> Enough o' meal's come in at Leith,
>   And herring at the Broomilaw,
> Cheer up your heart my bonny lass,
>   There's gear to win, we never saw.

Johnie's Greybreeks, he also could do ample justice to.

> Altho' my love's gane far awa,
>   Whar guns and cannons rattle o',
> Alas that he should chance to fa',
>   In some unhandy battle o'.
> And I'll clout my Johnie's Greybreeks,
>   For a' the ill he's dune me yet,
> And I'll clap a clout aboon a clout,
>   And see to turn the wun about ;
> For I hope to see, before I dee,
>   Our bairns dancing roun' us yet, &c.

After singing, he used to fetch a deep sigh, as if former days had crossed him, as doubtless they often did; then he'd give his exclamation, which always was *hech, aweel an hech,* and follow it, perhaps, by

> Up and waur them a' Wullie,
> Up and waur them a,
> Up wi' your lang pikestaff,
> And ding them down tae snaw Wullie.

In his disposition was a great deal of good nature and resignation; he had a contented face, and took his meat well to the last; he had got a circle of friends about him that he visited, and they fed him, but had the weather been bad, and he not able to get out to see them, he was then ill enough off, as he hoarded up nothing at home.

The worthy family of *Drumore* were extremely kind to him, and let him want for nothing they could furnish him with; he was, perhaps, the best beggar that ever tried the trade, for he always got plenty of food and clothes without asking for them; and when a *kimmering,* a *kirsening,* a *kirn* or a *wedding,* took place within his reach, he was sure to smell it out, for the sake of catching drops of his favorite luxury, whisky; and about the *new year time* he was often carried home to his *crue,* on a hand-barrow, just *mortal.* Tobacco he chew'd to excess, the *brew* of which ran in a brown rill from either *wick o' his mou',* as if it had been *trikle;* he knew well the persons who keep'd the best filled *spleuchans* in his part of the country, and also, *wha was best gien o' a' chow;* nor was he wanting of generosity; for when any well-wishers filled his *spleuchan,* he would present it again to them, to take a chew in return. The news of the country, or the *kintra-clash,* was well known to Bauldy, and he turned it to his advantage; all messages were bandied by him from house to house, *parties* were set, lads and lasses appointed to meet, all through Bauldy. In this respect he much resembled the celebrated Eddy Ochiltree. Children, where-ever he went, were very fond of him, and hung on by his *clickett staff* and *coat tails*. The servant wenches, though were often very much displeased with him, because of his questions, and his opinions of them, he was such an accomplished master of human nature, that he knew exactly what would please, and what not; these girls would rather have endured any thing, as a banter from Bauldy; his words pierced their very marrow, and made them shake at the centre.

He got very soon acquainted with strangers, and with loungers like himself, he bore the bell—was quick at detecting lies—he knew falsehood, he said, by its very *unnatural sough*; he never cared much about the servants of any house; ay, the *gude man* and the *gude wife* were those he warmly inquired after—he had wisdom in this too——.

Praising the *bairns before the mither's face*—this was too, one of his unfailing plans—saying that "*sic a ane* had just the *bonny een* of its mither, for he minded weel what they were like at fairs lang syne—that there was na sic a spangin clever hizzie on a' the kintra-side." Politics and newspapers he was always very fond of: still inquiring at those whom he thought skilled in these matters, how the war was coming on, and how that " fell fallow, Bonny, was skelpin through?" then, if he was told " that there lately had been a great *stramash*, many towns sacked, many men killed, and so forth," with tobacco-sap, dropping brown from his chin, he'd exclaim, *aweel an hech*——.

He died the other year, in the parish of Kelton, when he was above eighty years of age. The following epitaph on him, was one of my boyish crimes:—

EPITAPH.

Come, gather roun, and laugh or grane,
At what is said upon this stane,
Bout him aneath't, a famous ane,
    Wha's name was Bauldy Corson.

Gude faith, he was a cheel gie rare,
Bout fortune no a preen did care,
Yet fu' and merrily he did fare,
           The jovial Bauldy Corson.

He sang and drank, and damned awa,
For virtue cared na much ava,
Tell'd tales for fun, that did beat a'—
           The happy Bauldy Corson.

Ye wha can tak a bowsan drink,
Whan that your purses hae the clink,
Upon your brither here come think,
           And weep for Bauldy Corson.

Ye wha are unco mim i'e mou,
Wha at a dram do snuff and grue,
Mind he beneath was no like you,
           Despise than Bauldy Corson.

And seem to say he's gane to hell,
Amang his friens for ay to dwell,
Wha kens but ye a far waur cell,
           May get than Bauldy Corson.

What wad ye say, ye holy crew,
Wha goodness ay seems to pursue,
If he was blessed aboon you't you,
           The glorious Bauldy Corson.

Wha little Bible ever read,
Bout preachers ne'er did fash his head,
Nor learned ought but natnre's creed,
           Enough for Bauldy Corson.

If that his crimes sometimes were great,
His heart did often feel that heat,
Which made it sweet, and heavenward beat,
           The queer chiel Bauldy Corson.

But let him sleep aneath the sod,
Soon wi' him we'll hae our abode,
Than may our sauls flee up to God,
           And see auld Bauldy Corson.

BAWKS—Jousts, couples, &c.; beams for holding the roofs of houses steady.

BAWKS o' LAN—Pieces of land the plough misses in ploughing it. " Lae na banks in gude beer lan," is a phrase, meaning, that in telling a story, to dash right onward, and if any thing of an immodest nature seems to be in the way, to stop not for it.

BAWS.—The calves of the leg.

BAWSENT.—Having a white stripe down the face; applicable chiefly to brute animals. Cows with this mark, or horses, are commonly called " *bawsies.*"

BAWTIE.—A fond name for a dog.

BAWXTER.—A mighty personage of some kind or other. When it is said of such a one, that he " beat Bawxter, and Bawxter beat the de'il ;" it places that character high. Methinks this—*Bawxter* is Baxter, who wrote that well-known religious book, the " Saint's Everlasting Rest ;" he combats in it, with strong reasons, the devil, and may be said to overcome him whiles, which may have raised the saying, " That Bawxter beat the de'il."

BEARDIN THE LASSES.—The art men have of rubbing their beards on the cheeks of the girls; those men who have the stoutest brush are the best *bearders*; it does not answer the cheeks of delicate ladies, but country girls are fond of it, as those who can beard must be men—those who cannot, are *beardless boys*, with nothing but *goarlin hair* on their *chafts.*

BEARDOCS.—Small fresh-water fish with beards.

BEASENIN.—That fat thick matter which is drawn out of a cow's udder after she calves; when boiled it becomes excellent food.

BEASTIES.—An affectionate name for brute beasts; also one for vermin.

BEBB.—We are said to *bebb* ourselves with any thing, when we fill ourselves too full—the tide when full is said to be *bebbin fu*—the word comes from *bibe*, the Latin and English word.

BECK.—To bow; to be ceremonious.

BEDALL.—A grave-digger; for why, he " beds" us mostly " all."

BEDRALL.—A person so lame or disordered that he is obliged to remain constantly a-bed.

BEDRIDDEN.—We are said to be bedridden when healthy we sleep long in bed, and when we get up are not refreshed; for we have overdone nature by snoring so long; we have insulted her modesty; we have rode the bed so long, as it were, that the bed has got the upper hand and *rode us.* Whence the name.

BEDSTOCK.—The strong beam of wood which runs along the front of a bed. " Before I lie in your bed, either at *stock* or wa," as the old song says.

The following lines on the bed, wrote by Benserade, a French poet, and translated by Dr. Johnson, I still think good—

> In bed we laugh, in bed we cry,
> In bed we're born, in bed we die,
> The near approach a bed doth shew
> Of human bliss, to human woe.

BEE.—A small hoop of either brass or iron, put on the end of sticks to hinder their splitting.

BEEK.—To bask; *beeking*; basking.

BEEL or BIEL.—A shelter.

BEELINS.—Suppurations; bilious tumours in the flesh. Those reapers who have the bad luck to reap " *thrisly corn*" are troubled very much, poor souls, with " *beelin thumbs*;" " *prods*" otherways; prickles of hawthorn when " *picked out wi' preens*" from their poisoned cells; in our hands and feet whiles, are eaten by the *kintra-folk*; for they say, " eating the *prod-hinners* the wound *to beel.*"

BEER AWNS and BUTTER.—The beards of beer mixed with butter. When those creatures called " *Gian Carlins*" wont to meet with any one alone on *halloween night,* they stuffed it with " *beer awns and butter*;" a mixture by no means very agreeable to either the throat or stomach.

BEERBUNTLINS.—Birds as large as thrushes, and somewhat like them in plumage; common amongst grain, particularly *beer*, when growing; it is from this, and because they are of the buntin species of birds, they have their name; they are not good flyers; and they keep their feet hanging when they fly, like young or wounded birds.

BEERFEY.—Anciently the piece of best land about a farm. This was the craft, the only place that received a spoonful of manure—the only place where it was thought *beer* would grow.

BEES IN THE BRAIN.—People, after they have been " fou," feel, as they are returning to their wits again, a bizzing and " singin" in the head, which are called the *bees o' the brain*; also, when they are getting intoxicated, they feel these fanciful insects.

BEES-SKEPS.—Baskets made of straw and briers, as houses for bees; when a hive needs one of these mansions, it is rubbed with green leaves and old honey in the inside; then peeled sticks are put cross it to support the combs, and a standard post down the middle. And if this work is done before the hive needs it, the people say, " *they'll no need it that year, as bees like nought done a forran.*" Sometimes rascals of bee-men set " *toom-skeps*" in their gardens, to allure other people's hives into them. Such characters never thrive though on a " *kintra-side.*"

BEE-STANES.—Stones in the form of a sector, to set bee-hives on.

BEET.—To add fuel to a fire; taken figuratively, to add to what needs little addition.

BEETLE.—A wooden implement with a round heavy head; the pestle of the " kitchen," used for " champing" potatoes and other purposes. Some large farmers have four beetles playing away in the " *meiklepot*," when cooking food for their reapers, playing away all at once.

BEETS O' LINT.—Sheaves of green flax.

BEEYARDS.—Apairies for bees. Quarry-holes fronting the south make the best bee-gardens.

BEGGAR BODIES.—Beggars.

BEGGAR PLAITS.—Cresses in the skirts of garments. Beggars weeds are frequently plaited this way, from their lying and sitting on them ; hence the name.

BEGGAR'S BED.—The bed kept in farmers barns for beggars.

BEGGAR'S OWREWORD.—An old song called the beggarman's owreword runs this way—

> Through the streets o' Auld Reekie a beggar stravaged,
>   And a merry auld beggar was he,
> Though his breeks and his plaidy were baith unco ragged,
>   He could laugh, he could dance, ay, and relish a spree.
> When he'd meet wi a gentleman fat and weel bagged,
>   His honour he'd cr'ae for a single bawbee ;
> And say, while his hat on his staff he outwagged,
>   *A wee things a help, as the wran said,*
> *Whan she gaed ance, and pish'd i' the sea.*
>
> A little and little to meikle soon rises,
>   'Tis the high way to riches we see,
> To be adding, and adding, our purse soon surprizes,
>   Tho' the lump at the first be scare worthy a flee.
> And this is the way too our reason advises,
>   If we wad hae wisdom look gleg wi the e'e,
> A thousan times better than sillar the prize is ;
>   So than let us claught it degree by degree ;
> *For a wee things a help, as the wran said,*
> *Whan she gaed ance, and pish'd i' the sea.*

BEGGAR'S STAFFS.—These staffs are known from all others by their greasy sleekness. Irishmen speak of the juice of a " beggar-man's staff ;" it is likely there is such a thing.

BEGNET.—A bayonet.

BEGOUD.—Began.

BEIN.—Snug ; warm ; happy, &c.

BEINK.—A long form or seat.

BELLIBAN.—A band of leather or what not, which is made to pass under the bellies of horses, while each end is made fast to the *shafts* of the cart, to hinder them mounting when the cart is a loading.

BELLIBUCHTS.—Curious hollows in the sides of some hills, not running in the longitude way, as hollows mostly do, but the contrary.

BELL-TOWLIN.—Bell tolling. The ringing of the bell.

> As the fool thinks,
> The bell clinks.

This old snatch has truth in it. Whittington, the celebrated man with the *cat*, thought the London bells rang his wish; and so did *Bell Allan*. At first, hopeful girl! she thought the bell said,

> Ting towlin—Bell Allan,

as a warning for her to listen; then it sounded respecting her lovers,

> " Awa Peter Busby,
> " And a' thy kith and kin;
> " I'll follow Robin Fisher
> " Through thick and thin."

BELLY-FLAUCHT—Belly-broad.—When any person falls *belly-flaucht*, it means *a fall* on the broadest part of the belly.

BELLY-TIMMER.—Any kind of very strong food is so termed, as porrage, sowings, brose, &c.; such plank the *kyte*, as it were, with durable timber, or " *clag to the ribs*," as the saying is.

BELTON.—The third day of May.

BEMMLE.—A bad ill-shaped man; a bad walker.

BEN.—The innermost room of a house.

BE NAETHING THE LOUDER.—A common curling phrase. It is used as a direction given to a player—the which is to throw his stone so that it may gently hit another stone, and displace it a little, but not to give it any additional force on that account, more than if he were not to hit it.

He is not to give it *powder*, and shove all to *lochhead* of desolation, but simply to *brak an egg*.

BENGAIRN.—A lofty mountain in Galloway. There is little remarkable about it. It was one of the stations of the trigonometrical surveyors; and from its top on a clear day three or four kingdoms may whiles be seen, if we consider the Isle of Man as one. It is about three thousand feet above the level of the sea.

BENJIE.—The name for Benjamin.—Two lovers, Benjie and Phemie, figure in a song. It may here be given by the way.

PHEMIE AND BENJIE.

Ay just awa's ye cam' Benjie,
   Straught out owre the hill ;
For never will thy clavers, Benjie,
   Through my heart gae thrill.
Whan I was poor, ye bar'd ye'r door,
   And didna care for me ;
Now fain ye wad—Benjie lad,
   I canna suffer thee.

O dinna tell me sae, Phemie,
   Ye hae better sense ;
I lo'ed ye many a day, Phemie,
   Or ye gat the pence.
Do ye no min' the ball sae fine,
   Whar ye did partner me ?
And the wud sae gay, whar mony a day
   I leamed nits wi' thee.

That's a mere clatters, Benjie,
   Ye ne'er lo'ed me ava,
Let me dress as I wad, Benjie,
   In my best sae braw—
My poplin gown, wi' trimmin' roun'
   Which sae weel fitted me,
Ne'er drew your e'e the least ajee—
   I'se no be fash'd wi' thee.

Wi' than I'll just awa, Phemie,
   Ein out owre the burn,
There try gif I can stay, Phemie,
   And nae mair return.
Try to forget thy hair o' jet,
   And bonny blinkin e'e ;
There feel distress for happiness,
   Because I ha'e na thee.

Feel what ye please there, Benjie,
But ne'er thy fancy crowd
Wi' joys that wives will bring, Benjie,
Wives wha ha'e the gowd.
Gae af thy wa's, and herd the craws :
Thou'rt far frae being slee,
Wha ken's but yet, that I may get
Nae better lad than thee.

What's this ye tell to me, Phemie?
I'm na up to this.—
O tell me't owre again, Phemie—
Tell me wi' a kiss.
O what is this! O what is bliss!
How kine thou art to me!
Now—now—ye tell, ye lo'e mysell
As dear as I lo'e thee.

And wha cud lo'e thee ill, Benjie?
That was never me!
I only meand to try ye, Benjie—
Now thy heart I see.
Whan I was low thou wert my Joe,
Aneath the greenwud tree:
Now I shall share Fortune's fare,
My Benjie dear, wi' thee.

BENNLES.—Things dry and brittle, as reed.

BENSLE.—A bleak, cold place. A place where the frost wind finds easy admittance. Also a person with a saucy air—as much thinking that he does not care a d——n for the world. We say, *sic a fallow gangs wi a great bensle*, or has on a great *bensle.*—He passes the poor with a sneer, and capsizes the infirm with a laugh—his bosom is a *bleak place*, a *bensle*,—cold unfeeling blasts whistle round his frozen heart.

BENT.—The open fields.

BENTY-GRASS.—Coarse grass, which grows in marshes.

BESSIE.—A name for Elizabeth.

BEST MAN.—The male friend a bridegroom selects to attend him through the season of marriage. Commonly this "best man" is considered by the bridegroom his "*best crony*" when he rambles the country to invite to the wedding. This chief man attends him when he is about to

take the hand of the bride in the marriage ceremony.
This man stands beside him, and ungloves the hand.
This man, so highly favoured, attends him too at the
" *kirken*"; and, on the whole, is often as happy looking
as the bridegroom. Widows choose widows, and sometimes married men, for their " *best men*," never pitching
on any of the unmarried.

BEUK—Book. The Bible.

BEUST.—Grass two years old. Having stood through winter, it is withered. Is there a Galloway farmer who does
not know what a *tuft o' beusty grass* is? Not one. And
I hope now that all my readers are as knowing, as to that
question, as them.

BEVEL—Of the perpendicular. A wall made to lean in is
said to be *beveled* so.

BEVERAGE.—The first sweets of any thing. When a
young girl gets any piece of new dress, she slyly shows it
to her *Joe*, who gives her a kiss, which is taking the *beverage* of the article in question. And when he gets any
thing, they kiss again, which is giving the *beverage*. The
bridegroom takes the *beverage* of his bride by kissing her
the instant the marriage ceremony is over; but if any
other person be so nimble as to have a kiss before him,
that person gets the *beverage*.

BIBBLIN.—Weeping and sobbing.

BICKER.—A wooden bowl.

BICKERIN.—Making quick motions. One running fast is
said to *bicker*. One fighting fast is also said to *bicker*,
from such I infer the meaning.

BIDE.—Abide.

BIG.—Build.

BIGGIN.—A hut.

BIG-ON.—A term at the game of channelstone, much used
by my worthy and social friend *Drummore*. If a stone
lies near the *cock*, and guarded, yet thought to need a

double guard, if not a triple. The order from that side who has *in* the stone, is commonly to *big-on*—to guard away—to "*block the ice.*" And the command of the other party is mostly, when things are in this situation, to come up *wi' a' the powther i'the horn and waken the guards.* Old wary curlers, however, take a different plan. They won't *waste* stones on the guards. They sail them past the sentinels, nigh *wutter .length,* obtains a *Inring,* plays on it, and not unfrequently drives out the winner, thought by t'other side to be even almost too secure.

Bill—The bull—The king of the byre. Black-coloured bulls with "*wee-lugs*" are those thought most of by Galloway farmers. Black is the favourite colour for cattle over all the country.

Billhippie—An ox with bull-hips. Such animals please not the squeamish eyes of cattle-dealers. I once heard one of these *valuable* characters say, that a *billhippie* was fit to damn a drove.

Billhuik.—An hedge bill.

Billilue.—See Whillilue.

Bills eag.—An old bull castrated.

Billtory.—A name for a restless bull.

Billy—To make a noise as oxen. These *billy,* when they smell the blood of their kind, the whole herd gather round, with vengeance in their eyes, and tear up the ground. Bulls, on such mighty occasions, are the most forward, and lead on the furious concert.

Billy Bell.—This is rather an out-of-the-way little song.

BILLIE BELL.

Hech! how! Billie Bell!
   Whar hast thou been wan'ering?
Up in heaven, or down in hell?
   Ye beat the deil for dawn'ring.

Hast thou got a hizzie yet,
   To streek down by thy side, Billie?
Or canst thou no ava, man, get
   Ane to be thy bride, Billie?

E

I ha'e a' hame daughters sax—
   Wilt thou come and see them, Billie?
And gin ane o'them thou'lt aux,
   I'se be na ill t'thee, Billie.

I'll gi'e to thee a bonny cow,
   Gin thou'lt tak my Nannie, Billie,
Ane Crommie wi' a brocket mou',
   And they ca' her brawnie, Billie.

But gin thou'lt no fancy her,
   And ratherest wad ha'e Meg, Billie,
A less tocher maun her ser'
   Twa grey geese and a Steg, Billie.

Or, if thou better likes the e'e
   O' my wee Jeany, Billie,
My turkey-cock I'll gi'e to thee,
   And the breeding Peanie, Billie.

As for my Tibbie, Nell, and Kate,
   I ha'e nought to gi'e them, Billie,
But my blessing air and late :—
   Sae come awa and see them, Billie.

BILLY MARSHALL.—The famous Gallovidian gypsey, or *tinkler*. He was of the family of the Marshall's, who have been tinklers in the south of Scotland time out of mind. He was a short, thick-set, little fellow, with dark quick eyes; and, being a good boxer, also famous at the *quarter staff*, he soon became eminent in his core; and having done some wonderful trick by which he got clear off, he was advanced to be the chief of the most import-ant tribe of vagabonds that ever marauded the country. The following was that trick :—He and his gang being in the neighbourhood of Glasgow when there was a great fair to be held in it, himself and two or three more of his stamp, having painted their faces with *keel*, they went to the fair and enlisted, getting each so much cash. They then deserted to their crew in the wild mountain glen, leaving the soldiers without a single cue whereby to find them. For all, Billy once really took the *bounty*, joined the army, and went to the wars in Flanders; but one day he accosted his commanding officer, who was a Galloway gentleman, this way: " Sir, ha'e ye ony word to send to

your friends in Scotland at present ?" " What by that ?"
returned the officer, " is there any person going home ? "
" Ay," continued Billy, " Keltonhill fair is just at hand.
I ha'e never been absent frae it since my shanks could
carry me to it, nor do I intend to let this year be the first."
The officer, knowing his nature, knew it would be vain to
try to keep him in the ranks, so bade him tell his father
and friends how he was; he also gave him a note to take
to his sweetheart. So Marshall departed, was at Keltonhill fair accordingly, and ever after that paid much respect to the family of Maculloch, of Ardwell.

It is not my intention to give a lengthened portrait of
this character, as one of the above family, who personally
knew him, has done this for me, and much better than I
could, in Blackwood's Magazine. Suffice it to say, that
the *Corse o' Slakes* was a favourite haunt of his. There
did he frequently way-lay the unwary, and sometimes de-
prived them of both life and purse. Billy's gang were
seldom ever beat by any others. When they met at fairs,
he generally drove all before him; for the Irish took up
with him from Down and Derry,—and who can overcome
them at the handling of the *stick ?* To those country
Cock Lairds who were kind to him, he would do them
no injury, but all the good in his power; whereas, those
who were his foes—Billy was upside with them.

He would not have cared to have *taken up lodging*—he
and his core—in one of these gentlemen's *kills*—to have
purloined the greater part of the poultry, and roasted them
with the wood of the roof of said *kill*—to have there
staid a week, perhaps, in spite of every body—gone away
at his own time—and left a world of desolation behind
him. It was in one of these scenes that he drank, *May
ne'er waur be amang us*—a toast that can be construed in
many shapes. Thus did he flounder on through a long

life. When he got old, his people, though in a great measure, forsook him.

It seems that he had both the good and bad qualities of man about him in a very large degree. He was kind, yet he was a murderer—an honest soul, yet a thief—at times a generous savage—at other times a wild Pagan. He knew both civil and uncivilized life—the dark and fair side of human nature. In short, he understood much of the world—had no fear—a happy constitution—was seldom sick—could sleep on a moor as soundly as in a feather-bed—took whisky to excess—died in Kirkcudbright at the age of 120 years—was buried there in state by the Hammer-men, which body would not permit the Earl of Selkirk to lay his head in the grave, merely because his Lordship was not one of their incorporated tribe. Such was the end of Billy Marshall, a brother of Meg Merriless.

BILLY MARSHALL'S SONG.

Merry ha'e I been making a cutty,
   And merry ha'e I been making a spoon,
Merry ha'e I been courting a bonny lass,
   Merry ha'e I been whan I had dune.

Sorry ha'e I been whan I was drubbit,
   And mad wi' mysell whan my noddle was sair ;
Mony a time ha'e I sworn't, and ha'e broken't,
   That wi' the aik kibblings I'd never fight mair.

Drunkensome aft ha'e I been at Kirkcubrie,
   And at Auchencairn I ha'e aften been fu' ;
And wi' my Meg Lundy, baith week-day and Sunday,
   Wi' skilting we've bebb'd oursells till we wad spue.

Fifty fat bairnies now I ha'e gotten,
   The wanton sweet bizzies war ay fond o' me ;
Wi' them I wad row on the burn-banks sae sunny,
   Bargallie kens weel I had mony a spree.

Sae here's to the giens growing thickly wi' hazles,
   Ay here's to days I will never see mair ;
And here's to the tinklers, wallets, and cuddies,
   Whilk dadjell ilk year to braw—Keltonhill-fair.

The following song too is thought to have been ranted in Billy's core :—

Whan Jock and me war married, we war a happy twa,
We laugh'd thegether a' the day, and kiss'd the night awa ;
Sae thick and thrang, or it was lang, the bairnies round did squeel,
And Jock and me the nappie lo'ed—sae a' gaed to the de'il.

We had twa kye, we pawn'd them baith, the sty we cleared, and a' ;
Our cocks and hens too, by my faith! and wadding braws sae braw ;
We drank like fish frae caup and dish, fu' cantily atweel,
But wullawuns wi' tinklers now—we dawner to the de'il.

I lead ae weanie in my han', there's twa upon my back ;
My spawls ha'e ne'er a hoshen now, my pouches ne'er a plack ;
My gudeman fallows after, wi' the cuddy, powks, and keel :
Its alter'd days wi' us. How-hum ! we're a' gaen to the de'il.

But gin my auntie Kate was dead, and hidden i' the mools,
My Jock and me, again shall be, a pair o' ranting fools ;
Than we'll can clash, about our cash, and dress frae head to heel ;
For we shall heir her pursikie, in spite, man, o' the de'il.

Than we'se fling down the hampers, and dance a merry jig;
My Jock will crack his whup, and sing, and birl me in a gig.
We'll lash awa, and dash awa, and drink like mad and breel ;
For what the hell cares Jock and me, tho' we should gae tae de'il.

EPITAPH ON BILLY MARSHALL.

Weel tinkler Billy, here you are,
   The king ance o' the core, man;
We wat ye were a kettle rare,
   Whan ye did see sax score, man.

O brawly ye could clour a croon,
   And make a nose play gush, man ;
Ye liked weel to bleach a loon—
   Your cudgell was na frush, man.

Gude faith, ye were na joke ava
   Amang yer randy lasses ;
And cheels wha did the ramhorns thraw,
   Wi' a' yer cuddy asses.

The whisky just in noggin-fu's,
   Ye, 'thout a howst, cud slot, man ;
Ye were na ane wha boaks and spues,
   And brashes't up the throat, man.

Sae, Billy, rest thy crazy banes,
   Thy soul, belike's in hell, man ;
We only guess that there it granes,
   For wha the de'il can tell, man ?

Yet if ye're got to the right shore,
   Ye may be unco' glad, man ;
For, counting ilk infernal splore,
   Sma' was the chance ye had, man.

The duddy de'ils, in mountain glen,
   Lamenteth ane and a' man ;
For sic a king they'll never ken,
   In bonny Gallowa, man.

BILT.—A short thick man.

BILTAN.—Moving with the air of a thick short man.

BINKED-SHOON.—Shoes which were at first too large for the feet that were to wear them, and the leather naturally bending inwards, they become at last too small—full of " *binks*" or bends.

BINN.—A man of strong *binn* is a man strongly built and bound—crop of good *binn* is a good strong crop.

BINWUD—Wood-bine. I once tried my hand at song-making, and produced the " *Binwud Tree,*" which I here give with great deference—shewing forth what a *modest* and *wonderful* poet I, the youth, am—who will be a *beau* before my *granny* yet.

Sing hey for the Binwud tree,
   O ! sing how for the Binwud tree ;
For there the lads and the lasses wad meet,
   And daff 'neath the Binwud tree.—*Chorus.*—

There did Jock and his Mally Malinn
   Meet aften thegether awee,
And tho' the jade had an unco din skin,
   It grew white 'neath the Binwud tree.
            Sing hey, &c.

There Maggie wha swore she detested the men,
   Kiss'd wi' Tammy the Peanerflee ;
His whushers fu straught to her heart gaed ben,
   As they lay 'neath the Binwud tree.
            Sing hey, &c.

O ! mony hied there a sprogan ateen,
　Wham few wad expect to see,
Wi' bonny red cheeks and blinking e'en,
　And courd 'neath the Binwud tree.
　　　　　Sing hey, &c.

For. it grew in a neuk by yon bonny burn side,
　Adown i'the flowery green lee ;
And the mavis she lilted wi' meikle pride,
　I'the bowers o' the Binwud tree.
　　　　　Sing hey, &c.

But there cam a pizioness blast frae the south,
　And destroy'd a' our e'ening glee ;
O ! custom genteel—is the devil in trouth,
　It has wallow'd the Binwud tree.

　Then sing hey for the Binwud tree,
　　And sing how for the Binwud tree ;
　For there the lads and the lasses wad meet,
　　And daff 'neath the Binwud tree.

BIRKENSHAW.—A sunny place of all kinds of brushwood, a poet's country; there they roam unseen amang the Birks and yellow broom, and tune their pipes.

BIRKIE.—A would-be gentleman.

BIRKY.—A rustic game at cards.

BIRL.—To whirl.

BIRL THE BAWBEE.—Sport the cash for drink, is so termed ; also halfpennies are tossed up at the beginning of some games, to learn what side has the right first to play ; this is called " *Birlin the Bawbee.*"—See more of this article under the title *Heads or Tails.*

BIRND-MARKS.—Marks made by burning. Sheep are so seared on the side of the nose with red irons, that the owners may know them.

BIRNS.—Burned, or ratherly chared heather—the spikes.

BIRR.—Whirr.

BIRSES.—The bristles of swines manes.

BIRSEY.—Full of bristles.

BIRSLE.—To bristle.

BIRST.—A little person full of impudence.

BIT.—A small piece of any thing.

BITTS.—Those jointed pieces of iron which are put in horses mouths of course, but used allegorically in the country for a *dram* of whisky on certain occasions. When a man is wet and trembling with cold, give him a *cauker,* and you take the *bitts* out of his mouth.

Will ye no tak the bitts out o' my mouth the day, is a common phrase by those who long to have *drink* from their *neebours* when they meet on market-days in *Clauchans,* and after much *hargle bargeling* is gone through, a *gill* is decided on, so the party slide slowly and diffident into the *yill-house.*

BIZZ—Buzz. Hair all tossed on end, is said to be in a *bizz* ; this comes from *"Frizz,"* the English word.

BLACK A VICED.—Of black complexion; probably this comes from " *Black a faced."*

BLACKBIDES—Blackberries. This term for that fruit not very common.

BLACK DOUGLASS.—Perhaps the greatest villain ever known in Galloway; his den was the castle of Thrave, a befitting keep for the tyger; he keep'd the country round him in awe for many a day; even the Scotch kings could make nothing of him. He caused Lord Kirkcubrie, M'Lellan, to be hanged by a rope from a projecting stone in his castle wall, yet to be seen, and took his dinner calmly while his hangmen were doing so. Some say he was *" durked"* in Annandale, but how he came by his death is uncertain; however he did not die a natural death. More or less particulars of the wretch may be known by peeping into any book almost which treats of Scottish antiquities.

BLACK-LEG.—A kind of murrain or plague amongst cattle. The disorder for common seizes first on one of the hind legs, and this leg, when the animal dies, (which is in less than twenty-four hours mostly from the time struck) is of a black colour; whence the name. Sometimes they are touched first with the distemper in the eye, and other parts of the body. Young cattle are more subject to it than old; and it is always the best of the flock that die, though all perish that take it, there being no cure as yet found.

Plans for preventing it are practised—bleeding, purging, what not; these plans are often attended with good. Too old pasture is thought to be nothing in favour of it, and all allow that it is highly infectious.

BLACK MORROW.—Who this man was, baffles all antiquaries.

Tradition has him a *"Blackimore,"* and says he haunted the forests south of Kirkçudbright; a natural wood there, is yet called the *"Black Morrow Wud"*; there he stopped during the day, sallying out on the neighbouring country at night, and committing horrible outrages. Also, that having found his retreat, which was beside a cool spring, in the dark forest yet called the *" Blackimore's Wall,"* a barrel of spirits was brought by the people, and poured into the spring well one night when he was out on his rambles. Next day, having drank of the fountain as usual, he became touched with the grog, and fell asleep, snoring profoundly; his foes then rushed on him, like the Philistines on Samson, and *" dirked his heart wi' mony a deedly hole."*

So goes tradition—but my opinion, if it be worth any thing, is, that he was no *" Blackimore;"* he never saw Africa; his name must have been *" Murray;"* and as he must have been too an outlaw, and a bloody man—gloomy with foul crimes—*" Black"* prefaced it, as it did *Black Douglass,* and that of others; so he became Black Murray. Antiquarians say the sum of 50*l.* was offered by the king for his head, dead or alive.

That one of the *M'Lellans,* of Kirkcudbright, took to the wood single-handed, with a *dirk,* found the outlaw sleeping, and drove it through his head. With the cash he bought the estate of *Barmagauchen*, in Borgue; the foundation of the " *head on the dagger*" in the M'Lellan's coat of arms.

BLACK-PISH-MINNIES.—Black pismires.

BLACK SOLES—An assistant courtier. A male messenger between a man and his love. There is a meanness in any man working with such characters; it shews he has not a soul to dare to speak to a woman, nor a heart to love one.

BLACK WUNTER.—The name for the last of the crop brought in from the fields. The *harrester*, whose lot this job is, takes as good care as he can to avoid its being generally known, until he has it done; as if it be, the others assail him with all filth for bringing in such a sad thing as *black wunter*.

BLADDERSKYTE.—A silly foolish person, as easy " *skyted*" aside as a " *bladder*."

BLAE.—Blue, or light blue.

BLAE-BERRIES.—Billberries.

BLAE-BOWS.—Blue flax bells; the flowers of flax.

BLAIDRY.—Foolish chat.

BLART.—The noise which any broad thing makes falling amongst sludge or mortar.

BLASHY-WATHER.—Wet stormy weather.

BLASTIE.—Any ill-disposed youth.

BLATTER.—To talk fast; to rattle.

BLAUDS.—Broad pieces of any thing.

BLAW.—Blow; to puff any thing.

BLAW O' THE PIPE.—A whiff of the pipe.

BLECK.—A blackguard; a " kintra-cooser."

BLECKS AMANG WHEAT.—Milldew.

BLEDNOCH WATER.—The chief river in the shire of Galloway or Wigtownshire; it runs through a fertile track of country; it is a fine fishing stream; and where it falls into Wigtown Bay, at *Innerwall,* good salmon are caught. There are traces where ancient battles have been fought on its banks; and some warm fancies have the river's name from *"Bled-enough."*

BLEECH.—A stroke.

BLEER E'ED.—Having sore eyes; dim with tears and dried tears.

BLEEZE.—A blaze; also to blazon.

BLELLUM.—An ignorant talkative fellow.

BLIBBANS.—Ribbons of any kind of slimy matter.

BLICHAN.—A person useless for any thing.

BLIN—Blind.

BLINBARNIE—Blindharry.   The game.

BLINCHAMP.—A very singular rustic game; when a bird's nest is found, such as a *Corbies* or *Hoodicraws,* or some such birds that the people dislike, the nest is *herried,* that is to say, the eggs are taken out of it, and laid in a row a little from each other on the grass; one of the players has then something bound over the eyes to blind them, a stick is put in his hand, so he marches forth as he thinks right to the egg-row, and strikes at it; another tries the *champing* after him until they thus, blindfolded, break them; hence the name *blinchamp.*

BLINK.—To wink.

BLINKED MILK—Milk distasted. It gets so in warm sultry weather, the heat, as it were, ferments it. *Gude wives* have it *fired,* but the origin of *blinked* is, that it is witched; *blink'd* at by a *foul e'e.*

BLIN-MENS-BAWS—A kind of dried fungi, or mushroom; being balls, as it were, of a fine dark brown dust; this dust is doubtless blinding to the eyes, hence the name; they are common on the pasture fields during summer and harvest, particularly if the weather be dry; when they are young, they are white inside and out like other mushrooms, yet detested by " *catchup brewers*" for reasons best known to that " *valuable*" tribe.

BLINNIE.—A person mimicating the blind.

BLIRT.—The exterior of a mare's uterus.

BLOCK THE ICE.—A curling term, the same with " *big-on,*" to block up with guards the run of the stones, so that none of them may take out a guarded winner.

BLUCHANS.—Little salt-water fish, about the size of *Burn-trouts.*

BLUCHTANS.—Pieces of the dried stem of the mugwort; they are hollowed tubes; boys blow haw-stones and what not through them; hence the name.

BLUE BOYS.—Bad boys.

BLUE-GOWNS.—Old soldiers, with a " *pass*" for begging; they got a blue-gown and a shilling Scots, for every year of the king's age; there are none of them now wandering the country. *Eddie Ochiltree* will hand them down to posterity.

BLUESTER.—A bully of words.

BLUMF.—A stupid loggerhead of a fellow, who will not brighten up with any weather, who *grumfs* at all genuine sports, and sits as sour as the devil, when all around him are joyous.

BLUNNER BOAR.—A blundering fool.

BLURR.—To blotch the paper with ink when writing.

BLUSHIONS.—Bulbs of water; blisters of the flesh.

BLUTTER.—A foolish man, rather of the idiot stamp.

BOACK.—To vomit.

BOAF.—A name for a foolish dog.

BOAL.—A square niche in a wall for holding little *needfus'*; such as *Grannies specks*, and *cuttypipe*, with the *bane-kame* and single *carriges*.

BOAS.—Any thing full of emptiness.

BOCHLE.—An awkward footed female.

BOCHLES.—Old shoes, or shoes that have been worn by awkward shaped feet.

BODE.—An offer.

BODDLE.—A small Scottish coin, the sixth part of an English penny, and the half of a Scotch plack.

BODDUM.—The bottom.

BODIES o'BORGUE.—The people of the parish of Borgue; so called by the natives of neighbouring parishes.

BOGG-BEAN.—The trefoil herb of the marshes.

BOGGIT.—Stuck fast as in a soft bog.

BOGGLES.—A general name for all beings which create an *earieness* in man. In Scotland, more boggles are seen and heard of than there are in all the rest of the world; how this comes to pass may be difficult to define, but so it is. In every country of a similar form, composed chiefly of hill and dale, rocks and wild mountains, we find the natives having their *boggles*; the Welsh and Swiss are this way, and many others. But what have they in comparison to the Scots? what are their *knockers* and *reckers*, to *warlocks* without end, *worricows, kelpies, spunkies, wraiths, witchies,* and *carlines?* what, a mere nothing-accounts of these supernatural beings will appear in their proper order, and show that the Scots are a nation not only famous for religion, war, learning and independence; but also for superstition, which practically proves this point in moral philosophy, that fear attends the brave, as modesty does the worthy; and in proportion as the intellect is weak or strong.

BONELLO—A bon aller amongst parting friends. These meetings are generally merry to the last, they are then extremely sad.

KIRRCORMOCK'S BONELLO.

Kirrcormock's blyth lairdy, or he gaed awa,
To fight and to florrie, through wide India,
Invited his neebours about ane and a',
          To g'ie him a merry bonello.

And sure it wad been baith a sin and a shame,
For ony ava to hae drunted ahame ;
The de'il a ane did sae, fù' gladly they came,
          And breel'd at the lairdie's bonello.

The barmen did rattle their flails ow're the bawks,
The millers did hushoch their melders in sacks,
And hung the best braws that they had on their backs,
          To flash at the funny bonello.

The hizzies a tramping their claise at the burn,
That day they had nathing to whine 'bout nor yurn ;
In their bowies wi' barehochs, they plunged their turn,
          And fluchter'd about the bonello.

The mowdieman cuist down his petals and traps,
The herd left his hirsle amang the green taps,
And the milk-maid she scrubbed and scyringed her naps,
          And hasted awa tae bonello.

For sic an a shine, was seldom ere seen,
Auld Scotlan' did vow she had ne'er wi' her e'en
Beheld ought to match'd since the " Kirk on the Green,"
          'Twas a noble conducted bonello.

In the welkin fu' hie, the moon beamed bright,
Ne'er a clud came across her the hale o' that night;
How the lasses, fu' charming, did skip in her light,
          Up the glens to the darling bonello.

And mony a laddie, wi' bosom sae warm,
Half carried his dearie alang on his arm,
For the hizzies that night, the frost-bitten cud charm,
          It was an enchanting bonello.

The hale was delightfu—the binks they were pang'd,
Time about roun' the laugh and the blether ding-dang'd,
Fowk could na a' sit now, were they to be hang'd,
          Sae af gaed the dance and bonello.

What huzzas now did follow—the kipplings rang,
On their taptaes what couples did jicker and spang,
Whan the pipers play'd up, how they fimmer'd alang,
          Heels cracking to cheer the bonello.

The mowdieman's shoon being sparrable paved,
How he duner'd, and hooh'd, and thumped, and raved,
While the strools, that the barnmen the barley wi' kaved,
        Gaed clampering through the bonello.

In jugs and decanters, and noggins and kits,
The drink it did circle, and mirth took her fits;
Nae glumfie chiel sat, wi' his sneers and his skits,
        Scrutinizing the famous bonello.

How the breasts o' the bare-necked lasses did heave—
Round pair after pair, Love's nets she did weave,
Frae ither fu' easily hearts they did reave,
        O ! the joys o' the lovely bonello.

Thus, wi' dancing and drinking, the night slided by,
Till Sol, wi' his gowd gilt the Easilin sky,
And mony a drunken chiel ouzily did ly,
        A bumpling wi' the bonello.

Kirrcormock himsell was as fou' as a witch,
He danced till his lisk was beset wi' a stitch,
For a', while his shanks after him he cud hitch,
        He keep'd up his glorious bonello.

Sair wauchled the hizzies were or they gat hame,
Some seem'd in a dalldrum, yet fu' o' game ;
And twa'r-three moons after did swaul i' the wame,
        Wi' hougheling at the bonello.

For the sake o' auld Scotlan, sae every gude chiel,
Wha meaneth to lae her sud tak his fareweel ;
Or else wi' a vengeance be flung to the de'il,
        And in hell hand his cursed bonello.

BONSPIEL—The highest game at curling—the chief *spiel*. When one parish, for instance, challenges another to play it, at the famous Scottish game of curling, or *channlestane*, that bout on the ice is called a *bonspiel*. The best players on these occasions are selected to play, and when not only their own honour, but that of their parish is at stake, they do, or at least strive to do, their very best; though often good players are put into such a flutter at these times that they lose the *steadiness of their han'*, and play badly : those who keep unmoved amid the crowd, and pay no attention to either damns or huzzas, play always best. The parishes of *Borgue, Sorby,* and *Closeburn,* rank amongst the first of the curling communities in the south of Scotland.

Sometimes *cock-lairds* challenge other to fight a *bonspiel,* and often these concerns turn out to be wars indeed. The following poem depicts a *broolzie* of this nature :—

THE BONSPIEL.

In Auld Scotlan' whan winter snell
  Bin's up the fosey yirth,
Than jolly curlers hae a spell,
  O' manly fun and mirth :
Whanere the ice can har'ly bear
  Ahame lie hurkling nane,
Wha liketh independant cheer,
  And can a channel-stane
                    Owrhog that day.

But whiles our grand peculiar game,
  Which ithers a' surpasses ;
Is hurt by Gomfs, weel worth the name,
  Vain bullieing senseless asses :
Akin tae them brave Hallions twa,
  Laird Nurgle and Laird Nabble,
'Bout wham I mean tae croon awa,
  Or, like a wilesteg gabble
                    A while this day.

Their habits, tempers, a' are bad,
  They're saucy, glunchy, greedy ;
Lan' they alike ay nearly had,
  And tenants starving needy :
For far abroad they baith were bred,
  Sae are o' kindness scarce ay,
A savage life they lang had led,
  And lash'd puir Massa's arsie
                    On mony a day.

To curling they did baith pretend,
  Sae challeng'd ane anither ;
Their farming slaves a han' maun lend,
  And neither whinge nor swither ;
Twall on a side, the place Loch Lum,
  The rink just forty ell ;
The bet a puncheon o' gude rum,
  Upon the ice itsell,
                  Fu' fu' that day.

And 'ere they did the play begin,
  Ilk stamock gat a cauker,
For, nane did think it was a sin
  Most bonnily to tak her.
Ahin the quickly toomed glass,
  How the wee finger twirled,
Than up in air a bawbee was,
  For heads or tails hie birled
                To lead that day.

Laird Nurgle had that triffing luck,
  Sae his first player led;
The stane to his direction stuck,
  But by the cock it fled;
At which began to fidge the laird,
  And muttering to blame him;
Laird Nabbles' man nae better fared,
  For Nabble loud did damn him,
                At first that day.

" Lay your stone right upon the tee,
  " My sickar handed fellow;
" My broom, if you're not blind, ye see,"
  Fat Nurgle now did yello'.
The trimling player stells his tramps
  Wi' mony a stamping stog;
Af gangs his stane, and ay it clamps,
  But hoh portule, a hog—
                It grunts that day.

What language now frae Nurgle fell,
  His phiz had on a horrid thraw;
What oaths he let, ne'er heard in Hell,
  Warm frae the Gulph o' Florida.
Lean Nabble than gaed out the word—
  " Be white ice to the witter;
" You're, ye are not worth a t—d,
  " Ye seem tae hae the sk——r,
                " Or bloit this day."

O! was na that a darling game,
  And worthy imitation;
Ye wha do understand the same,
  Ye standards o' our nation—
Had they been on Loch Duddingston,
  And no Loch Lum, we're thinking,
Few ends indeed they wad hae thrown,
  But aff been hissed linking,
              Fu' fast that day,

F

Whanere a Scotchman turns a slave
  He is na worth a boddle ;
Before the brave—below a knave
  Will cringe, they'll want the noddle.
Though there are some, were wae to tell,
  Feet soles are fond o' licking,
Will stick to tyrants, even to Hell,
  And bear their sneers and kicking
              Frae day to day.

But still the bonspiel drives awa,
  The ice was weak and slagie ;
The stanes wad scarce gang up ava,
  They grew sae unco clagie.
Ill nature pued down every brow,
  The lairds they swore and choked ;
There common sense did loit and spue,
  And wisdom aften boked
              Wi' a brash that day.

Thus, frothing on ilk noble side,
  Wi' blustering wan a game ;
A' corked were alike wi' pride,
  A Gomeril's near the same.
This minute was a bullierag,
  And that a blue erruction ;
At length did burst the meikle bag
  Which caused the destruction
              O' the speil that day.

As Nurgle raved about the cock,
  A stane came up the rink,
And hit his heel a canny shock,
  On that wi' joy we think—
For down he whurled upon Loch Lum,
  Some crawing cockaleerie ;
And span awhile upon his bum
  Like Tontom, or queer peerie,
              About that day.

But sprachling up a madman now,
  See how he lays about him ;
Laird Nabble cudna see his crew
  Abused—never doubt him.
A battle general began,
  Wi' brooms and neives they linged,
And mony a wee bit foolish man
  Was getting himsell swinged
              In stile that day.

Till hah ! the lochen gaed a rair,
  And af in blawds divided ;
Down sank the gows amang the glaur,
  Or else the water lided.
Yet han' in han' they reached dry lan',
  Up to the chin weel cooled ;
Then hame puir draggled cuifs they ran,
  Magnificently fooled,
            And dub'd that day.

Dear social honest countrymen,
  Let despots never dinnle
Your manly bosoms—for will then
  Nae pleasure through them trinnle.
Detest those sooking turkey-cocks,
  For ever jibing, jeering,
And heed as little's, yon grey rocks,
  Their guldering domineering
            On ony day.

Boo—To make a sound like bulls. These animals make three kinds of noises, expressed by the words *booing*, *crooning*, and *billieing*. Two Galloway priests, once passing a fellow who was good at flinging every thing into rhyme—quoth the one to the other, " I hold ye a sixpence, *Clinking Charlie* will be beat with what I say to him ?"—Done, says the other : so, when they passed the poet, the priest held out his finger at him, sounding *boo*, when the man of clink instantly returned—

    " Mr. Scott and Mr. Boyd
    " O' wit and learning they are void ;
    " For, like Billjock amang the kye,
    " They boo, at fowk as they gae by."

It is needless to add, that the clergymen slunk away, somewhat offended at the retort of *Clinking Charlie.*

Boonmost—Uppermost.

Boost—Must.

Borgue—One of the most singular and celebrated parishes in the south of Scotland, and one too of the very best that is to be found in any country. The following poem, by an old bard of the name of *Hackston*, belonging to the said

F. 2

parish, I here give, altered somewhat of course to suit my own foolish taste, and, perhaps, partly wrote by *mysell,* as my muse is quite ready with her aid, when any thing occurs, *poor jade,* that she can help me to—

THE PARISH O' BORGUE.

Blest be the bard wha can twine out his lays
To any grist, in thae great twining days;
Wha can plait cables, whan he has the thread,
Within the haurns o' his uncommon head :
Can send his muse to India for a time,
To wallow sweetly in that luscious clime
'Mang ladies, harams, and delicious flowers,
Melodious groves, and lovely vernal showers;
Or up amang the cluds, the clever wench,
Far frae yirth's beauty, or her unco stench,
To step about amang the starns, and see
A thousan' queer things wi' her gledgin' e'e ;
Car' takin tho' to keep in sight o' hame,
For fear some hule might scare her flight to fame,
And ow're a comet's tail gae lay and skelp her.
Without ane being near at han' to help her.

    For me, I care na tippence whar we go,
Whether tae lift, or fumart holes below ;
Whether to bonny isles ayont the sea,
Mull Jellies Hallan, or the *Brig o' Dee,*
Whar *Brumstane Dallies* fired a peat-stack,
And brunt a *pedlar* ance to get the *pack ;*
Aroun the moon, or *Muncraig's* gurly shore,
Whar pasper grows, and slavering pellocks snore ;
Whar *Connel* fell and brak his neck and scull
Ane Sabbath day, whan herrying, lucky Gull,
Adown the heugh the *chiel* reel'd a' to brash—
His banes and eggs met an unwelcome crash.

    Enow, tho' *Borgue,* my muse wi' pith and glee,
Means thee to croon, for, faith, thou pleaseth me ;
And I've heard singing 'bout some spout or burn,
Perhaps, na better than our ain *Pullwhurn:*
'Bout hills and tomacks too, faith, by the gross,
Perhaps na bonnier than the *Mool* or *Ross ;*
Wi' shores and caves whar gurly wuns do blo',
As by *Nockbrax* and ancient *Carlines co'.*
O! famous parish for the *Browns* and *Sproats,*
The like o't's na on this side John o' Groats.
True honest chiels and merry bunts o' lasses,
I've tooted wi' ye mony whusky glasses,
Spent mony a happy day amang ye trouth,
And ay ye hae keep'd me sappie 'bout the mouth.

There'*s* *Blair o' Senwick,* what a darling cheel,
May he ne'er feel the clutches o' the De'il ;
For weeks thegether he has keep'd me swimmin
In Hollan gin wi' him how aften raemin.
Auld Muldroch too, I wuss him ay fu' hale,
At the *saugh ligget*—mony a worthy tale
We twa hae gat, and cracking, drunk our fill
O' hame made maut and sometimes trickle yill,
While *auld Maminn,* the hule for clubbing lees,
For nursing flowers, and skepping hives o' bees,
Sat, like a sage, aside the chimlew lug,
And fancied queer things owre the faeming jug.
The *Deacons,* an uncouth, but clever fallow,
He is na dult, gude faith, he's nae way shallow.

And at the Ross, wi' yawcking *Johnie Dowall,*
And *Manksmen* gabbling frae the *manor-hole ;*
What naggins hae we drank o' smuggled rum,
Just hot frae aff the *Isle o' three legs* come.
Sic *joach* cheers me, it cows ought ere I foun',
Except the lovely blinks o' *Mary Cun ;*
Sweet Mary, shining wi' a thousan' charms,
The loveliest saul ere lay in *Hackston's* arms ;
What happy hours upon the buesty grass
O' *Carniehill* I hae towzled wi' my lass.

Borgue lads delight to marry lasses bonny,
Yet scorn to gang frae hame to seek for ony ;
They'd tak a sister o' their ain, by Jove,
Afore they'll through anither parish rove :
Sae blest am I gets ane as brights' the sun,
Without gaun far the bonny *Mary Cun.*
Nae Sillar sawnies on the *Borness* shore
Can sparkle like the e'en dang *Hackston* owre ;
Nae waving tangle, at low-water mark,
Can match her hair for shading light and dark ;
Nae sleek wee cobbles, on the wave-washed beach,
Beshape her bosoms—that they canna reach ;
But bletherin this ways, unco silly fun,
For nought on yirth to me's like *Mary Cun ;*
But e'n thout her, *auld Borgue* I wad adore,
Ay, every rummling-kirn about its shore :
Tho', my dear Mary, i'the mirkest night,
Maks me run far, to hug my lassy tight,
The *Plunton Castle* howlets wild may cry,
And ghaists about *Barrloch,* yawp—" Hackston fle,"
Cullraven's auld gibb cats eternal mew,
Mossney's ten-headed gomf might come in view,
And ilka collie after me might run,
Hackston should see his deary *Mary Cun.*

O ! *Mary Cun* and *Borgue* to me are dear,
And shall be sae while alive can steer ;

Whan I am dead, may they their hoary bard
Clap i'the mools o' *Senwick's* lane *kirk-yard ;*
Aside the auld gude friens wha mony a day
Took pity on my haffets growing grey,
And at my head set up an auld sea sclate,
Wi' thae words on't, coined in my curious pate—
" Here *Hackston* lies, *Borgue's lourat* mony a year
" Without his saul—whar's it, we canna hear ;
" He liked rhyme, was fond o' the wee drap,
" And now he sleeps as sound as ony tap."

    But why thus talk, whan I'm a sturdy man
I'll aff tae chieftain curlers on *Nockann,*
And see the fun, the pith o' meikle banes,
Sends whunnering up the rink the channel-stanes,
I'll ablins get a dram o' whusky there,
Syne I'll be crouse as ony tipped hare.
Kirkcubrie, Twinholm, Girthon, canna craw,
Borgue bids them kiss her ——, she beats them a'
At bonspiels, ay, o' what a shilpet crew,
Sic pewtring bodies, curse me, ne'er I knew :
Come never here, ye druken hallion *Sloan,*
Wi' a' your flum, let us in Borgue alone ;
Borgue is a pure, a spotless lawland clan,
Chain'd heart and hand thegether man and man :
Nae grubbing strangers here dare cock their nose,
Puir bodies may, tho', she be kind to those,
Wi' ony ithers, soon she is insulted,
Forbes can fley them, faith, frae out the pulpit.
Wi' faces, ay, as white as ony starch,
They wad be joustled clean out owre the march,
For mang our clints and hags, and rashy bogs,
Chiels do appear, can claw a fallow's lugs :
A glorious squad they are, baith one and a',
They're no hauf matched in a wild Gallowa :
While *Hackston* doth their sprightly bairnies teach,
While *Forbes* can like ony stentor preach ;
While bonny lasses in the *Boreland* thrive,
And now't in *Senwick Parks* can southward drive ;
While *Samuel Cloon,* in *Ross* can sit fu' cross,
While peats are got in *Plunton's* glaury moss ;
While craws at *Barmaguachin,* yearly big,
And lasses at the kirk look unco trig,
Borgue shall be famous throughout auld Scotland,
Her *woo'* and *hinnie* never left on hand.

BORGUE-HINNIE—Borgue honey. This article is of such good quality, that the fame of its excellence spreads far and wide. In London there is a sign, with *Borgue-hinnie for ever,* wrote on it.

Boss—A fat consequential man.

Bossie—Bosom.

Bou—To bend.

Bouch—One of a curr-dog's barks.

Boutgate—When a plowman starts from one *landen* or *headrig*, plows to the other, and returns to where he broke off, he is said to have gone a *boutgate*; as also the distance which mowers can go at a *sharp*, or with one sharping of the scythe. This is also termed a *boutin or boutgate.*

Boukin Linen—Boiling linen webs with lees, in order to lay them out to bleach.

Bouls—The bended handles whereby several vessels are moved anywhere.

Bowerock—An huddled lump of any thing. *Big on to the bowercock,* a term at curling, and means, to direct the stone to where a number are already laid.

Bowertree-puff.—An hollow tube made of *Bore tree,* used by *kill-men* to blow through, and rouse their *seed* fires, or fires fed by the husks of corn.

Bowie—A washing-tub.

Bowkail—Cabbage.

Bowlhive—A deadly distemper, common amongst infants.

Bowloch—A person with ill-shaped legs.

Bowls—Basons of a small size, made of earthern ware.

Bowt—An iron bolt.

Bowt.—To start up suddenly is to *bowt up*; as a person, when come up to the surface again, after plunging beneath water. This word, and the English " boyant " are one and the same.

Bow-wow—A dog's bark, when he first smells strangers.

Bowze.—A set-to for some time at eating and drinking.

Bowzie.—Looking fat like. A man is said to be so that fills his waistcoat well.

Boytoch.—A thick short little animal ; bad at walking.

Bra or Braw.—Well dressed ; neat.

Brack.—A break.

Brack an Egg.—A curling phrase, given by the directors of the game to those about to play ; and means, that they are to strike a stone with their's, with that force that it would break an egg between them at the point of contact.

Brae.—The brow-side of a hill.

Brag and Pairs.—A rustic game at cards.

Bragwort.—Mead. A fermented liquor, made from honey : a *wort* that can *brag* all others for being so good. Hence the name *bragwort*. After the bees are *smuiked* in the *hinharrest time*, the *gude wife* takes the *kaimes* out of the *skep*, and lets the *hinny* drop out of them before the fire ; when this is done, she takes these combs or *kaimes* and steeps them in water. This water, warmed and quickened with *barm*, composes *bragwort*. It is an extreme sweet and pleasant drink ; when put in bottles it is apt to break them. That person is a particular favourite in that house, when, by making a call, he is treated with a draught of *bragwort*. If he be a young man of fair character, looking out for a wife, and this house be a place where fair dames are, he is sure to taste *bragwort*. It may be called with propriety the " lover's drink."

Braiggle.—Any old, unsafe article—as a large gun with a large lock.

Braird.—Corn as it appears above the ground a little after it has been sown, when it begins to " beard."

BRAIRDED-DYKES.—Fences bearded with whins, thorns, or other brushwood, to hinder cattle from getting over them.

BRALLION.—An unwieldy man.

BRANGE.—To kick, to plunge, and knock things to desolation, like a mad horse.

BRANKS.—Old wooden bridles, also a disorder of the neck.

BRANNER.—A brander.

BRASH.—A watry fit of sickness.

BRASHLOCH.—Rubbage.

BRATCHIE.—Indian rubber. That elastic gum which comes from the Indian tribes, used for defacing the marks of wadd, or black lead.

BRATS.—Aprons ; also rags ; also children in rag

BRATT.—The scum of any fluid.

BRATTLE.—To rattle.

BRAUN.—An old boar.

BRAVELY.—Very well.

BRAWCHTON.—Any thing weighty and unwieldy.

BRAWD.—Any large rude article.

BRAWLY.—The same with bravely.

BRAWNET.—A colour made up of black and brown, mostly relating to the skins of animals. A " nowt beast o' a brawnet colour " takes a south-country man's eye next to that o' the " slae black."

BRAWS.—Dresses. The grandest of these are generally farthest " ben " the wardrobe. Hence we say of any one when we see them more gaudy than usual, that the " boddom o' the kist has been a looking at ——."

BRAXY.—A disorder prevalent amongst sheep, and in general a very fatal one. The animal soon dies after in-

fected, and there is no cure for it as yet discovered that
can be said to avert the evil. Sheep in good condition are
those it makes great havoc of. That kind of weather
with hoar frost after rain is the worst for it; shepherds
then are sure to have much mortality amongst their flocks.
Braxy is a malady attended always with an abominable
stench. Strangers unused to it cannot for some time suffer it at all. Their smelling organs will not endure it; and
much longer are they in bringing themselves to be able
to eat the flesh of the poor animals who perish, let it be
boiled, stewed, roasted, or any way dressed. All the spice
in the world will not keep down the noxious smell. The
braxy effluvia keeps still uppermost: the *daught* pre-
dominates. In truth, it is not a very wholesome food.
Those feeding much on it become blotched, and not unfrequently are troubled with that filthy disease, the *yaws*.

BRAXY-HAMS.—The hams of those sheep which die of the
braxy. When the *herd* finds any of his flock dead of that
distemper, if they can stand *three shakes*—that is to say,
if they be not so putrified or rotten but that they can
stand to be thrice shaken by the neck without falling to
pieces—then he bears them home to his master's house
on the *braxy shelty*. What of the carcases can then be
ham'd, are done, and the rest of the flesh made present
use of by the family. The hams thus cut out are hung
up in the *smuiky brace*, until they are quite dry. They
are then bound in bunches, like so many hare-skins,
and suspended on *nags* and *clicks*, in convenient parts of
the roof of the kitchen, and used now and then for
very singular purposes. As for instance, when a club
of *burn trout fishermen*, or one of *muirfuel* sportsmen,
come the way of the house, they are hospitably entertained
at table with plenty of *braxy ham*, and other dainties; for
the natives of the moors are a kind people, and generally
keep what is understood by a *fu' house*. Now I am not

sneering at present; but honestly saying, that a *male o'*
sic food, washed down by a few glasses of *peatreek,* or
tumblers of *bragwort,* please a hungry *kyte* very much,
and cause one to fall in love with mountaineers. For
braxy is by no means bad food, when ham'd; the smell
then in a great measure leaves it. Likewise these hams
sometimes adorn the saddle-bow of a moorland lover,
when he starts a horseback to *seek a wife,* and are considered to aid him much in making his *putt-gude* with any
girl he takes a fancy for, particularly if she be a *laich
fiel lass;* though he is often disappointed in this specu-
lation. However, on the whole, there is worse furniture
to be found in a house, in cold, snowy, wintry weather,
than plenty of *braxy ham.*

BRAXY SHELTY.—A little rough poney kept by moor farmers to bring home *braxy sheep.*

BREASTED.—Leaped, by first throwing up or over the
breast. Those who mount horses without stirrups, are
said to " breast on to their bare backs." Girls sneering at
short little men, often say, " that they cudna breast a ratton
af a peat."

BRECHAMS.—Collars for horses; anciently they were made
entirely of straw, and called " Strae brechams."

BRECKAN.—The fern.

BRECKANY BRAES.—Rural solitudes, growing with fern;
the haunts of innocence and rustic poets.

BREEDS.—Breadths. Girls talk of how many *breeds o'
prent* will make them a *frock.*

BREEKS.—Breeches.

BREEL.—To reel; to make a noise.

BREEST-BANES.—The breast-bones of fowls. They are
bones of a forked figure. Two persons engage to pull
the fork apart with their *little* fingers. They draw against
each other, and the person who gets the largest share of

the bone left in hand when it breaks, is said will be married first.

BREEZE.—To bruise.

BRENTBROWS.—Having a smooth forehead, not wrinkled.

BREW.—Opinion. This word deserves further consideration. " I ha'e nae great brew o' that man," is often said, and means, " I have no great opinion of that man." Also, " I ha'e a good brew," which signifies the reverse. Now, this " brew " cannot be allied to " broe," sap or fluid of some kind, but may be to " brow," the front of the brain, as those who read *phizzes* place much dependance on what they find on the brow ; still this comes not to the point. I am flung back to " brew,"—and this may mean, to make, to conceive ; as ale is *brewed*; for we are said to be " brewing " when we are thinking. So the word, for all, may come from this : " I ha'e nae great brew."—There is no brewing in the brain of any consequence.

BRICHT-LINTIE.—A bird of the linnet tribe.

BRIDLING RAPES.—Ropes which hold down the thatch on stacks. They are woven into the *owrgaun anes,* or those which are vertical over the *concern,* and are not rolled up like them when made, but twisted together in a longer shuttle form.

BRIG.—Bridge.

BRILCH.—A short thick impudent person.

BRISKET.—The breast.

BRISLIN.—Bristlin.

BRITHER.—Brother.

BROACHES.—Wooden spindles to put pirns on, to be wound of.

BROCHEN.—A fat mixture to feed young calves.

BROCK.—Refuse of any thing ; rotten straw.

BROCK.—The badger.

BROCKET.—Like a badger in colour, black and white.

BROCK-HOLES.—Badger dens.

BROD.—Board.

BRODS.—Window-shutters.

BROE.—Sap, juice, &c. of any thing.

BROESE.—Broth.

BROGGLE.—To make a bad hand of a job ; to be unhandy.

BROICH.—To be warm and sweating much, is to be in a " broich " with sweat.

BROOLZIES or BROOZLES.—Rows in the rural world. The old poem of " Christ's Kirk on the Green" is of this nature ; also an unknown one, here to follow, termed

THE BEE-HIVE.

Whan May comes in wi' mochey showers,
    And blinking snns, sae warming,
The bees, amang her bonny flowers,
    Are smioking and swarming.
Frae bud to bloom they bizz wi' speed,
    For virgins ay they're striving ;
Young queens their cores abroad do lead
    To where the merry hiving
                Will haud that day.

And aften far they'll tak a flight
    Owre hills, and hags, and mosses ;
Before they think it's time to light,
    Which mony a body crosses ;
As was the way wi' Archy Bell,
    Whan his tap swarm did flee
Out owre Bentouther's buesty fell,
    And down tae Lowdenlee
                Fu' straught ae day.

This Archy was a greedy curse,
    And glie'd at things about ;—
He pat the bawbee in his purse,
    But seldom took it out.
His mind was no as braids ane's loof ;
    He had na heart ava :
Was just a grubbing, shyling cuif,
    Fu' fit to gi'e ill jaw
                The lee lang day.

A bee-man lang the chiel had been,
   Keep'd mony a winter stale,
And sell'd the hinny ay aff clean,
   Wi' bannock-wax fu' hale.
Na bragwort ere was brewn by he
   For scuitifu's to sloken,
A stang about the neb, or e'e,
   Wad har'ly make him gloken—
                On ony day.

Amaist, like Bonar, he a skep
   Cou'd paise and sleely han'le ;
The smooking them ne'er made him weep,
   Wi' lowing brumstane can'le.
Their dying sough did please his lug—
   That sad confused lamenting ;
But feelings he had nane to tug,
   Which throweth some, repenting—
                On mony a day.

O, is it na a horrid thing,
   Sic myriads to slaughter,
For a' the cash the prize can bring,
   And yet to do't in laughter ?—
Which Archy unco often did,
   And snork'd his snuff fu' cheery ;
At length, however, he was chid,
   And ne'er again was merry—
                Wi' bees ae day.

The hive which warped owre the fell,
   As formerly was stated,
Was followed warmly by himsell—
   O how he pech'd and sweated !
And now and then would glowre for it
   Up i' the lift uncloudy,
Than something whiles wad keep his fit,
   And whurl him heels owre gowdie—
                Wi' a thud that day.

Whiles too as thus he rowd, and sten'd,
   And clinched it awa,
He'd slonk adown, or ere he ken'd,
   A miry, quacking qnaw,
Or glauroch, far aboon the knee,
   Through some blue rashy gullion,
The hive ay keeping in his e'e,
   A grim disjasket rullion
                He was that day.

Thus driving down on Lowdenlee,
   As hard as he cou'd smack,
Against a whunstane dyke gaes he,
   Rebounding arset back.

Queer rings o' mony a different hue
  Did whirl afore his een ;
Some were a yellow, ithers blue,
  And some were livid green—
            We true that day.

The dwamel aff, he skellie's roun',
  But cou'd na see a bee ;
Ay, sure he heard their bizzing soun',
  Tho' them he cou'd na see.
But whether it was the bomf he got,
  That made his lang lugs tingle,
He ken'd na, and away did trot,
  Again what he cou'd wingle—
            That weary day.

Till Girzy Grey, down i' the lee,
  A cross-grained wrinkl'd wicker,
Sees Archy wi' her reeked e'e,
  And cries, " Whare's this, ye bicker ?"
" Come here, gudeman, and len' a han'—
  (" O dinna by me hasten)
" And let us skep gin that we can
  " My gude tap swarm here casten,
            " This bonny day."

" Ye lee, ye bitch," (roars Archy out)
  " I won'er o' ye Grizzel ;
" Ye'll get some day for it, I doubt,
  " A whaling till ye whizzle.
" The hive is mine ; it flew frae hame
  " About an hour sincesyne,
" And after it I was na lame :—
  " D'ye think that I shall tyne
            " My bees this day ."

" Your bees !" (quoth she to Archy Bell)
  " Faith, that's a tale indeed !
" O, Archy, man, to de'il in hell,
  " Ye're cantering wi' speed.
" Though I be auld, and often 's c'ad
  " A wallow'd, wicked scranny,
" Dread ye the claws, my sneeling lad,
  " O' feckless Wullcat granny,
            " Or curse this day."

Baith own'd the hive, tho' it was thought
  To neither to belang ;
Baith owre it stood, and raged, and fought,
  And scrated, punsed, and flang.
Baith got a skep, and baith wad hae't,
  In their's to make its mantion ;
But nane o' them had luck to get
  The *Queen's* most gracious sanction
            Upon that day.

Up rase her swarm, frae whar it hang,
  In bunch below a broom,
And did the haveralls nicely staug,
  Weel worthy sic a doom.
How Archy swaul'd, and roun' did loup!
  How girn'd the wizen'd spirran,
For some crawl'd up, and hov'd her doup,
  And did na miss her birran,
                    'Tis said that day.

Whaever tweillie about bees,
  Thae bees will never thrive,
Nor thae saes Providence decrees
  Wha fashes wi' the hive.
" Let a' industrious tribes alane !"
  True Wisdom's ay resounding,
Sae will this world wi' grief ne'er grane,
  Nor broyliments, confounding
                    Appear na day.

BROUNIES.—Nocturnal beings, which thrashed farmers'
corn, and did other laborious jobs, for which the *gude
wives*, as Milton says, " had the cream bowl duly set."
They were seldom seen. Some think they were of no
supernatural origin, but distressed persons, who were
obliged to conceat themselves, and wander about, during
some of the past turbulent ages.

BROWST.—A brewing, a mighty making of any thing.

BROYLIMENT.—A mighty commotion of some kind or
other. When a black bank of clouds is seen to rise in the
south, and a noise or mighty *soughing* of the sea is heard,
then a *brooliment* of the weather is at hand. Indeed,
rookeries, or storms of any kind, are fully expressed by
the word. It is still connected, one way or other, with a
broil.

BRUCKLE.—Brittle.

BRUCKLE-BREAD.—Brittle-bread.

BRUFF'D.—Thickly cloathed.

BRUGH ABOUT THE MOON.—A kind of thin hazy va-
pour which seems to infold the moon sometimes. We
behold it between her and her radiance, but are not aware

of its existing, was it not for the moon; as, but for this sign, the nocturnal sky seems without clouds or mists of any kind. The *brugh* or ruff, round the silvery orb, is very beautiful—so white and snowy just before the disk— then shading away, till the cicrumference of the fold is drawn by the intruding darkness,—whiles it is called the *faul about the moon*, or fold. The signification of *brough* is a gathering of foul matter, a collection of rubbish; so when it is seen, those skilled in the weather prophecy that there is going to be some *onfa'*, or other—either of rain or something worse.

BRUNSTANE.—Brimstone.

BRUNSTANE CANNLES.—Matches made of paper and brimstone, to suffocate bees.

BRUNT.—Burnt.

BRYME.—Salt brine.

BUBBLIEJOCK.—A name for the turkey-cock.

BUBIES.—The breasts.

BUCHANITES.—A singular sect of religious fanatics that first made their appearance in the neighbourhood of Glasgow about fifty or sixty years ago. From thence they came to *Buchan ha'*, in the parish of Closeburn; and now the remnant of the core remain at a place in Galloway, called the *Crooked-ford*, a place about eight or nine miles west from Dumfries. Their founder was a Mrs. Buchan, the wife of a dyer in Glasgow. She was a very tall, strong woman; or, in the Scottish, a *strapping hizzie*. Her husband and her having had some dispute, she flung aside her *litt pots*, and left off the colouring of matter for the colouring of mind, and was so fortunate as soon to have many followers, all dipped in one *dye*. Amongst these was a fellow of the name of White, a *colleged priest*, as he was termed,—a fellow who had been bred up for the church in some university, but having a weak brain, unfit

to hold the learning that was poured into it, he so became
a fit subject for waiting upon Mrs. Buchan, and frantic as
she could possibly be.   White, however, aided her cause
very considerably.   He was quite an Abbo Bekar to Ma-
homet.   When the innocent country people heard that a
real priest, a minister of the word, had become a *Bu-
chanite,* they gathered in from all quarters, and became
so likewise.

One of her chief tenets was, that all who followed her
and her doctrine would go to heaven without tasting of
death, like Elias, and that too, on a certain day which she
prophesied—for she always wished to be looked on as a
prophetess, and that she alighted on earth at the *Clauchan
o' Thornhill,* from heaven, keeping still the *litt rats* in the
gorbals of Glasgow out of sight.   At long and length the
glorious day arrived on which they were all to be taken
to the regions above, where endless happiness existed, and
pleasure for evermore.   Platforms were erected for them
to wait on, until the wonderful hour arrived, and Mrs.
Buchan's platform was exalted above all the others.   The
hair of *ilka* head was cut short—all but a tuft on the top,
for the angels to catch by when drawing them up.   The
momentous hour came.   Every station for ascension was
instantly occupied.   Thus they stood, expecting to be
wafted every moment into the land of bliss, when a gust
of wind came ;—but, instead of wafting them upwards, it
capsized Mrs. Buchan, platform and all ! and the fall
made her all *hech* again on the *cauld yird.*   After this unexpected downcome, she fell into disgrace by her leaders,
and her words had not so much weight with them ; still,
however, a great number clung by her ; and one night
(she having been ailing for some time before) a fit came
on her, out of which she never recovered ; but her dis-
ciples, thinking it to be a trance into which she had fallen,
expected her to awake ; but no signs of this appearing
for some days, and her body beginning to have a putrid

smell, they thought it prudent to bury it in the earth beside the house; and by her have been laid all those of her
sect who have since died.—So ends the tale of *Lucky Buchan.* She would allow none of her followers to marry,
or have any love-dealings with other; so the tribe soon
weeded away and became thin. It is said that there were
many *bastard bairnies* appeared amongst them; but that
they hardly ever let them behold the light. Be this as it
may, their general character all along has been quite
harmless. They were, and yet are, a very industrious
people, and have been long unmatched at making *Wee
Wheels* and *Chackreels,* plying the turning-loom to great
perfection. They are all, however, of rather a wild frantic nature, and seem to want " some *pence* of the shilling,
a penny or more." After all, they have been an odd concern; and to think they arose in Scotland, a place

" Whar lair and light, are at sic a height,"

is a thing to be wondered at. Many pamphlets and songs
have been wrote respecting this species of Mahometans;
but none of them that I have seen seem to have any
touches of talent worthy of remark.

BUCKBEARD.—A kind of hard fog, of a white nature,
which is found growing on rocks—often it is seen in the
form of a wine-glass, or inverted cone, and looks very
beautiful; it is not used now-a-days for any thing I know
of, but anciently the witches found it an useful ingredient
in a charm mixture.

BUCKIES.—Fruit of a certain kind of brier. There are
three species of " buckiberries" in the country—a long
green kind, good to eat, grows on lofty bushes; another
much like them, but grows on higher bushes, and never
ripens well; and a third kind, about the size of a sloe, or
larger, and of the same colour, which grows on a dwarfish
brier, thought to be somewhat poisonous.

Buckie Lice.—The seed of the buckie; it much resembles lice.

Buckin.—Striking.

Buckle.—To fix.

Buck nor Croon.—An animal is said to be unfit to do either of these, when it can neither strike nor make a noise, though willing to do both.

Bucks and Kids.—A school-game. See " Dools."

Buck-teeth.—Outstanding tusks.

Buffer.—A boxer—a Crib; a blackguard—a man detested amongst men.

Buff nor Stye.—A phrase which signifies—I know nothing about it, neither more nor less, neither in one respect nor in another.

Bufft.—The noise of a blow given on soft subjects, which may be well conceived from this quotation from " *Christ Kirk on the Green*"—

> " He hit him on the wame a whap,
> " It bufft like ony blether;
> " But ha! his fortune was and hap,
> " His doublet made o' lether—
>   " Saved him that day."

Bught.—A sheepfold.

Bulb or Bulboch.—A disorder with sheep; when infected, they drink water until they swell and burst; when swelled, they are of a bulbous form—hence the name.

Bulla.—Brother.

Bullirag.—A dispute with words—" words that often come to blows."

Bullisters.—Large sloes, common on sea-shores; for there the sloe thorns spread on the beach like wall fruit trees, as it were, on the walls before the sun.

Bumbees.—The wild humble bees. There are three kinds of these bees common in Scotland—the black, the *braw-net*, and the brown. The first has its nest deep in the ground, and they are generally found in very large colonies together; the second build and breed under ground too, but not so deep as the others; and the third, or brown, always on the surface. The sting of a wild bee is not so venomous as that of a tame one, neither are the *bumbees* so fierce as the others; but will fly buzzing round and round, and seldom dart in to sting—their *bykes* are robbed for common, without much trouble. The honey of *bum-bees* is also quite weak and watry to that of the others; nor do they display great handy work in the formation of their combs; theirs are no hexagonal tubes, but dirty glo-bular figures; they are no craftsmen in truth, nor yet near so nimble as the others in comparison; yet who does not love to hear them in the spring *bumming* amongst the *sillarsaughs wi downie buds,* or the opening leaves of the *plaintree.* In an old riddle the three kinds are thus spe-cified—

> " As I cam owre the tap o' Tyne,
> " I met a drove o' Highlan' swine;
> " Some o'm *black,* some o'm *brown,*
> " Some o'm *rigget* owre the crown;
> " Sic a drove o' Highlan' swine,
> " I ne'er met on the tap o' Tyne."

Bumclock.—The humming beetle of the evenings.

Bummin.—Humming.

Bummle.—To fumble.

Bumpkin brawly.—An old dance, the dance which al-ways ends balls; the same with the " Cushion" almost.

> " Wha learn'd you to dance,
> " You to dance, you to dance,
> " Wha learn'd you to dance—
> " A country bumpkin brawly?
> " My mither learn'd me when I was young,
> " When I was young, when I was young,
> " My mither learn'd me when I was young,
> " The country bumpkin brawly."
>
> *Auld Sang.*

The tune of this song is always played to the dance.

BUMSHOT.—When any plot gives way with us, we are said to be *bumshot*.

BUMWHUSH.—When any thing has made a noise for some time, and is then quashed, it is said to gone to the *bumwhush*. This is too often the way with people of great popularity; they have their day, then go all to the *bumwhush*.

BUNJELLS.—Burthens of straw; fern.

BUNKER.—A long chest, answering also for a seat.

BUNN.—A hare's tail.

BUNSE.—A short thick little girl.

BURD.—Bird.

BURD ALANE.—Bird alone.

BURIAL HOUSE.—The house of mourning; the house wherein lies a corpse awaiting interment; it is termed the *burial house* but for one day, the day of the burial.

BURLY WHUSH.—A game played at with a ball. The ball is thrown up by one of the players on a house or wall, who cries on the instant it is thrown to another to catch or *kep* it before it falls to the ground; they all run off but this one to a little distance, and if he fails in *kepping* it, he bawls out *burly whush*; then the party be arrested in their flight, and must run away no farther. He singles out one of them then, and throws the ball at him, which often is directed so fair as to strike; then this one at which the ball has been thrown is he who gives *burly whush* with the ball to any he chooses. If the corner of a house be at hand, as is mostly the case, and any of the players escape behind it, they must still shew one of their hands past its edge to the *burly whush man*, who sometimes hits it such a *whack* with the ball, as leaves it *dirling* for an hour afterwards.

BURN.—A small river of water. These rivulets are frequently very poetical objects in nature, when they steal

" 'neath the lang yellow broom," or when " 'neath the brow the burnie juiks ;" and on so. *Tannahill* has a good song called *You Burn Side* ; and here follows a new one, of an original stamp, termed—

THE SUNNY BURN BRAE.

My auld cronnie Pate has his sweet, sweet Kate,
 And my darling Nannie I hae, hae ;
Wi' her I roam, the meadow and the howm,
 And row on the Sunny Burn Brae, Brae—
And row on the Sunny Burn Brae.

Her shining hair is a yallowish fair,
 And her e'en are as black as the slae, slae ;
O ! were she in my arms, to towzle her charms,
 Again on the Sunny Burn Brae, Brae—
Again on the Sunny Burn Brae.

O ! her singing to hear I do lo'e dear,
 'Tis sweeter than the lammies mae, mae ;
But to kiss her mou' is like Heaven I true,
 On the green and Sunny Burn Brae, Brae—
On the green and Sunny Burn Brae.

My heart she has ta'en, O ! I find its clean gane,
 And I hope she'll ne'er let it gae, gae ;
Nor the want o't I'll no mourn—as her ain ane in return,
 She gaed me on the Sunny Burn Brae, Brae—
She gaed me on the Sunny Burn Brae.

By the hinnysuckle tree, adown the flowery lee,
 I like weel on the e'ening to stray, stray ;
But the hinnysuckle tree is nought ava to me,
 Like my love on the Sunny Burn Brae, Brae—
Like my love on the Sunny Burn Brae.

BURNBECKER.—The bird known also by the name of *waterpyet*, having a white breast, while the rest of its plumage is black, and a frequenter of burns or streams of water ; it keeps its body in continual motion—*beck—becking*—hence the name *burnbecker*. It is one of the poet's favourite birds, not for its singing, for it sings none, nor for its beauty, having also little of that ; but because it haunts places of deep solitude—lonely burns—where also do the bards of nature.

BURNBLADES.—A large broad leaved plant. which is found growing on the banks of burns.

BURNT-STANES.—A curling term. When a stone in motion hits another in passing slightly, it is said to *burn* on it; sometimes when they *burn* or rub rather roughly, they are said to have got their *burthen*; that is to say, they have got as much of their motion retarded by one stone, as hinders them to damage any more; and when a stone in motion hits the feet, or the *broom* of any player, not on the same side of the game with that stone, it is allowed to be played over again; but if it hit one on its own side, it is thrown off the *ice*; for why it is a *burnt-stane*.

BURRBLE.—Any thing in confusion. When a pirn of yarn in winding runs into disorder, it is then in a *snurl* or a *burrble*.

BURR-THRISTLES.—The strongest of the thistle tribe. There are five kinds of thistles common in Scotland—the *burr* or *horse thristle*; the *corn thristle*; the *moss thristle*; the *swine thristle*; and the *Scotch thristle*.

BURSEN KIRNS.—Those *kirns* which are cut with labour. Thus, if the last of the crop cannot be got cut by the *shearers* for all they can work until night be set in—then they say they have had a *bursen kirn*; they have *burst* themselves almost before they got the last cut or *kirn* shorn.

BUSHES.—Iron or brass rings in the centre of wheels, to keep down friction.

BUSKET.—Neatly dressed.

BUSS.—Bush.

BUT AND BEN.—Kitchen and parlour.

BUTT.—A mark. " Bowbutts," little hillocks of earth common in Galloway; there are mostly two of them found near other, within 150 or perhaps 200 yards; they were the places shot at by our forefathers, when practising with the ancient weapons of war—the bow and arrow.

BUTTERMILK GLED.—A bird of the falcon tribe; it is of a cream colour, of the size of the common *kite*; some think it is the male kite, but this cannot be so. It seems to be a bird of emigration; and, by its visiting us in winter, bespeaks it comes from some arctic nation. Indeed, *Greenland* is seen in all its moves; it is savage and cold-hearted. No *burd o' prey* gives a *clocken hen* a greater *glocken* than the *buttermilk gled.*

BYE-HIM-SELL.—Deranged in the intellect.

BYKE.—To whinge; to weep and sob.

BYKES.—Bee-nests; also nests of angry people.

BYLES.—Gatherings of bile on the body.

BYNALL.—A tall lame man.

BYNG.—A rude lump, or heap of any thing, such as a pit full of potatoes.

BYRE.—A cowhouse.

BYRE-PLAID.—A plaid used about byres.

BYRE-WOMAN.—The girl about farm-houses, whose duty it is to look after the cows during the winter season; these girls for common are strong-boned persons, as able to give a good lift as a man. There are always two chief female servants about houses of this kind, called the " byre-woman," and the " kitchinwoman," the cold half of the year; and the " *outane*" and the " *innane*" the other half; for in summer cows are put out of the *byre.* I have heard that Nicholson our poet has wrote a poem, ycleped verses on the " *Death o' a Dairymaid.*" I wish I saw them.

BYRRAN.—The female nymphæ.

C.

CA'.—To call; name; and drive.

CABBAGE BLADES.—Blades of the cabbage plant, used to wrap soft matters in, as butter.

CABROCH.—Stinking putrid flesh; food for the ravens and greycrows.

CADGELL'D.—A person having got a rough ride is said to have been *cadgell'd*; cadgell, being to carry after a rough manner—

> " Fate ne'er intends us twa auld hags,
> " Twa *Billy Newals*, or *Sawnie Rags*,
> " To cadgell, keel, and ronnet bags—
>   " Owre a' the kintra Geordy."
> *Epistle to George Wishart.*

CADGER.—A carrier on horseback.

CADGER TE CREELS AND A'.—An expression representing a cadger and all his appurtenances.

CAED.—Calved.

CAER BENTORIGUM.—A beautiful Roman camp in the parish of Kirkcudbright; it is on the top of a commanding hill, and surrounded by deep trenches; a more entire thing of the kind is not in the south of Scotland; some think it was one of the posts of Agricola.

CAERSLOOTH.—An ancient fortress on the sea shore, in the parish of Kirkmabreek, Galloway; it is a strength by nature of the first kind; a deep chasm cutting its site from the main land, above twenty feet in width, and above fifty in depth; over this has been thrown a draw-bridge; and as the sides of the rock all round are extremely steep, it is wonderful to conceive how a foe might gain possession of it; yet here it was that—

> " Wallace lap, and Carlie clam."

He first threw his broad sword over the yawning chasm— did the mighty Scot's patriot; then followed it by making a tremendous leap himself. His fell, comrade Carlie durst not try that trick, but went down the precipice, and *clam* up to the assistance of his friend—what brave fellows— was a place ever taken by storm in such a manner—there did they *lay on* like devils. Wallace took his great sword, which was like the *rafter* of a house, both hands to the handle, and mowed the southeron loons down before him; some of whom, rather than receive a *fleg* from his metal keen, leaped over the *heugh*, where they were dashed to pieces below.

On the main land, and just beside where the grand entrance had been, stands a large smooth faced stone, with many characters cut on it, but what these import no antiquarian as yet can tell.

CA'ES.—Calves.

CAFF.—Chaff.

CAFFIE-HEAP.—A heap of oats before they are winnowed.

CAIRN HATTIE.—A large Galloway mountain; on its top a cloud generally reposes—a cowl or hat as it were—hence the name *hattie*.

CAIRNS.—Hillocks of stones; whiles they are built with care, but oftener not; they are common on the tops of hills; a number of them were built prior to dykes, as marks, to shew *lairds* the *marches* or boundaries of their possessions. In ancient burial grounds they are met with too; our ancestors, like the natives yet of every uncivilized country, huddled a number of stones on the graves of their dead.

" *I'll throw a stane to your Cairn,*" was a phrase used in the days of yore, and expressive of a kindness that would be shewn persons even when dead—by throwing a stone now and then to the *cairns* on their graves. Chieftains of course then, and people of note, would be honoured with the largest *cairns*.

CAIRNS-MOORS.—There are three large hills or moors in Galloway, called " Cairns-moors"—

" Cairns-moor o' Fleet,
" Cairns-moor o' Dee;
" But Cairns-moor o' Carsphairn
" 'Sthe biggest o' the three."

They are about a couple of thousand feet above the level

of the sea. *Yirns*, otherways eagles, build their nests on them—and amongst their wild rocks are pieces of beautiful spar found, termed by the country people *Cairns-moor diamonds.* I have heard, too, of the *door of the Cairns-moor of Fleet*, which is a very large cave that runs away into the interior of the mountain, as yet, like the *Piper's Co' o' Cowend*, unexplored.

CAKIE.—The excrement of children.

CALLAN.—A young person, either a boy or a girl.

CALLERIN O' THE BLADE.—A slight rain by which the blades of grass are cooled and refreshed.

CALLION.—Any thing old and ugly.

CAMRELL.—A piece of wood used by butchers, notched on either end, used in hanging up carcases by the hind legs.

CAMSHACKLED.—A quadruped is so, when its two fore legs are " *langled,*" or confined with a chain, so that it cannot leap.

CAMSTEERIE.—Restless; given to quarrel.

CANGLIN.—Wrangling; foolishly disputing.

CANKERT.—Cross-grained; ill-natured; fretful, &c.

CANKERT KING COWAN.—An old farmer wretch, who lived at a place, some years ago, called the *Blairs o' Cree*; he was extremely bad to his wife; in short, there was not one good quality about him. An Irish bard, who had been stopping sometime in his neighbourhood, and who knew his character well, would make a song on him—the which I here give; because it contains some genius, and is wrote not only to a Galloway air, but in the Galloway language; some of the ideas however bespeak green Erin. It gave me some furbishing ado before I got its grammar, measure, and clink, in a fair looking passable way; but indeed the *confessions* of an old blackguard will never look well—

My name's Johnnie Cowan the king o' queer fellows,
    The devil the like o' me ere ye did see ;
My lungs they are stronger than ony smith's bellows,
    Sae far frae the grave than I surely maun be.
But like the horn'd howlet that's a' the nicht screeching,
    'Bout cuikin o' victuals am a' the day teaching ;
On washin o' dishes too I'd mak a preaching,
    Wad bet on sermon ere ranted on Cree.

I never am weel but whan discontented,
    Sae my wife and me we do seldom agree ;
I lather her aften and never repent it ;
    I wuss she wad tak the hint some day and dee.
I'd rather be boxin and scaulin the women,
    And riving their cheeks till the bluid it came streamin',
Than hae a brade river o' wine to gae swim in,
    Exceeding in bigness the water o' Cree.

For how to get rich it is a' my desire,
    Before that on whisky I'd spen' ae bawbee ;
I'd rather sup sna brew that's made at the fire,
    My neebors ken weel what a miser I be.
I hunger my wyme, and my back I keep duddy,
    For how to save sillar is a' my hale study ;
Ne'er think it ought strange tho' I girn in a wuddie,
    Ay auld farmer Jock at the Blairs o' the Cree.

The first wife I had was a hule o' a woman,
    But death was sae kind as to click her frae me ;
To whripe for the dead is a sin unbecomin,
    Sae never a tear left my blinkers for she.
Afore she tirl'd owre my prayers war fervant,
    Death cam and the cheel did na gang 'thout his yerrand ;
But than my hale blame was I kiss'd my ain servant,
    Like mony mae else, on the water o' Cree.

Sae whan I had gotten my auld Lucky burried,
    My joy it rase up to highest degree ;
O ! than my hale thought was again to get married,
    For 'thout a bit hizzie I never cud be.
I rade af on my naig than and conrted my Rosie,
    As plump as a pig and as gay as a posie ;
But little thought I she was frien to auld Nosie,
    The bawdy house-keeper on the water o' Cree.

I took her for nane o' your gigglin gawkies,
    Tho' she had a vile gate playin wink wi' her e'e ;
Her kisses war sweeter than frosty potatoes,
    Ilk time that a smack o' her mou' I did prie.

I swore by my soul, I could swear by no greater,
　That I was quite wnllin my dear wife to make her;
If she'd na comply o' the auld boy might tak her,
　For me Johnnie Cowan on the water o' Cree.

But afore she wad join me in sic a contraction,
　Three hunner pounds interest I yearly bond gie;
And being in lo'e faith about to distraction,
　To a' her proposals I quickly did gree.
And now my auld pow she has neatly adorned
　Wi' thae vera things that I sae meikle scorned;
For now like a big Irish bill I am horned,
　And croons out my wrath on the water o' Cree.

And now my guid neebors sae douce and religious,
　I beg this ae favour frae you whan I dee;
Ye'll rip up my memory through distant ages,
　And this epitaph ye'll get printed on me.
Here lies the remains o' Cankert King Cowan,
　A miser, a cuckold, a pickthank, a loon,
And a lustfu' auld rogue—his match was ne'er known
　Wha farm'd ance the Blairs on the water o' Cree.

CANNLESMAS-DAY—Candlemas-day. The way in which
this day is held at country schools, is tolerably expressed
in the following poem, written by a youth of fifteen—

CANNLESMAS DAY.

　Whan February's flaughts o' snaw
　　Besark the infant year;
　Whan ne'er a bonny flower ava
　　Upon the howms appear;
　Than Cannlesmas at kintra skools
　　We haud in merry stile;
　Nae skolar's fash'd wi' buiks and rules,
　　But ilka ane dis smile.
　　　　　　Wi' joy that day.

　Behold Gillronnie's family braw,
　　Gaun owre yon Whunnie hill
　Wi' faces clean, snod daickert a',
　　By mammies greatest skill;
　And see how crouse their father looks
　　As he steps up ahin them,
　Thinking by how they learn their books,
　　That meikle pith is in them,
　　　　　　To shine some day.

　Sic fathers are auld Scotlan's pride;
　　The far famed haunt for learning,
　What nation i'the warle wide
　　Like her in its discerning—

Her manly independent youths
  Can never live 'thout knowledge;
And deep they're shawn the science truths
  In mony a thacked college,
          By night and day.

There Dominies are fain to teach,
  Tho' scrimpet be the salary;
And gif they play the sooking leech,
  They're whistled down wi' raillery;
And youths there be 'mang moorland fells,
  Far frae a' rural Athens,
Wha pore awa, and learn themsells
  Wi' pleasure and wi' patience,
          For mony a day.

But ha! The croovie-skool is seen
  In loop o' yonder burn;
The scraws and heather keep it bein,
  The bairns wi' cauld ne'er yurn.
Frae out its conic comic lum,
  The reek is thickly rowing;
Within—hear what a din and hum
  Frae skolars thickly scrowing,
          A' there this day.

Adown the deep snaw wridy glen,
  What knots are coming posting,
How merrily they onward sten,
  And o' their cocks are boasting;
For midden cocks het fra the bawks,
  They bring te daub and batter,
And may be some for a' their cracks
  Will get, and what the matter,
          Their licks this day.

And now the crue is panged fu',
  On binks they a' are seated,
The Dominie's ay glowering through
  To see a' kindly treated;
He waleth ay the wee anes out,
  And plants them roun' the fire;
The big anes drive the jibe about,
  The de'il the ane dis tire,
          And gaunt this day.

Douce Elder John, than ca's the names,
  The barnies than do ease;
Their pouches wagging by their wames,
  Wi' their intended bleese;

Some saxpence brass—a shilling bit,
  And some gie twa or three ;
Gif that they be inclined to sit,
  As king and queen ye see,
          Upon this day.

And o' peep at the Dominie,
  Was ever monarch gladder ;
See how he e'es the white money,
  And pockets up the cauder ;
Wi' perfect joy the body smirks,
  And fain wad fa' a laughing ;
He snirtles wi' his neb and snirks,
  Than's fluttering and laughing,
              Puir cheel this day.

Roun' comes in jugs on whiteairn traes,
  The sweet brewn whusky toddy ;
" Come whomeld owre, the waiter says,
  " Twill hurt na honest body;"
Than Carvie Kebbuck featly cut
  In sonsy oblong dasses,
Wi' bruckelie scly owre the glut,
  What stiveron this surpasses,
          Nane—nane, nae day.

O 'tis a noble rustic sight
  To see sae mony youths ;
Their Dominie a serving right,
  While he sae minds their mouths ;
A dram is worth a million thanks,
  A thousand fluent speeches ;
For in the breast it plays its pranks,
  While they the heart ne'er reaches,
          On sic a day.

Ablins amang the younkers here,
  Just pure frae nature's glens ;
Some may be heard o' yet elsewhere,
  As wonderous fowk—wha kens
A patriot stern, a poet wild,
  A Wallace or a Burns,
Sae 'mang the prodigies be stiled,
  But time makes few returns
          Like them ilk day.

Some o'm doubtless wunna fail
  O' being plowmen strong,
Or fit to swing the weary flail
  The gloomy wunter lang ;
Or some may chance be hardy tars,
  And swash upon the ocean,
Or sodger lads for bluidy wars,
  To fight without promotion,
          For mony a day.

Nae matter tho' they now a ring
        Do form fu' wide and braw,
And into it their cocks they fling,
        The chanticleers do craw ;
But ablins there is ane o'm game,
        Steel spur'd in fighting order ;
Sae some saft faes he soon dis tame,
        And some my chap dis murder,
                        Perchance that day.

The battle by, again the punch
        Comes sweiling roun' the binks ;
The eater nulls the hearty lunch,
        The drinker dreeps and drinks ;
The fun is fairly at a height,
        Nae ceremonies hamper,
Wi' faces red and hearts fu' light,
        They out and hameward scamper,
                        Wi' glee this day.

The anld fowk left now closer draw
        O' care their sauls unfankle,
They canna lae the pig ava
        While it sounds pinklepankle ;
Whan naething mair frae it dis seep,
        Wi' than they move the shankie,
And bicker through the glens sae deep,
        Fu' jollock, blythe, and swankie,
                        Right cheels that day.

CANNLESMAS BLEEZE.—That offering or present pupils
make to their " Dominies" on Candlemas-day. Anciently
it used to be a large candle, one that could give a good
" blaze ;" hence the name " bleeze ;" now-a-days " hard
cash" is thought gives as pleasant a light.

CANT.—A little rise of rocky ground in a highway ; also
to " cant" any thing over, is to tumble it off the perpendicular, or over it.

CANTER.—The motion of an animal between the trot and
gallop.

CANTRIPS.—Witch spells, incantations, or the black art
witches use, when going on with their witcheries : various
snatches of Cantrip rhyme are yet afloat on the atmosphere of tradition, not unsimilar to what Shakespeare in-
troduces in his tragedy of Macbeth. Surely, the mighty

bard of nature had been no stranger to *Cantrips*—with his—

> " Toil and trouble, toil and trouble,
> " Fire burn, and cauldron bubble."

I may give two of the many specimens I have of these curiosities—

> In the pingle or the pan,
> Or the haurnpan o' man,
> Boil the heart's bluid o' the tade,
> Wi' the tallow o' the Gled ;
> Hawcket kail, and hen dirt,
> Chow'd cheese, an chicken-wort ;
> Yellow puddocks champit sma',
> Spiders ten, and gellocks twa ;
> Sclaters twall, frae foggy dykes,
> Bumbees twunty, frae their bykes !
> Asks frae stinking lochens blue,
> Ay, will make a better stue :
> Bachelors maun hae a charm,
> Hearts they hae fu' o' harm :
> Ay the aulder, ay the caulder,
> And the caulder ay the baulder,
> Taps sna white, and tails green,
> Snapping maidens o' fifteen,
> Mingle, mingle, in the pingle,
> Join the cantrip wi' the jingle :
> Now we see and now we see,
> Plots o' poaching ane, twa, three.

Such, I suspect, is a *cantrip*, respecting bachelors and blackguards ; but the mysteries in it are not to be seen through. The other I here give, is much of the same nature, only it seems more concerned with the female creation—

> Yirbs for the blinking queen,
> Seeth now whan it is e'en ;
> Boortree branches, yellow gowans,
> Berry rasps, and berry rowans ;
> De'il's milk frae thrissles saft,
> Clover blades frae aff the craft ;
> Binwud leaves. and blinmen's baws,
> Heather bells, and wither'd haws ;
> Something sweet, something sour,
> Time about wi' mild and dour ;

Hinnie suckles, bluidy fingers,
Napple roots, and nettle stingers;
Bags o' bees, and gall in bladders,
Gowks spittles, pizion adders;
May dew, and fumarts tears,
Nool shearings, nowts neers,
Mix, mix, six and six,
And the Auld maids cantrip fix.

CANTY—Happy, healthy, cheerful, &c.

CAPPERNOITED—Intoxicated, giddy, frolicksome, &c.

CAPPIN—A piece of *green hide,* firmly tied to that half of the *flail* called the " *soople,*" so that the " *midkipple,*" another piece of hide, may connect it to the other half the " *hand-staff.*" Flaxen-hair'd *Frank* was the *boy* who could both tune a flail and a *fiddle.*

CARLE—An old tall man; also a tall rustic candle-stick.

CARLINE—An old woman, though more often used to express some supernatural being.

CARLINES Co'—A very small cove on the west side of the river Dee, and one of the most lonely and romantic any where to be seen. When the bloody *Grier o' Lagg* and the *Douglass's* hunted the *Covenanters* over hill and dale, a poor man of the name of Dixon took up his abode in *Carlines Co',* and lived the whole of the time that foul persecution lasted, on the shell-fish he gathered on the sea-shore beside him, the which he found means to broil on a fire by night: thus he eluded the foes of his clan, the foes of God and man. The mouth of the cave is quite covered with brush-wood; at the farther end, or *benmost bore* of it, remains yet his seat—a square sea-stone: on it I expected to find an inscription of some kind or other, but was deceived. The *Assmidden,* and other remains of fire, to be met with, together with the general appearance of the cave, left no doubt on my mind but that it had been once inhabited, and for a considerable time—

" There sat the lanely trimmling wight,
   " Fear hardly let him draw his breath,
" For every hour, by day and night,
   " He dreaded 'that he'd meet his death.

" A day o' storm—a night fu' black,
   " War seasons whan his soul had ease ;
" Light e'er flung him on the rack,
   " Grim terror did poor Dixon tease.

" He lang'd na for the brade bright moon,
   " But wish'd her ay ahint a clud ;
" Whan morning came he griend for noon,
   " The darker—less his heart did thud.

" Gif that the heron ga'e a scraigh,
   " While stegging on the saunie shore ;
" Or shelldrake mang the crags, a squaigh,
   " His cauld sweat gush'd frae every pore.

" He'd shade the binwud door aside,
   " And through the wunnock sleely peep ;
" And whan he saw nought but the tide,
   " He hurkled ben, and hauflins fell asleep."

CARLINS O' CAIRNSMUIR.—A poem of strange Carlines.

Come, draw roun' the ingle ane and a',
   And our merriest tales gae tell ;
Let us begin wi' the norland lad,
   The lucky Abram Fell.
The true heir was he to Dinwudie,
   That braw state by the Tweed,
Whar mony a how, lay for the plough,
   And hill for the sheep to feed.

Whar hinnie sweyd down the whiteclaver,
   And the wallies head did ben',
Whar the herds shoon gather'd the yellow wax,
   And the nowt did fu'ly fen' :
For the wunter's sna, scarce lay ava,
   On that warm and beilie gruu,
And the hie leaf'd tree, on Dinwudie,
   Ne'er dreaded the gurly wun.

Now Abram he was luiked on
   As a gye lucky boy,
To be the only ane wha wad,
   The bonny place enjoy.
The lasses a', aroun the ha',
   The lairdies daughters fair,
Did blink on he their blythest e'e,
   And dinked wi' ane air.

But whan young Abram gaed to claim
  The richts to his estate,
Than he did learn sic unco news
  As made him luik fu' blate.
His Enbruch scribe, o' the black gown tribe,
  Did let him plainly see,
There was ane skin, they cudna fin,
  Some deed 'bout Dinwudie.

And od the want o' this parchment,
  Did hurt young Abram sair ;
He dawner'd by the Pentlan' hills,
  And whriped through despair.
Sair he did weep, then fell asleep,
  And soundly snor'd awa ;
And he did dream, as it micht seem,
  But 'twas 'bout Gallowa.

" Get up ! get up ! a voice did say,
  " And gang's the wun dis bla',
" Till thou dis fin thysell, Abram,
  " In boony Gallowa.
" And there gae dance, a while wi' chance,
  " And thou skalt meet or lang
" Something, my dear, thy heart will cheer,
  " And set a' right that's wrang."

Sae merrily up young Abram lap,
  The wun blew frae the north,
And being yaul', he soon lost sight
  O' the green banks o' Forth.
Owre Enterkin he fast did rin,
  Through Minniehive and a,'
And soon cam he, aside the Dee,
  In bonny Gallowa.

He gat a fishing-wan' and fished
  The Geds wi' meikle glee,
And wi' a gun pirl'd the Muirfule,
  As they wad whurrin' flee.
At ilka fair, lo he was there,
  And wha was there like he,
Wha had his grace, wha had his face,
  A' lo'ed him to see.

And nane did lo'e the laddie mair
  Than charming Katie Bell,
The lovely saul amaist ran daft
  About young Abram Fell.
Her e'en war blue, that lovely hue,
  And the bonny hair had she,
In siller and gowd, it glancin' flow'd,
  And she sang wi' mely odec.

Mang the fairy dales o' Gallowa
  Nane was sae fair as she,
And the only daughter too she was
  O' the lairds o' Burnilee :
Ten thousan' poun', he cud pay down,
  Upon her wadding day,
But wha durst gang, and court there thrang,
  Nae chiel durst luik that way.

For the laird did think, as sae he micht,
  Her match cud no be foun' ;
Nae lad he thought sae guid as her
  'Tween the sea and the sun.
And whan young Abram to him cam,
  He thought the same o' he,
A broken laird, o' sma' regard,
  Did please na Burnilee.

" Forsake my daughter and my ha',
  " To Abram he did say,
" How durst ane sneaking beggar-boy
  " Come sae far af his way.
" Awa, awa, lae Gallowa,
  " She hates thy face to see,
" Click up ane leg, and gang and beg,
  " Brave laird o' Dinwudie."

Sae glad was Abram to jump on
  His twa steave shanks and flee,
As fire sprang frae baith the e'en
  O' the laird o' Burnilee.
And Katie fair, did greet fu' sair,
  The lad glowr'd roun' to see,
And saw her fast, held roun' the waist,
  By twa strong chiels or three.

Sweet saul, in durance she was laid,
  And watched nicht and day,
And ay she raved 'bout young Abram,
  In the chaumer whar she lay.
And ay she cried, and ay she sigh'd,
  " I'll ne'er wed ane but he,
" Wi' him in rags, owre the muir-hags,
  " I wad beg happilee."

Sae Abram tuik his rod again,
  And fish'd about the Dee,
But o ! his heart was unco sair,
  'Bout the maid o' Burnilee.
And dull he turn'd, he bitter mourn'd,
  Then brak his wan in twa,
Gaed doyl'd about, and lay without,
  Amang the frost and sna'.

And she, for a' her keeper's strick,
  The bonny Katie Bell,
Was lost ae morn, and whar she was,
  There cudna ane o'm tell.
They sought her far, owre hench and scaur,
  And up and down the Dee,
At last they cam, to whar Abram,
  In doolfu' dumps sat he.

They question'd him gif he had seen
  The lovely Katie Bell,
But satisfaction they gat nane
  Frae the doyl'd Abram Fell.
Sae frae their rout, forfouchten out,
  They back returned a',
And said, " they had sought for the maid
  " Owre a' wide Gallowa."

But tho' that they had sought the wuds
  And glens whar warlocks beek,
They hadna foun' sweet Katie Bell,
  Wham they had gane to seek.
They now despair'd—likewise the laird,
  That her they'd nae mair see,
Sae nought but grief, without relief,
  Was heard bout Burnilee.

They ne'er thought that the Carlins had
  Convey'd the bloomin bairn,
To their grand palace in the muir,
  The hie muir wi' the Cairn.
Through the mirky air, in their arm-chair,
  The damsel they did ride,
Until they came to their house o' fame,
  Sae elegant and wide.

For carpets o' queer ureie hues,
  Bespread the lightsome floors ;
The sillar silk did co'er the wa's,
  And gowden hang the doors.
And music rang, and minstrels sang,
  Auld Scotlan's airs sae sweet,
And fairies did dance, but didna prance,
  Wi' airy mettled feet.

But tho' they nursed, dear Katie Bell
  Wi' mair than Minnies care,
And gaed her ay the best o' food,
  Whar on hersell to fare ;
She pined awa, and no ava
  Cud either eat or sleep,
But ay, alane, wad sab and mane,
  And scaudin' tears wad weep .

The Carlins they did brawly ken
  What a' wi' her was wrang,
Sae they wud seek young Abram Fell,
  And please her ere 'twas lang.
Whar the hazles bud, in Kirdle wud,
  There they did fin' the boy,
And up the moor, to their ha' door,
  They led him wi' great joy.

The wun had mony a hole blawn out
  O' his breeks and his coat,
His elbucks bare, glowr'd glibly forth,
  He was na worth a groat.
But soon they fed, and soon they clad,
  The doyloch Abram Fell,
And by their slicht, soon had him richt,
  To see fair Katie Bell.

But first they led the hopefu' lad
  Through the auld palace gay,
The Carlin Queen did toot her horn,
  Gian Carlins led the way.
Upon ilk head, the bonnet braid,
  Sat like ane cowl o' sna,
Their hinnerliths, in spangl'd claiths,
  They flaiper'd ane and a.'

And some o' them had nebs fu' lang,
  And whisking chins o' hair,
Wi' e'en that lowed like can'les bricht,
  Whan i'the mirky air.
And their sandal shoon, gleam'd like the moon,
  Their upper robes seem'd green,
Fu' fit war they, as weel to fley,
  Gif meet them late at e'en.

At first young Abram maist had swarf'd,
  His Carlin frien's to see,
He glowr'd to east, he glowr'd to west,
  And wildly row'd his e'e.
But they gaed a dram to young Abram,
  Whilk daldrums scared awa,
Whan he drank it, faith he grew fit,
  To bauldy luik at a.'

'Twas speerits o' their ain making,
  It ne'er through worms fu' warm,
Cam wi' a steam, nor was it brewn,
  By laying too the barm.
The best o' wine, or brandy fine,
  Was naught to it ava,
It was the drink, that gard ane wink,
  And crously gab awa.

Sae on young Abram they did lead,
　Through rooms and lobbies gran',
And grander too did things appear,
　Whan he cam nearer han '.
What shining chairs, what flichts o' stairs,
　What saft beds did he see,
What things for ease, what things to please,
　What things for lug and e'e.

At length he to a winnock came,
　It was a winnock braw,
Through it was seen ilk fertile nuik
　O' bonny Gallowa.
The Nith, the Cree, the darling Dee,
　War seen a rowing sweet,
And just below, did wamplin flow,
　The Minnoch and the Fleet.

They led him next to whar in state
　The water kelpies were,
And sic a sight he ne'er had seen
　As the sight he saw there.
What eerie chiels, war thae queer de'ils,
　How eldrich sough'd their words,
Their vera forms, seem'd made for storms,
　For spates and faeming fords.

Neast, to a place mair on tae east,
　He was let ha'e a view,
O' wizzards, witches, warlocks, and
　The crooning worricow.
And boggles queer, whilk he did fear,
　For a' his bauldness great,
Ranked in raws, wi' tusky jaws,
　Whilk raised the cauld sweat.

And brownies too wha barried,
　Kind farmers mows o' corn,
They thumped them the leelang night,
　Then dawner'd there at morn.
Thae chiefs he did see, o' the swingin tree,
　In ane strange auld chaumer there,
Their claes war brown, frae the heel tae crown,
　And strang like tykes they were.

Ane housefu' was it, o' as odd fowk
　As Abram Fell ere saw,
The like o't's no in Scotlan', nor
　In countrees far awa.
Whan thus he had seen, the Carlin Queen
　Her tootin horn did yell,
Her waiters a' then fled awa,
　And quoth she to Abram Fell—

" Abram, my lad, thou hast seen a'
   " The fowk wha wi' me do dwell ;
" Thou hast seen them a' but ae sweet ane,
   " Ane I keep for thysell."
Then open flew, a door she knew,
   And in gaed Abram Fell,
There met alane, his lovely ane,
   His darlin' Katie Bell.

What joy was there, what true love there,
   What claps and kisses sweet,
Whan thae twa youthfu' creatures did
   Sae unexpected meet.
How they wad talk, how they wad walk,
   How they wad warm embrace,
And the heavenly smile, just a' the while,
   Adorning ilka face.

Join hans', join hans', a Carlin cried,
   And a queer Carlin was she;
Join han's, join han's, for now ye shall
   This moment married be.
They joined han's, in wedlock ban's,
   The loving happy pair,
And the Carlin said, be not afraid,
   Ye'll never synner mair.

And she fix'd roun' baith their wrists a bee
   O' the black ivoree;
And said, as lang's ye wear this bee,
   Ye'll here fin' dwalling free.
Then music sweet, to mettled feet,
   The minstrel fays did play,
And Abram Fell, and Katie Bell,
   Did dance wi' ither gay.

Thus did they spen' the hinniemoon
   Wi' meikle mirth and glee,
And ae day Abram gaed to see
   The Carlin's libraree ;
Whar auld buiks stood, wrote afore the flood,
   And mony a charming sang,
To the light lang lost, ance Scotlan's boast,
   Lay there i'the archives thrang.

While thus he read, and rummaged awa,
   What did he chance to fin,'
Mang mony anither auld charter,
   But his ain sair sought-for skin.
The richts sae free, o' Dinwudie,
   His lairdship by the Tweed,
Now the joy o' our twa, was nae way sma,'
   De'il hae't cud it exceed.

They bade farewel to the Carlin's kind,
  And to bonny Gallowa,
Then posted af out owre the hills
  To the norlan warl awa.
Sae Abram Fell and Katie Bell,
  And their friens' lived happie a',
Sae Burnilee and Dinwudie,
  And mair befel the twa.

CARLINWARK LOCH—The most beautiful sheet of water in the south of Scotland ; and if we except Loch Lomond, Loch Katerine, and some others of the lovely highland lakes, we have nothing to match the Carlinwark in Scotia ; and even these highland lochs are rendered more beautiful than they are, by the pen of Sir Walter Scott. This lovely place lies about eighteen miles west from Dumfries, beside the thriving little village of Castle Douglass.

When beheld on a summer's evening, when the weather is fine, when the sweet gay lasses are out strolling on its banks, and the pupils of Isaac Walton out in boats angling ; when the trees on the woody islands are green, and the blackbird whistling amongst them, why the thing becomes Killarney at once, and not much behind Winander, the haunt of the lake poets. It is wonderful indeed, that a *laker* or two does not arise about the *Carlinwark*. I have heard of *Gerrond* and *Kelvie*, but what are these; they have both a little of the poet about them, but notihng of the Wordsworth and Wilson school. Show Gerrond a flock of fat wild-ducks within the range of his *swivel*, on the lake, and you show him a scene he much more admires than quivering sun-beams, hues of azure, and other fine things. As for Kelvie, he might give us the poem of the *Carlinwark Loch*.

CARRCAKES—Cakes made of eggs and oatmeal.

CARREEN—To lean to a side.

CARRIGES—The religious catechism.

CARRPIN—Teazing, with vexatious talk.

CARRY—The motion of the clouds, a driving over Heaven's face before the wind; anciently it was thought spirits carried them so—see more of this in the article *Lift.*—

" Ne'er a star peeps through the carry ;" hear to the soft language of poor *Tannahill,* a bard or songster of the first kind, who drowned himself in the Clyde, when between forty and fifty years of age, in a fit of melancholy despair. Scotland, for all the warning she got with the early fate of Burns, and for all the stigmas deservedly piled on her, for his account, also shut her eyes on poor *Tannahill,* never changing him from the low situation of a *Paisley weaver*—no wonder that his tender heart could not withstand this treatment. I here give three verses to his memory, which I consider tolerable—

> Ha, melancholy mirky wight,
>   Grim Heckler o' the feeling soul,
> Hast thy ow'rpow'ring gloomy might,
>   On our sweet sangster set sae foul.
> The tears frae nature's watshod e'en
>   Row murmuring down mony a rill,
> And nought is heard by hillocks green,
>   But doolfu' wails for Tannahill.
>
> For a' the charms o' tenderness,
>   His harmless bosom warmly felt,
> And thae his muse did sweet express,
>   His melting heart made ithers melt.
> His bonny *Jessie o' Dumblain,*
>   Wi' lo'e auld Scotia's sons dis fill,
> E'en *Sleeping Maggie* maks us fain',
>   A darling bard was Tannahill.
>
> Tho' *gloomy* was his winter here,
>   And tho' his friends war dowie dull,
> The *Highlan' Laddie's* sangs are dear,
>   He was ane *Harper* true frae *Mull.*
> Burns, baith can make us laugh and weep,
>   He gars our hearts extatic thrill,
> Wha wi' him can sweet pathos sweep,
>   Nane, nane ava, but Tannahill.

CARSELAN—Level loamy land by a river side.

CARSONS—Water-cresses.

CARTES—Cards.

CAST—A throw, a turn, a change, &c.

CAST o' CORN—As much oats as a *kill* will dry at once. Over all Galloway, this quantity is about six bolls.

CASTLE o' RAEBERRY—One of the castles of the family of M'Lellan, in Galloway. It stood on a promontory on the shore of the Solway Frith, in the parish of Kirkcudbright ; steep precipices flanked it all round, except the neck towards the main land, and cross this has been a deep trench, with a draw-bridge over it. The word " *Berry*," comes from the German *berg*, a lofty hill or mountain, and quite beside it is one of these large hills ; for all such a place of *strength* as this castle was, it was not strong enough to keep out *Black Douglass of Thrave ;* the tradition respecting his capture of it, is here told in an old song. It seems they had used boats about it, as an antiquary lately discovered a boatway, cut through the rocks beneath, on the shore.

RAEBERRY CASTLE.

I met wi' a man the ither night,
　And he was singing fu' merry,
How Black Douglass, the bluidy wight,
　Was gonked at Raeberry.

For the Maclellan lap owre the scaur
　Wi' his naig, and swam the ferry,
He snored out, owre Barnhoury Bar,
　And left far ahin Raeberry.

O ! he has sail'd the Solway sea
　Without either ship or wherry,
And saved his craig frae being drawn, did he,
　Owre the castle-wa' o' Raeberry.

For curse confound the de'il o' Thrave,
　His necbors he dis herry ;
But Gallowa will never be his slave,
　Nor the braw lord o' Raeberry.

CASTLE O' THRAVE—The strongest castle in Galloway, and the most famous. It is a large square building, with hornworks, on an island in the river Dee. Francis Grose, the celebrated antiquary, gives a good account of it in his *Antiquities of Scotland*. It was anciently an infernal place, and many were the foul deeds there done ; even at this day one shudders to inspect it : its thick walls, narrow windows and staircases, its rooms arch-roofed, and the dungeon yet remaining in perfection, make the blood freeze. I have seen no *old castle* (and I have seen now a good many), which conjured up scenes of ancient barbarism, and murder, more than this one ; it seems as if it had been built for the sole purpose of conducting savage deeds. It was the seat of the *Black Douglass*, one of the most horrible devils that ever appeared in Scotland ; he made his very king tremble for him, and hanged M'Clellan, Lord Kirkcubrie, against his order.

The following verses of poetry I may here give, as respecting this fellow, and his *Castle o' Thrave*, or *Trief*, as in the ancient records of the house of *Kenmore* it stands ; probably it is connected with *reive*—to rob, being quite a den of robbers and murderers :—

On a bonny green isle in the water o' Dee,
As it rows frae the ken to the Soloway sea,
Stands the tower of the baron, the fell bluidy knave,
And the name o' his keep is the Castle o' Thrave.

He has strung Lord Kirkcubrie owre his castle wa',
The worthy M'Clellan o' wild Gallowa ;
The dumb sough o' vengeance we hear frae his grave,
And it shall be answered at Castle o' Thrave.

Mons Meg we'll drag out, and we'll thunner him down,
We'll skelp him to hell, where his frien's will him crown,
We'll show him what's honour, and how we'll behave,
By dashing destruction on Castle o' Thrave.

Let him rally his rebels through a' Gallowa,
We care for them not, we shall conquer for a' ;
We'll rush on our faes like the far-fetched wave,
And sweep to damnation the Castle o' Thrave.

CASTIN O' BEES—Bees are said to be " *castin*," when they are swarming. Sometimes, when the insects are in this state, they fly far away from their parents before they hive or alight, in spite of all the *pistols* that are fired, and *water* that may be thrown amongst them by their watchers, which is the cause of many a warm race to the rustics. The poem of the " Bee Hive" illustrates a haunt of this kind. See the article *Broolzies*.

CASTIN PEATS—The art of cutting peats out of a moss with a *peat-spade*. " Good casters" are always the chief men about a moss.

CASTIN UP—The art of making little arithmetical calculations. A mower once regretted to me that he had not learnt algebra at school, for then he could have " *cast up jobs*" on the *nail o' his thum.*' Also, " *castin up*" is a mean way of reproaching persons, by reminding them of some little guilty slip in " youth," or of some crime of their ancestors. Such conduct frequently leads to serious broils. A man on horseback came up with another rider like himself, while going to a Dumfries *Rude fair* once, and quoth the one who overtook, " Whar come ye frae, gude man, gin ane might spear :' e'en out o' the *parish o' Cowen,*' replied he ; " I was thinking sae (returned the first), for, like a' your parish fowk, ye sit far back on the hinder part o' the beast." " Ablins, (quoth his companion) and whar come ye frae, is a fair quastion for you now to answer." " O, am Mr. K ——, of R——," he replied, " I just thought sae (quoth the *Cowend* man), for I see the stedd o' the gallows that hanged *Henry Gregg*, on your back." On *casting up* which they at each other with *loaded whups*, and the forward Mr. K. was left sprawling on the road.

CAT—A small lump of manure.

CAT and CLAY—Straw and clay, used in making rude partitions through cottages.

CATAN—Tempting to battle, by poisonous language.

CATCHIE—Quick at taking the catch. It is said of those expert at this, "That if they war as keppie as catchie, they would make gude shepherds' dogs."

CATCRAIG—A sugar-loaf rock in the river Fleet, covered with juniper-bushes. Tradition says, a monster of a wild-cat was once killed on it.

CATKINDNESS—Selfishness.

CAT-LILLS—A kind of punishment inflicted by grown-up people on those who are not so. It is done by pressing the fore-finger into the hollow place at the root of the ear. Let all beware of doing this, for it has not unfrequently been the cause of death, the cause of bursting blood-vessels of the head.

CAT OUT O' THE POWK—A phrase, signifying the letting out of a secret.

CATSTANE—A large stone placed behind rustic fire-places.

CATSTRAN'—A very small stream.

CATWHUNS—A low-growing ferny species of whin, good coverts for the Scotch wild-beasts.

CATWUTTED—Of a savage humour.

CAULDRIFE—Cold-blooded; also easily affected with cold.

CAULDSIDE SHARPIN-STANES—Stones found in a burn, in the farm of Caulside, parish of Kirkmabreck, famous for making hones of, to sharp edge-tools. Tradesmen tell me they are before the best " Barskimming," or *Water o' Ayr* stones, and that no Welch, nor Norway " *Rag*," can give an edge with them. The " *pile*" being so wonderful.

CAULL—A dam cross a river, made on purpose to raise the water for mechanical, or other concerns.

CAUM—A mould for casting bullets.

CAUMSHELL, or CLAMSHELL, or MAYSHELL—A beautiful white piece of shelly or boney matter, in shape somewhat like a lady's slipper, frequently found driven in upon our shores. It is reduced by *nowt doctors* to a fine powder, and blown through the hollows of quills into cattles' eyes which have motes in them, such as *flichters o' caff,* when the sharp dust instantly causes the animal's optic orb to be flooded with water, so that it winks much, and by so doing, cuts the scum and obstruction away. What these bones or shells are, like many things else, I have not discovered, nor do I know that any have : some say that they are formed on the breasts of certain sea-fowl, which moult them now and then ; others, that they are the bones of a fish called the *clamfish* ; and others again, that they are of a coral nature. I would wish to know what some great naturalist says respecting them. Linnæus, the famed Swede, will have them to be the *scallop shell (ostrea opercularis),* and to this clings Dr. Jamieson, the great Scottish lexicographer, a person whom no Scotsman can praise too much, who has given the world a dictionary unmatched for the learning and antiquarianism contained in it ; and considering that nothing of the kind but some few glossaries had been done before, the work truely becomes a wonderful compend ; yet, as to the term under consideration methinks, with all due deference to the Doctor, that it is not of kin to the old French word *clame,* a pilgrim's mantle, but to the Galloway *scaum*—scum, because its use is in taking the scum off eyes. Now, in Scotland there has been a fashion of prefacing various words with S : as *swhirrls, sturnills,* &c. ; now if this letter be taken off *scaum,* we have *caum,* which is the popular name by which the shell is known.

CAUMSTANE—Fuller's earth, used by scourers.

CAUP— A shallow wooden vessel.

I

CAUPED—Curved, bended in curves.

CAUP SNAIL—The snail which inhabits the black shell, common about old gardens and castles.

CAUVEGRUN—Our place of birth.

CAUVE REEDS—Rennets; stomachs of calves, for curdling milk. The same with *rennet bags*.

CAWDAH—A soft substance extracted from linen, for the benefit of wounds and sores.

CAWKER—A dram of spirits; also a shod for a shoe of iron.

CHACK—A lunch; also a crush between stones.

CHACKET—Squeezed suddenly, checked.

CHACK REEL—A piece of machinery for winding yarn. At every " *hank*" it winds, it gives a " *chack*," or clack. It is not a very true instrument, as the circumference of the wheel enlarges with the threads, as the winding continues.

CHAFTS—The blades of the jaws.

CHAMPED—Mashed.

CHAMPED POTATOES—Mashed potatoes in milk and butter; one of the very best of dishes. I defy the most skilful French cook that ever lived, to make a dish of a more delicious nature; and no confectioner's shop in the kingdom has any thing to compare with them : they are truly glorious *belly timmer*.

CHAMPIS—An exclamation of seeming surprise.

CHANNLE-STANE—Curling, the game at the *ice*; also the stone a player plays with in the game. Some think the name comes from channle, the bed of a river, because round stones were got in such places anciently, which pleased our forefathers well enough to play with, before we found out the way of making them artificially. Others again think, as these stones have to be kept running in one channle as it were upon the ice, that they have had their name from this. It is hard to say which is right; so, I shall content myself by saying, that there is not a more manly or a better game played on the earth than the channlestane.

CHANROCK—A channel of round stones.

CHANTY POT—A chamber pot.

CHAP and CHUSE—To select.

CHAPMEN—Pedlers, hawkers, &c. Scotland, famous fo many things, is also famous for her pedlers. Anciently, the Scottish pedlers in Poland were a respectable body; now they keep nearer home, and travel about in England, and in general, are a class very highly thought of; neither Englishmen nor Irishmen make such pedlers as they: indeed, the English try it a little, but not so the Irish, and an Irish pedler is always as mean a looking object as is to be met with; the wares he hawks are of the lowest kind, in truth, he knows not the proper way to shoulder a bundle. Scotsmen are naturally fond of this business; for why, they detest slavery. A young Scotsman of spirit, before he will be bowed down with his nose in the earth, and become a labourer to his superiors, will be a pedler. He is then soon his own master, and the business being of a wandering nature, leads him to see curiosities, a thing the sons of the north are fond of; and, after acquiring some money at the trade, he leaves it for something of a more honourable name. Thus then, it is no discredit to Scotsmen, the *pedling* trade. I know not of any other which can match it, as a stepping stone for young men of common talents, that they may leap on to from a humble situation, and from thence to something better.

CHAPMEN'S BED—A bed reserved in farm-houses for the use of *chapmen*, and other wanderers.

CHAPMEN'S DROWTH—People are said to have this *drowth,* drought, or thirst about them, when they are not only in need of some fluid to slake it, but food to take with it. It is called the *chapmen's drowth,* because pedlers of a low class, in calling at country houses to vend their wares, complain often to gude wives that they are *drowthy,* which means, if they have any food to spare in the pantry, they will not *cast out* with a *cull,* or piece of it.

CHAPMEN'S SLAUGHTER—There is a lump of stones in the north end of the parish of Borgue, termed so, as two " *chapmen boys,*" coming from a fair once, disputed, and slew each other there, by stabbing with pen knives.

CHAPPIE—A name for a young man.

CHAPPIT—Choppit. " He *chappit* a bargain," he struck, he choppit a bargain. No bargain stands good unless hands be chop'd over it ; the buyer's hand must be slap'd into the seller's, then a purchase is made ; in truth, this ceremony seals the matter.

CHARKIN—Speaking like pyets, or weazles.

CHARLIE—Charles.

CHARNLE-PINS—The pins on which the hinges of machinery turn. A man is said to miss his *charnle-pins,* when he is so intoxicated with spirits that he cannot " stand steave in his shoon," so *fou* that he loses the centre of gravity, and *gaes heels owre gowdie.*

CHAUMER—A chamber, from old French *chaumere,* a little hut. This *chaumer,* or *chammer,* was a kind of detached room of the farm-houses of yore : here slept all the young men belonging to the family. The *chaumer,* as it were, was their apartment, the place they could call their own ; in it were their beds and *kists,* what not. This was the place of all merriment ; thither came *cronnies* to see *cronnies* ; here were lasses brought by their *Joes* and courted ; here the country clash sounded ; here were songs sung, tales told, *dams* played ; here the *gude man* or *gude wife* seldom made their appearance, unless they were given to mirth ; and many old men of cheerful natures preferred sitting in the *chaumer ateen*, to any other place about the house. To close though, I do not know that we have so much fun and hilarity now as our *forebears* had in the *chaumers o' auld lang syne.*

CHAWCHLIN—Eating like a swine.

CHAWLIN—Eating in a sickly manner.

CHAWNER—To talk much and whine.

CHEEK for CHOW—Tête-a-tête ; cheek by jole.

CHEEL—A man ; a male person.

CHEEP—To cry as some birds.

CHEEPOCK—The female Nymphæ.

CHEESECLOUT—The cloth wherein cheeses are made.

CHEESEGIRD—A girth which is put round cheese when a making.

CHEROK-OKIE-OK — The lark's first note, in a May morning—

> Cherokee-okee-okee
> Sang the lark, as she did flee
> Up amang the cluds, and sing
> Ae bonny sunny day in spring.
> The sang a bardie did translate,
> The sang did rin this vera gate—
>
> Now is the season for me,
>   The rest I care little about ;
> I can sing, I can soar now wi' glee,
>   My note and my wings they are stout.
>
> Not as when the winter winds blaw,
>   And freeze my lang tae to the sod,
> Whan aft through the night's in the snaw,
>   I maun tak up my cauller abode.
>
> Higher yet shall I soar i'the sky,
>   My dewy breast dry in the sun,
> Then down on the sclent shall I fly,
>   And to my warm nest I shall run,

CHEESLE—The moulding dish wherein cheeses are cast. " Never jump out o' the cheesle ye hae been chirted in," is a favourite proverb, and means, that though fortune may smile on us, let us not forget the humble way in which we were bred.

CHIMLALUG—The cheek of the fireplace.

CHIRKIN—Making a noise as the adder sometimes does.

CHIRKLE—To grind the teeth on other, as sheep are in the habit of doing.

CHIRMS—Small bastard fruit.

CHIRPERS—The insects, house crickets ; when they leave a house on a sudden it forbodes evil, when they visit, the reverse.

CHIRRIN—The noise grasshoppers make in sunny weather ; they do it by rubbing their thighs quick against the body.

CHIRT—To squeeze.

CHITTERIE—Small backward fruit, or small bad potatoes.

CHITTERIN—Trembling with cold, so that the teeth chatter on other.

CHITTLE—To shell oats as birds do.

CHITTLER—A small bird of the tit-mouse species.

CHOLLERS—Lumps of fat beneath the chin—double chins.

CHOW—To chew ; also a quid of tobacco.

CHOWKS—The upper parts of the throat.

CHUCKS—A game with marbles played by girls.

CHUCKY—A name for a hen ; also the henwife's call for the poultry.

CHUFFY—Fat, chubby, &c.

CHULDERS—The same with *Chollers*.

CHUNS—The spring or " *sprootings*" of potatoes.

CLABBER—Any soft dirty matter.

CLAGGY—Cloggy, sticking, &c.

CLAITH—Cloth.

CLAMPIN—Tramping after a noisy manner.

CLAN—A tribe which holds together.

CLANCH—A mannerless man, given to eating in the swinish stile.

WULL HULLYOCH.

Wull Hullyoch was as big a clanch
  As 'ere was kend by ony body;
Rasps and crabs he up wad cranch,
  His haurns wi' slawk and sludge war muddy.
The slunyoch's visage was fu' ruddy,
  His sillar up in meat he'd banch,
Whilk keep'd his hurdies unco' duddy,
  The beast had sure a strong digestive panch.

Whan bacon in the pan did crack,
  And gravie deep aroun' did sotter,
Than Wull his fipples red wad smack,
  He smell'd the imry like an otter.
And on the scent awa wad hotter,
  And sae hae at the roast a snack;
He'd glutt a cargoe till his knees wad totter,
  It took a clisk his pechan out to rack.

A greedy gormandizing cheel
  Has been detested, and will be for ever,
They wi' the kyte, belike the swauld woocreel,
  Dear modesty is seen to suffer never.
For, let a fallow ever be sae clever,
  This gies his character the bursen seal,
Whilk frae his name he'll ne'er be fit to sever,
  'Twill dog his hatefu' carcase to the De'il.

CLANJAMPHRY—A worthless blackguardish crew of people, throngest still on the Lord's day.

CLANTER—A jarring noise, such as proceeds from clogs walked about with in a house.

CLAPPER O' A MILL—The tongue of the mill; beside the *hopper*, set in motion when the mill is set in motion.

CLAPPIN—Fondling, toying, &c.

CLARRIED—Besmeared with mud.

CLARTIE—Dirty with mud.

CLASHBAG—A person full of low mean stories.

CLASHES—Low, idle, scandalous tales.

CLASHMACLAVERS—The same with *Clashes*.

CLATCH—To besmear with mud.

CLATTERBAG—The same with *Clashbag*.

CLATTER-BANES—Those bones which move when we chat.

CLAUCHAN PLUCK—A village of the genteel name of
Lawriston. It is seated in the moorlands, has learning
and peat-stacks about it; and has turned out on the world
some wonderful characters.

CLAUT—An implement used in cleaning office houses,
roads, streets, &c. It has a broad semi-circular mouth,
placed vertical to the shaft. A young fellow, who had
been out of the country a little while, pretended, when he
came back, to know nothing of the mother country : even
this tool, which was reclining against a wall, its name
seemed to have fled his memory. " Come, what devil do
ye call this," said he to his rustic friends, laying his foot
rashly on the mouth of it, when the shaft sprang up, and
hit him in the face. " O! d—n the *claut*," he exclaimed,
not waiting for an answer from his humble companions ;
the name striking him by a strange association.

CLAVERS—Nonsense.

CLAWS-CRUNTS—Old trees, which cattle rub themselves
against.

CLAY'D UP—Eyes are said to be so when boxing has
blinded them.

CLECK—Idle chat.

CLEEDIN—Clothing.

CLEPPS—Pieces of bended iron, used for hanging pots
on fires.

CLEPPIE BELLS—People of the name of Bells, who aided anciently the persecution of two Christians on the sands of Wigton. They tied them to stakes on the sand, and left them to perish with the coming tide. When asked how the poor wretches behaved, when the sea was coming foaming about them, they said, " that they *clepped* round the *stobbs* like partons, and prayed," viz. wreathed round the stakes ; after which saying, they were always called " *Cleppie Bells,*" and the fingers of their hands grew strangely together, which deformity yet attends their race.

CLEUCHS—Wild steep woody glens, the abode of foxes, owls, and other such animals.

CLICKY—A turned headed staff ; also to be quick at catching.

CLIENS—Small heaps of stones.

CLIERS—Thick saliva, which obstruct the windpipe.

CLIMPETS—Sharp pointed rocks.

CLIMPIE—A person with a strange lameness.

CLINCH—To halt, to walk on one foot.

CLINKEN Co's—Caverns which make a tinkling noise when stones are thrown into them.

CLINKER—A blow.

CLINTS—Little awkward lying rocks.

CLIP—To cut with scissars.

CLIPE—A person scanty of good manners, who has little in him, as the people say, but what the " Ram-horn spoon puts."

CLIPPIE—A person with too neat cut clothes.

CLOCHERS.—Mucus matter which is coughed out of the throat ; thick phlegm, termed by some *fat spittles* ; the sound a person emits when throwing out *Clochers,* is too called *clochering.*

CLOCKIN HENS.—Hens which are or have been hatching; to scare them from clocking, *gude wives* plunge them into cold water.

CLOCKS.—Beetle insects.

CLODDOCHS.—The same with *Cliens*.

CLODDTHUMPERS.—Rollers.

CLOGGS—Wooden shoes, iron bound; they are all numbered according to size. Ploughmen generally use " *tens*;" so in the country, cloggs are not unfrequently called " *tens*."

CLOITED.—Fell easily.

CLOOTER.—The noise a bad delivered channle-stone makes on ice.

CLOOTS—Hoofs.

CLOTCHD.—Sat in the broadest and most slovenly way.

CLOUT.—A slight blow.

CLUDDY WATHER—Cloudy weather. The colour of the sky rules the colour of the sea; if the sky be a deep blue, the sea is a deeper; the denser the medium the darker the hue. The sea at no time is of a more sable hue than when the land is covered with snow, and sky loaded with black clouds.

CLUES—Balls of winded thread. Witches had their " *blue clues*," to aid their necromancy. One at the stake going to be burned, on the *Barhill* beside Kircudbright, said, if they would bring her " her ain *blue clue*, which she had forgot a hame," that she would lay open her art. The *clue* was produced, she took one end of it and flang it into the air, and after muttering a few words, vanished in a moment. To win the *blue clue* in the *killpot* on *hallo-ween*, was a serious matter before Burns made the world laugh at it.

CLUNK.—That noise which is produced when a cork is drawn out of a bottle.

CLUSTER o'STARS.—The constellation of Orion, to the naked eye there seems to be no such obvious cluster of stars in our hemisphere as this; so has been particularized by country people in all ages.

CLUTTER.—A piece of bad stone building, particularly if it be " *dry ware wark.*"

Co'.—Cove.

COAGIN SHEEP.—Shearing the wool from off their necks before the great days of *sheep clipping* come on; this is done for the purpose of saving that wool which would otherwise fall off before the season mentioned.

COALLS.—Little hay cocks.

Co' O' CAERCLAUCH.—One of the most celebrated coves in Galloway; it seems to have been used as a subterranean castle by our forefathers; a *clauch* or *clauchan,* or small village, as secure as a *caer* or castle; so the literal meaning of the whole may be, " the cove of the armed or defended village." Tradition says, that no human eyes ever beheld the *back side,* or farthest extremity of this cave; that a dog once went in at its mouth and came out at the *door o'Cairnsmoor,* a place nearly ten miles from it; and when the *tyke* did come out he was found to be all *sung* (singed), as if he had passed through some fire ordeal or other.

COBB.—A blow.

COBBIN EWES.—Shearing the wool from off their udders, so that their lambs may freely get to the teats to suck.

COBBLES.—Large sea-beach stones.

COCKABENDIE.—I dare hardly, for the sake of modesty, explain this term; when such is seen to be the case, readers may make a rough guess what it is.

COCK AND PAIL.—Spigot and fauset.

COCKAWINNIE.—The method of carrying persons with a leg over each shoulder.

COCKE'E.—The circles which surround the " Tee," or mark played at in curling.

COCKFAIR O'DRUMADDIE.—The name of a fair which never existed, but yet is frequently talked about. When a farmer, for instance, has unsaleable goods in his possession, he is bid take them to this fair; when persons a bargain-making, cannot agree, they tell others that they will at this fair; and when a young woman cannot get a husband, she is told that her only chance is at this place; so imagination has some use for the *Cock fair O'Drumaddie.*

COCKOLEARY-LAY.—The cock's matin, or morning crow.

COCK'S EGGS.—When hens are about to give over laying, they lay small eggs like dove ones; these are said to be produced by the cock, there is no yolk in them.

COCKUM.—A name for the cock.

CODGER.—A hearty old fellow.

CODSLIP.—A linen bag in which are put pillows.

COGG.—Any flat surface not lying horizontal, is said to be a *cogg.* An old carter, fond of whisky, would often *birl the bawbee* with his horse, to know whether it should have a *stimpert* of corn, or he one of grog; one cold day, trying the turn of fortune this way, the luck fell on the side of the poor beast, when he bawled out, " That's no fair; that's a *cogg;*" so he *birl'd* away, until the luck came to his side—the inhuman wretch.

COGGLE-TE-CARRY.—The amusement with the board laid over the fulcrum; a person gets on to each end and has an undulating ride.

COGGLIE.—Unstable.

COLE.—To dress by cutting.

COLLY.—A dog; also a coward.

COLLYSHANGY.—A worry either with dogs or men.

COMMON CORN.—Oats of that kind where each grain
hangs by itself upon the stalk; not like the other kind
termed " *potatoe corn*," where two grains always hang
together; there is little of this " *common corn*" now used:
the other kind just mentioned has superseded it, as thought
to be both more prolific and " *early*," which has caused
the other " *common*" over all the land anciently, to be
now branded with the epithet of " *late corn*."

CONGLUMRIFIED.—Conglomerated—stupified with a mixture of many foolish thoughts when applied to man, as it
generally is.

COOL-STANE.—A stone whereon the famous *Laird o'Cool*
(whose ghost will afterwards be spoken of) used to sit;
it is in the farm of *Cool*, parish of Buittle, and no man
dare touch it. A bold mason once would, but as the
people say of him, " he had never after anither day to do
weel;" he fell under it, and got his bones almost squeezed
to a mummy.

COOTIKINS.—Spatterdashes.

COOTLE.—To make a noise like ducks, when they are talking to each other.

COOTS.—Ancles.

CORBY—The raven. This is one of our most singular
birds; he seems to feel more pleasure in flying than any
other, and goes through many antics in the air, tumbling
himself on his back frequently; he cares nothing about
storms, and in fine calm days he will on wing circle often
the top of some high hill; his nature, however, is very
savage, and when domesticated, as he easily is, he prides
himself in doing all the devilry he can.

CORKIN-PREEN.—A large pin.

CORKLIT.—A whitish kind of fog, used in dying; it is taken from rocks, and feels like cork-wood, hence " *cork*" the name, and " *lit*" being a dye.

CORNCLOCKS.—Beetles common amongst corn.

CORNCRAIK.—The bird Landrail; its young ones are black, and they run among the grass like as many mice.

CORNKIST.—A chest to hold corn, common in stables.

CORNS.—Circular stones about two feet diameter, used for grinding malt, and anciently other things, before the invention of water-mills.

CORSE—Cross. Saxon.

CORSE o'SLAKES—Cross of rocky hills. *Slakes*, in Saxon, meaning rocky hills, or rocky brows. In Galloway there are no roads so wild as the one which leads over the celebrated pass of the above name, between *Cairnsmoor* and *Cairnhattie*; it is a perfect Alpine pass, and was a haunt of *Billy Marshall* and his gang in the days of yore; even yet it is frequently selected, as a suitable station for the " bludgeon tribe."

CORSICROWN—A simple game. A square figure is divided by four lines, which cross other in the crown or centre; two of these lines connect the opposite angles, and two the sides at the points of bisection; two players play, each has three *men*, or *flitchers*; now there are seven points for these men to move about on, six on the edges of the square, and one at the centre, the *men* belonging to each player, are not set together as at *draughts*, but mingled with other; the one who has the first move may always have the game, which is won by getting the three men on a line.

COSH.—Snug, happy, &c.

COTMAN.—A cottar, one who lives in a cottage, a bound servant to a farmer; this man is always looked on as the second in command about a farm-house; he receives his wages, or what is termed his benefit, not in hard cash, as other servants do, but in meal, barley, potatoes, or what not; the keeping of a cow, or *cows-grass*; he is the most useful of all servants, because the most settled; he interests himself more in his master's affairs, and looks after his property as if it were his own, and generally fills his station very respectably.

COTTRILL.—A nail in the head of a plough, by which it is drawn.

COUK.—To sort, to arrange, &c.

COUM.—Culm, refuse, dust, &c. See "*Peat-coum*."

COUMMIE EDGE.—The edge of a tool is said to be so when it does not seem to be good steel, nor well polished.

COUP.—To overturn.

COUTHY.—Frank, agreeable, &c.

COW.—A besom.

COWANS.—Those who would wish to know the mysteries of free masonry, without being regularly initiated, a thing both mean and foolish to attempt; mean, because they are cowards, and dare not go boldly forward like men; foolish, for unless they do so, masonry they never, never can know, no not the slightest thing about it; they may rail against the ancient and glorious institution, because they are held in ignorance, a thing which harms it nothing, for masonry, while time remains, will always find patrons in warm-hearted, social, and independent men. All other arts but it, of man's formation, some-time or other decays, and are reeled rotten into the bastile of oblivion, it alone remains the oracle of ages, and stands on a foundation so deeply grounded in nature, that no storm, though ever so rude, can make it in the smallest totter.

COW'D.—Made a coward of.

COWDIES.—A name for cows.

COWT.—A young horse.

CRACKET.—Split, deranged, &c.

CRACKSIE.—Talkative.

CRAE.—Crave.

CRAFTIN LAN.—Good green fields of the nature of croft.

CRAIG.—The throat, also the neck.

CRAIG O'HERONS.—The herons having the long *craig* or
neck; these birds get extremely lean in body about the
dark o' the moon, or when the moon is about the change,
because they see not then to fish, and are birds that feed
mostly by night; and being of a gluttonous nature, it is not
a *wee thing* that serves them; indeed, the heron is a bird
that may be well said to eat itself *out of ply,* for it is
always very lean; a stranger to this bird, on seeing it fly,
would think it very weighty, by the trouble it seems to
sustain itself in the atmosphere, but this is the reverse; it
is on account of its bulk and lightness, the wind can drive
it almost where it will, it is a very timid bird; come upon
him unawares, while wading about in a lonely pool, he has
not the fortitude to get under way, and may be caught. This
is the bird that vomits the *shot star,* that clear gluey matter found in fishy marshes; instead of being a production
of the lofty regions of aether, as long fancied; it is now
found to proceed from the greedy *gizzerons* of *lang-necked,*
or *craig o'herons.*

CRAIK.—An unneedful noise.

CRAIMS.—Stands, forms, &c. whereon open-air merchants
expose their wares.

CRANCH.—The noise that teeth make, in eating unripe fruit.

CRANES.—Long poles, with notches fixed to them, for the
feet to stand on; while they are used in wading rivers, a
water three feet deep has frequently been passed over with
cranes.

CRAPP.—The essence of whey, extracted when the whey is boiled, off the top, called in England " *float whey*," it makes very healthy food.

CRAPPIN.—The crop of birds.

CRAPPIT—Cut short. The rebels in Ireland were called *crappies*; for why, they had the hair of the head cut short ; see the song of " *Laury O'Broom, Sir*."

CRAPPS—Crops. Produce of harvest.

CRAW-PLUKIN—Threatening for faults committed. " I hae a *craw* to *pluck* wi' you" is often said by those who have thought themselves injured, to those whom they think have done them an ill turn.

CRAWS—Crows. These birds are said to begin to build their nests always on the first Sunday of March, and there is some truth in this, though it does not still hold good ; also, that they are always throngest at work on the Lord's day, when building; this will not just stand the test either ; we think them thronger on that day than on any of the week days, because, on that day we are resting from labour ourselves, so more at ease to remark ; they follow not our example.

CRAWTAES.—Flowers of the hyacinth species, common in wild woody glens.

CRAWTT.—A small insignificant person.

CREECH.—Grease.

CRESPIESTOOL.—A little seat.

CRIFFLE.—A large hill in the south-east corner of Galloway. I have seen many funny conjectures made about the derivation of its name, as of the devil ; and also the famous wizzard Michael Scott, having it once in a " *creel*" fixed round their bodies with a rope, that the rope there broke, and the " creel fell," so from that taking the name ; however, I cannot see the use of giving the fancy such a flight, in order to come at the thing wanted. Does " criff " in

K

no ancient norlan tongue signify "cliff?" I think it does, or else it is a corruption of "cliff," and as for the other half, it surely comes from " fell," a wild rocky range; so putting the two together we have " Cliffell," which is as near the name " Criffle" as the other " Creel-fell," and surely nearer the representation of it, for it is a place entirely composed of cliffs and fells.

CRIFFLE DIAMONDS.—It is strongly reported that this hill is full of these precious stones, but never can any of them be obtained; sailors passing it on the sea in their barks by night, are said to see them sparkle in the cliffs, but when they haul their wind, and go ashore in boats to get them, their guiding radiance vanishes, and so they come aboard sadly disappointed. Inventive fancies have suggested the firing of cannon balls at them through the nocturnal gloom; then finding in day-light the places struck by the bullets, which would be in the neighbourhood of the rare minerals; but I know not whether this plan has ever been yet tried.

CRIMP.—To plait, to " frill," &c.

CRINKY.—A rod of iron, with an hook at the end.

CROCK-EWES.—Old ewes which have lost *mark* of *mouth.*

CROCK-PIGS.—Large vessels of earthen ware for holding butter.

CROICHLE.—To cough often but not loudly, the sickly cough; those of consumptive habit are always " croichlin."

CROITTOCH.—A lameness which often assails the feet of cows and oxen; some cure it by drawing a hair rope through the split of the hoof; others, by pouring into that place, that burning thing " aquafortis."

CROMEK.—An English gentleman of the name of Robert Cromek, whose memory every Scotsman ought highly to respect. He was born in Yorkshire, had a genius for engraving, but a greater for a particular species of literature—the songs and manners of the days of yore; the works of Burns first gave him a bent this way, nor could he rest being so charmed with the muse of our great bard, until he took a trip to Scotland, and gathered the " reliques of Burns," a very amusing work, for which he was made a member of the Antiquarian Society of Edinburgh. Having published this book in London, he again set sail for the land of song, with his legendary wallet, and having arrived in the fertile regions of the south of Scotland, he soon was enabled to fill his budget by the aid of a bard he there *forgathered* with, and Mrs. Coupland, a lady at Dalbeatty, Galloway. This lady's exquisite taste in poetry furnished him with some delightful matters. O! would she but publish the effusions of her own muse, what a treat would this be to auld Scotland. The bard our enthusiastic Englishman fell in with, was no less a one than Mr. Cunningham; he met with the poet amid his rural haunts, singing of all the sweets of nature; and as I have heard, Mr. C. presented him with some of his poetical pieces, in order to have his opinion respecting their merits, the which Mr. Cromek ratherly sneered at, which caused the bard, when he shewed him any more of his productions, to say they were of the *olden time*, the which bait he greedily swallowed; whether he ever was aware of the songs being all mostly Cunningham's is not for me to say; he has lauded them as being extremely good, and as belonging to that part of the world; in doing so, he has said but the truth; now, why should there be such a jangling abroad in the world about this and similar things? if a poem be met with decidedly good, matters it much whether it was written in this or that century; the works of Ossian, the Song of Hardyknute, Chatterton's Poems, and the Nithsdale and Galloway song, 1 admire as much for my own part as if they had been all known as well about dates, places, every thing, as the poems of Burns.

K 2

Mr. Cromek had certainly a very just idea of what composed a good song; his taste in this respect seems to have been great, and considering the land he passed his youth in, it is wonderful to conceive how well he was acquainted with the manners of the Scots, the nature of their songs, and expressions of their language; worthy man, he died of a consumption in London sometime in March, 1812, when but a young man, leaving a widow and two children. Mr. Cunningham has given a sketch of his character, which is to be found in the front sheets of a spacious edition of a poem called the "Grave," by Blair, published by Ackerman, bookseller, *Strand.* He never wrote very much himself, but was very active, gathering rarities and getting them *pressed.* On the whole he was a man in every sense of the word, whose memory deserves not to be neglected.

CRONIE.—An agreeable friend.

CRONOCH.—The air of an old song, the Earse, Coronauch.

CROOK.—A piece of iron with clicks to hang pots on fires with.

CROOKIE.—Any thing crooked.

CROON.—The melancholy music of the ox.

CROOVIE.—A little snug, strange-shaped hut or den.

CROOZIE.—A broad-bottomed candlestick.

CROUSE.—Merry, high in spirits.

CROWDIE.—A thin mixture of oatmeal and warm water, not so thick as " porritch," nor yet so fat as " brose."

CROWL.—A dwarf.

CRUDDS.—Curds.

CRUDD-SAE.—A shallow tub to hold curds.

CRUE.—The same with *Croovie.*

CRULGE.—To stoop, to cringe.

CRUMMIE.—The name for favourite cows.

CRUMMIES PUNCH.—Grog, half water, half whisky.—
Crumbie, a Priest, who was once a placed preacher in
Kirkcudbright, amongst the many divine things he taught
his flock, this species of *Punch* was one, and it seems to
outlive all the rest; yea, and hand his reverend name down
to posterity; *Crummies Punch* will live as long as the
Crook o' the Lot or the *Pilgrim's Progress*.

CRUMPIE.—Any food brittle to eat.

CRUMWHULL's GIBB CAT.—A queer Galloway Poem—

In Gallowa now some hae heard
　O' Auld Crumwhull's Gibb Cat,
Or may be no—the de'il the odds,
　Let bards alane for that——

And there's o' them wad rather hear
　About ane big Gibb Cat,
As o' the grandest richest king
　On Gowden throne ere sat ——

Or warrier faeming on a naig,
　Owre blude besumped fields,
There splitting pows—there jagging hearts,
　And jingling on shields ——

Or statesmen thumping 'ither down,
　Wi' a' the pith o' chat,
Ane nobler theme than them by far,
　Is Auld Crumwhull's Gibb Cat——

Wha worried ance a fumart dead,
　And shook him after him,
Wha did the girnell o' Crumwhull
　O' rattons aften thin——

Wha crumpet mice like raisings up,
　And mony anither thing,
Wha aft upo' the knee wad loup
　O' Auld Crumwhull and sing——

For Auld Crumwhull wad straik his back,
　And ane sleek grey back had he;
Than wad he cock his tail fu' straught,
　And nyurr awa wi' glee——

He lo'ed the auld man unco' weel,
　For why he used him sae,
As selfishness had the Gibb Cat,
　And men the same whiles hae——

Ay, ay, the maist o' mankind hae
　　Enough atweel o' that,
There's some o' them mair selfish far
　　Than ony grey Gibb Cat——

Wha seem to sing a friendly sang,
　　And act a friendly part,
But hoh anee their sellie tugs,
　　Warst at the rotten heart ——

Frae death's door nane they wad relieve,
　　Tho' that was in their power,
Unless fu' sure they wad be paid
　　For doing 't ten times owre——

What think they, no' that they'll see heaven,
　　O! sure they can't think that ;
For heaven they'll never, never, see,
　　Mair than Crumwhull's Gibb Cat——

Whan e'er had ony thought to lae,
　　The kind place o' Crumwhull,
Mair than to lae the ocean has
　　Ane keckling sea-gull——

But Auld Crumwhull through perfect age,
　　Was ta'en to his lang hame,
Sae his bien ha' and a' his lands,
　　Anither laird's became——

Wha brought fell tykes about the house,
　　Whilk had nae sense ava,
For they did hunt the gude Gibb Cat,
　　Frae dear Crumwhull awa ——

He ran tae wuds, and lived upon
　　Young gorbs which he did fin'
In burdies nests and ither things,
　　Whilk sleekened his skin——

There turn'd a wullcat true did he,
　　Ane mad and furious pest,
And sleeped ay on taps o' trees,
　　In some snug corbie's nest——

The boys wha used to roam that wud,
　　And gather leaming nits,
Wad sometimes by the fell Gibb Cat,
　　Been flung in fearfu' fits ——

They heard him myauing mony a time,
　　Whan de'il the myau gaed he,
And saw him too, whar he was not,
　　For what won't terror see——

And whan a mither wanted whiles,
Her squaching bairnie gude,
She'd fley'd frae greeting a' at ance,
Wi' the wullcat o' the wud ——

Nae witch e'er wond in Binwood glen,
Was sic a fount of fear,
Nae gaunting ghaist in auld kirkyard,
Made sic a tale sae drear——

Nor need we wonder at the thing,
For flaming grew his e'en,
And mair than that he grew a cat,
The like was never seen ——

Thus thrave the awsome Gibb for years,
What bawdrons was like him?
What puss had e'er his whusking tail,
Or yet his strength o' lim'?——

Ane winter time, lang lay the snaw
Twa gude ell deep and mair,
Whilk pat *Sir Gibbie* to his wits,
For food wharon to fare ——

He kend a farmer just hard by,
Made aften sweet milk cheese,
And raw'd them nicely on his deals,
As *yallow* as ye please——

Af in a bonny moonlight night,
Ran the grimalkin there,
Broke through the wunnock in a crack,
And on them sweet did fare——

He broke the *scroof* o' three or four,
And left them sad to see
By the gude wife at scregh o' day,
And mad as she cud be——

Revenge was vow'd wi' mony a curse,
Against the thief unkend,
The next night they wad sit and watch,
And try his tricks to mend——

Wi' swooples, spurkles, beetles, fows,
The family a' war arm'd,
And haith they faun' use for them a',
For they war sair alarm'd——

Whan in cam spanging to the cheese,
The hule and wha was that,
Lord save our sauls they yelloch'd a',
It is Crumwhull's Gibb Cat——

By the chulders he seised on the gudewife,
    And soon wad hae stap'd her breath,
Had na her man, her sons, and daughters,
    Barried him to death ——

A wee thing did na kill the chiel,
    He fuff'd, he bit, and spat,
Sae merry Scotsmen now ye'll ken
    About Crumwhull's Gibb Cat——

Tho' for the moral o' the tale,
    Let nane that moral tell—
May every birkie watch his saul,
    And haud it out o' hell.

CRUPPLE.—The curple; the article in horse housing; well known to the *Monkland* people and others, who pride themselves in " *riding gear.*"

CRUTTLINS.—The refuse of soft food.

CRY'D—Proclaimed in church. Those proclaimed do not attend church on that day, nor none of their near relatives, which is Scotch modesty—

THE SONG OF BENJIE KELLAUCHEN.

Chorus.   *Owre the wil' waves I followed my Mary,*
        And owre the blue hills o' the lan' far awa,
        But I never faun' her, till back I did wan'er,
        A' hame wi' her mither at Gillyburnha.

O! the sweet jade had her notions romantic,
    She welcom'd me back wi' a glowre o' disdain;
She laugh'd at my justles across the Atlantic,
    And ne'er gaed a sigh at my tales fu' o' pain.

She had at her parties the beaux of the clauchen,
    And mony a young lairdy fu' goofish and braw,
But deuce a bit card cam' to puir Benjie Kellauchen,
    Never a kin' invitation ava.

Yet ay I did lo'e her, and ay she was bonny,
    O! nane like my Mary ava I cou'd see;
My heart ay beat queerer for her than for ony,
    Altho' she wad seem unco' cauldrife to me.

I gat unco' dowie I cou'd na be cheery,
    I dawner'd about the Saughligget and sigh'd,
Ay dreading ilk day at the kirk that my deary
    On some ane or ither but me wad be " *cried.*"

But what's come about think we—I've gat my Mary,
    For a' the cauld cluds that atween us did blaw,
'Tis the natur' o' women to shuffle and vary,
    But gin we are sicker we won them for a'.

Owre the wil' waves, &c.

A SONG BY BENJIE KELLAUCHEN.

O! my love she is fair,
And modest and neat,
O! charming's her air,
And her lips they are sweet;
Let her dress how she will,
Enchanting she's still,
O! she makes me to gaze, and she makes my heart thrill.

Full many a maid,
I have loved to kiss,
But my lips ne'er were laid
On a sweet mouth like this;
When the hills hide the sun,
When the evening 's begun,
Then, then, to my darling I swiftly do run.

And she waiteth for me
By the banks of burn,
'Neath the brown hazle tree,
Where the merle doth sojourn;
The fairies dance round,
On the flower covered ground,
O! that is the place where true pleasure is found.

To her I do give
My hand and heart free;
O! would she but live
In contentment with me,
I would shield her from harms,
With the power of my arms,
And enjoy evermore the delights of her charms.

CRYING PIPES.—Little pipes made of straw, which children make a noise with; the humble doric reed.

CRYING SIN.—A sin fancied to be large.

CRYING WIFE.—A woman in labour.

CRYN'D—Shriveled, contracted, &c.

CUBB.—A dull fellow.

CUBBERT—Cupboard.

CUD.—A lying young man.

CUDDLE.—To lie with other lovingly.

CUDDOCHS.—Black cattle a year old.

CUDDROCH.—A timid worthless youth.

CUDDY ASS.—An ass.

CUDDY AND THE POWKS.—An ass with bags hanging about it; also a school game—two boys join hands and feet over the back of a third, the which creeps away with them on hands and knees to a certain distance, and if able to do this, he, the *cuddy*, must have a ride as one of the *powks,* on some others back.

CUFF o' THE NECK.—The back part of the neck; that part where bitches and cats carry their young by, when they wish to remove their lair.

CUIF.—A blockhead.

CUIST.—Did cast.

CULL.—A lump of hard food.

CUM'D.—Grain is said to be *cum'd* when it has begun to *sproot* or bud ;—the *cum o' maut* is the advancement the bud has made—the length it has grown; by this, *maut-men* know if the grain has been long enough kept moist before they *kill-dry* it.

CUMMER'D—Cumber'd; hands are said to be so when benumbed with cold.

CUNDIES.—Hare holes through dykes. Poachers set girns in these to catch the game. One set a strong brass wire one, once; this he did in the gloaming; in the morning when he looked at it, there was his own dog hanged in it; he took out the dead *tyke,* set it again—looked at it next morning, and there's his own *bawdrons* leaping and *scraiching* in it; he had much ado in setting her free, then swore he, that " *girns he wad never set mair.*"

CURCHIE—Curtsey.

CURLY-MUCHY—Mouth-thankless.—See the article *Nyaph.*

CURR.—A shepherd's dog.

CURRBAWTY.—The art of seeking quarrel; some people, to their misfortune, are good at this, for they too often find it, and are frequently sadly *forfoughten*; there are some again who can steer their way through this life, bad as it is, and never have a battle with any body. I once heard a *cheel* say, " that a *worry* refreshed him—that it claw'd his back, and that he could not live if now and then he had not a *brattle* with his fellows ;" for my own part " I relish quietness at a price too much," as Pomfret, says ; and should any write against this queerish book and myself, with the high swinging language of damnation, mine *eldritch* jaw should never be opened in self defence ; the *broosle* they should have without fighting for it. I hate the mean art of *Currbawty* as I hate the devil ; what is the use of making this world worse than it is ? Let us take a laugh in it whenever we can.

CURRCUDDY or KIRRCUDDY.—A singular rustic dance, now common to be seen danced on the stages of theatres by buffoons. The dancers *curr* or sit down on their hams, with their hands joined beneath their thighs, and so they hop about, and go through various evolutions.

CURRMURRIN.—That noise in volcanic bellies, ready for eruption.

CURRY-KAME.—A comb for cleaning horse hides.

CUSHADO'ES—Cushet-doves. These are the most destructive birds in the south of Scotland, and they are not so bad yet as they will be. Plantations introduced them, and as the one thrives so does the other. They take no warning when one of them is shot, like crows.

CUTTIE-MUN—A short person, with an extremely small face. This face is said to be like a *mun*. Dr. Jamieson has *munn* to be a short-hafted spoon, and adds, it is a Galloway word. In this I differ from him ; *cutty-horn* or *cutty-spoon*, is the name I have heard, *mun* always applied to a little face. I have sometimes thought this *mun*, this word of perplexity was derived from moon, *cuttie-moon*, a little moon of a face : but this will not do well either, for we have a phrase, when speaking of a man with a large face, that he has a face as *brade* as a *moon*. I am sorry to leave the word baffled. The doctor thinks that it may come from the islandie, *munn*, the mouth ; now it is not the mouth that is the thing which makes us say a face is like a *mun*, it is the little circumference of that face. Old people, on the grave's brink, are said to have faces shrunk into that form.

CUTTIE-PIPE—A short-shanked pipe ; great smokers dislike any other kind of pipe than this, as also a new one. The English, in this respect, are not so, they must have long-shanked new pipes to every spell of smoking.

CUTTIE-SPOON or CUTTIE-HORN—A short-shanked spoon.

CUTTS—Those bands of iron which encircle *swingle-trees,* or barrs of wood, by which ploughs and harrows are drawn ; there are three of them on each bar, one at each end, and a large one in the centre. They are called *cutts,* because before they were made of iron ; there was just a strap of home-made rope for each *cutt,* and these, in time, by friction, *cut* through the wooden bar.

> An art may alter, but its early name
> Clings closely by it, till it reaches fame ;
> And when 'tis there, the hold it does let go,
> For then 'tis held, tho' it may wish or no.
>   MYSELL.

CUTTS and CAPERS—Flashes and flings.

CUTTS and HANKS—Thread in a loose state before it is wove into a web.

CUTTY—Any thing short, scanty.

CUTTY-GLIES—A little squat-made female, extremely fond of the male creation, and good at winking or *glying* ; hence the name cuttie-glies. Poor girl, she frequently suffers much by her natural disposition : to be short and plain, it seems this is the class of females destined by some infernal law to become prostitutes.

CUTTY-WRAN—The wren, the little nimble bird: how quick it will peep out of the hole of an old foggy dyke, and catch a passing butterfly. Manx herring-fishers dare not go to sea without one of these birds, taken dead with them, for fear of disasters and storms. Their tradition is of a " *sea-sprit,*" that haunted the " *herring-tack,*" attended always by storms, and at last it assumed the figure of a wren and flew away. So they think when they have a dead wren with them, all is snug. The poor bird has a sad life of it in that singular island; when one is seen at any time, scores of Manxmen start and hunt it down.

D.

DA'—A fond name for father, a contraction of daddy.

DAB—To pick like a bird, or peck.

DABBLE-DOCKS—The last candles that are made at a *making*; they are *dabbled* as it were in the *dock*, hence the name. Also persons battered with storms, having all their clothes wet, are called *dabble-docks.*

DAFFIN—Toying with women under night.

DAFFY-DOWNDILLY—The lovely yellow flower daffodil, or lily.

DAFT—To be deranged in the mind; also some are thought to be " daft," who are worth two wise folks. A strong natural genius is, for common, thought to be so when young.

DAGG—A cut of earth.

DAICH—Dough.

DAIDLE—To stroll about carelessly, and tipple and loll.

DAIDLIE—A loose frock, worn by children over their other clothes, called in England " pin-afore."

DAIKERT—Dressed, sorted, set to rights, &c.

DAIMEN—Rare, odd, &c.

DAINTIES—Delights, delicacies.

DAIVERT—A little oath, also to be *stun'd* with a blow.

DAIZ'D—Fail'd, decay'd, not fresh, &c.

DALLDRUMS—Foolish fancies, " he has ta'en the *dalldrums*,"
he has got foolish ideas into his head. I can say nothing
respecting the derivation of this word, but such is its
meaning.

DALLIED—Tarried.

DALLION—A person whose clothes befit not his body,
being too large for it; also, that person has a singular
foolish gait in walking.

DALLOCH—A flat of fat land.

DALLOW—To dig with a spade.

DAMBROD—A draught-board.

DAMDYKE—A mound of earth flung across a stream, to
confine the water, for mechanical affairs. " Spates"
often drive these dykes before them, to the grief of millers
and others; a very worthy and singular miller, of my
acquaintance, once told me the following :—" I had been
in at the market, and *ablins*, I might hae taen a gill or twa
mair than was right, nought mair likely. I had been in
' *Dinnies*' by the Brig, too, and minds o' me, haeing a
twelie wi' Lucky. But let thae flees stick i'the wa'. After
I had lifted Gillronnie brae, I foun' mysell soberin, sat
down on a taff-dyke, and took a look o' the lift. The moon
was wadin deep, and there was a damnable sough i'the sea
owre the Ross. I saw a spate brewin plainly, every clud
the carry brought whiskin by, tell'd me. I thought o'
my *damdyke*. The brod maun be lifted wi' the screw the
night ony way, or it will be a' to the pot or morning. This
said I to mysell, started, catched clicky again, pat a chew

o' *Jeannie's* best i'my mouth, and held straught on to the *dam.*

" But whan I cam in sight o' the *Milton,* frien' Johnnie's wather-glass cam i'my head. I had heard o' certain gentlemen farmers consulting the *' mercury,'* sae I, for ance, wad consult it too. Gaed in tae house—Johnnie was na gane lie, I foun' him taking a blaw o' the pipe owre the fire, wi' the *mowdieman.* Quo' I, ' how's the glass the night, man ?' we're gaen to hae a wather brack, that's my notion o't, sae I maun down tae dam, and lift the brod, or I'll hae nae dam i'the morning."

" Howt's fool," quo' *Johnnie,* " we're gaen to hae nae spate. *Auld Guthrie* has filled ye wi' thae babbles as ye cam' by now, the glass is up, awa atween *fair* and *dry*; but we'll tak the cannle, and look, gin ye like, there's nae fear o' your dam the night ony way." We did sae, the thing was as he had said, the mercury was up, awa by " fair and dry." But gang out man, and look at the lift, and hear the sough i'the sea ; gif they look na like a spate, they cheat me, quo' I. " Howt's fool," quo' he, " its your ain lugs that sough the night, and wha kens but your e'en may be a wee thing glazed too. We'se hae a glass o' whusky owre this ony way." To this I was " nothing loath," as the great Milton says, for by this time, wi' sweating, drinking water, and chewin tobacco, my mouth was got dry, and a " *wrack*" had gathered brown roun' my lips, like the wrack on the shore roun' the sea. Ae glass brought anither ; him and me tae jawner, and whan I gat hame, lord knows. I wakened i' the morning wi' an awfu sair head ; the ducks I heard giein queer eldrich squakes about the " *lade.*" I pat on my *mill-claise,* and gaed out: the wun was awfu' ; the rain was fa'in in stoupfu's. I set af to unscrue the dam wi' a haste ; but or I wan haufway till't, there its coming meeting me, rowin just afore a sea o' water. I had eneuch ado to wun out o' its range. The hale was fearfu' to look at ; on it roared and famed, covered my bit meadow with sods, nor did it rest till it rolled into *Mollock Bay*, making the sea, as far as the *Netherlaw Head*, muddy. What cud I do; to fret needless, but wha cud keep frae't. " Let it lie there," quo' I, " there's nae faith to be pitten in *whusky* and *wather-glasses*."

DAMS—Game at draughts.

DANDGELL—A person much the same with *Dallion*; also a large thick top-coat.

DANNER—To wander carelessly.

DANTON—To fright, to intimidate.

DARCK—A day's work. " A darck o' peats," a day's work to obtain peats; this clause is in many a poor man's bargain with his master. " Darck" sometimes too, rather extends beyond a " day's work;" thus, we say often when a hard job is done, which has taken the work of weeks, " that that was a *darck* indeed."

DARG—The noise a spade makes when darting into soft earth.

DARK o' the MOON—That period of the moon when she is in conjunction, or changing, or ratherly the first and last quarters of the moon's age; she is then but little seen by us, and leaves our nights, while she remains so, to the utter dominion of darkness. " *Parties*, in the country," viz. meetings among friends, are never fixed to be held during this season, and several wild animals which roam during the night for prey, get lean in flesh at this absence of the radiance of the nocturnal queen. The fox and owl miss her light very much, but none more so than that bird we call the *craig o' heron*; it is then nothing but a *rickle o' banes*, covered with feathers, and has given rise to the saying, when any one is down in flesh, like an *Edinburgh Student*, that he resembles the *craig o' heron* at the " *dark o' the moon*."

DARROCHS—Oak woods, or places where oaks grow, the word is quite *earse*.

DARNIN STOCKINGS—The art of mending hose; the art
of hiding, or " *darning*" faults.

DASH'D—Browbeat, abashed, put out of countenance, &c.

DASHELLED—Beat, battered, and washed by bad weather.

DASSES—Cuts of hay, the way hay-stacks are taken down,
cutting them with knives in " *dasses.*"

DATIL-IT-TIT-TIT-TAY—The first note of the wren's song.

DAUD—A blow, a fall, a piece, &c.

DAUDED—Abused, hurt, &c.

DAUGHIE-DAY—A warm, foggy day.

DAUGHT—Any thing having a wild, unnatural taste with it,
is said to have a *daught*, and though this taste be not felt
for some days after the thing has been eaten, still it is said
to have left a " *daught*" behind it.

DAVIE DRAP—A little black topt field flower. Children
amuse themselves on the *braesides i'the sun*, playing at
hide and seek with this little thing, accompanying always
the hiding of it with this rhyme, marking out the circle
in which it is hid, with the fore-finger—

> " Athin the bounds o' this I hap,
> " My black and bonny *Davie-drap*,
> " Wha is here the cunning yin,
> " My Davie-drap to me will fin."

DAVIE EDDIE—The chief of our Galloway idiots. His
native clauchan is *Garlieston*. Once he leaped into a boat
there, and drifted out to sea with it; was some nights on
the wild element, till picked up by a boat, twenty miles
from that port. He is fat, and " *hotters*" about the
clauchans with boys after him, always smiling. He has as
much sense as to take food and coppers when they are offered him; and, like a true idiot, will not work for any
body. He seems to have some ear for music, as all fools

have, and might probably, who knows, have been learned
to write rhyme.   See more of him in the article " *Naturalls.*"

DEACON MA'MINN—The Borgue philosopher. This was
quite a Dr. Franklin, if he had had his industry ; but,
wanting that (except for me), he would have sunk into
oblivion. The Deacon was a rustic of no common intellect : it is pleasant to reflect on his vast mind, even though
it was rude.   Had he received the benefit derived from
education, there is no saying how far he might have ex-
plored the ocean of science; what unknown lands he
might have found ; and what gems, by diving, he might
have brought up to light.

For the greater part of his life (and it was not a short
one), he lived in a little hut beside the *Glebe of Senwick,*
and wrought just at labouring work, hoeing whins,
quarrying stones, &c. He seldom was a bound labourer,
he was ratherly what is called a *jobber,* taking little *spells*
of work from those who had them to give, and doing them
at his leisure, for the Deacon would never allow himself to
be a hard worker, his great mind insisted frequently for
time to reflect on the various works of nature which presented themselves before him. He was fond of Botany,
and had a little garden filled with flowers, fruit-trees, and
bee-hives. All the Gardeners in Galloway knew the Deacon, and would have come twenty miles and upwards, for
the one purpose of having a *crack* with him. With them
he exchanged visits and plants, and was a welcome guest
in all the hot-houses, parterres, and orchards, the wide-
spreading country could boast of. His gooseberries were
still of the first kind, and when they were in season for
eating, his garden was like a little fair on Sundays,
with people tasting his mellow fruit. Such was the Deacon ;—he is now in his narrow bed, poor man : the house
where he lived is in ruins, his berry-bushes withered, and

covered with nettles, and *robin-rin-the-hedge*, while some
of his " garden flowers" are now to be seen " growing
" wild." Yet the fond memory of some conjure up the
rustic sage, and some of his shrewd remarks seem as if
they were not going to be forgot. When the minister
of his parish died, some of his warm friends thought of
erecting a monument, with a suitable inscription thereon,
to the memory of his departed Reverence, but ere doing
this, they thought it would do no harm to have the Deacon's opinion on the matter, when he gave his *showthers a
hotch*, and answered, " Wi' I ken na what ye wad say
about him, but that he's *there* ;" meaning, as much that his
body lay *there*, and there required no more in justice to be
said : so the idea of a monument was blasted by the Deacon's sarcasm. Though it was known that the Reverend
gentleman was never much admired by him, as when he
(the priest) met with our philosopher, at *diets o' examine*,
it was always his way to set upon and question hard the
Deacon, respecting the knotty points of our faith ; yet
even there, he could not get the better of him so well as
he wished, as, whenever a cramp question was put, the
Deacon would shake his head, and say, " He cud na cle-
verly tell that," the which answer compelled his Reverence
to tell it himself. When asked by an acquaintance once
what he thought of the sermons of the above-mentioned
priest, if he considered them true to the point, or if he
" backed weel out wi' Scripture ?" " I ken na (quoth the
Deacon), he preaches *loud*—ay, he's *loud*," meaning as
much that he made a noise, when speaking, and nothing
more.

When some *Sutors* in the *Gate-house* started from the
stall, and began to harangue a multitude respecting their
evil ways, the Deacon thought " Preaching would soon
be *gaun wi' water*," like any other piece of mere machinery.

His inquiries after the wonders of nature were of the first kind. The tides of the ocean, the thunder, the clouds, and the stars, cost him many reflections; and far did his mind penetrate into the ways of Providence. Wild too, did his fancy soar, and out of *hale claith*, as the saying is, he could shape a wonderful story. His imagination was perfectly exuberant; he not only knew the ways of men, and the various turns of nature, but he seemed also as if he had spent many a day with witches and warlocks; dined with water kelpies; and danced with fairies. With these visionary beings, he still seemed quite at home. By the strange tales he struck out, and the distance his mind was above his brother rustics, was he honoured with the title of *Deacon:* his christian name was James. He was a great artizan, as so were his sons, quite masters of all kinds of turning, centric and eccentric; they made *distaffs* and snuff-boxes, unmatched for handy craft.

It may be said of the Deacon, as it is said of not a few, that he was gifted by nature with powerful talents, but blasted by the laws of Fortune.

DEAD-DAYS—Those days the corpse of a person remains before it is buried; no ploughing, nor opening the earth in any shape, is allowed to go forward, when such is the case in a farm.

DEADILY—A school game.

DEAD-MATCH—A close match.

DEAD-THRAWS—The throws of death. To the man of feeling, there is not a more horrible sight to be seen, as a fellow creature in this wretched state; how alive we are then to the power of death, and how grieved to the soul that we can render no relief. I was never able to stand the scene but once, and will never try it again, unless abruptly compelled. I do not think death itself will be more difficult for me to endure than that appalling scene was. Once too, that restless being within me, Curiosity, dragged me to see the execution of a young man, when in Edinburgh, but she'll drag well if she drags me back again to see such a spectacle. I was not myself, Mactaggart, for a month afterwards, my mind was so disordered with the sight. In a curious way wrought the phrenzy (as I am one who speaks my mind), I tell this. I felt an inclination, both during night, when dream after dream whirled through my brain's airy halls, and in the day-time, to do some crime or other, that I might meet with a similar fate. Whether this is ever the way with any other person, I cannot tell, but so it operated on me, and which has caused me ever since to say, that *hanging*, instead of scaring from crime, has a strong tendency the other way. May God keep me far from seeing again any in the *dead-thraws*.

DEATH ON SKYTCHERS—Long, lean, ill-made people, are said to be like *Death on Skytchers*—Death on skates; for this fell foe of our race is fancied, by all nations, to be a *rickle o' banes*, yet he *skates*, or moves quickly about.

DEBUSHED—Debauched. I am always fond of inserting those little scraps of poetry I have about me when they suit the article, and I think this at present on the *Death o' a Debauchee*, is quite a-propos :—

> And sae my merry ranting Tam
>   Has turn'd the nuik at last,
> Weel did he lo'e a wench, a dram,
>   And lived unco' fast.

> Few ance cud dance and drink like he,
>   And woo a bonny lass :
> For he attended every spree,
>   And freely flashed his brass.

> At waddings, raffles, jerkins, balls,
>   Blyth Tammie ay attended,
> He boxed well in midnight brawls,
>   And sae his days he ended.

> His pouch o' cash was seldom light,
>   For his auld scrubbing dad
> Left him a weighty purse to right,
>   And set him floreing mad.

Thus the father spent his days
  In grubbing misery ;
The son, tho', did reverse his ways,
  And died a debauchee.

Sillar's ay the root o' woe,
  Whatever view we take,
It is the miser's wretched foe,
  And oversets the rake.

Sae Tam, ye're now gane to the grave,
  That tavern cauld and grim ;
Nae parties there do ill behave,
  There a's in sober trim.

Your landlord Death, in quitness keep:
  The chaummers o' his Inn,
There cursed clamour queemly sleeps,
  The wicked's ill-fared din.

For you the yillwives here lament,
  And drunkards sound thy fame,
May they, unlike thee, here repent,
  Or they gae to lang hame.

What madness this, to plunge downright
  In black damnation's pool,
To love the night, and hate the light,
  O ! foolish man ! fool ! fool !

DEEP DRAUGHT—A long deep-drawn plan. People, this way, for all their uncommon craft, seldom thrive. The world holds of them as of a weeping crocodile.

DE'IL DOGS—Black dogs, met with under night, have long been called dei'l-dogs ; and it is confidently thought by many, that the Prince of Darkness *trounces* through this world in the form of a black dog : even Burns has him— the Piper at Allowa Kirk to the Witches—

   " A towzie *tyke, black*, grim, and large."

DEI'L'S BUCKY—A bad boy.

DE'IL'S BUIKS—The Devil's books, the cards, generally called the *De'il's buiks* by that sect of religious persons called the *Hill fowk*, for they will not touch the cards, and consider them the first books in the Devil's library.

De'il's Club—Many people fancy that the Devil carries a club with him wherever he wanders, and whatever object he is allowed to touch, from that moment it becomes his property, as when he touched the Man of Uzz anciently. Thus, at that season of the year called Michaelmas, he is said to touch with it the black-berries, or to " throw his club over them," none daring after that period to eat one of them, or the " worms will eat their ingangs." That boy too, who personifies an infernal being at Yule time, with face besmeared with soot or *grime*, and a sheep-skin belted round him with a straw rope " wooly side out, and fleshy side in," as the song of Bryan O'Linn goes, this boy bears in one of his hands a club, and in the other a frying-pan, as he rambles from house to house with his comrades, in white weeds; and, in one of his rhymes, ·thus describes himself—

" Here come I, auld Beelzebub,
" And over my showther I carry a *club*,
" And in my hand a frying-pan,
" Sae am I no a jolly auld man."

See more of this article, *Yule Boys.* There are many, however, who dread not either the *auld boy* nor his *club*, but are something, as the poet said of *Ingleby*, the female who lately astonished Scotland, by laughing at fire; her flesh remained unhurt in the strongest flame that could be made; she could too, lick with her tongue, a red *gaud o' airn*, and lap up a mouthful of boiling lead—

·" If *Ingleby* ere gangs to hell,
" Auld Nick will ken na whar to throw her,
" She'll stand his bleezes like himsell,
" He'll no can make a *penny* o' her."

People should really be more afraid than they are of that pit wide yawning; and I myself should reflect oftener on the matter than I do, for I find I have not been an *unco' gude boy.*

De'il's Dizzen—-The number 13.

De'il's Milk—The white milky sap of many plants, called so because of its bitter taste. There is much of it in the stem of the *swine thistle.*

De'il's Needle—A large insect common in the latter end of summer. Its body and wings are about one length, that is, three inches. It haunts mosses and moors : it bites hard when caught, and is called *adder-bell* in some districts in Scotland. Some say it stings, but this it does not ; and whether its bite be poisonous or no, I have not yet learned, nor do I know the name insectologists give it. Frequently two are seen flying together, and in conjunction. It is an insect not much beloved in the country, and tall men of a bad disposition, are not unfrequently called *De'il's needles,* and sometimes *De'il's darning-needles.* See, for more respecting them, in the article *Robin Aree.*

De'ilry or Devilry—To illustrate this word, I may give the poem named the " Devilry o' Drummorrel." When I say *the poem* at any time before I give it, I do not mean to say it is a *poem* well known, a *poem* that has been printed, and all the rest of it ; I only mean it is a *poem* that I never before beheld the *light.*

> Daft Davie had a farm,
>   And it was ca'd Drummorrel,
> The soil o' it was na warm,
>   Bent grew on't and sorrel.
>
> His lairdy had a daughter fair,
>   Nane like her sae bonny ;
> She had the e'en and the hair
>   Nature gies na mony.
>
> Wooers cam frae every airt
>   To court the lovely Nancy,
> But it was hard to shog her heart,
>   No ane o'em could she fancy.
>
> She cared na for a common cheel
>   De il the single spittle,
> Some lord she thought might answer weel,
>   Her whimsies were na little.

Blawn up wi' meikle pride hersell,
  And helped by her mither;
She cared na what did wisdom tell,
  It never made her swither.

Wi' her did Davie fa' in love,
  And wha at that need won'er,
Whan wi' that passion she did move
  Younkers mony a hun'er.

He dawner'd, doyl'd about the farm,
  His heart ay beating queerly,
Raving about her every charm
  And how he loe'd her dearly.

" O ! Nannie, thou's a heavenly queen,"
  He aften owre repeated;
" The like o' thee nae man hath seen,
  " Nor got his fancy heated."

Upon his farm there was a co',
  Which travellers did admire;
Our lady ae day to't wad go,
  It being her desire.

Drummorrel gat a scent o' this,
  And down tae co' gaed linking,
In hopes the cheel to get a kiss,
  Wi' meikle plotting thinking.

He crawls into the farthest nook
  O' the auld curious chaumer,
And there the benmost bink he took,
  Whar Nick learns witches glamour.

Wi' ladies and wi' cannle-light
  Fair Nancy now did enter,
To see the famous rustic sight,
  It was a daring venter.

Davie e'es the lovely maid,
  Lord, how his heart was thumping;
He sees her coming half afraid,
  And he's prepared for jumping.

He letteth first an hideous yell,
  Then claughted at the lassie,
Wha thought him het just out o' hell,
  O sadly scared was she.

Her comrades let the lantron fa',
  And out they sprawchled scraighing;
Lang wast or they cud speak ava,
  For fainting maist, and peching.

Than quoth Drummorel to the girl
  " Do this, or I can't save thee ;
" Gae wed, or down I will thee whirl,
  " Gae wed, Drummorrel Davie."

Sae let her gae, she wauchled out,
  Puir thing she was na fearie,
It was the De'il, she didna doubt,
  Whilk had made her sae earie.

And Davie, wi' his wilyart voice,
  Lay i'the cavern roaring ;
He raised an awfu' eldritch noise,
  Wi' squeeling, squaching, snoring.

And strange to tell, or it was laug
  He gat the darling lady,
Wi' joy he owre her daily sang
  A happy life-time had he.

Thus Drummorrel's devilry
  May show the world that wildness
Succeedeth to a high degree
  Aboon the calm o' mildness.

There is something about this poem which reminds us of the tale of " Daft Jock M'Clean," so I may also give it. Jock was a curious enough human being ; not altogether wise, and one could not say he was quite an idiot either ; yet he was mostly allowed by all who had the *honor* of his acquaintance, to want a few *pence* of the *shilling*, as the saying is.

Well, the fellow wandered about the *nit-wuds* and *burn-sides*, and one lovely sunny summer evening he met with a certain Nobleman's daughter. This young woman was extremely bonny ; her eyes bewitched poor Jock M'Clean the moment he saw them, and made him stand fast : so the wretch stood and gaped and panted, and glowered after the yellow hair'd maiden, until she went out of his sight past a turn on her walk. He went home to his mother in a sad state ; love was burning him up alive. Sleep—he could get none ; and how to have a kiss of the fair charmer, puzzled him much. At length he hit on a plan : he knew of a crab-tree in full bearing : he went and pulled the

fruit, and rowed them along the fair lady's accustomed
walk, ending the row in a deep recess of the wood, in a
dark *binwud* grove. The bait took ; the lady, out strolling, seeing the crabs placed in this manner, followed
the train away into the deep grove, where *Jock* lay in am-
bush to receive her. He clasped the sweet soul in his
arms ; she screamed ; he kissed ; she fainted—he let her
fall, and ran. Some people working near by, hearing the
cries of the young lady, came to her aid : soon they caught
the poor daft fellow, who simply told the whole cause of
the uproar. The lady pardoned and pitied him, saying,
" That if he had come and told her what he wanted, he
would have got it, without putting himself to so much
trouble, and her in such jeopardy." For the fellow's
craft, however, she gave him a suit of new clothes, and a
more flashy fellow than he was, came not to the Belton
Fair of *Kirkcubrie* that year, and some girls were not
ashamed to admire *Daft Jock M'Clean.*

DELFS—Marks of animals feet in soft land.

DEMENTED—Deranged in mind. Some girls go *demented*
about some men. This is a turn of mind I am not up to :
if the men have injured them, then it may be accounted
for ; but for pure love, it beats me quite.

DE-NETTLES—A kind of nettle common in corn-fields, and
hurtful to the reaper's hands.

DEUCE—The Devil ; *deuce a bit,* devil a bit.

DEUG—A long tough man.

DEUGLE—Any thing long and tough.

DIBBLE—A piece of pointed wood for planting with.

DIET o' EXAMINE—An examination of honest Christians
by their parish priest about religious matters, points of
faith, grounds of salvation, what not. Wise priests examine now none at all ; others, not so wise, or perhaps
wiser, examine the youths of their flocks, a thing surely

quite right; and others, more foolish, still examine all " *hand owre head*," the young and the old, a thing in many respects very far wrong; nothing but impudent country-folks can answer properly any questions at these meetings. The modest, and they are still the great majority, can answer nothing: how can they; whenever they speak they are laughed at, and timidity debars them finding words for their ideas: yet still I think more of the religious principles of that person who can answer not a word, than of that who can. The one is mostly found to have the darling heart, and the heavenly light therein; the other we find to have goodness only " *lip-deep.*" At these *diets*, the priest, and many of the *heads* of families, have a " *diet*" indeed, of good *beef* and *greens,* as they are mostly held at the *wealthiest* of the country people's houses.

Anciently, when the minister withdrew, and took *terror* with him, a fiddle was introduced, and dancing, drink, and fun kept up to an early hour next day, which pleased the taste of many as well as the question of " *effectual calling.*"

Din—Noise of any kind.

Din—Dun, the colour. " Its a mercy dinness is na *sair*," quoth an eminent wit to a certain auld *Lucky* who had the Ethiopian's skin. " How that gude man (quoth she) wi' had it been sae, he returned, you and me wad hae been keeped in eternal *torment.*"

Dinge—A blow, or *dinnage.*

Dingle Dousie—A piece of wood burned red at one end as a toy for children. The mother will whirl round the ignited stick very fast, when the eye, by following it, seems to see a beautiful red circle. She accompanies this pleasant show to her *bairns* with the following rhyme:—

> Dingle dingle-dousie,
> The cat's a' lousy:
> Dingle dingle-dousie,
> The dog's a' fleas.

Dingle dingle-dousie,
Be crouse ay, be crouse ay ;
Dingle dingle-dousie,
Ye'se hae a brose o' pease, &c.

DINK—To walk with a more affected air when in dress than when not so.

DINNLE—To quiver, to shake, &c.

DINTED—Struck, as with love.

DIRDUM—A battle with words.

DIRLIN—Acute pain, from scaulding.

DISH'D—Sorted, put in dishes.

DISHALAGO—Coltsfoot; a broad-leaved herb. Some use it as a substitute for tobacco : it is a bad weed when it gets into land ; there is no getting it out again, it roots so deep.

DISH-A-LOOF—A singular rustic amusement. One lays his hand down on a table ; another clashes his upon it ; a third his on that, and on so. When all the players have done this, the one who has his hand on the board, pulls it out, and lays it on the one uppermost : they all follow again in rotation, and so a continual clashing or *dashing* is kept up ; hence the name *dish*. Those who win the game are those who stand out longest, viz. those who are best at enduring pain. Tender hands could not stand it a moment : one dash of a *rustic loof* would make the blood spurt from the top of every finger. It is a piece of pastime to country lads of the same nature as *Hard-knuckles*, which see.

DISHCLOUT—The cloth dishes are washed with.

DISHNAP—The vessel dishes are washed in.

DISJASKET — Fatigued out ; low in body, mind, and clothing.

DISSLE—Trial severe of any kind.

DOACH—A waterfall ; or a trap for fish in a waterfall.

DOACH's o' TONGUE-LAND WATER—The waterfalls of the Dee. Their roaring noise is heard afar. Traps are set in them to catch salmon fish.

DOAF—Without animation, lifeless. The earth of a garden is " doaf" when, though it seems fat, nothing will grow on it but weeds. That part of the body is " doaf" which is devoid of feeling.

DOAFFIE—A lifeless fellow.

DOCHTIE—Strong beyond appearance.

DOCKENS—Dockweeds. Mine worthy original *Saddler Halliday* was once asked by a gentleman—what was the best method of extirpating *dockens* out of gardens? " Take a spade, quoth the *Saddler*, and howk them out dinna lae, a single talon o' the root ahin; wash and lay them on the yard-dyke to dry; then burn them; that's the best plan I ever kend." In truth it surely was a most effectual one.

DODDLES—Hard pellets of dirt which form on the tails of sheep. When they begin to get young grass to eat in the spring, they make a rattling noise on other when the animals run.

DODJELL REEPAN—A beautiful wild flower common in marshy places. It is something of the figure of the feather in some soldiers caps; of a conical form; not unlike a head of Indian corn, or a *firrtap*, the common colour of it is a lovely red, but sometimes it is seen white; its smell is very fine, and its root is of a bulbous nature, and very much like the body of an infant from the waist downwards. I have been thus particular, because I cannot find it hinted at in any books of botany that have fell in my way, and for some other causes which will just now be told. There are few districts in Scotland which have not their own name to this plant; in Annandale, and by the *border*, it is *meadow rocket*; in the west, and greater

part of Ireland, *mount caper*; the *yirbwives*, my famous
herbalists, tell me that this *yirb*, above all others, should
not be known to man; that's to say, its virtues should
not be known to him; but as I have come to know what
these virtues ascribed to this plant are, without these old
females leave, and without promising to any one I should
keep the important *mystic*, so I fail not to tell it.

The roots of *this herb* then, when decocted, that is,
boiled, and then mingled with a *lukewarm* lover's-meat,
the female will get burning in love with the male who did
it, although she was very indifferent about him before, as
soon as she has swallowed the mixture, and will follow
her object through thick and thin, in spite of all opposi-
tion, until she obtains her love adored. How far this
holds true I cannot say; persons have been pointed out
to me who have tried the same with success; and the tales
respecting which are indeed wonderful pieces of fancy.
But much I am inclined to think that this *reepan* or *rocket-
juice* is a composition of mere nonsense; had there been
any reality in it, I should not have been the first to give
it to the world; for nothing of a hurtful nature to mankind shall come from me, if I am aware of it. Methinks
this sap will aid Cupid nothing more than a *sploit o' tobacco brew*. There is a poem in my wallet, entitled
" Something on the death *O' Dodjell Reepan,* a game-
keeper ;" whether it is my own production or no I cannot
exactly say; it smells something of my *ugly fist*. It may
here be given, though there be nothing in it about the
plant in question but the name :—

> And Dodjell Reepan's dead and damn'd,
>   The poacher's whistling do tell ;
> And he's hung up on a nag to be ham'd,
>   In the reekiest neuk o' hell.
>
> Mony a brute he laid fu' caul,
>   Wi' his twa barrled gun ;
> But death himsell at last did maul,
>   And thought it noble fun.

He miss'd a fit on the tap o' a dyke,
  Ae day there lay wrides o' snaw,
And into ane o'em the petty tyke
  Head foremost wi' a dart did fa'.

He kicked wi' fury three times at the sun,
  Whan he was a smooring fast ;
But, alas, the scalbert's days war run
  In the snaw wride he graned his last.

Mony a puir cheel the hallion did trail,
  Wha had may be shot a paitric or hare,
And ram'd him 'thout remorse i'th auld stinking jail,
  Whar the day-light ne'er did stare.

For him a shepherd's collie durst na bark,
  Nor a loving gibb-cat gie a mew ;
The corbie durst na croak, nor the flecket-pyet chark,
  Else to death wad he them pursue.

Ae day he ram'd his han' in a fumart hole ;
  The hole was i'the auld Taff-dyke ;
But sic pertness the fumart cudna thole,
  Sae snacked the thum' o' the tyke.

And sank its alson tusks to the white hard bane,
  Whilk pizioned the thum' for ay ;
And till he gat its head besnang'd wi a stane,
  Black bawdrons wad na let gae.

It wad hae gard a hauf-dead body laugh,
  To see Dodjell louping about,
And gieng the hearty scraigh and squagh,
  While the fumart hang by him fu' stout.

The harmless brock too he punsed in his den,
  And worried him without grief,
Altho' auld brocksie ne'er ruffled a pen,
  O' the game burds charged by the squeef.

He nicher'd unco aften like a new spean'd foal ;
  Was scooling and glieing ilk gate ;
His clyping manners wha cud thole ;
  He gat aft a braw clowr'd pate.

He's gaen heels-owre-gowdie i'the mools ;
  Let him *lie there*, his mourners are few ;
He was as mean a hyple as ere graced fools,
  And a hatefu'er wratch nane ere knew.

For God sake ye lairds wha be sportsmen mad,
  Scare sic vile trash af yer lan',
Unless they be cronnies for ye base and bad,
  And *wee tricks* do best understan'.

DOIT—A copper coin; the half of the boddle; the twelfth of an English penny.

DOITED—In a state of dotage.

DOLLY BEARDY.—In Galloway now slumbers a singular old song and dance, called *Dolly Beardy*. After going through a world of trouble with great pleasure, I got a *hint* respecting the song, and here is the result of that—

> Dolly Beardy was a lass,
> De'il the like o'r on the grass,
> Her lad was but a moidert ass,
>> Hey, Dolly Beardy.
>
> Dolly Beardy had a leg,
> Ay, and she cud mak it fleg,
> And sometimes she was got wi' egg,
>> Hooh, Dolly Beardy.
>
> Dolly Beardy had a cow,
> Black and white about the mou',
> She keeped her ay rifting fu',
>> Smock, Dolly Beardy.
>
> Dolly Beardy she cud whud
> About the bonny birken wud,
> In spring time whan the saugh did bud,
>> Sweet, Dolly Beardy.
>
> Dolly Beardy lo'ed a cheel,
> His heart was cauld, it cudna feel,
> Sae him and her gaed baith tae de'il,
>> Ha, Dolly Beardy.
>
> Dolly Beardy steek thy een,
> They do confound us whan their seen,
> We lang to cuddle thee ateen,
>> Dear, Dolly Beardy.
>
> Dolly Beardy's blinking e'e
> Fairly hath dumfounder'd me,
> She is a hizzie fu' o' glee,
>> Mark, Dolly Beardy.
>
> Dolly Beardy ye hae craft,
> Dolly Beardy we are saft,
> Gallowa 'bout thee's run daft,
>> Hech, Dolly Beardy.

DOMINIE—A schoolmaster. *Dominie Hutchison o' Clauch-enpluck*, author of that learned work the *Infant*, price *one penny*. One of the rarest schoolmasters in Gallo-

way, and quite an original.   He is up to all the various
branches of learning, and teaches his scholars on the natural plan; that is to say, whatever be the bent the Dominie
checks it not; so his pupils become fond of him, and
full of love.   Many he fits out for college, and some
kirks in Scotland have his pupils preaching in them.

To his various lore he adds that of Æsculapius; and
the Dominie's medical skill is in high repute in the Moors.
None can " *bluid*" with him; none can remove *virulent*
so and so's, like he; and none can die without receiving a
visit or two first from the *Dominie*.   I conclude with him
at present; but the article *Peatnuik* will bring the philosopher again on the carpet.

Donsy—Neat, clean, honest-like.

Dool—Sorrow; also a place of refuge.

Dool-hills or Doon-hills.—There are several hills in
Galloway whereon have stood castles and other strengths
of yore, termed *Dool* or *Doon-hills*.   These places of
refuge seem to have existed prior to the Roman invasion,
as the name *Dool* or *Doon* is never given to hills whereon
are the remains of Roman camps; the labours of these
hills then belong to the ancient British or some Scandinavian wanderers.

Dools—A school game; and school games are by no
means things unworthy observation, as many of them bespeak matters of the olden time; the one of *dools* then,
amongst others, hints at something of this nature; the
dools are places marked with stones, where the players
always remain in safety—where they dare neither be caught
by the hand nor struck with balls; it is only when they
leave these places of refuge that those *out of the doons*
have any chance to gain the game, and get in, and leave
the *doons* they frequently most; this is the nature of the
game.   Now this game seems to have been often played
in reality by our ancestors about their *doon-hills*.

DOOL-STRING.—A piece of black crape put round the hat, to show the world we are in *dool* and sorrow; mourning deeply about the death of some dear friend or relative; the nearest of kin to the deceased have commonly the largest *dool-strings*. When this piece of fashion is considered a little philosophically, it shews itself a thing of vanity at once; those always feel the keenest sensations of grief who wear nothing of the kind. I have seen fellows with them hanging half down their backs, attending the funerals of their wives, who God knows if they felt very *severely*. Genuine sorrow is like charity, it detests all shew and ostentation. Some hypocrites never unrobe their chapeau of the dool-string, but keep it constantly on for years together, though in course of time it has changed its hue from black to brown, and become frumpled, like a piece of dry sea-weed.

Auld Barrclye was a character somewhat of this kind; he used frequently to take a trip over to the Isle of Man in quest of cattle. In one of these rambles he was attended by a celebrated wag, nicknamed *Sheerness*; they had been riding out on little Manx ponies in search of their object one day, and were returning in the evening, to pass the night in the gay little town of Douglas, when Sheerness intimated to his friend Barrclye, that he would ride forward and see to find proper accommodations for them and their shelties, which was agreed on. Away scampered *Mac*, and on galloping up the principal street, he bawled out repeatedly to the populace, " To clear the street, Barrclye's coming;" which astonished the Manxmen much. They imagined by this that Barrclye must be a lord or duke, of mighty eminence, attended by a grand retinue; so they housed instantly, and filled every window, as anxious spectators of the coming scene. But lo! how were they deceived, when, instead of the glittering cavalcade their fancies had drawn, rode hobbling into the amphitheatre *Auld Barrclye*. Hissing and hootings instantly began, followed by an attack on our old drover and his poney, who could not withstand the shock of rotten eggs with which they were assailed, gave way. Barrclye was unhorsed, and for once lost his old hat and dark brown *dool-string*.

DOON-HEAD-CLOCK—A yellow flower common in the fields. When the flower fades away, a fine down is left behind on its head. Rustics, to know the time of the day, with their tale of it, pull this plant, and puff away at its downy head; and the number of puffs it takes to blow the down from off it is reckoned by them the time of the day. So comes the name *Doon-head-clock*.

DOONS—The same with *Dools*, which see.

DOTTLE—The little piece of half burnt tobacco left in the pipe after smoking, useful when another pipe-full is to be consumed in lighting it.

DOUCAT—A dovecot.

DOUDLIEDOO—A song of a singular amorous nature.

DOUHALL—An easy-minded man; one who rather wishes himself to be considered a fool. Such characters are by no means rare.

DOUKER—The British bird cormorant. See more of them in the articles " *Mochram Laird*" and " *Scaurt.*"

DOUKIN—Bathing.

DOUNDRAUGHT—An oppressive load.

DOUNWOTH—A declivity.

DOUP—The hinder end of any thing. The *doup* of a candle, the *doup* of the day, &c.

DOVERIN—Slumbering.

DOW—To be able.

DOWIE—Melancholy

Down-lying—A woman is said to be about so when she is on the eve of introducing another sinner into this world.

Down-sitting—A place to sit comfortably down in. The lasses are often not very willing to wed lads who have not a *down-sitting*, like myself, to take them to ; and a lad not unseldom looks out for a lass who has the *blunt* ; one, which were he married to, he would have no trouble with, such as providing various things for *pleneshing* and *taking up house* ; one whom he might just draw in his chair, and sit down, without giving himself any concern about the troubles of this world. Many of our *auld Scotch songs* are nothing more than accounts of down-sittings, which our lads have from time to time laid before their dears, in order to entice them to marry. Allan Ramsey causes Roger, in his famous pastoral, to give Jennie an inventory

> " O' a' the woo' he did at Lammas sell,
> " Shorn frae his bob-tail'd bleaters on the fell,"

and of his other effects. But the strangest detail of a *down-sitting* I have any where heard of, was that of the laird o' the Knows's, to a young milliner in Garliestown—

> I hae fifty acre o' gude white lan',
> And a meikle meadow that's yearly mawn,
> Twa hunner acre o' muirs and craigs,
> And as warran' as meikle o' wild moss hags ;
> I hae twunty stirks, and a dizzen yell nowt,
> Wi' hay to gie them, when they hungry rowt ;
> I hae four-score ewes, twa-score o' them's tippet,
> And weighty their fleeces wey whan they are clippet ;
> Twunty gates I hae now, I ance had but nine,
> A sow and a boar, and sax ither swine,
> Twa tykes, sax cats, but ye'll see them a',
> My bonny young lassie, gin ye'll come awa.
> How happy we'll be in my father's auld house,
> We'll sit and we'll clatter wi' ither fu' crouse ;
> Ye'll link on the pan, and fry braxy hams
> While the herd and me try a game at the dams.
> For o! in my kitchen the hams do hing
> Sae thrang they canna get room to swing ;
> I hae sackfu's o' carrots, and sybows and pease,
> How fuely we'll live, my dear lass, at our ease ;

My peatclaig is fu' o' links o' gude peats,
Whilk the breath o' the north sae finely heats,
And my presses wi' blankets are weel panged a',
As thou shall't see, lassie, gin thoul't come awa.

The milliner, methinks, would have been foolish if she had not left the bare trade of the *needle* for the laird and his *down-sitting*.

DOWPDOWN—Squatting; or to squat out of sight suddenly.

DOYL'D—Crazed in mind.

DOYLOCHS—Persons doyled. Burns, the poet, was for many years thought to be " *doyled*" by those who lived with him and saw his ways. This was when he was composing those poems which nature's library will ever contain.

DRABB—A colour between white and dun.

DRABBLES—Droppings when sipping food.

DRACHLED—Wet, covered with mud.

DRAIDGIE—A funeral entertainment. The following is a question, " Whether it is more proper to have a feast on a person's entering this world, than one when it bids farewell ? "

The case much depends on circumstances: if it be an *heir* to an estate that has made *entrée*, then a roaring feast over him cannot be thought improper; but if any other almost, it is not just reasonable to do so. Why should we rejoice at a being's coming into this world so full of sin, crime, trial, wretchedness, and woe? Surely, it is rather mockery to hail it with gladness into a land of sorrow. Was it into a paradise, the thing would be proper; and when it is a child of poor parents, the thing is a burlesque on common sense. On the other side of the question, an old bachelor, *turning the corner*, and leaving behind nothing that will miss him, is not unlike the heir in the other case. A good *dredgie* over him cannot be far wrong. Let the gossips take a hearty bumper over him,

and wish his soul a safe landing on the far distant shore:
That shore to which many a *Columbus* sails for, but
never returns.

But if it be any other, the thing has not reason with
it to say it is right; for all others almost will be missed and
mourned for by some.   Moreover, we know not how soon
we shall follow, so should not be merry.   Were we sure
we should all go to Heaven when we died, then might we
rejoice at the death of a friend; but this we are never
sure of.   The question therefore, nearly hangs on even
balance :—

For not to be ashamed to live,
    Nor yet afraid to die,
What would I not with pleasure give,
    If had the giving I.

A million earths', if they were mine,
    Composed of solid gold,
I'd give, without remorse or whine,
    To have my soul inrolled.

Perhaps there is a den in Hell
    A fitting up for me,
Where I eternally must yell
    In horrid misery.

Never to have a moment's ease,
    Nor feel one spring of joy,
For torturing demons, who will tease,
    And all delights destroy.

O ! would some angel in mine ear
    This intimation sound—
" Mactaggart, thou ha'st nought to fear,
    " Heaven hath thee worthy found.

" In patience wait a little time,
    " Soon thou shal't be at rest,
" Be in the grand Empyrean clime,
    " Amongst thy Father's blest."

But long on earth I may remain
    In doubt and darkness drear,
A sinner marked with many a stain,
    Before such things I hear.

And there's a chance I never may
    Hear such like things at all,
Yet for them I will ever pray,
    Tho' I should downward fall.

I read the Scriptures, and believe,
But whiles I them forget,
Vice her webs around me weave,
And I can't break the net.

I'm told it is the heat of youth,
And that 'twill wear away,
O! would it so, and let the truth
Ne'er leave me night nor day.

DRAPPIE—A little spirits.

DRAPPYKINS—Drops or drams of spirituous liquors.

DRAP-RIPE—Drop-ripe.

DRAW—A curling term, meaning to give the stone all the pith in the arm.

DRAW A WUTTER SHOT—A curling phrase, signifying to give the stone so much strength that it may slide the length of the mark, and no farther.

DRAWING CUTS—Casting lots; pieces of straw or wood are cut of various lengths, according to the numbers that mean to try their luck. One then takes and arranges them in private, putting all their ends close together in one hand, so that none of them may project beyond one another; the other hand is laid on this, so that nothing may be seen but the ends. So the drawing goes on, and the one who draws the longest *cut* is Jonah of the party. *Bessie Bell and Mary Grey, they war sic bonny lasses,* that their *Joe,* by Allan Ramsey's advice, *draws cuts* to know which he shall have.

DREADNOUGHT—A top coat.

DREE—To endure.

DREECH—To be plodding, constant at work, steady as the water running.

DREEL—To drill, to exercise soldiers. When *volunteers* lately started in every parish to defend the country, in case of a Bounaparte invasion, a country laird who commanded, or *dreel'd* a party of these raw military lads, used frequently to forget the technical words of command, when he had need of them, to the no small amusement of both his *company* and its spectators. Once, when the order should have been, " Rear rank, step forward," he cried out, forgetting the proper term, *back raw stan forret*. At another time, when " right about wheel" should have been the thing, he came out with the homely phrase, *come roun' like a ligget*. I should have liked to have heard this captain's orders at such a place as Waterloo.

DRESSER—A piece of furniture in kitchens for holding *plates, bowls, noggies,* &c.

DRIBBLE—A small quantity of spirits; a few drops, not mighty gush; a *dribbling day*, a day that does not know well whether to be wet or dry.

DRIDDLE—To saunter, to step about carelessly.

DRIFFLIN—Raining slowly.

DRIFT—A flock, a drove, also intention.

DRINGIN—Not working, hanging about.

DRIVE A RIG—A person is said to be able to *" drive a rig"* when able to reap as well as other reapers, and as fast. He is thought to be a youth of strength who can do this at fifteen years of age, and the rustics applaud him accordingly; though I would advise all young lads not to strain themselves for this praise, they will get no thanks for it when old age attacks them sooner than it should do, bringing with it a thousand evils, as they may plainly see if they look round them. Be not men, therefore, in any respect, until nature says it is full time.

DRIVING THE PLEUCH—This is done away with in Scotland now, and it would be well for the farmers of England if they did so also. It is the using a number of horses far more than needful, and employing a man more than enough to manage one plough. This man, or rather boy, was called with us anciently, the " *driver o' the pleuch*," and had mostly a poor life of it from the plough-man, or the one who steered the plough, as, when any thing went wrong, the boy was always blamed. Sometimes these boys would have got angry, drove the horses fast, run the plough against rocks, and caused the crusty old ploughman to be flung breathless from the *stilts*, with a broken rib or so.

DROCHEN—A very short little man. I have heard some say of such, that " they cud na breest a ratton af a peat ;" that is to say, they could not mount unto the back of a rat, even of a turf, being so short ; and that when they were on horseback, they look like a *tade on a tammock*; a toad on a little hill.

DROGGET.—Woollen cloth strangely dyed, worn by coun-try girls ; it is a slatish blue.

DROUGHT.—Dryness.

DROUKET.—Drenched, as with rain.

DROUTHY.—Inclining to dryness ; some tiplers are still in that state, and would drink *fire and brimstone*, and put them in a *brandy glass*.

DROW.—An undefinable quantity of water.

DROWNING THE MILLER.—We are said to be *drowning the miller*, when we are pouring in too large a quantity of water among the whisky to be mixed into grog ; and when we over-do the thing thus—we have *drowned the miller* ; the phrase is very ancient, and comes from a just cause ; if too much water be let run on a mill, the wheel becomes *drowned*, as it were, and will not move the machinery ; now, if the *big* or *outer wheel* be drowned, the miller may be said to be also drowned, for he is flung, idle, and useless, when his mill will not work. " Dinna drown the miller then," ye who take grog by a time, for it will render the machinery of your frames no good; swallow little water, and then the *miller,* which is in this case the heart, will not be *drowned,* but beat away quite active.

DRUCKENSOME.—Inclined to drink to excess.

DRUMMOCK.—Cold water mixed with oatmeal.

DRUMMYLAN.—Wet land of gentle curves, and of cold till bottom.

DRUMS.—Curved wet land.

DRUNTED.—Petted, huffed, &c.

DRUNTS.—Fits of pettedness.

DRUTTLE.—An useless, good for-nothing person.

DUBSKELPERS.—Persons who ride fast on horseback— " And send the wash (or dubs) about on both sides of the way"—Like John Gilpin.

DUDDERON.—A person in rags.

DUFFART.—A dull person.

DULLBERT.—The same as above.

DULSE.—Sea-weed which grows on the rocks; some are fond of eating it.

DULLTS.—That pupil at the foot of his class.

DUMCHASERS.—A species of male sheep, which seem to be eunuchs by nature; they chace and spoil the ewes in the rutting season.

DUMFOUNDER'D.—Stupified, quite overthrown, foundered in some voyage of ambition.

DUMMIE.—A dumb person; or one so deaf that will not hear.

DUMNED.—A hard, constant step in walking.

DUMPLINS.—Puddings made of sheep's blood, fat, and oatmeal.

DUM-SWAUL—Dumb-swell. A swell of the ocean, that maketh no noise; commonly these swells are the largest waves that are seen before storms and after them. Sailors dread no waves but those which curve at the top, or are made up of *broken water*. It is singular to see these large waves, called *Dumb-swauls*, when there is no wind, when the weather is quite calm, this is only though a little before the coming of the tempest. The cause is the undulating motion of the mighty waters; when this motion is given to the deep, it spreads over it much quicker than the hurricane which gives it; the storm enters the "*wame o' the waves*," as *Eddie Ochiltree* would say— silently it rolls on, till it encounters the rock-bound shore, and there in surges wild it roars. I wonder what makes this *Eddie* so often cross my mind, it is because he is the most poetical character ever *Scott* drew, and will live the longest of all his original family.

DUNNERBREEKS.—A person, such as an old cobler, with breeches so *barkened* or stiff and *sleek wi' dirt*, that they *dunner*, when struck, like a dried *sheepskin*; that is to say, makes a noise like distant thunder. I have seen a somewhat curious poem, which I may here give, ycleped

THE DEATH O' Dr. DUNNERBREEKS.

What doolfu' news are thae we hear,
Our tenner hearts will never bear,
They canna stan' sic thumps ava,
They'll burst befuter'd ane and a'
Down sink our spirits faith wi' speed,
For Dr. Dunnerbreeks is dead.
The mighty Dr. pang'd wi' lair,
Or rather wi' infectious air,
The lengthen'd lecturing representer,
The original experimenter;

His haurn pan was ay sae fu',
The mirkest scene he cud glowre through.
He drew out wonners by the slump,
The deepest ocean he cud pump,
Just at a glance he mair wad ken,
Than half a hunner thoughty men,
The theory o' the yirth at ance,
He lighted on as if by chance;
And set at nought the silly clatters,
O' ithers wi' their lues and waters,
For being an acute discerner,
Nae Hutton was a match nor Werner;
Sae weel he kend the lay o' Stratas,
His judgment ne'er contained erratas.
He traced the cause o' burning mountains,
And queer Icelandic boiling fountains,
Shaw'd reasons mair than ony can show,
Why bursteth out the fell volcano;
'Twas just as reek comes frae the lum,
Or wun frae out his ain braid bum;
For he delighted much in air,
He lo'ed his nether end to rair,
And ae night as he gaed to bed,
Wi' supper in his kyte weel fed,
Composed o' unco mixie maxies,
Whilk stough thegether waur than braxies.
He thought he'd an experiment
Try then, tho' he shou'd it repent;
Whilk was to ken if he was able,
Gin kyted air was inflammable,
Like oxygen, or hydrogen,
As said by mony chymic men.
Sae did he find his bounded wame,
Contained meikle o' the same,
For he cud never stir nor stoop,
But out in strings twad quickly proop;
And whan he let it frae him flee,
Without restraint unsmother'd free.
The room wharin he was wad dinnle,
Ay a' the plenishen wad trinnle;
Weel then he fin's a quantom form,
Sae he prepareth for the storm,
To ken exactly gif it was,
Composed o' a flaming gas.
He gat a burning glim then ready,
To hand it too, wi' hand fu' steady;
What was the singular effect,
Say ye wha sit and deep reflect,
Ye wha do owre ilk ither craw,
In drouthy arts like Algebra.

Wha lye and think, and think again,
And plot awa wi' haurns in pain;
The truth o' here, is sad to tell,
A tragic fate our sage befel,
The tears frae baith our een do drap,
And on the yird do light and hap.
The grand experiment proved fatal,
The Dr. fell, and lost the battle;
His f—t took fire in a crack,
And to gasometer flew back,
When there the blue inflated air,
Exploded wi' tremendous rair,
And at the time the bag did burst,
Some say *philosophy* he curst.
Thus went the man wi' mighty head,
Thus *Dunnerbreeks* gaed to the dead,
Was buried deep amang the mools,
In corner set aside for fools;
There let him sleep, there let him *smell*,
His saul wilt stink the de'ils frae hell.

DUNSH.—To but, to push, &c.

DUNT.—A blow, also to palpitate.

DUSTY.—A name for a miller.

DWAMLE.—To faint, or look like fainting.

DWAMLOCK.—A very sickly person.

DWINING.—Pining, decaying.

DYKE—A fence. Anciently dykes were built for confining mankind to certain portions of the earth; as those the Romans built in Scotland, to keep at bay the daring Scots; and that one by the Chinese to hold out Tartars, considered one of the wonders of the world; now they are only used to inclose brute cattle; some people make a trade of building dykes, one of these must have been *Davie the Dyker*, as the following Poem doth testify:

What horrid news are thae we hear,
Owre true they be, we fear, we fear,
Our een begin to brew the tear,
       Wi' sabbing speed;
Puir Davie wham we lo'ed dear,
       Is smother'd dead.

The sclateban o' the quarry shott,
Afore our worthy out o't got,
And crush'd him lifeless on the spot,
         Without remorse ;
Sae he was carried to his cot,
         Ane mangl'd corse.

O ! dreadfu' shocking news thae be,
The body we'll awa and see,
Upon his back, and eke his knee,
         We aft war borne ;
Us boys about may lang for he,
         Lament and mourn.

He never fley'd us frae nor fun,
The bluchton and the billet gun—
Ay glakes that birl'd in the wun,
         Did Davie make ;
By him too dragons ne'er the sun,
         Their tails did shake.

And was there ever ere his like,
At bigging o' a strang *Stanedyke,*
He was na fractious, dip na fyke,
         For meikle doon ;
He sought for, through-ban's that wad *rike,*
         And capes wad croon.

His dykes had ne'er the sleek'd skin,
Ne'er fair without and fause within,
He didna *batter, line,* and *pin,*
         To please the e'e ;
There ne'er was heard a clanking din,
         Whar bigged he.

A rickl'd rood ne'er left his han',
His dykes for centries will stan'
A *slap* wi' clutter's never fa'en,
         In ane o'em pet ;
May they the name o' he puir man,
         For ages get.

Owre moor and dale for mony a year,
May Davie's famous dykes appear,
Ne'er bilged out wi' wather-wear,
         But just the same ;
As whan puir cheel he left them there—
         To bear his name.

Nae wadder fleet can owre them jump,
If e're they try't back on their rump,
They will recoil wi' whulting bump,
         E'en *Rigling Rullions ;*
Wi' rattling doddles arset stump,
         Our down gae brallions.

Had he been wi' the chaps lang syne,
Wha wad the ancient Scots confine,
(The Romans war they if we min')
    Wi' meikle dyke ;
Brave *Grahm* wad been waur to haud in,
    The norlan tyke.

Auld Agricola had na ane,
In a' his core cud bed a stane,
Let learn'd historians write, and grane
    Out what they fike ;
Wi' our puir Davie they had nane,
    Cud big a dyke.

The thing is queer to think o't yet,
For a' the fowk the Romans beat,
Our countrymen they ne'er cud get
    Squeez'd 'neath their pride ;
Our Claymores gaed them a' the pet,
    Sair tools to bide.

But Davie, what's a' this to thee,
It wunna change the stern decree,
Whilk sinners us we sadly see,
    For ever mair ;
In thy cauld den thou soon will't be,
    Our hearts are sair.

Wi' you nane cud the Gellock wield,
The yellest craigs for you boud yeal'd,
What hoolochs down ye clantering reel'd,
    At ae gude *prize* ;
And junrells till the echoes peal'd,
    O' munstrous size.

Wi' *jumper* too, ye whiles wad bore,
And make the rocks wi' powther roar,
Whilk scar'd the *pellocks* frae the shore
    Wi' smacking fin ;
What Maukins too wad scud afore
    The dunnering din.

O' war we rhymesters sae profite,
As epitaphs on thee to write,
To thee the muses should indite
    (Our honest Cronnie) ;
Ane that nae saul alive cud wyte,
    'Twad be sae bonny.

But hoh-ance we'er a' unfit,
The attempt wad only be a skit,
For want o' pith then, we'll submit—
    " Na faith (cries out,
Ane honest muse) come hae at it,
    " We'll do ne'er doubt."

" Our dyker Davie, flesh and bane,
" Is streeked un'erneath this stane,
" But sure to heaven his saul is gane,
           " Gif ony gangs ;
" The rulers there, o' never ane,
               " Deserving't wrangs."

DYKIE.—A little bird of the chattering species, common
about old *Dykes*; it is of various colours, lays five small
white eggs, and is not unlike a cock sparrow, but not
quite so large.

E.

EAKIN—Adding too, making larger.

EAK o' WOO'—A kind of oil that is on wool when newly
shorn from the sheep.

EASLE—Eastwards.

EAZLES—The eves of houses.

EBBIE—Ebenezer, the name.

ECHO-STANE—A black hard stone, full of holes, common
in meadows and bogs. They can be made into good,
channlestanes. Their cavities make them of a sound-
returning nature, hence the name.

EDDIE—The name for Edward.

EEKED—Joined to.

EENOW—Even now.

E'ENSHANKS—This term has the same meaning with
Ancrum or *Antrim*, which see. It was that food our
ancestors took about five o'clock in the evening, now designated by the title of *four-hours,* and being thus taken
about the close or end, or *shanks of e'en,* or evening, the
name *E'enshanks* arose. At an *E'enshanks* neither tea nor
sugar made their appearance; no Indian nor Chinese
spicery were to be seen. Magellan had then doubled Cape
Horn, nor Gama, its brother, Good Hope. Nothing

N

but Scotia's *hard-foun' food* graced the table in these days. The poet would never have had cause to spout the following verse extempore, upon a young lady who took no sugar to her tea, (as is the way with many a delicate *Miss*), gif the feast o' *E'enshanks* had yet existed—

> " Methinks, my dear, you scorn the sugar-bowl,
> " Yes, leave't to those who're sour and tough ;
> " For o ! my darling, lovely soul,
> " Thou art already *sweet* enough."

EERIE—Terror, fear, &c.; for beings of a supernatural stamp many are afraid to walk alone under night; these are of an *eerie* nature.

EETCH—The adze, the carpenter's tool.

EGGED—Stirred up.

EIN—Even, direct, &c.

EINING FOWK—The country people had a fashion some time ago of pairing the young folks about ; that is to say, if a young man had taken a girl to be his partner at a dancing school, or if he had been seen speaking to one about the *kirk-stile*, or any other popular *gathering*, these two were instantly *eind*, evened to one another; and when a pair became thus *eind*, the very *clash* of the parish brought them soon to be *cried*. So this *eining* did some good to the cause of marriage. Now, however, people are got more *hard i'the mouth*, and set such a small value on *clashes* and sneers, that *eining* fowk becomes a vain trade. Manners, somewhat similar to these, will be found treated upon in the article—*Gaun to a House*. For some-time past, the matrimonial market has been far from being *brisk*, like many others, so that in some parishes a wedding has not taken place in a *twallmonth*, which is the space of a year in time :—

> What's come owre the lads, lasses,
>   Hae they ta'en the thraw,
> Whan sae few o'em marry, lasses,
>   Few or nane ava ?

Cupid, waefu' cheel, lasses,
  His dear arrows a',
He has shot awa, lasses,
  Fairly shot awa.

Bachelors grow grey, lasses,
  Frosty they are a',
They lae ye to grow auld lasses,
  Rising scories twa.

This wark will never do, lasses,
  Never do ava,
Nature, ay, respect the lasses,
  Gar us, feel thy law.

Again fill Cupid's quiver,
  And bid him shoot awa,
For the lasses, never, never,
  Maun be despised ava.

ELDEN—Firing.

ELDRICH—An *eerie* sound. The shrieking of a ghost, any wild supernatural noise that creates fear.

ELF-ARROW-HEADS—Triangular pieces of sharp flint-stone, which our forefathers pointed their arrows with. They are sometimes found in Galloway, as they are all over Scotland, and being of stone, not of steel, are found as perfect as when used in war, for flint rusts not. They are called " *elf-arrow-heads,*" because it was long thought they were the workmanship of elves, and used by them when shooting children, cows, what not. They were indeed used by curious elves, as in the 25th verse of *Hardyknute*—

> " The king o' Norse, he socht to find
> " With him to mense the faucht,
> " But on his forehead there did licht
> " A sharp onsonsie shaft.
> " As he his hand put up to find
> " The wound, an arrow kene,
> " O ! waefu' chance ! there pinn'd his hand,
> " In midst betwene his e'ne."

ELFGIRSE—A kind of grass *yerbwives* find, and give to cattle they conceive injured by elves.

Elfrings—On old pasture land, that slopes about at right
angles to the rays of the Midsummer sun, circles, of all
diameters, from three to thirty feet, are to be seen; and
these circles are beautifully defined by a kind of white
mushroom growing thickly all round the circumference,
except about a foot or two in some; these spaces, un-
studded with fungi, are called the " *elfdoors,*" the openings
by which the elves go into their circle or ring to hold the
lightsome dance. As superstition crows over philosophy,
when the latter is not able to point out the errors of the
former, so with *elfrings* she has every reason almost to
clap her wings, for no sage nor naturalist hath yet shewn
the cause why these *rings* are formed. For my own part,
I have marked the matter with all the attention I am capable of giving any thing, and yet must I own myself partly
overcome with it. That they are formed by the solar rays,
I doubt not a moment; no animal on the earth has any
thing to do with their formation, because, on places where
the ground is not of the same declivous nature, these
rings deviate from the true circle, and the unevener the
slope, the greater the variety of circles, or ellipses of various eccentricities; and where the rays strike at about a
right angle to the plane, there they are of equal radii.

But here comes the difficulty ; if the figures and situations of the *elfrings* prove them to be the work of the sun's
rays, how do the sun's rays produce them? Before the
mushrooms grow, the grass of the ring seems as if it had
been withered by a scorching heat ; now, this must either
proceed from lightning, or from the sun; that it proceeds
not from the former is evident by the form of the *rings*,
for mathematically it can be shewn, that on the plane
where is described an ellipse, if that plane had been of
the same angle with that on which is described a circle, that
ellipse would have been a circle also, which seems to
prove that the circles, let them be of what form they will,
have all one grand centre, which is the sun, and that they

only vary because their planes vary. Lightning could *singe* out nothing of such regularity. About the summer solstice, the rings are first observed *singed*, and in August they get covered with mushrooms : this is a natural consequence, because wherever grass is *singed* or blasted, there start up clusters of the mushroom tribe.

I have heard of coup-de-soleils or sun-blows of the tropical climates, and of people who have suffered by such blows; but I have never seen the account of any one respecting how the sun inflicts them, and am inclined to think that the way in which he does the one, he also does the other. Were there for instance a ray of the Midsummer's sun confined in a tube, and the motion of this ray marked, on the *hillside*, from his rising until his going down, I am almost sure that we would behold the manner in which the grass is scorched and the circles struck out. But I leave the matter until future observations can be made. As for the elves having any thing to do with them, is at least rustic nonsense ; let the superstitious hold it out so or not. For,

> Like the mermaid and unicorn,
>   Talk'd oftener about than seen,
> Are warlocks and worricows,
>   And elves upon the green.
>
> They all are cattle that
>   Do feed upon the Fancy's farm,
> And they love those fancy pastures best
>   That are fertile and warm.
>
> The poet's *nowt* they truly are,
>   And if he keeps them fu' and hale,
> When he brings them forth to market
>   He will meet with a sale.
>
> But if they are not fat and good
>   His sale will be but small,
> The critic butchers sneer at him,
>   They will not sell at all.
>
> For their beef, when lean is bad,
>   It will not take the salt and keep,
> And it plays the curse with honest folks,
>   And makes them fall *asleep*.

ELFSHOT—A disorder with cows.

ELLWAN' o' STARRS—Those three bright stars of the first
magnitude, or at least of the second, in the northern constellation Lyra, the harp, I believe, if memory can be depended on.   These stars are among the most obvious to
naked eyes of any that bestud the welkin.   Them, and the
" Cluster," as the country people call the constellation of
Orion, the Hunter, and " Peter's Pleuch," otherwise Ursa
Major, or the Big Bear, strike at once the most rustic of
astronomers, and have struck them more than the rest in
all ages.   In the ancient poetic Book of Job a verse says,
" Cans't thou bind the sweet influences of the Pleiades,
or loose the bands of Orion ?"

Now, what are the Pleiades, but those seven bright stars
in the constellation of the Big Bear above mentioned,
called, some time ago, Charly Wain, but more anciently,
Peter's Pleuch, and Orion, the Cluster ?

These stars then which draw the attention of men in all
ages deserve particular consideration, and none more so in
my opinion, than these three, called by the Scotch the
" Ellwand," from their seeming to the eye to be about
equally distant from other, and in a straight line.   Who
knows yet but this ellwand may indeed be used as an ellwand for measuring all over the earth.   It is long now
since an universal standard, for measuring has been called
for by the philosophic world, and none to give satisfaction
hath yet been produced.   The earth has been actually
measured with a chain, I may say, from Pole to Pole, for
this purpose chiefly ; and the great complaint always is,
the changeableness of the works of nature.   The earth
alters of itself ; the Poles flatten away, the Equator keeps
swelling out, the large luminaries of heaven are always
altering in size and situation with respect to the earth, and
nothing but the stars in any propriety can be said to be
fixed.

From them then let a standard for measuring be taken, one which will not alter, and one whose original may be easily referred to by all nations. And what shall we better get than the " *Ellwand o' Starrs,*" a measurement held out to us by nature as it were. Let the apparent length of this *ellwand* be taken, either by beads on a line, or holes in a flat slip of wood, and so we may form an *universal ellwand.* The natives of Iceland, Tombuctoo, Pekin, Washington, and London ; yes, the great body of the inhabitants of the earth, be their situations on it where they will, will understand by this at once the foundation of the measure, for the constellation in which is the " *ellwand*" being Orion's Girdle (nigh the range of the ecliptic) ; it may be seen every uncloudy night by mostly all men on the globe.

EMMERS—Embers.

ENLANG—Endlong. I have heard country people frequently discussing about the propriety of these sayings ; the first is, " *I came owre the brig.*" This is wrong they argue, it should be, I came *enlang the brig,* the other meaning as much that I went over the *side* of it or *ledge,* and into the river. Now, both expressions are perfectly right. I came over the bridge, and I came endlong the bridge, are *one* and the *same* thing ; for why not as well come *over* the bridge as the road comes, as go *over* its side. Secondly, " It is not right to say we are going *up* when we are going *south*; we should always say *down* to the *south,* and *up* to the *north.*"

Now it is not proper nor right to say whether we are either going up or down when going either south or northward. There is no occasion to add either the one or the other. Up and down refers to high and low ; and the *south* is just as high as the *north.*

EPPIE—The female name Euphemia. Who ever heard my
old witch, *Eppie Foggiehorn,* sing

> O ! my love was a fairy,
>   And could dance round the moon,
> My path, too, was airy,
>   In the welkin aboon :
> But a damn'd worricow
> Cam between us somehow,
> And hath sinner'd us now,
>   The auld grim badger loon.
>
> Sae nae mair on the carry
>   We will ride now away,
> And in regions sae starry
>   We will never mair stray ;
> For we're baith in the dark,
> O ! Hell is our mark,
> And auld Nick is our Clark,
>   He tells us what to say.
>
> Then the sea it may ebb,
>   And the sun it may shine,
> I hate whan my neb
>   Smells on earth aught divine.
> Arise thou black blast,
> Obey every cast,
> Let the warl stand aghast,
>   And the tempest be mine.
>
> Now the deep is in foam,
>   Now the sky it is black,
> Now the wild water's roam,
>   And the waves ither smack.
> Fling the yirth af her whirl,
> O ! strike her a skirl,
> That nae mair she may birl
>   On her auld batter'd track.

EVEN DOWNPOUR—A shower of rain which fulls almost
perpendicular from the clouds. These showers are frequent
in sultry weather ; and, when the air is charged with electricity, they are something akin to the water-spout.

F.

FA—Fall; also to become.

FADDOM—Fathom, plumb, &c.

FAE—From; also foe.

FAEDUM—Witchcraft.

FAEM—Foam. In stormy weather, the foam which gathers on the margin of the sea is often lifted by the wind and carried miles into the country.

FAGGED—Fatigued.

FAGGENS—The weary ends of any thing.

FAIGHLOCHS or FAISHOCHS.—Sorry working labourers; always seeming busy, yet putting little work *past* them.

FAIR-FARRAND—Open, free, inclined to flattery.

FAIRIES—These beings are yet often to be seen and heard of in the south of Scotland. One came to a *gudewife* once, and wished her to give an " *awmons*" of meal. The mistress complained she had little meal in the house. " Gie ay, (quoth the fairie) a part o' what ye hae to a poor body, and ye'll never lose." The wife obeyed her, and, continued the fairy, " sae lang as ye never look into the *girnel* ye shall ay bring plenty o' meal out o' it wi' your hand." She did so for some time, but one day feeling a curiosity to behold the exhaustless store, she looked in, and there was an empty *girnal*; so ever afterwards she had to fill it herself.

Another time a man met on an evening a funeral. The people with it seemed fatigued, and desired the honest man " *to tak a lift o' the corpse.*" " I'll do that (quoth he) in *gude's name,*" which he had no sooner said than they all disappeared, leaving him with an empty coffin. The man died soon after. This was a *Fairy Funeral.*

FAIRINS.—Presents given at fairs.

FAIRNTICKLES.—Freckly spots on the skin.

FALLDERALLOES.—Foolish unneedful things.

FANKLE.—When cloth is in unrid folds, it is said to be in a *faukle.*

FANNERS.—Machines for winnowing corn.

FANKED.—Warped in cloth.

FARKAGE.—A bundle of cordage, so confusedly warped, that there is no ridding it out; or a bundle of various things in a similar state.

FARKLE.—This word, and the one above, are one and the same; none of them, be it known, are what the Latins called " *verba recens ficta,*" new coined words, though I am not able to ferret out their proper derivations.

FARLE O' BREAD.—A cake of bread of oatmeal, bent with toasting.

FAUGH-BLUE.—Bleached blue.

FAUGH-LAN.—Fallow land.

FAUL ABOUT THE MOON.—Fold about the moon.

FECKLESS.—Weak in both body and mind.

FEEDING O' FROST.—A slight thaw, amid frosty weather; after thaws of this kind, the frost commonly becomes more severe than ever; hence they are said to *feed* the *frost.*

FEERIE.—Fearless, strong; a *fearie auld man,* a hale old man, considering his age; strong amid the years of infirmity; a *fearie wight,* a being that can endure much trouble:

> " Wallace Wight, upon a night,
> " Did burn the barns o' Ayr,
> " And claw'd the croons o' southern loons,
> " Whilk they mind ever mair."—
>
> *Auld sang.*

FEGGS—Faith. Upon my *feggs,* upon my faith.

FEIGH.—An exclamation of disgust.

FELL.—The broad muscles of the body; it is between the *" fell and the flesh,"* say country doctors, that water in the " dropsy," gathers.

FELL.—Strong, hardy, perhaps from having good muscles.

FELL.—Biting hard ; also, a wild rocky range.

FELL o' BARULLION.—A lofty *fell,* or range of high hills in Wigtonshire, famous merely for the name; where find we a stranger name for a mountain than *Barullion?* *Barool,* the chief mount in the Isle of Man, is somewhat like it, but not so sounding ; and as for *Etna,* *Heckla,* or mount *Blanc,* they have nothing to say to it on this score; even *Chimborazo,* the loftiest in the world, has not a more lofty name.

FEND.—A way of living on the border of want, but not in absolute want either.

FEWLS.—Fowls, if large.

FIB.—A lie, an untruth.

FILLIE-TAILS.—Little ragged clouds, something resembling uncut *horse-tails,* hence the name, they forbode windy weather :

> " Whan frae the south whusk filly-tails,
> " Than hie ships wear low sails."—
>
> *Auld say.*

FIMMERING.—Moving the feet swiftly, either in dancing or walking; yet moving them at the same time with a singular grace of person.

FINNIE.—A feel with the hand, or ratherly a feel which returns with good tidings to the senses ; persons purchasing grain, generally estimate the price of it, by its *finnie,* or the way in which it feels :

> " A wat May and a winnie,
> " Bring a fu' stack-yard and a finnie."—
>
> *Auld say.*

The meaning of which is, that a wet and windy May month, is such weather that makes crops grow good; so that they fill the stack-yard, and the grain feels weel.

FIPPLE.—The underlip; when dull about any thing, we are said to "*hing the lip*;" and when those around wish us rouzed, they say we would answer well for eating *Peelock potatoes*; for why? we might be cooling one in our *fipple*, while eating another.

FIRED.—Milk is said to be so when it gets ill tasted, in sultry weather; also, any part of our skin, injured by walking in warm weather, is said to be "*fired*."

FIRE-FLAUCHT.—A broad body of firey meteoric matter, frequently seen flashing through the regions of the atmosphere; the common name is a *fire-flaucht*, but sometimes a *firey dragon*; and some say "they have heard them fa' in the sea aften, and gae fizzing to death," which is reckoned a great kindness of Providence; for had they lighted on the land, "The Lord be near us, it is thought they wad hae cramped the folk up rump and stump, wi' *tusks* o' red *gaud* airn."

FIRESPANG.—A quick tempered person.

FISSLE.—To make a rustling noise.

FITSTEDS.—Marks of the feet.

FITTIE.—Having good feet, safe enough to walk with; also an imaginary personage, of an extremely useless nature, with which we compare real persons, as "ye're as useless as *fittie*," or ye can do a certain job, "na mair than *fittie*."

FITTING-PEATS.—The art of setting peats on end to dry.

FIZZING.—Hissing, the noise red iron makes when flung in water, or ale in bottles when uncorked.

FIZZIONLESS.—Sapless, without pith.

FLADGE.—A broad-bottomed person, any thing broad; the same with bladge.

FLAFF—A puff of wind, raised with one's hand, or a fan.

FLAIPER.—A foolish person, both in dress and manner; more particularly if this manner aims at something out of that person's sphere of action.

FLAIPERING.—Flashing about in foolish clothes.

FLAKES.—Parts of fences which cross *barns*; they are a kind of gate hanging the wrong way.

FLAPDAWDRON.—A tall ill-clad person, viz. clad in clothes not befitting the body.

FLAUCHT.—Any thing broad.

FLAUCHTERS.—Broad turfs.

FLAUCHTER-SPADE.—A spade for fleying land.

FLAUMING.—Flaming, exerting, &c.

FLAWS.—The points of those nails which hold shoes on horse-hoofs; the smith twists them off when they get through the hoof.

FLECKED.—Pied, black and white.

FLEEING-BUSS.—A rapid burning fire is said, to *go* like a *fleeing-buss*, or a *whin-bush* on fire; for when one of these bushes is set fire to in a windy day, we think by looking at, that the blaze is, as it were, taking the bush with it, before really it has it consumed; hence *fleeing-buss,* or *fleeing, flaming-buss.* The cause of this optical delusion is, that by looking at a rapid burning fire, our eyes dazzle; they mount with the flame, as it were, and take with them the what feeds it also—it is just refraction; we see the *sun,* after he is in truth set.

FLEETCH.—To insist and whine; to entreat kindly.

FLEETER—A full. A bumper.

FLEG.—A swinging blow; also, to walk with a swinging step.

FLEGGIN. Walking fast.

FLEUCHING.—Any thing very light; to what it seems, more in bulk than weight, the *light chaff* or *flowing*, is sometimes termed *fleuching*, but more commonly light grain.

FLEUKS—Flounder fish. Boys, in the neighbourhood of sandy shores, have great work; *tramping fleuks*, which is accomplished by wading softly on the sand banks; and when the feet *tramp* on the backs of the fish, they are held, until the hands dive and grapple them more secure.

FLEUPS.—Broad feet.

FLICHAN.—A light person, and small.

FLICHTERS.—Light flying flakes, such as of snow; when the snow, at the first of a storm, is like fine dust, as it comes from the air, it is a sure sign that the storm is going to be one of long continuance, but if the *flichters* be broad, it will *upple* sooner. It is the same way with the drops of rain. Rain never falls in large drops long, and never falls in large drops at all, unless there is much heat in the atmosphere. For warm water runs through a sieve much sooner than cold; from this we may infer the cause of the severe snow storm, when it begins to fall like dust, or what is called " *snastowre*:" for then a most intense cold prevails, caused by a frosty air, and dense clouds.

FLIM—Film. Matter of a mucous nature, which gathers in the throat. *Tipplers* say, "that a dram o' strong *farintosh* in the morning, cuts the *flim*."—See more of this under " *Floam*."

FLING.—To drive with the feet in walking.

FLINGBAG.—A bag or wallet for the shoulders.

FLINGSTICK.—A rowly-powly man.

FLIPE.—To peel, to *flipe* the skin of any part of the body; is to peel or strip it off.

FLIRDS.—People of a vain, silly, dressy disposition.

FLISK.—To fret, to flaunt, to whisk the tail, &c. as an ill-natured horse does.

FLITTING.—Removing from one place to another; also the things removed. " As ane flits, anither sits," is an *old proverb.*

FLOAM.—The same as *Flim.* I am rather at a loss to know whether this word is a corruption of *Flim,* thin pellicle, or phlegm humours of the stomach, probably the latter.

FLOCHTER.—A person looking extremely big, and wishing all eyes to observe.

FLOGGAN.—Walking fast.

FLONKIES.—Waiting men, lackeys; I wonder gentlemen keep so many of these creatures about them; for, instead of adding any thing to their dignity as noblemen, they detract from it.

FLORY.—A very dressy person.

FLOWPEATS.—Peats of a soft nature, cut out of flows.

FLOWS.—Large soft marshes, of a spongy nature, haunts of snipes ; and it is fine fun to wade in them, and shoot at these nimble birds on the wing; to catch young wild ducks too, in them, is a favourite job with sportsmen when they have good water dogs.

FLUGARIES.—Nonsensical pieces of dress, furniture, or any unneedful article of a foolish appearance ; a person fond of such is called a *flugarie* : also one mad in love is said to be in a *flagarie*; the words mean the same, for be it known they are burning for a mean person, or one quite out of their station; perhaps this word, and the Latin *flagro,* " to burn with love," may be of a kin.

FLUMRIE.—See *Sowens.*

FLUSH.—A wet soft piece of land; also, to be too liberal in flinging away money.

FLUSTER.—A person is said to be in a "*fluster*," when seeming more drowned in business than needful, and driving all to destruction.

FLUTHER.—To flutter in dust, as chickens and partridges do.

FLYAM.—Those large tangle sea-weeds, which grow round shores; yet the tide seldom ebbs from around them.— There are few finer scenes than those seen out of a boat, on a calm sunny summer day; down amongst these tangle one is most forcibly struck with the abode of nymphs of the sea; the tangle waving so beautifully beneath the translucent fluid, and sweetly gleaming in the darkened sun beams.

FOARDSDAY.—Thursday.

FOGGIN EWES.—Old ewes, past the days of lamb-bearing.

FORE-NICHTS.—The fore part of the winter nights; in summer there are no *fore-nichts*. They are the spaces of time between gloaming and going to bed; spaces taken of the long nights, and added to the short days, as it were. But of all the hours which wing their way over a peasant's head, none are so dear to him as those of the *fore-nichts*. For if he has a wife and family, then he may be said to enjoy them and be happy. If he be a bachelor of social disposition, then he is out at *parties* amongst is *neebours*, or some of them are with him; and if he be of a studious habit, then he may read books, enjoy himself with feasting on literature, and pondering the abstruse sciences.

Many a famous self-taught scholar the *fore-nights* have made in Scotland; many a notable tale and song they have produced; they are the delights of all classes of *kintra folks*, to none more so than lovers, and the rare sons of rustic genius; these latter revel in extacy during this season.

Wunnoing, otherwise cleaning corn; knitting stockings, *muffetees,* and *loofies, cobbling shoon,* and what not, may somewhat run contrary to the employments of pleasure; yet, still the joy of joys is to be found in the *lang wunter fore-nichts.*—Dear to my soul is the country; long was I a *Ruricola.*

> O! but I love the country well,
>   But true I love its labour ill,
> Sweet 'tis in rural world to dwell,
>   But sour to mow, and shear, and till.
>
> And this proceeds all from the heart,
>   For some delight to sweat and toil,
> Dear nature scorn—and relish art,
>   Poor greedy grubworms of the soil.
>
> They never hear the burdies sing,
>   They never feel the evening breeze,
> In vain, for them primroses spring,
>   Or leaf, in majesty the trees.
>
> Give them the what their kytes will cram,
>   Or lumps of ore to fill the purse—
> They want no more, all else they damn,
>   What I consider joy, they curse.
>
> But let ilk man, pursue his plan,
>   Let all have liberty of soul,
> Let every man, stand by his clan,
>   And slavery have no control.

FORFOCHTEN.—Sorely fatigued.

FORGETTLE.—Having a bad memory.

FORNENT.—Over against, right before. A female which dances right before her partner.

FOU.—Intoxicated with spirits; also, a full of any thing.

FOUMART.—The polecat; anciently *foulmart,* from its horrible smell; *mart,* from its being of the species of martin.

FOURPARTDISH.—An old measure, the fourth of a peck.

FOWS.—The house-leek, said to cure the dropsy.

Fows—Prongs. Forks for hay.

Foy.—A parting feast; the same with *Bonnello.*

Fozzie.—Not solid, porous, &c.

Fractious.—Fretful.

Free.—Any thing brittle, such as free-stone.

Freets.—Superstitious observances, with respect to omens good or bad, more commonly bad; the greater part of which now a-days, though they be observed, are not paid great attention to; yet, on the whole, they are ratherly respected. A *cup o' saut* is yet put on a corpse, from the time it is *straughted* until it be coffined; also the dead are waked with great solemnity. The shoes are yet twisted of the hoofs of mares before they bring forth their young, and they are by no means allowed to *foal* in stables. An horse-shoe is put thrice through beneath the belly, and over the back of a cow that is considered *elfshot. Elfgirse* is given to this cow; a *burning peat* is laid down on the threshold of the *byre door*; she is set free from her *stake*, and driven out; if she walks quietly over the *peat*, she remains uncured; but if she first smells, then lets a *spang* over it with a *billy*, she is then *shaned*, cured. If at the funeral one at the *handspakes* misses his foot, and falls beneath the bier, he will soon be in a coffin himself. If we are on the way to *rid an errand*, yet forget something, we will have no luck that day. A hare, to cross our path, is a bad omen. If a knife be found lying open on the road, few will dare to lift it. Even a *preen*, if the *broadside* is not found lying towards the face, will not be touched. A broom or *cow* is thrown after curlers, when they leave a house; this is *shaning* them good luck, and the *blue dead lights*, which appear before a death, what omens are they; these lights are seen in the air, about the height a corpse is carried, and *bobbing* up and down, the undulating motion of corpse bearers: they are seen to leave the house where the person is to

die, and go to the grave where the interment will take
place; to *kep* these lights is not right conduct; a man did
so once, when the corpse came to *that* place on its journey
to the grave, there a fear came over the burial folks, they
could not move farther, until the man told the tale of
the *dead light*; three things are ay *sonsy*, but why need
I note so? I could tell more than a hundred, without
being any way exhausted; let these be a *swatch*, however,
I shall still continue saying a little more on the subject
with respect to those *freets*, which come from one generation to another, in the shape of little rhymes:

> " Sit and see, the swallow flee,
> " Gang and hear the gowk yell,
> " See the foal afore its minnies e'e,
> " And luck that year will fa' thysell."

Which means, when we are sitting, the first time we see
the swallow flying; walking, when we first hear the cuckoo;
and the first foal we meet with, if it be before the eyes
of its mother, that will be a fortunate year. The great
anxiety young women are in to know any thing about the
husbands they are to have, gives rise to numberless *freets*;
one of these is, when the new moon is first beheld, they
sally out to the green *braes* in bevies, and there each pull
a handful of grass, saying, at the same time,

> " New moon, true moon, tell me if ye can,
> " Gif I hae here a hair like the hair o' my gude man."

Viz. Among the grass pulled, which is carefully searched,
and if a hair be found among it, which is generally the
case, the colour of that hair determines the hue of the
expected *gude man*'s."

The three first days of April are called *borrowing days*,
and the *freets* of them run so—

> " March borrows frae April
> " Three days, and they are ill ;
> " The first o' them is wun and weet,
> " The second it is snaw and sleet,
> " The third o' them's a peel-a-bane,
> " And freezes the wee burds neb tae stane."

Magpies cause other curious *freets,* according to the number of them seen at any one time together.

> " *Ane's* sorrow—*Twa's* mirth,
> " *Three's* a burial—*Four's* a birth,
> " *Five's* a wedding—*Six* brings scaith,
> " *Seven's* sillar—*Aught's* death."

A mist about the last day's of the moon's age, brings with it a *freet.*

> " An auld moon mist,
> " Never dees o' thrist."

It is said of February—

> " That February fills the dyke,
> " Either wi' the black or white."

And of Candlemas day—

> " Gif Cannelmas day be fair and clear,
> " We'll hae twa wunters in that year."

And " Gin the Laverock sings afore Cannlesmas, she'll mourn as lang after't."—I conclude with the following bunch of *freets* :—

> " *Grumphie* smells the weather,
> " And *Grumphie* sees the wun,
> " He kens whan cluds will gather,
> " And smoor the blinking sun ;
> " Wi' his *mouth fu' o' strae,*
> " He to his den will gae ;
> " Grumphie is a prophet, wat weather we will hae."

> " Whan we steer the greeshoch,
> " Gif the lowe be blue,
> " Storms o' wun and weather,
> " Will very soon ensue."

> " Whan flares o' Easlin light,
> " As the sun starts frae his bed,
> " Make the cluds a bluidy sight,
> " Changing them frae blue to red,
> " Or the blazing cheel wuns owre,
> " The Keystane o' the lift ;
> " The weather wet will pour,
> " For the wun it will shift,
> " The wun it will shift, and the deep it will swaul,
> " The faem it will flee, and the broyliment will brawl."

FRENCH BUTTERFLEES.—The common white butterflies ; the *Pontia* of learned insect men, I believe, and of the class *Lepidoptera*; when war raged between this country and France, our patriotic youths hunted these poor butterflies over hill and dale, armed with *whun cows,* and destroyed as many of them as they possibly could; having the idea that they really were from France, and being of the colour of the French flag, white, decided the matter. The red butterfly was called the *British* one, the *Apatura* of naturalists; it was venerated; to slay one of them was considered a horrid crime.

FRETTIE—Fretful. Many people are naturally so, and keep their circle of acquaintances about them in *het water.* Give them the whole world, they would not be half contented; the following is a rhymed sketch of a

FRETFUL FARMER.

We hate to hear a body whining,
For ever frettie and repining,
          Like Robin o' the risk;
He never wears a joyfu' e'e,
Nor taks a laugh right merrilee,
          The blockhead ne'er looks brisk.
    There's something wi' him ever wrang,
    He's yawping ay a yammering sang.

Wi' nature he is ay at war,
And wi' her weather he dis spar,
          For never half she pleases;
Altho' his crap waved rich and gude,
Tho' swaul'd his nowt wi' beef and blude,
          Sweet joy-his heart ne'er eases.
    Nor wadna tho' the hale yirths skin,
    Belang'd to him baith out and in.

Wi' a big rent he is na racket,
His lair claps on him nae *strait jacket,*
          He may be a *free* farmer;
May plough whare'er he will, or maw,
And he has bonnie bairnies twa,
          Wi' ane wife just a charmer.
    Nae matter still, still the poor saul's yurning,
    And ever about naithing mourning.

Weel really he deserves to get,
Ane actual something for to fret,
       Sin he be sae dooms keen o't;
We wadna wonner but or lang,
The fool maun sing anither sang,
       And kenna what's the mean o't.
 Like yon big bairn wha whumper'd ay and grat,
  Gat frae a' Wulliewan ance what it ne'er forgat.

Than will his corn look well i'e braird,
His scythes row owre a famous swaird,
       And no a silly whittery ;
Nae fleuchan than will grow his wheat,
His peelocks will be sweet to eat,
       And no puir scabbed chittery.
 The weather then won't be owre wat or dry,
  But pleasure than flow baith frae yirth and sky.

At nature ay to girn and thraw,
Whan she's doing us nae ill ava,
       Is sure a sin infernal ;
And even suppose she sooks the purse,
Still her we ne'er sud dare to curse,
       But wi' her live fraternal.
 A man has power whiles owre his fellow man,
  But nature scorns it do he a' he can.

Whane'er she likes a storm she'll blaw,
Either o' rain, or hail, or snaw,
       And we puir sauls maun bear it;
For no a single doit cares she,
Whether wi' it we happy be,
       Or whether we do sneer it.
 Sae Robin think and look about ye fool,
  Or gang some months to Reason's Boarding School.

FRILS.—Ruffles.

FROAD.—Froth.

FRUSH.—Unsound, decayed, &c.

FUDD.—The tail or *bunn* of a hare.

FUDDLE—A spell at tippling.

FUDJELLS.—Fat contented persons.

FUFF.—To puff.

FUFFLE.—To tuffle.

Furbeast.—The horse which walks in the furrow when ploughing.

Furder.—To aid, to prosper.

Furthy.—Forward.

Fyaam o' auld Glens—It is a thing quite impossible for me to express the meaning of this *fyaam*, or fume proceeding from old glens, except to keen naturalists, who have felt it. It is the scent of Melancholy, as it were, in her abode in lonely glens. So soon as the smelling organs feel it, the soul is alive to all the charms of solitude, and to unutterable objects in the wild bosom of nature. It is a something like the poet's " Hollow hum in the dark green wode."

" There is a pleasure in the pathless wood,
" There is a rapture on the lonely shore"—Sayeth *Byron.*

And Byron is a wild strong bard, with some little errors hanging about him, thought great by some, whereas the truth is, they are the mere dust on the sandal soles of mighty Madam Genius.

What curse is this within my brain.
　Which sinks me thus so gloomy sad,
With beating heart, and head in pain,
　Upon the point of running mad?
Am I a sinner black and bad,
　And know not how I can repent,
Knew I my crime, I would be glad,
　And bear with peace my punishment,
But what I am, I know not the extent.

My mind, I feel's a mighty wilderness,
　A mass of something quite irregular,
Which sadness wisheth to compress ;
　But o'er the world 'twill stretch afar,
Tho' *alligators* fling their jaws ajar,
　And snap their tusks in fell array.
Beyond yon moon, ay, and yon argol star,
　Will fancy wing her sunward way,
And scorn the clouds that would befoul the day.

Shall savage man, with all his gold,
　Be fit to clip the poet's wings.
Or turn his heart by freezing cold,
　And cut its tenderest feeling strings ?

Nay, he defies unmanly things,
 In spite of fortune energy doth burn,
And genius, like a giant springs,
 Tho' gloominess the brains may churn,
All what's not independant he doth spurn.

O ! happy he again would be,
 To stroll along yon sunny shore,
Or by the glen and hawthorn tree,
 Sweet nature's self but to adore.
But oh, how mad, how sick and sore,
 The breast is too devoid of love ;
O ! would this withering gale blow o'er,
 And let the rustic bard go rove,
Singing his song, and trusting in his God above.

How wavering is the human mind; full of changes.
Melancholy gives it strength ; all great minds have felt a
great deal of melancholy—from gloominess to gaiety
how swiftly it alters.

Hah, ha, this morn how merry's a
 The tyke, he laughing barks,
The cock ay now and than dis craw,
 The lift's fu' o' cheery larks.

The pyet wags her tail fu' green,
 Plays hap and charks awa,
Whiles on yon tammock she is seen,
 Then wi' the hoodicraw.

The de'il the haet dis girn and snarl,
 And snuff wi' wrath and blaw,
For Jock's come back to the rural warl,
 Gieing mony a loud gaffa.

Poets and poetry *dumfounder* me ; let them get hence,
and the *Fyaam o' the auld Glen.*

FYABBLES.—Foibles ; foolish things.

FYACHLE.—To work at any thing softly ; to *fyachle down,*
to fall softly down. *Fyachling,* moving about in a silly
manner, and seeming to work at something in a *feckless*
way.

FYKES.—Trivial troubles.

FYKES FAIR.—A singular fair, held annually at the *Clauchan o' Auchencairn*; it begins at *ten o'clock* at night, con-
tinuing to the morning, and through part of the next day.

All the drinkers, *floriers, cutty gliers,* and curious folks, attend from all parts of Galloway; and when so many such characters are met, any one may conclude, what for a fair it is; that it is one of the most blackguard gatherings in the south of Scotland.

FYLE—Make dirty.

" Her face wad fyle the Logan water."—BURNS.

G.

GA'—Gall.

GAB—The mouth; also to talk pertly.

GABBIE LABBIE—Confused talking; the way in which we think foreigners talk when we know not their language.

GABBIT—Did talk.

GABERLUNZIE—A wallet.

GABERLUNZIE MAN—A man who carries a wallet.

GAIG—A rend or crack in flesh brought on with dry weather.

GAISLINS—Young geese.

GAISTCOAL—A coal, that when it is burned it becomes white. They are more of a stone nature than coal.

GALDROCH—A greedy, long-necked, ill-shaped person,

GALLBUSSES — A shrub which grows plentifully in wild moorland marshes. Its leaves are something like the willow, but its scent is different from that of any other shrub. The scent of it is extremely strong, and though it be cut, retains its fumes and freshness for many months. It is thought to be able to extirpate insect vermin out of rooms. I wonder something is not tried with this astonishing smelling plant; who knows but it is highly medical.

GALLOWA—A large district or shire, ranging along the south
of Scotland, anciently much larger than now, stretching, in
the days of yore, from the English border to the Irish Firth,
a distance of more than a hundred miles. Its breadth has
not varied much, being naturally cut off, as it were, from
the rest of Scotland, by a range of wild bleak moors.
This has continued much the same. It had its own kings
once; *Galdus* or *Galders*, whose tomb and name yet exist
in the country, was one of them, and it is thought Galloway had its name from him, which is not unlikely. *Murray*, in his literary account of the district, quotes various
authorities respecting the name, and in this, shows considerable genius and research, though, as to the true derivation, it yet remains doubtful. The manners, customs, and
language of the peasantry differing widely from those
belonging to the rest of Scotland, I was induced to say
something respecting them, being fond of curiosity, and I
have not confined myself to the Galloway of modern days,
but to the ancient *Gallovadia*, *Gallwallia*, or *Gallwegia*,
for doing which, if any thank me, it is well, and if none do
so, I have myself to thank, which I do with boldness ;
because, in saying what I have said, I have felt great pleasure, so should *thank myself* that I found out this little
source of happiness; and even had those manners and
what not, not differed so widely as they do from their neighbours, still I would have said something respecting them,
not that I may know matters that the world knows not,
and perhaps cares little about, and not that I like to hear
myself talking, but just to show, that the peasants, though
an extremely modest race, have bred one amongst them
full of impudence.

GAMF—An idle meddling person.

GAMPIN—Gaping, like an half-hanged dog.

GANG O' WATER—The water that is brought from the well
at once.

GANSH—To snap greedily at any thing, like a swine.

GAR—To cause, to make do.

GARDY-PICK—An expression of great disgust.

GARDY-VINE—A large beautiful oblong-shaped glass bottle, used for holding spirits. It is from the German, " a gin-bottle."

GARTEN—Garter.

GATES—Goats. *Gate-skin,* goat-skin.

GATE-WHEY—The whey of goat's milk. People of consumptive habits drink it; so a draught of goat's whey, and a week's recreation in the moors, are as much relished by people living on sea-shores, as these latter places are to the moorlanders.

GATIN-CORN—That bad plan of drying grain, by binding the sheaves near the top, spreading them wide below, and setting them on end singly. They dry, to be sure, pretty soon, but then they are loose, and wet as soon; so, if it be variable weather, they commonly are rotted useless.

GAUCY—Jolly, well-dressed and well-fed.

GAUN to a HOUSE—About forty or fifty years ago, *visiting* in the country was a very serious matter; that is to say, there was no such thing as *kintra neebours* going to see how other were at their houses, unless there was some urgent business in hand between the parties, and even if there were, the visitor would seldom go into the house, but execute his mission, or what not, on the green in the open air; for if he had, he would not have come out again, if a young man, without having himself *eind* with one of the daughters of that establishment, which being done, marriage had to ensue. The natives waited for the *pair* to be *cried* every Sabbath-day that came, in the *kirk,* and if no proclamation took place, the fellow was badgered and bantered about the girl where ever he went; at *shoot-*

ings, kirns, prentice-loosings, &c. The poor lassie would never be matched to another; so his soul would give way to the foolish scandal and *country clash* afloat, and he would enter the matrimonial state to get clear of them; thus, *gaun to a house*, as it was called, proved to be a sad matter often, if the lads and the lasses had not previously engaged other at *kirk-stiles*, or some such famous courting *houfs* or haunts.

GAUT—A male swine.

GAUTSAME—Hog's lard.

GAVLE—Gable of a house.

GAWKIE—A foolish girl.

GED—The pike, the fresh water shark.

GEDWING—An ancient looking person; an antiquary, and fisher of geds.

GEE—A species of madness. " My wife she's ta'en the gee," as the *auld sang* goes. My wife is taken some mad fit, and is almost unmanageable.

GEENS—Wild cherries.

GELL—A rend, an open in any thing, such as in wood.

GELLOCK—An iron crow-bar for making " *Gells*" or rends, useful in quarrying stones.

GELLOCKS—Insects which haunt the " Gells" of rocks, probably of the earwig species. It is lobster shaped, about an inch long, of a black colour, inclosed in a hard rind. They bite savage-like, and their bite is attended always with a little poison.

GEMMLE—A long-legged man.

GEORDIE WUSHART—An eminent rustic bard, and one of the most honest and social of men. He is chief salmon-fisher on the Dee, but was born and bred somewhere on the Scottish border. In his ways all—he is quite an origi-nal; every motion of either his body or mind attests it. He can tell the most humorous tale without giving a single smile with his countenance : he will have all around him in a roar of laughter, and himself sitting the while as serious as Socrates.—He is one of the most patient and contented men on earth, nor is this happy temper annoyed by him having a hell of a woman for a wife, as the unfortunate sage lately mentioned had, for, on the contrary, she is a worthy and amiable female.

As to his poetic talents, few there are who have the pleasure of estimating them, as they have not yet been fairly laid before the world's mycroscopic eye; but I, for one, have been honoured with a peep at his MSS. in their present state, so am able to say what I think of them, which, without the " decimal fraction of a doit's-worth of flattery, I say they are extremely natural and pleasant, and ought to have got a squeeze in the *press* long ago." There is not much wildness and madness about them; they are simple and halesome, not unlike the strain of Allan Ramsay.

His *General Review* and *Eternal Almanack* are indeed superior to most rustic poems in my knowing. Their plots, and the way in which they are handled, prove *Geordy* to be a man of genius. He is not only a poet, but a very clever mathematician, understanding Algebra well, and can engrave beautiful sun-dials. I once sent him a dial of rather a singular construction, when he thanked me as follows :—

I gat the dial that ye sent,
It was ane handsome compliment,
And thanks are due on cent. per cent.
          In gratitude frae Geordy.

I ne'er saw ought like it afore,
I glowered at it owre and owre,
The farer I did it explore,
          It gaed mair joy to Geordy.

O ! cud I write the vera best
That ever was in words express't,
'Twas due to thee boon a' the rest
          That ere sent ought to Geordy.

But, O, alas ! my muse is dull,
The pen is frail, and thick the scull,
But for the deed ye'll tak the wull
          Frae a well-wisher Geordy.

Though there may be rather too much *sweet oil* in these
thanks, yet any one of penetration may see they flow from
a tender and good heart.   In truth, there is no man more
beloved by all who know him than Geordy.   His honest
face brightens up every company he is in ; whether that
company be in the *Hall o' Barniewater, Auld Ned's Anti-
chamber,* or *St. Cuthbert's* Mason Lodge.   He is fond of
shooting, and in Galloway there is none can wield a *double
barrlie* so well as Geordy.   When the game springs,
whether on foot or wing, he takes a snuff deliberately,
brings the gun quitly up to his e'e, lets fly, and if he
misses, it is a *wonder.*   But, to give a further proof of his
poetic powers, and firstly then, a piece, entitled

THE THOW.

The bitter-biting frost now seems to fail,
    And safter zephyrs wave the leafless trees,
How quick the thow dissolves the snaw and hail,
    And sets the ice-bound waters at their ease.

The chittering burdies, draigglin forlorn,
    Now find their sustenance with easy care,
Nor do they come at e'ening and at morn
    To touch the borders of the schoolboy's snare.

The wakefu' lark, that by the early dawn,
    Wi' vocal notes doth warn the approach of day,
When that the flakey snaw o'erspread the lawn,
    Amaist became destructive Famine's prey.

But now the sun extends a warmer glance,
    His cheering rays again doth gladness bring,
A' nature now enjoys unbounded dance,
    And welcomes back the sweet returning spring.

Again the *finny tribe* will glad the stream,
  The artfu' *angler* a' his wiles will try,
The cheerfu' ploughman whistling by the team,
  His *master's* place will faithfully supply.

Rejoice, rejoice a' nature at the sight,
  Again the fields resume a verdant green,
Again the woolly flocks do take the height,
  Aud lowing herds are in the vallies seen.

The above poem is tolerable, but had it been more *Scotchified*, I would have liked it better ; however, he makes this up in his answer to a friend who sent him some good snuff—

MACABAA.

Sir—I gat yer sang wi' the fine Macabaa,
  For which I gie naething but thanks that are sma,'
To see sic a poet, and *few* there do *know it*,
  Why do ye *conceal sic a talent ava?*
There's some silly asses wha clim ap Parnassus,
  And think there to shine on the poetic *law*,
But truely *I tell ye*, few, few can excel ye
  In yer funny wee sang o' the rare Macabaa.

Your halesome advices sae canty and braw
  About the drap whusky, the saul-case and a',
Ye surely are right, for by day and by night,
  We sud keep frae the hizzies whan tippling awa.
But now ae request I maun ask o' ye neist,
  Altho' it be bracking discretion's gude law,
Neist time ye gang north, by the Clyde or the Forth,
  Ye maun bring me a teat o' this same Macabaa.

Lang life to yersell than, the mistress, and a',
  May happiness crown ye by Harmony's law ;
May your faes ay be few, and your friens ay enew,
  Until your last breath on this warl ye draw :
And through a' our lives, wi' our friens and our wives,
  May temperance ay be the rule to us a',
Wi' a wee drap o' Toddy to nourish the body,
  And sometimes a teat o' the gude Macabaa.
Fare-thee well then, my worthy *Geordy.*

GERROND the POET—What a difference there is between this bard, and the one just sketched. John Gerrond the *gow*, and George Wishart the *sage*. The first, an honor to the Muses, the other a disgrace. He was bred a black-smith; went to America; drank and *frolicked* in the world *beyond* the flood; came back again, tilting over the *white top'd* surges of the *Gulf of Florida*, to use his own language, then published at various times stuff he termed poems; shameless trash, appearing as if they had been dug out of the lovely bosom of an *Assmidding*.

For all there is much about him deserving my attention. Some genuine madness, vanity, and folly; and I will dare to say, that if he had had ten times more industry than what he has, he would have wrote some tolerable verses, as his madness is ratherly that of a poet's. In truth, his *Red Lion Frolic* is as fine a specimen of *gowishness* as I have seen. He says he is the first of *Vulcan's sons* who strives to climb the *sliddery brae*, and that as music was first produced by striking on an *anvil*, he expects that even something greater yet may be produced in a *smiddy*, and that nothing ever came from those whose ears hear little but the *chirping* of the *yarn-beam*. Indeed, was not the tender *Tannahall* a weaver; poor *Gerrond*, I won't hurt thee, thou hast been injured much already by the destiny of thy stars; for Burns, you say, was very lucky in appear-ing at the time he did. He got just the start of you by a few years, and took up all those subjects which was befit-ting your muse: just so; but if he had never wrote, neither would ye have done so, nor ever have thought that *Halloween* and the *Holyfair* were *frolics* that a poet could make exist to eternity; so *Gerrond* is a strange creature, and perhaps there never was any being moved about more independent than he in *clogs* and a *ruffled sark*, for which he has my highest praise; for poverty, in all its shapes, he values nothing. Give him a glass or two of whisky, and he would not call the *king* his *cousin*; and no one deserves a *glass* more than he, for he both loves it dearly, and will give thanks for it either in *clink* or other-

ways. The *Peatmoss* is his longest poem, beginning
with

> " Some delight to sing o' battle,
> " Whether victory or loss ;
> " But whaever owre a bottle
> " Sang the scenes o' a Peatmoss."

While ranging for *subscribers* once through the country,
a priest was so impudent as to tell him he was *no poet.*
" Don't you think (returned our hero), that the Almighty
is as potent now as he was in the days of old ?" Surely,
(replied the priest.) " Wi than (quoth Gerrond), he has
opened the mouth of another *ass* to-day, methinks." This
retort was not so far amiss ; on the whole, he is a harmless
soul, and reels about like a true poet, contented, in rags,
and commonly as *fow* as the Baltic. It is far from me to
discourage the efforts of genius ; I am quite on the side of
a young poet, if I have any penetration to see he is on the
right side o' the dyke ; but, hoh, ho, *Gerrond* was never
there, and is too old now to *speil* over. Merit will work
its way, under a million disadvantages, to the Temple of
Fame ; nothing else will do. But oh !

> " Ilk clauchans pang'd wi' goafish bards,
> " The de'il a mailins free o' them ;
> " Tie their bladders to their tails,
> " And owre the brig o' Dee wi' them."

Auld Galloway song.

GIBB CATS—Male cats.

GIE—To pry.

GIEAN CARLINS—A set of carlins common in the days
away, but now so much unknown, that account of them
is almost lost. They were of a prying nature, and if they
had found any one alone on Auld Halloween, they would
have stuffed it with " *beerawns and butter.*"

GIEING UP THE NAMES—The ceremony attending the
giving in to the Precentor the names of those to be

P

cried or proclaimed to church congregations, previous to marriage ; so that any who wish to object to such and such matrimonial concerns going forward, may do so ; they have then the power to fling down sixpence, and protest against proceedings going farther, a thing seldom done. Though they be *cried* three times, if the three *cryings* be put all past on one day, as is now commonly the case, the *Precentor's loof* must be better *creeched* than if he took three separate days to it, which is the strict point of church law. Those *names* are generally given in on a Saturday night. The parties meet in a public house ; no females attend ; the father or brother of the bride is her representative ; the bridegroom is present, and his *best man,* on the Precentor being called in to the meeting (a business he generally likes, as he gets plenty both to eat and drink for nothing), the *names* are wrote down on a slip of paper ; the bride's name by one of her relations present, and the bridegroom's by his *man* ; after this is done, the *bowzing* goes merrily on ; the whisky punch dashes about like *dishwater* ; all present get fuddled, and the Precentor worst of all, as *fow* as a witch.

Such is the *fourth bout,* in the regular routine of a proper matrimonial transaction ; first *taking the notion* ; secondly, *courting* ; thirdly, *getting consent* of the *auld folks,* and *buying the braws;* and fourthly, *gieing up the names* ; then comes the *crying,* the *wedding,* the kirking, and lastly, the *taking up house.*

GIEZIE—A person fond of prying into matters which concerns him nothing.

GIFT O' GAB—Having power to gabble.

GILL—This word comes from the same root as *gell.* It is, as it were, a small *rend* in the earth ; a little glen, through which runs a brook. A *gill,* a *glen,* a *cleugh,* and a *haugh,* are all of the same family, but differing in magnitude, all excavations of this planet caused by the running of water.

GILL—A leech. This word, and " *gell*" are one, for the leech is a creature that makes " *gells*" in the flesh. The word *gell*, I am not sure whether it is of Norman or Erse extraction ; I am inclined to think the latter. If cream be rubbed on those parts of the body where leeches are to be put, they will take hold sooner than without it. The bite of a leech is poisonous when newly taken out of its native place : they should be kept some time before used ; the water they are put in should be changed every day, and that water should be much of the nature of their native water, of an half putrid nature, for it is on the viewless animals of this water they live. Spring water is death to them, and they should have, if possible, fresh air. A bottle is not a good thing to keep them in ; it should be a wider vessel, with a lid holed like a sieve.

The wound they make is of a singular shape, something like the letter Y ; three legs striking off from a centre, having the angle of sixty degrees between them. Nature, thou art a wonderful mathematician ; what wound would answer so well as one of this form, both for letting out blood, and healing soon. Like the bees, with their hexagonal combs, no other solid would answer them so well. Leeches deserve attention ; when we wish them to vomit, nothing but their mouths should touch the salt.

GILL-GATHERERS — People who gather leeches in the marshes. These are commonly old women: they wade about with their coats *kilted high* ; the vampires lay hold of them by the legs, when the *gill-gatherers* take them off, and bottle them up. These persons have commonly a long stick, called a *gill-rung*, with them. When they come to a deep hole, they plunge in it with this, and start the leeches, singing a strange song at the same time to the rouses of the pole. Annexed to this, is *Mally Messlin*, the *gill-wive's* one :—

> Gilly, gilly, gilly,
> Come and sook thy filly ;
> Hear'st thou Mally plunging
> Wi' the rung a runging ?
> Bubbles up are boiling,
> Am kirning and am toiling ;
> Ye dinna hear my swashes,
> For blue seag-roots and rashes :
> My gilly, striped gilly,
> Come and sook thy filly.
>
> Let me see ye wimple,
> And make the water dimple ;
> Start now frae the boddum,
> Tho' it I canna fadom :
> Come and see thy Mally,
> The body's living brawly ;
> Tho' warroching in mires,
> Puir Mally never tires ;
> Come awa, my gilly,
> And sook thy filly, filly.
>
> My under-cotie's hie now,
> Gif ony bodies see now,
> The water's boon my knee now,
> Aye faith, aboon mid thee, now,
> Amang my yallow spawlies,
> There ye come and crawlies ;
> Bonny's the moss lilly,
> But bonnier far my gilly :
> Now thou sticks, my gilly,
> Sook thy filly, filly.

GILL-HA'S—Snug little thatched huts erected in *gills*, or small glens. These are often, in Galloway, and other places, the birth-places of genius. Out of these issue young men, whiles excellent at climbing the slippery Mount Parnassus. The *Ettrick Shepherd* was doubtless born in a gill-ha'. They are the famous archives for legendary tales ; there are the cream of the milk of ages ; the food of pleasure.

GILL-PIES—Young tight girls, looking out for husbands.

GILL-RONNIES—Glens full of bushes, haunts of poets, and people a *sproging* ; sweet rural solitudes.

GILL-TOWALS—The horse-leeches. These leeches are of no use to man, as the others are; they won't bite when wished. The country people, however, think otherways, and would not allow one of them to be " *laid to*" for a good deal, as report goes; that if they be " *laid to*," they won't, like the others, " fall off," but continue sucking so long as they can get a drop of blood, while the life-stream flows out of their *nether end*, whence the name " *Towals*," or tails, leeches at either end.

GILLY-GAWKIE—A long-made and rompish girl.

GILLY-GAWPOCK—Nearly the same as above, only the other is, or was, the name of a farm once in Galloway. " Gaping glens" may be about the English of it.

GINNERS—The gills of a fish. " I gaed my way on tae saun the ither day, and raised a pickle bait (quoth the celebrated John M'Clellan), and wad awa, and try the fishing. The wun was aff the lan', so I thought I might get a cod or twa about the *Laird's Point*, or aff the *Red-craig*, but I had na row'd the boat to the ' *witch wive's haen*,' whan the wun cam ahead, and I was obliged to bring her to aff the *Oyster Craig*. Weel, there I sat, and gat naething but plenty o' wee ' *bleuchens*,' but owre i'the afternoon, just as I was thinking on starting for hame, I fin' an awfu' tugging at the line, owre the scullrow; my coat I flang aff, the better to manage the meikle fish, drew the ' *dart click*' to me, to double huik him, whan I brought him near the tap o' the water. Sae up I brought him slowly, the biggest *fluik* ever I saw; nae common pan wad hae ta'en him in at hauf a dizzen times. I brought him safely intae boat; he had swallowed the bait greedily, the huik was sticking in his ' *ginners*.' I took out my knife, ripped up his un'er-jaw, to get back the huik; but just as I lifted him, to fling aft a bit, lord ! he gaed a de'il's wallop, slipped out o' my han', and o'er the

gunnel o' the boat again intae water. I let dive after him
wi' my arms to the oxters, but he slided awa. O! I was
vexed ; I drew up the penter, gaed awa ashore to *Meg* wi'
the tear in my eye. Sinsyne, I hae thought it was na a
fleuk, but some watch in the shape o' ane, may be, *Eppie
Hanna,* gif that be sae, she has sair *ginners* the day, be
she whar she wull.

GIRD—A hoop, a blow.

GIRDS O' THE WUN—Blasts of the storm.

GIRNELL—A box or barrel for holding oatmeal.

GIRSE—Grass.

GIRSE-GAWD—Cut by grass. Those who run bare-foot, as
" *herds*" do, know well what these cuts are.

GIRSLE—A gristle.

GIRZY or GRIZZLE—Name for grace.

GLAKES—Playthings for children.

GLAUMER—Witchery, the black art. Man can do nothing
supernatural, yet he has powers to make some of his
weaker brethren think he can. Man can invent singular
things, and so bemistify them, that others may gape and
wonder ; but there is no genuine glaumer about him, nor
there is no glaumer at the present day in existence, unless
the eyes of fair females contain a little.

GLAUMS—Instruments used by horse-gelders, when gelding.

GLAUR—Soft mire or moss.

GLEBORING—Talking carelessly.

GLEDGE—To hang about thief-like.

GLED'S-CLAWS—We say of any thing that has got into
greedy keeping, that it has got into the *gled's claws,* where
it will be kept until it be savagely devoured.

GLEED—A comfortable little fire, when the embers of the
gleed are stirred, and a blue flame appears, it betokens
bad weather.

GLED'S-NESTS—Nests of the kite. These are common in moorland glens : they build there on what the shepherds call *scurrie thorns*, low dwarfish thorns ; and these nests, when *young gleds* are in them, are kept well filled with mice and moles, which proves that this bird not only preys on animals of its own tribe, but on quadrupeds. It is a greedy bird, the kite, and extremely useless in bearing up against the rudeness of winter ; one would think, that when the frost and snow reduced the little birds to a sad forlorn state, that those of prey would then be feasting. This is not so, though ; a mark of the wisdom of Providence : cold sets upon the prowling vagabonds in a manner that naturalists have not found out ; for, frequently in winter, they not only want strength of wing to catch their prey, but can neither kill nor eat it when it is catched, as I have often seen proved.

> " The tod's a beast no easy fed,
> " Lykewise the burd they ca' the *gled*,
> " The wasp, the speedard, and the ged
>   " Are greedy curses ;
> " And factor Jock is damn'd ill-bred
>   " Wi' our light purses."
>
>   *Auld poem of the Rent-day.*

GLEDS-WHUSSLE—Kites, when they fall in with prey, give a kind of wild whistling scream. We apply this, metaphorically, to the ways of men, in the phrase, " Its no for nought the *gled-whussles* ;" meaning, it is not for nothing that greedy men whistle ; it is the good fee makes the lawyer whistle.

GLED WYLIE—The name of a singular game played at country schools. One of the largest of the boys steal away from his comrades, in an angry like mood, to some dyke-side or sequestered *nuik*, and there begins to work as if putting a pot on a fire. The others seem alarmed at his manner, and gather round him, when the following dialogue takes place :—

They say first to him,

> What are ye for wi' the pot, gudeman?
> Say what are ye for wi' the pot?
> We dinna like to see ye, gudeman,
> Sae thrang about this spot.
>
> We dinua like ye ava, gudeman,
> We dinna like ye ava,
> Are ye gaun to grow a *gled*, gudeman?
> And our necks draw and thraw?

He answers,

> Your minnie burdies ye maun lae,
> Ten to my nocket I maun hae,
> Ten to my e'enshanks, and or I gae lye,
> In my wame I'll lay twa dizzen o' ye by.

The mother of them, as it were, returns,

> Try't than, try't than, do what ye can,
> Maybe ye maun toomer sleep the night, gudeman;
> Try't than, try't than, Gled-wylie frae the heugh,
> Am no sae saft, Gled-wylie, ye'll fin' me bauld and teugh.

After these rhymes are said, the chickens cling to the mother all in a string. She fronts the flock, and does all she can to keep the kite from her brood; but often he breaks the row, and catches his prey. Such is the sport of *Gled-wylie*.

GLENKENS—A glen amongst rocks. This is the largest and wildest glen in Galloway, extending into many parishes. In the heart of it is the *Loch o' Ken*, a lovely lake, *Newgalloway Clauchan*, and the ancient seat of the *Gordons* of *Kenmore*. It is a most romantic place : it was on his way through it (in riding from *Dumfries* to *Gate-house*), that *Burns* composed the chief of national songs, " *Scots wha hae wi' Wallace bled.*" He did this during a storm of rain : the storm, and the wild situation in which it catched the poet, must have aided those uncommon manly breathings of the song to burst forth. He was accompanied in his journey by his friend, *Mr. Sims,* who wrote out the story. Galloway, then, must have some share in the honour of giving birth to the famous effusion, and a *small share even,* is surely a great honour.

GLENT—To gleam suddenly, or a sudden gleam of light.

GLIBB—Quick, sharp, more so than needful. A person too quick, as it were, for the world, or " *glibb,*" is generally disliked.

GLIBBANS—A *glibb* person.

GLIFF—A transient view of any thing.

GLISK—A glimpse of light. A little light flung suddenly on a dark object. *Gliff* is the short view; *glisk,* the little light which gave the short view.

GLITT—Oily matter, which makes the stones of brooks slippery in summer.

GLOCKEN—A start from a fright.

GLOIT—A soft delicate person.

GLOSS—A comfortable little fire of embers.

GLUMF—A sulky fool.

GLUNCH—To look sulky.

GLUNDY—A fellow with a sulky look, but not sulky for all : one who deceives by appearances ; also a plough-ridder.

GLUNNER—An ignorant sour-tempered fellow.

GLUTTED—Swallowed.

GLYING—Looking with one eye.

GOAVE—To gaze with fear.

GOITS—Young birds unplumed.

GOMF—A fool, or one who wishes to seem so.

GOMRELL—The same as above.

GONKED—Cheated.

GOOL—The seed of wild herbs. That seed which is taken out amongst corn.

GOOSETS—Pieces of cloth set in at certain angular points of clothing, so that they may better befit the body. Little out-lets, as it were, well known to the sewers of *white-seam.*

GORBLE—To eat ravenously.

GORDED LOZENS—Panes of window-glass, in the time of frost, are so termed. What beautiful objects like trees do there appear in the frigid season.

GORLIN-HAIR—The first hair which grows on body or *beast.* That hair on young birds before the feathers cometh.

GORLINS or GORBS—Young birds.

GORROCH—To mix and spoil porridge, or such food.

GOTH.—An exclamation, and a bad one, for it is no less than a molification of the sacred word God; *goth man, goth ay, goth this,* and *goth that,* are by far too common sayings; many are led to prologue their words by them, who know not the meaning of the language they are using; let all desist from tampering with this word in the time to come; let *goth* become obsolete, so will we be respecting the name of our Almighty Creator; also, let *haith,* which is used for *faith,* sink to oblivion.

GOU—A bad taste or smell.

GOURLINS—The black bulbous roots of an herb with a white bushy flower, good to eat, called *Hornecks* in some parts of Scotland.

Gow.—A name for a fool.

Gowdie.—Mr. John Goldie, a young gentleman, for some
time editor of the "Ayr and Wigtonshire Courier," born
and bred in Ayrshire, but being the manager of this newspaper, and it having ado with part of Galloway, of course
it behoves me to take notice of him. And I do this with
much pleasure, for why, I consider my friend very worthy
of it, he is a *poet*, that's enough ; yes, and a poet too,
agreeable to my taste, as also I should think of every
peasant in Scotland ; and I would much rather be a bard
that could *kittle* up the feelings of the country folks, than
one who was a favourite at court ; but the truth is, a
peasant's poet is also a prince's, for who are not moved
with the mellow voice of nature ? it thrills through the
breast enstarred, as quick as through that covered with
the corner of a plaid ; it works its way to the heart, be
that heart in what situation it may. Mr. Goldie has certainly much of the right ore about him, ready to be brought
forth, and (without much amalgamation with other metals),
stampt in that mint, which issues out the genuine coin
that endures for ages. Lately he published a volume of
sweet little pieces, some of them reminded me not a little
of the strain of Tom Moore. He is the author of that
song which took such a hold of the stage in the days of
dandyism, and partly helped to bring these *toy-shop* gentry
into ridicule ; it begins with, as many know,

> There's the wealthy widow Watt,
> She's as ugly as her cat,
>   She's toothless, dull of hearing, crooked and bandy O !
> Tho' her skin's as dark as my hat,
> Yet her cash can cover that,
>   For the cash you know's the thing that's for the dandy O.

When editor of the newspaper, he was the means of bringing many a gem out of the gulf of oblivion ; he lent not a
deaf ear to the whisperings of Genius, but freely gave the
goddess a *corner* whenever he heard her voice. He was one of

the chief instruments by which was completed with so much *eclat* on the *banks o' bonny Doon*, a monument to the memory of Burns, or ratherly a land-mark to guide the pilgrim in after ages to the venerable Kirk Allowa ; as also the one who constituted an *Ayr Burn's Club*, to commemorate the anniversary of the bard in his native town ; on the whole, this gentleman's conduct has not been unlike that of Mr. M'Diarmid's Dumfries, to be afterwards spoken of ; he has the love of mankind and literature at heart ; is like myself now driving away in London, so God speed the *wark*, and ever sing " success to the cause." I may here treat my readers to an effusion of his muse, never before in print :—

THE FOUNDLING.

When sick or wae, the puir man's wean
   Kens that a mither's smile is sweet,
The joyless orphan left alane,
   Aboon a father's grave can greet ;
Sic bless alake is no for me,
   For ne'er has't been *my* lot to prove
How sweet's the blink o' mither's e'e,
   How warm the glow o' father's love.

My birth-night saw me at yon door,
   The cauld, cauld yird my cradle's place,
And winter's snaws were driftin o'er,
   My sichtless e'en an tender face ;
December's blasts were blawin chill,
   An cauld an nippin was the air—
The mither's heart was caulder still,
   That laid her sinless baby there.

The han' that fed and cled was kin',
   An aye sall be richt dear to me,
But warmer luve I fain wad ken,
   Than warmest gratitude can be ;
A mither's luve I fain wad share,
   For oh! this heart to love was made—
Wad hear a father's e'enin prayer,
   Ca' Heaven's blessins on my head.

When join'd wi' younkers in their play,
   I whiles forget a mither's wrang,
But when the weet or closin' day,
   Gars ilka playmate hameward gang ;

O ! then I fin my bosom swell,
    Wi' feelings that it lang has nurst,
And yearn a parent's love to feel,
    Till whiles I think my heart will burst.

When seated by the ingle side,
    Some neighbours blythsome, weans I see,
While luiks that speak a father's pride,
    Are beamin frae their father's e'e ;
I strive to chock the burstin sigh,
    And dicht awa the burnin tear,
Syne luik upon yon gouden sky,
    An houp I hae a' father there.

Mr. Goldie has a half brother, a sailor, now settled in
South America, who seems, by what I have seen of his
MSS. to have very much of the rustic poet about him,
and as he is strikingly original, I cannot refrain from
giving a few verses also of his—

" A tar I am, proud o' the name,
    " And a head fu' hie can carry O !
" I've conquering fought, and will again,
    " Or I loss my Charming Mary O ! "

" I've cross'd the wide Atlantic sea,
    " And been in regions dreary O !
" But a bonnier lass I never saw,
    " Than my lovely Irwine Mary O !"

Again, behold the man of genius in another strain.

" I left Paisley about 1 P. M. with my little frigate in
tow,—stood through the moor,—reached Neilston at half
past two,—the weather squally, with some rain.   Brought
to, at the Black Bull, got some grog for myself and
storeships; breeze *freshens* ; fell in with a *strange sail*, on
the homeward-bound passage ; stood on for Stewarton,
under a press of canvas, wind S. S. W. took a ship in
distress in *tow* ; ran on for Killmaur fore land, parted
convoy, dropped anchor with my girl for the night, though
still in good *sailing* trim."

But my favourite piece of this poet's is, his " Elegy
on Robbin Smith," a wandering botanist ; here his rusticity

indeed, refreshes me, the following verses are a specimen :—

> Mourn, mourn, ilk sympatheezing frien,
> Let sorrow's tears fa' frae your e'en,
> The queerest shaver e'er was seen,
>   I'll tak my aith ;
> Lies in below that sod sae green,
>   Poor Robbin Smith.

> The hauf o' *terra firma* owre,
> He trod in quest o' yirb and flower,
> Through ilka glen and wud he'd cour,
>   And by-way path ;
> But death at last led to his bower
>   Poor Robbin Smith.

> Whan father Addie was the laird,
> O ! Eden's ance delightfu' yard,
> He delved awa—and never cared,
>   Nor dreaded skaith ;
> Weel, every plant that e'er he rear'd,
>   Kend Robbin Smith.

> He wi' great skill too, cud explain,
> What brought the snaw, and what the rain,
> The sun, and moon too, he made plain,
>   War warls baith ;
> Our ancient dads war a' mistaen,
>   Quoth Robbin Smith.

> 'Bout every fish, and every shell,
> In sea, or river, he cud tell,
> E'en frae a beardoc to a whale ;
>   Nor was he laith,
> To learn puir doaffies like mysell,
>   Kind Robbin Smith.

> The mawbag o' a butterflee,
> Weel dried and stuff'd, ahame had he,
> The baw too, o' a midges e'e,
>   Its dirk and sheath ;
> Wi' belts o' mony a queer bumbee
>   Had Robbin Smith.

> And strings on strings o' seddar's eggs,
> Wi' mony a creature stuck on pegs,
> The skin o' beetles, flees, and clegs,
>   Blawn up wi' pith ;
> But hoh anee ! dung af his legs,
>   Is Robbin Smith.

The roons had he o' Eve's first sark,
A snuff box made o' Noah's Ark,
The stane king Davie did the wark,
     O' Gulliea Gath;
The knife too, whilk slew Mungo Park,
     Had Robbin Smith.

Amang the lasses whiles he ran,
And gard them sometimes *coup the cran*,
Forgie ye hizzies gif ye can,
     He's tint his breath;
Just *frailty* like anither man,
     Was Robbin Smith.

Ye bretheren o' the rake and dibble,
O! let your e'en a twalmonth dribble,
Weel may ye greet and yurn and bibble,
     And flee in wrath
At death for withering like a stibble,
     Puir Robbin Smith, &c. &c.

Such a Poem is not amiss; I am in love with the Poet, and intend, some day or other, to publish his works, which I have beside me; I am going to write to him, in America, such a genius should not be kicked to a corner.

Gowk-spittles.—A white frothy matter, common on the leaves of plants about the latter end of the summer, and beginning of autumn; in the interior of these spittles, a little insect is always found, some say a young *cleg*, or gad-fly, and that it lives on this froth until it be strong enough to hop elsewhere; these *spittles* are said to be the *gowks* or cuckows, as at the season they are in the greatest plenty; this bird gets hoarse, or seems, by its voice, to have a *clocher* or spittle in its throat, ready to void; but the truth is, this matter is the production of some insect, and perhaps for the purpose already spoken of.

Gowl.—A sharp howl.

Gowpen.—The cavity two hands can make when their sides are laid together; or the quantity of any thing that cavity can hold, the double of a " *neifu*'."

Gowsted.—Boasted.

GRABS.—Little prizes.

GRAMASHES.—Overall hoze, to ride with.

GRANNIE—Grandmother. These old women are always fond of giving advices to the rising generation; what follows, is a specimen of this :—

> Howt's Bauldy my boy, ye're gaun a' to devil
> But hearken yonr grannie a minute or twa,
> Puir body, she wishes ye'd learn to be civil,
> And no fling your health and your sillar awa.
>
> This rinning at night, Bauldy, which ye delight in,
> And bairning the hizzies wharever ye gang,
> Is vile wark I true, and weel worthy the righting,
> Believe me ye waur yoursell unco far wrang.
>
> Come marry thy Maggie wha liv'd wi' the Millar,
> And sifted the meal that was grun at the mill,
> Wi' her ye'll fin pleasure in wauring your sillar,
> And get man o' a war'ly comforts thy fill.
>
> Than I shall bequeeth thee my five hunner marks man,
> And gie thee a shielling to bide in and a',
> She'll mak a' thy claise, and synn a' thy sarks man,
> For thou canna do, but a wiffie ava.

GRANNIE MOIL.—A very old, flattering, false woman.

GRASSMEAL.—The grass that will keep a cow for a season.

GRASSNAIL.—A long piece of hooked iron, which has one end fixed to the blade of a scythe, and the other to the scythe's handle ; so, that (as mowers say), " her runt may sleep steady i'the *den*."

GRAULSE.—A young salmon.

GRAY BEARDIE.—A bottle of the larger class, made of earthenware ; it is made to hold generally about three gallons, but whiles they have *double lugs*, and hold a much larger quantity ; the *whusky pig*, in farm houses, is a *pig* of this kind: " hae ye ought i'the *pig* the day," is a common salutation, when friendly neighbours meet at others houses ; and although whisky be not mentioned, it is well understood to be the thing wanted ; answers to salute are various, such as, " I dare say there is a *dreeping*,"—"Ay, I heard the gude wife say it could *pinkle pankle*," &c.

GRAY-HEADS.—Heads of grey-coloured oats, growing among others that are not.

GRAY STANES.—Here and there, over all the face of the country, round gray stones make their appearance; there are two things which strike us strongly on looking at this scene " what brought them there," and " what made them of a globular form," that cause which brought them to their present situations; also, has been the cause of rounding them; it is evident from these *stanes* alone, that some awful revolution has taken place at some distant period, on the earth, and this revolution has been a tremendous flood of water.

GREDDON.—The remains of fuel, the sweeping out of the *peatclaig*; the same with *coom*, almost, only the first brings the idea, that stones and earth are among the remains, the second not.

GREEN LINTY—The green linnet. This is a beautiful bird easily tamed, but it can sing none.

GREESHOCHS.—Fires of embers; a *greeshoch* is much the same with *gleed* and *gloss*.

GRIER O' LAGG.—Grierson, laird of Lagg, in the parish of Dunscore I believe, anciently, the infamous persecutor of the stern and worthy covenantors, the accomplice of the base Claverhouse, and one of the most infernal villains Scotland ever gave birth to; not a church-yard do we go into throughout all the land of Galloway, but we meet with stones, perhaps cleared of their fog by *Auld Mortality*, testimonies to the inhuman fact; there we think we hear the poor martyrs speaking from their graves, and informing us how they were butchered by the bloody *Grier o' Lagg*; the heart melts with the detail of their fate, and we feel ready to revenge the cause, were that

not done for us already; even on our wild moors, and
in our dark glens, we trace the fell tract of the savage.
The tower yet remains in a partly ruined state, where he
lived when *at home*, it is a small square keep full of loop-
holes; when the venerable old man, *John Bell*, of *White-
side*, begged of Grierson a little while to pray, before he
was shot, the murderer replied—" What, devil, have ye
been doing, have ye not prayed enough these many years
in the hills ?" was there ever a colder, and more unholy
expression ? poor John was slain in the parish of Tongue-
land, February, 1685. " Robert Grierson, of Lagghall,
was a persecutor for upwards of ten years, and though
excommunicated for being an adulterer, and every thing
bad, impertinently obstinate he keeped still being Justice
of the Peace." When he was dying, tradition says, that
he made a wish to have his feet bathed in cold water, but
the moment they were immersed, they made it *fizz, and
boil wi' hellish heat*; indeed, to this day, the horrid word
hell, is ever coupled with his name; the country people say sometimes, when enforcing a fact, " that they are
as sure such and such is the case, as they are of the laird
o' Lagg's being in hell," and about the time of his death
which happened in 1700, a ship at sea met with a
singular *sail*, a chariot drawn by six horses, and conducted
by three drivers, all of the Pandemonium stamp, coming
plunging and snoring over the wild waves, attended by
black clouds, vomiting forth thunder and lightning. The
sailors hailed, *were bound*, when the answer received was,
from Hell to Colinn. This was the vehicle sent to bring
Lagg to the land of Demons.

When his bodily remains were a taking to the kirkyard
for burial, the horses employed in that service seemed to
be much fatigued, and at a certain place on the road they
stuck up altogether, could go no farther, and appeared
ready to perish; a gentleman present, sent home for four
of the strongest horses in his stud, yoked them in to the

dead carr, they drew it, indeed, to the place required, but the poor animals were so *forfoughten* out with the job, that they could do nothing afterwards while they lived ;—so much then, for *Grier o' Lagg* ; those wishing to know more of him, may consult the *Cloud of Witnesses*, a good book, and those bunches of tales in prose and rhyme, which help to bound out the wallet of every ballard hawker in Scotland.

GRINNING HARES.—The devilish art of setting gins in holes of dykes, or on walks, to hang hares; this is the meanest way of all poaching, there is no sport with it, being purely for gain, and truly savage.

GRIST.—The texture of yarns ; also, a miller's fee for grinding. The phrase, " he has got anither grist to his mill now," means, he has got another way of making a livelihood.

GROOZLE.—To breathe uneasily.

GROUF.—To sleep restlessly.

GRUE.—To nauseate.

GRUESOME.—Frightful, but that kind of fright which brings on vomiting.

GRUFF.—A short, thick, well-dressed man.

GRULCH.—A fat child.

GRULL.—A stone bruised to dust.

GRULLION.—A mixture of various food ; a hotch podge.

GRUN.—Ground, a farm ; also, any thing grinded.

GRUNS.—Sediment of any liquid matter.

GRUPPING.—A disorder amongst steep; it *grips* them in the neck, as it were, rendering them unfit to turn their head but one way.

GRUSHIE.—Fat, flabby, &c.

GUDDLE.—To botch with a knife, to cut rudely.

G<small>UDE</small> F<small>ATHER</small>.—Father-in-law.

G<small>UDE</small> M<small>ITHER</small>.—Good mother.

G<small>UDE</small> M<small>AN</small>.—The master of the house.

The Gallovidian way of the old Scotch Song,

THERE'S NAE LUCK ABOUT THE HOUSE.

There's nae luck about the house,
There's nae luck ava,
What luck can be about the house,
Whan our gude man's awa.—Chorus.

There's no an hour in a' the day,
But something gaes athraw,
The servants a' are master's grown
And nought is done awa;
The cauves brak through the milking slap,
Their minnies pawps they draw,
The de'il a kebbuck now I get,
Or ought tae kirn ava—
There's nae luck, &c.

The tinklers they come up the gate,
To thieve and gie ill jaw,
Whan there's no a body i'the house,
To fley the de'ils awa;
The sheep grow mawket on the hill,
And sair themsells they claw,
And whan their hips are no laid bare,
Wi faith they dee awa—
There's nae luck, &c.

The bairnies winna gang tae school,
They trone it ane and a',
What care they for the Dominie,
Whan our gude man's awa;
The drovers they come smackin roun,
And bout their stots they bla,
But what ken I about yell nowt,
Whan our gude man's awa—
There's nae luck, &c.

The tod comes scoolin' frae the cleuch,
And snaps the laggies a',
For the terriers they winna hunt,
Whan our gude man's awa;
The fire claucht the raunle tree,
And brunt the lum and a,
For wha had I to sloken them,
Whan Archie was awa—
There's nae luck, &c.

O ! gin he war back again,
  'Twill be a month or twa,
Or his dear spouse will condescend,
  To *let him gang awa*;
For there's nae luck about the house,
  There's nae luck ava,
Na the fynt a luck's about the house,
  Whan our gude man's awa—
           O, there's no luck, &c.

GULDER.—To rave like a domineer, or angry turkey cock; to tyrannize.

GULDIE.—A tall, black faced, gloomy looking man.

GULLION.—A stinking, rotten marsh.

GUMPTION.—Wisdom, genius, &c.

GUMPING.—A piece cut of the *gump*, or whole of any thing; when a *banwun* of reapers are *kemping up a lan'*, the weak of course fall behind the stronger, and when a *shift o' riggs* takes place, those forward cut through their weak neighbours *rigg*, behind, duly opposite the place they left their own, so leave a part of that *rig* uncut, between them and the weak reaper; this piece is called the *gumping*. Two *cronnies*, or a lad and lass in love, never *cut the gumping* on one another, the cause for why, needs no explanation.

GUNPOWTHER.—A well known combustible matter, properly named gunpowder; an original poem I give here respecting it, which my readers may relish, as they think proper :—

Gunpowther thou's a won'erous thing,
Weel wordy that a bard should sing,
      A sturdy sang on thee ;
Some bard o' genius pang'd wi' might,
Weel up to art and nature's slight,
      And no a gow like me.
For true it is the haurns o' man,
Hae ne'er made ought to match ye,
As a strong tool, for death's snell han',
Damnation wha did hatch thee—
      In hell man, lie still man,
      We dinna want your name,
      Gae row there, i'e lowe there,
      Infernal is thy fame.

For you to sit and plot wi' death,
How best to tak your brither's breath,
               What sin was ought like this;
Auld Shanks was fit enough himsell,
For forming plots to nip us snell,
               'Thout adding your's to his—
Your stoure combustible and quick,
The sad black chymic nitre,
Made frae the hauf brunt shunner stick,
The sulphur and sautpetre—
               Invention—to mention,
               It gars the flesh to grue,
               For o' man—what foe man,
               To us has been like you.

The ancient arrows, darts, and slings,
To muskets be but harmless things,
               And cannons fu' o' grape?
Af nae brass shields the balls will bounce,
They come wi' a determined whunce,
               E'in on their course they shape.
Through beef and bane, and wud and stane,
Without a howst they whunner,
While roun' the air dis rift and grane,
Wi' artificial thunner—
               The auld wars—war bauld wars,
               Whan man wi' mau cud fight,
               But now faith, we vow faith,
               'Tis murder a' downright.

For now a feckless wabster chap,
Or far spent blackguard wi' the clap,
               Can bravely draw the tricker:
And reel a fae down on the fiel',
As fast's a strong-baned raekless cheel,
               And some will say e'n quicker.
Sae scalbert bodies limping spruce,
And scurrs belike the gallows.
Suit war as weel as Robbin Bruce,
Or glorious Wullie Wallace—
               Now strang men—and hangmen,
               And dukes are a' the same,
               A wight now, o' might now,
               By powther gains nae fame.

And now the castles ane and a',
Our father's thought wad never fa'
               In junrells are dung down;
'Twas powther caus'd them first to wag,
As they sat on the towering craig,
               And glowered a' aroun'.

Mons Maggies balls are battering rams,
Which hae the hardy crooms,
They dunch down strengths like wiggiewams,
And hornie wa's roun towns—
  They crash them, they smash them,
  And gar their gates to flee,
  While roareth, and snoreth,
  The mad artilliree.

E'en on the sea as at the Nile,
Whan Nelson grool'd the French in stile,
  Gunpowther shaw'd its might;
There blazing to the skies it sent,
The Franks chief boat La Orient,
  To light the fleysome night.

At Gibraltar too, we may
Gie it a puff o' flattery,
Whan Elliot het balls did play,
On Spanish floating battery—
  What burning, and yurning,
  And blawing up was there ;
  What whizzing, and bizzing,
  O' red shot every where.

But whar Black Smeddum best ye shine,
Is in the dark and dreary mine,
  'Mang orie craigs fu' yell;
For sad ye in a jumper bore,
The stratas stiff by you are tore,
  That laugh'd at wadge and mell.
Ye rive up Sweden's hard airn wyme,
And gars her trollies flee,
The clints we stew to gie us lime,
By you too, raised be—
  Thou's ne'er laith, to do baith,
  The what is gude and ill,
  Ye howk whiles, ye choke whiles,
  Ye quarry, and can kill.

Ablins that cheel wha did ye fin,
That gouty Chinese Mandarin,
  Or thoughty Jesuit ;
Invented thee for doing gude,
And no for shedding human blude,
  The job ye sae weel hit.
Gif sic was she slee bodies plan,
He's weel deserving praise,
And fame may hie exhalt the man,
Her tooting horn gae raise—
  Nae duel, fu', cruel,
  Perhaps did cross his brain,
  Nor battles, that brattles,
  Blude sumping mony a plain.

Whan men war huff'd wi' crabbit words,
They anciently drew out their swords,
   Sharp gleamers frae Toledo ;
And flegg'd at either dreigh and lang,
Till sculls and shields, fu' wildly rang,
    And thumbs and knuckles bled O !
A gash wi' them, was but a scart,
It only mair did warm them,
For blude they didna care a f——t,
A we thing didnà harm them—
    Nae fleeching, but bleaching,
    And skelping on at will,
    Was seen than, on green than,
    Fair play attending still.

But now a futtie banker's clark,
A flonkie ance wi' ruffl'd sark,
   Or hauf pay idle sodger ;
Will mak a flash, and tak the pen,
And gab bout honorable men,
    To raise some honest codger.
Till nought will please but pistols for't,
Its fit to gar ane scunner,
The worthy man is shot in sport,
For what's ca'd wounded honour—
    Nae neive now, maun deave now,
    The gentries ill faurd din,
    Nae stick now, maun lick now,
    The yeucky yallow skin.

Hech, nature's laws are laughen at,
Gunpowther thou's the cause o' that,
   Thou ticklish de'il uncanny ;
Had thou been kend in days o' yore,
Whan eastern blackguards fought and swore,
    Like Macedonian Sawny.
And that rough handled Cæsar chap,
Wi' nameless rascals mony,
Wha pranc'd about through blude and lap,
Like our de'il, Moderen Bonny—
    Our lan' now, o' man now,
    Wad had few *stocks* ava,
    Sic weeders, few breaders,
    Wad here been left to craw.

Fell fae to life, and love sae sweet,
Ye gar baith bairns and mither's greet,
   Sae fu' o' wae's thy tale ;
E'en beasts and burds, on lan and sea,
Sair dread the savage might o' thee,
    As Puss and Whaup and Wale.

The supple shank, the wing, the fin,
Are racers no thy match,
For like the flares o' light ye rin,
And deadly aft ye catch—
    Sae now than, adieu than,
    About ye I'll nae mair,
    Gae string than, or sing than,
    For my saul wi' ye's sair.

GURLIE.—Blustery, given to squalls.

GURNLE.—A strange shaped, thick man; also, a fisherman's implement, used in inserting "stobs," or stakes in the sand, to spread nets on.

GUTCHER.—Grandfather.

GUTTER-HOLE.—The place where all filth is flung out of the kitchen to.

GUTTRELLS.—Young fat swine,

GUTTY.—A big-bellied person.

GYTE.—Deranged, simply,

GYZENT.—Shrunk with the sun's rays; drinkers say of themselves, whiles that they are *gyzent*, when they have not been drinking for some time.

H

HA'.—Hall.

HABBERSACK.—A bread bag, French haversack.

HABBLE.—To hobble, to walk lamely.

HABBOCRAWS.—A shout the peasants give to frighten the crows of the corn fields, throwing up their bonnets or hats at the same time. A person once fell a sleeping and snoring in a church; the priest, being a dull orator, when the psalm began to be sung, he believed himself amongst the rooks, and started up, roaring with outspread arms, *habbocraws*, to the astonishment of the holy congregation.

HACKED.—Rough, cracked, &c.

HACKS.—Rocky, mossy, black wilds.

HACKS O' ANWOTH.—A very wild moorish place, in that parish of *Anwoth.*

HACKSTON.—An old Borgue bard, he had a vein for rhyme; some say but a small *vein*; he once wrote to the king, to know if he would have him be laureate. Subscribing himself *poet* and *private English teacher, parish of Borgue;* what a valuable curiosity would this address to royalty be; Oh! for a copy, but alas, I am afraid is is lost for ever. His song of *Paul Jones* is tolerable, and is not yet forgot by some :—

> " She came from Flambro' Head,
> " Did she not, did she not,
> " She was a ship o' dread,
> " Was she not, was she not," &c.

Blair, the queer laird of *Senwick,* was wont to have same fun with him, when a party of gentleman was with the singular landlord, *Hackston,* the poet, (who was commonly about the house) was allowed to come amongst the company; then whisky would be given him, a thing he was always very fond of, and so when they had him half drunk, they diverted themselves at the poor poet's expence; once they got a sword, and made the poor wretch believe he was about to be run through with it, but ere this was done they would grease the blade, so that it might transfix him a *sleeker* manner; it is needless to sketch the *auld wight* farther.

HAFFERS.—Sharing half in any thing.

HAFFLINS.—Half-ways.

HAFFMANOR.—Having land in partnership, between two.

HAFTED.—Animals are said to be hafted, when they live contented on strange pastures, when they have made a haunt.

HAG.—To hew.

HAGELOG.—A clog of wood to hew on.

HAGS.—Rocky, moor ground; the same with *Hacks.*

HAG-YARD.—A stack-yard. The phrase *" clear the hag,"* means, clear all out of the way.

HAINCHING.—Throwing, by springing the arm on the haunch.

HAIR.—A small quantity of any thing.

HAIVERS.—Foolish chat; idle conversation.

HAIVERALLS.—Fools, who talk *Haivers.*

HALLANS.—Mid-walls through cottages, composed of cross bars, and overlaid with straw plastered with clay, called *cat clay*; also, those abutments or batteries, built against weak walls to keep them from falling, are termed *hallans.*

HALLICKET—Fools. Thoughtless, restless beings, who cannot *haul*; who must be running every where, and talking a great deal on subjects they know nothing about.

HALLION.—A blackguard.

HALLOW-EEN.—Hallow-eve, or eve of All Saints. Before the incomparable Burns brought the superstitious observances of this night into ridicule, it was a wonderful one all over Scotland; and even yet, though superstition be laid aside, it is a night much attended to, and full of frolics; thus a large deep tub is filled with water, in which is put a large apple, so the rustics strip off their upper garments, and try to catch it with their teeth; this they find impossible to do, while it swims on the surface, so they dive down with it under the mouth, and when it strikes the bottom, they dart their tusks in, and so triumphantly brings it up.

A candle, and apple too, are hung both by one string, at one place; to have a bite of this, without burning the face, creates much fun.

Then songs are sung, and whisky goes round, which are cheering things, and if attended by a fiddle, much

more so. I have been speaking with respect to the way
the lower classes now observe it; the higher again meet
in large parties together, play cards, feast, drink,
dance, &c.

But I must own there is nothing so poetical now about
the matter, as was in the *days o' lang syne.* " When *blue-
clues,* fair water and foul, eating apples at glasses, washing sark-sleeves at *rare burns,* pulling *kailrunts,* &c. went
forward." I have seen the old plan tried too, but superstition cannot be mimicated,

HALLYOCH.—A term used to express that strange gabbling
noise people make, who are talking in a language we do
not understand. Thus, a club of Manxmen together,
are said to *haud an unco gabbie labbie o' a halyoch wi'
ither,*

HAMMER, BLOCK, and STUDY.—A school game. A fellow
lies on all fours, this is the *block* ; one steadies him before,
this is the *study* ; a third is made a *" hammer"* of, and
swung by boys, against the *block* ; it is a rude game.

HAMPERS.—Large baskets, carried on the backs of asses.

HANBARROW.—A spoked barrow, carried by the hands.

HANBEAST.—The horse a ploughman directs with the left
hand.

HANCH.—To eat like a swine.

HANNIE.—Handy.

HAN OWRE HEAD.—A phrase, signifying " choosing
without selecting ;" thus, in large droves of cattle, there
are some fat and others lean. Drovers, in purchasing
these, will sometimes take the good, and leave the bad,
this is called *shooting* ; others will take the lot as it is,
this is buying them, *hand owre head,* both plans are
ruled by the way the bargain is made, to leave *shotts* and
have all good, the price for each will be larger, of course,
than taking them at random.

HAND-REEL.—An old *reel* or machine, used for winding and numbering the hanks of yarn; while winding, the *auld wives* counted thus:—" There's *ane*, and there's no *ane*, and there's *ane* a' out."

HANSLE.—A morning lunch.

HANTLE.—A quantity of any thing, and it may either mean a large or a small quantity, there being no limitation to the term; " he has a *hantle* o' yon sillar dune now" means, that a good sum of the money is spent, but how much or how little it does not determine. An English woodcutter was assisting once to hew down a Gallovidian forrest, when a native came up to him and said, " he had a *hantle* o' that timmer down now." The Englishman stood mute, and the traveller, thinking him sullen, passed on; the other *bucherons* observing this, gathered round their fellow, and began to quiz him about not answering the man; " I knew (said our hero of the hatchet) well enough what the fellow said, but how could I answer him? If he had told me how many acres of wood he mean'd by a *hantle*, then I might have been able to give him some satisfaction."

HAPP.—To cover; also a cover.

HAPSHACKLED.—An horse is said to be so when an hind and fore foot are confined by a rope fixed to them; this is to hinder them to " hop" or leap.

HAP, STEP, and JUMP.—A way of taking three leaps— first hop, then step, and again leap.

HAP THE BEDS.—A singular game gone through by hopping on one foot, and with that foot sliding a little flat stone out of an oblong bed, rudely drawn on a smooth piece of ground; this bed is divided into eight parts, the two of which at the farther end of it are called the *kail pots*; if the player then stands at one end, and pitches the smooth stone into all the divisions one after the other,

following the same on a foot, (at every throw) and bringing
it out of the figure, this player wins not only the game,
but is considered a first-rate daub at it; failing, however,
to go through all the parts so, without missing either a
throw or a hop, yet keeping before the other gamblers
(for many play at one bed), still wins the curious rustic
game.

HAP WEEL—RAP WEEL.—A phrase, meaning " hit or
miss."

HARGLE BARGLIN.—Higgling, disputing about bargain-
making.

HARL.—To trail, a *harl* a trail.

HARRIST.—Harvest; sometimes *Hairst.*

HARRIST BROTH.—The broth made use of as food in
harvest, allowed to be the best *broth* to be met with in
the country all the year round, for then the vegetable
world is in perfection ; then indeed they sparkle with *rich
een,* and a *brose* made with the *broe* taken out of the *lee
side o' thé kail pot,* is quite an exquisite dish at this season, setting at nought the boasted skill of the French in
the art of cookery.

HARRIST MOON.—The moon in the harvest or Michaelmas time of the year. At this season she presents us
with one of the most vivid marks we have of the Almighty directing the movements of nature toward the good
of man ; by attending to her motions at this period, can
any rational creature deny the existence of Deity? it is impossible. Though we may know by the sublime science
of Astronomy—

> " That the *Harrist Moon,*
> " Rises nine nights alike soon," or will rise.

That as she is passing through one of her northern nodes,
or ascending, while the sun is southing beyond the Equator,
and descending, her march round the earth becomes as it

were obvious on the horizon; every night for about nine together, we find her having her thirteen degrees of more amplitude from the south, which are about her daily number, and so waning away to the north. Yet who gave her orders for this? who caused her wanderings to be this way at this season, and at no other? Who but he whom all should adore, in the fulness of soul.

By fixing her this way, how is the husbandman befriended, and when this is so, is not all mankind befriended? for the farmer feeds the world. Was the moon not to shine forth in harvest-time, was darkness to come on the moment the sun sank in the west, how much would it retard the gathering in the fruits of the earth; but as it is otherways, the farmer has the liberty of adding whatever part of the night he pleases to the day, in order to forward his labours, and assist him in *wunning up the year's wark*. Anciently though, this *moon*, which was called the *Michaelmas moon*, was hailed by some of our *ancestree* as a mighty useful thing for other purposes—viz. in *reaving* and making inroads, many a marauder made a good fortune in her beams. The *tocher* which a *doughty borderer* gave a daughter, was the result of his reaving during this moon. But surely Providence never intended her to favour such as the *Elliots*, the *Armstrongs*, and *Jocks o' the Side* of yore.

HARTSCAUD.—The heart-burn.

HASH.—An impudent young man.

HASHLOCH.—Waste, refuse, &c.

HASKY.—Husky, rough, &c. not clean nor smooth.

HASPLE.—A sloven in every sense of the word.

HATTIE.—A game with *preens*, pins, on the crown of a hat; two or more may play; each lay on a pin, then with the hand they strike the side of the hat, time about, and whoever makes the pins by a stroke cross each other, lift

those so crossed. It is quite delightful to describe the
Scotch games. Navigators sail away by the pole, and travellers pop their noses into Africa, yet bring not home
accounts of the manners of any people half so strange
as our own, when truly described.

HAUGHS.—Wide glens, with some level land in them, and
a river running down the middle. *Haughs, cleuchs, glens,*
and *gills,* are all of the same " genera," as a naturalist
would say, but different in species and character.

HAURK.—A term much used by *Scotch* foxhunters, when
the hounds find the scent of reynard in one of his keeps, or
challenge him ; the terriers or little dogs are brought to the
place, and desired by Nimrod to get below, far *aneath the
yird,* the which they will do without much entreaty ; but
when they come near the throne of his majesty, his *high-
ness* places himself so in a jamb or chink, that they cannot
get behind him ; there stand the little vicious creatures,
and keep up a continued barking. When the *hunter* hears
by them the situation they are in, he bawls down to
haurk to him, haurk to him, ye wee blasties; so, in defiance of the tusks of the fox, they seize on, and drag out
the crafty villain.

HAURL.—A female careless of dress.

HAURNPAN.—The scull.

HAURRAGE.—A blackguard crew of people.

HAVERON.—A goat a year old, gelded.

HAVOC-BURDS.—Those large flocks of small birds which
fly about the fields after harvest ; they are of different
sorts, though all of the linnet tribe. *Whunlinties* form
the greatest number.

HAWCKIN.—The noise made to clear the throat.

HAWKIE.—An affectionate name for a favorite cow. Burns
talks about " *twall-pint Hawkie*," *Hurly Hawkie* is the
call milk-maids use to call the cows home to be milked.

It is somewhat a curious song, that one of *Hurlie
Hawkie*; the world may have a sight of it :—

O yonder's my Nannie gathering the kye,
  Whar the e'ening sun is beaming,
Awa on the hazley brae down by,
  Whar the yellow nits are leaming.
    And ay she cries " Hurly Hawkie,
    " String awa my crommies, to the milking loan.
    " Hurly, Hurly, Hawky."
How sweetly her voice dinnles through my heart,
  I'll wyle roun, and her forgather,
Tak a kiss or twa, and than gae part,
  For fear o' her crusty father.
    And ay she cries, " Hurly Hawkie,
    " String, string awa hame to the milking loan,
    " Hurly, Hurly, Hawky."
Now a' in a flutter she lies in my arms,
  On the hinny smelling bank o' clover,
Wha wad be sae base as steal her charms,
  It shall na be me her lover.
    I'll let her cry, " Hurly Hawkie,
    " And wize the kye hame to the milking loan,
    " Hurly, Hurly, Hawky."

HAWK-STUDYIN.—The way hawks steadily hover above
their prey before they pounce on it ; they anchor themselves in the air, as it were, and always with their " bow"
or breast to the wind. No other birds but them seem to be
able to " bring to" in the ærial element ; no wonder this was
taken notice of by the ancients, as in the question put to
the Man of Uzz, " Dost thou know how the *hawk* flies ?"
Indeed, none can say how ; none human.

HAWSE-BANE.—That rise beneath the chin on the throat.

HEADIM AND CORSIM.—A game with pins. Pins are
hid with fingers in the palms of the hands ; the same
number is laid alongside them, and either *headim* or *corsim*
called out by those who do so ; when the fingers are lifted,
if the heads of the pins hid, and those beside them, be
lying one way, when the crier cried *headim*, then that
player wins ; but if *corsim*, the one who hid the pins wins.
This is the king of all the games at the *preens*, and let
it not be thought that it is a *bairn's play* ; by no means ;

it is played by lads and lasses as *big* as ever they will be, and by those whom age has again made young; the game is simple and harmless, and not uninteresting; the Peasant is as anxious about gaining a *preen*, as my *Lord Duke* would be ten thousand pounds; when the stakes run high, barnmen and ploughmen get noisy over them, and play open-mouthed, taking such hearty laughs whiles, that sparrows who have "taken up lodging for the night," in the *thacked easings*, flutter frightened from their holes. *Cheatery* is sometimes heard of in this game too; then is the saying sounded, "They wha begin to steal needles and pins, end wi' stealing horned kye;" (as the twig is bent the tree's inclined.)

HEADRIGG.—The ridge which runs along the ends of the others.

HEADS AND TAILS.—That plan for deciding matters by the "*birl o' a bawbee.*" The one side cries *heads*, (when the piece is a whirling in the air) and the other *tails;* so whichever is up when the piece alights, that gains, or settles the matter; *heads* standing for the king's head, *tails* for she who represents Britannia. Some will doubtless laugh at me for explaining things minutely which seem to them to be so well known as to need no explanation; I may just laugh at these in return, for there is not one in a hundred "could explain" what is—*heads* and *tails*.

HEATHER-BLEET.—The mire-snipe.

> " The *laverock* and the lark,
> " The *bawckie* and the bat,
> " The *heatherbleet*, the mire-snipe,
> " How many burds be that?"

There are some who must think awhile before they answer this question rightly, by saying *three*. The snipe is called *heather-bleet*, from her loving wild heathery marshes, and when soaring aloft, "*bleating*" with her wings, in the spring time. Yes, *bleating* with her wings, not with her mouth; she vibrates her wings quick against the air, causing the sweet bleating noise to take place.

HEATHER-COW—A heath-broom.

HECH!—An exclamation used almost on every emergency.

HECH-HOW!—The same as the above; only it is the name of the poisonous herb, hemlock, also.

HECH-HOW-HUM!—An exclamation much like those above, only, it is always accompanied with a yawn.

HECK—A hay-rack. Also the toothed thing which guides the spun-thread on to the pirn, in spinning-wheels.

HEDDLES—Those parts of a weaver's loom through which the threads come to be wove. They are connected with the " threadles," and can be altered any way at the weaver's pleasure, by his touching the " treadles" with his feet.

HEEZIE—A mighty lift.

HELL'S-HOLES—Those dark nooks which are dreaded as being haunted with bogles.

HELTER-SKELTER—Bounding forward, fearless of every thing ; not caring whether the way is right or wrong, confused or not.

HEMP-RIGGS—Ridges of fat land whereon hemp was sown in the olden time ; and in these modern days, when land is a praising for goodness, it is said to be as strong as hemp-riggs.

HENCHVENTS—The same with " gores," pieces of linen put into the lower parts of a shirt, to make that end wider than the other, to give " vent" or room for the " haunch."

HERON, the Historian.—Sketches of the life and character of this ill-fated Gallovidian, have now frequently been given, so I only mean to say a few things not spoken of by any. When he was in his seventeenth or eighteenth

year, he taught some farmers families in the *Parish o'*
Borgue. My mother had the honour to be one of his
pupils. He *lashed* his scholars sometimes dreadfully, for
his temper was easily ruffled. A *big lad* at his school
being called up for punishment once, the fellow burst out
" that he would not be *lashed* by any *Heron* that ever *lap
on twa legs* ;" so the teacher and he had a *set-to*, both came
madly to the *scratch*, the *dominie* was *floored*, his *bread-
basket* was almost broke on a *bink*, and from his nose
claret leaked profusely.

In those days he was a great reader : the book was never
out of his hand, and the manner in which he punished the
boys was hitting them a *skelp* on the side of the head with
a book, which made the tears start in their eyes. He fre-
quented the *loop* of a *burn* much : this was an out-of-the-
way *nuik.* Here did he study with deep attention the
mazy world of literature. When the house-maid would
have wanted him to come to dinner, in vain might she
have stood at a distance and called on *Mr. Heron* ; he
heard her not, being so deeply absorbed with his books, so
she had no other shift than always go, and *put at him* with
her hand, saying whiles, " O ! wad the burn rise some day
and swoop Heron afore't into the sea". These natural
touches, trivial looking though they be, strike at the foundation of this wayward character. He was fretful and
ambitious, fond to excess of learning ; had he read nature
though, more than books, it would have been as well for
his fame now a-days. He is not an original writer ; his
thoughts commonly are at second or third hand. Had he
given the world a history of his native *clauchan*, New
Galloway, I do not know but it would have been as much
to his fame as his *History of Scotland*, good though that
work be. His sentences are much too long, a reader is
apt to lose the thread of the discourse. Poor fellow !
but why say any thing against him ? few, few are born with

half his talents. The heart melts when thinking of his latter end ; had I been in London when he was inhumanly incarcerated in a lazar-house, if I had not found some means to relieve, I would have perished with him.

HET-AHAME—It is said of those who wander abroad when they have no need to do so, and happen to fare ill, that they " *war owre het ahame.*"

HET-BITCH—A bitch in her rutting season.

HET-DRINKS—Warm drinks of the cordial nature, which gude-wives bumper at "*Kimmerins.*"

HEUGHS—Precipices. Some of these in Galloway are very steep and deep ; perhaps those of *Cruggleton* and *Rascarrel* are the largest on the shore, but those of *Cairnsmoor,* in the inland, are far larger. Many kill themselves clambering about on these for birds' eggs and " *pasper,*" and cattle often fall over them no more to rise with the life. *Davie Maben,* an old cross-grained *Herd,* once quarrelled with his dog, when he catched him by the *hind heels,* and tossed him over the " *Raen Nest Heuch*" of the " *Netherlaw,*" exclaiming, when the poor *tyke* was suffering below, " Did you not know that I was a passionate man ?" Perhaps Shakespear or Scott have expressed nothing more genuine than this, of mad feeling.

HEY WULLIE WINE, and HOW WULLIE WINE — An old fire-side play of the peasantry, hinted at by *Cromek* ; but there are many ways of drawing out the merry concern. Suppose, seated round the *ingle,* in the *fore-night,* a large party of lads and lasses, full of mirth, beauty, honesty, and simplicity ; in short, *bairnies* of nature. One of the lasses, for instance, addresses one of the lads so—

> " Hey, Wullie Wine, and How Wullie Wine,
> " I hope for hame ye'll no incline,
> " Ye'll better light, and stay a' night,
> " And I'll gie thee a lady fine."

Then he answers,

> " Wha will ye gie if I wi' ye bide,
> " To be my bonny blooming bride,
> " And lie down lovely by my side?"

Again she—

> " I'll gie thee Kate o' Dinglebell,
> " A bonny body like yersell."

Then he—

> " I'll stick her up in the pear-tree,
> " Sweet and meek and sae is she ;
> " I lo'ed her ance, but she's no for me,
> " Yet I thank ye for your courtesy."

She—

> " I'll gie thee Rozie o' the Cleugh,
> " I'm sure she'll please thee weel eneugh."

He—

> " Up wi' her on the bane dyke,
> " She'll be rotten or I be ripe ;
> " She's made for some ither, and no for me,
> " Yet I thank ye for your courtesy."

She—

> " Then I'll gie ye Nell o' sweet Springkell,
> " Owre Gallowa she bears the bell."

He—

> " I'll set her up on my bed-head,
> " And feed her weel wi' milk and bread;
> " She's for nae ither but just for me,
> " Sae I thank ye for your courtesy."

Such is a specimen of the concern. The *lad,* before the questions are put, whispers to another, the girl he will stop with—so this one must be given, before the dialogue ends. The chief drift of this singular amusement seems to be, to discover the *sweethearts* of one another, and such discoveries are thought valuable, but not so much so as they were anciently.

HIDDLINS—In a hidden way, not open.

HIE-COCKET HAT—A hat with the brim thrice cocked. It is said to be " the life of an old hat to cock it." Anciently these hats were very commonly wore ; also hair tied and clubed in a *ribbon fang*; coats long in the waist with large buttons ; waistcoats with *pouch-flaps side on the thee*, and mostly of a *demity cut*, with broad *mother o' pearl* buttons ; breeches without braces, but with buckles and *buckle-flaps*, and these breeks were generally of either a hoddan grey or slate-blue colour ; stockings knitted ahame, with many ribs ; shoes sharp-toed, with buckles, and often with buckles and *fause-tags*. Thus adorned, *tag-rag* and *bob-tail*, our forefathers were *no joke*. A dandy at a country kirk in these times would have been hailed as a most astonishing object ; the *auld wives* would have thought " *it* had drapped frae the moon." The first umbrella that ever was braced in Galloway belonged to a *Sutor*, who *won'd* about the *Gate-house* fifty years ago ; he ran allwheres through the country to display the *farly*, and being at *Borgue kirk* one windy day, while coming over the *kirk-stile*, all eyes on him, a *gurl* came, when all sail was set, and away went the *tappin lift*, down came the pikes clashing about his *lugs*, and one of them transfixed his cheek to the effusion of *Crispan*'s blood. O ! but I glory to keek back into the days of yore, and take a laugh.

HIELAN FLING—A rustic dance.

HIELAN-MAN'S BURIAL—A funeral which lasts more than a day. These are common yet in the Highlands of Scotland, but rarely now to be met with in the Lowlands ; however, funerals nigh approaching to them sometimes happen. The mourners get " *fow*" at the *burial house*, and have a dancing time with the corpse on the road from thence to the kirk-yard. If the old " *freet*" be true " that those who fall when at the *handspake* aneath the

corpse, will soon be the corpse themsell," there would
soon be a good few corpses ; for at these " *druken*" concerns, the bearers are falling some of them every now and
then. The following is a verbatim account of one of these
burials :—" At length the laird o' the *Bowertree Buss*,
gaed his last pawt, was straughted, dressed, coffined and a' ;
and I was bidden to his burial the Tuesday after."

" There I gaed, and there were met a wheen fine boys.
Tam o' the Todholes, and *Wull o' the Slack* war there ;
Neil Wulson, the fisher, and *Wull Rain*, the gunner, too ;
the first service that came roun' was strong farintosh,
famous peat reek, there was nae grief amang us. The
laird had plenty, had neither a wife nor a wean, sae wha
cud greet. We drew close to ither, and began the cracks
ding daug, while every minute roun' came anither reamin
service. I faun' the bees i' my head bizzin strong,
in a wee time. The inside of the *burial house* was like
the inside o' a *Kelton-hill tent* ; a banter came frae the
tae side of the room, and was sent back wi' a jibe frae the
ither. Lifting at last began to be talked about, and at last
lift we did. ' Whaever wished for a pouchfu' o' drink
might tak it.' This was the order ; sae mony a douce
black coat hang side wi' a heavy bottle. On we gaed wi'
the laird, his weight we faun na'. *Wull Weer* we left ahin
drunk on the spot. *Rob Fisher* took a sheer as we came
down the green brae, and landed himsell in a *rossen o'
breers*: Whaup-nebbed Samuel fell aff the drift too. I
saw him as we came cross *Howmcraig* ; the drink was gaen
frae him like *couters*. Whan we came to the *Taffdyke* that
rins cross *Barrend*, there we laid the laird down till we
took a rest a wee. The inside o' pouches war than turned
out, bottle after bottle was touted owre ; we rowed about,
and some warsled. At last a game at the quoits was proposed ; we played, but how we played I kenna. Whan we
got tae the kirk-yard the sin was just plumpin down ; we

pat the coffin twice in the grave wrang, and as often had to draw't out again. We got it to fit at last, and in wi' the mools on't. The grave-digger we made a beast o'. Sic a funeral I was ne'er at afore ; surely, I ay think that it was na unlike a *Hielan'-man's Burial*."

I may follow the sketch of the *Hielandman's*, with

THE BIG MAN'S BURIAL.

Whan simmer suns were blazing high,
 And clegs made cattle startle,
Whan gussey in the dub did lie,
 And hardly gaed a spartle;
Frae Bath came hame to Oxterlee
 Lord Burble's stinking carcage,
Pack'd up in coffins ane, twa, three,
 A most infernal farkage
      To yird some day.

His honest tenant folks about
 Were glad the same to hear,
For lang the scurr had screw'd the snout,
 And damn'd the fa'ing tear ;
But that disease reserved by death
 For hallions sic as he,
Which works by *lice*, hotch'd out his breath,
 And left him to the e'e
      Grey sight ae day.

Now, as it often is the gate
 Wi' sic like purse-proud fools,
Whan dead, to lie a while in state
 Afore they gang tae mools,
Sae in a bonny airy room
 The great Lord Burble loll'd,
While clowns and chambermaids did come
 Grand torches to behold
      As bright as day.

What gowden bobs and siller corus
 Wi' raws o' tackets clear,
Did glister on the varnish'd boards
 That held the lousy peer ;
Through a' the lan' o' Gallowa
 The news like muir-burn ran,
And o'er the seas and far awa
 That death this nobleman
      Had down'd ae day.

And that upon the coming twault
  O' mochy sultry July,
He wad be rowed to his vault,
  Which beggars minded truly;
They left Maybole and Minnieive,
  Fu' ragged and fu' merry,
And mony a loon wha ne'er did thrive
  In counties Down and Derry,
                For that big day.

Behold them limping out the roads
  That led to Oxterlee,
Aud hurkeling in glen abodes,
  A dusty sight to see;
High were their hopes for food and cash,
  And drink to keep them strunting,
Which cures the yisk and waterbrash,
  And sets the pipes a lunting
                Sure grab that day.

What skinless cuddies hobbling by,
  What troops come flagging on
Frae the auld clauchan o' Dalry,
  And grim Damellinton;
What sarkless randy hizzies there
  Just bubbeling wi' bawdery,
Their hips, outkeeking did declare,
  They cared na much for gaudery
                To shine that day,

" Rike me out my blackish breeks,"
  Quoth Rab o' Braxy Brae,
To Mall, the wife—sae she them seeks,
  Deep hid amang the tae.
He claps them on his rustic doup,
  Sae hairy and sae yellow,
And af tae burial did loup,
  A raw-baned conntry fallow,
                To help that day.

And there was need o' some strong folk
  To en' him down the stair,
For faith, lead coffins are nae joke,
  They gall the shouther sair:
This, Factor Glunch did brawley ken,
  Sae sought the crowds fu' neatly
For sax or aught strong sturdy men,
  To do the business featly
                And right that day.

The first twa that he picked on
  War Rab and Jock the Tar,
Rough Jock wha mony a year had shone
  On board a man o' war ;
Than Putting Tam, Black Boxing Ned,
  And Pate, the mighty thrasher ;
Marle-throwing Wull, Leash Sam the Blade
  Wi' Jeamy Jirk, the smasher,
              To lift that day.

But tho' they war the strongest chiels
  That day upon the ground,
They often stagger'd on their heels,
  When his great weight they found ;
And coming slowly, step by step,
  Thus rather overpowered,
Hoch ! ane o' them a' fit did slip,
  Sae down his lordship low'red
              Fu' fast that day.

The swearing now fu' loud began,
  Crush'd taes were felt a' quaking,
And skin, torn aff a leg or han',
  Gaed subjects for coarse talking.
Fat Jock, the man-o'-war's-man damn'd
  Rab for a rotten lubber ;
While thrasher, Pate, the sailor blamed
  For nought but stinking blubber,
              And filth that day.

The tinklers on the gowany green
  Upstarted frae their hurdies,
And now about my lord were seen
  Outspuing bonny wordies ;
Nae bossness then they felt ava'
  Within the pow and crappin',
For plenty had been gien to a',
  And nane refused their chappin'
              To glutt that day.

Some well-dress'd bloods now seem'd to tak
  Upon them a' the trouble,
The ragabash were ordered back,
  And then began the hubble ;
For cudjells now war seen to bounce
  Aff sculls and bloody noses,
While, some unfit to stan' a whunce,
  Sten'd aff, and miss'd the doses
             O' that wild day,

At last the beggars clear'd the field,
  For wha could stan' their whunners?
The verra ploughmen had to yield,
  Wi' hides as black as shuners.
Then on four rollers they did place
  His lordship and his coffins,
And haurl'd him to his vault wi' grace,
  'Thout either sneers or scoffins,
           To close that day.

Sae snugly now he rots awa
  In hole below the grun,
Auld Shanky values no ae fla'
  Slump fifty thousan' pun'.
May every curse wha lives like he
  By vermin sae be crumped,
Yea, like him too, interred be,
  And in Hell bravely thumped
           Wi' pith, some day.

HILCH—A singular halt.

HILLANS—Small artificial hills of any thing.

HILL-FOWK—Those truly religious and independent people, the Covenanters, well known to all the world ages ago,
and the inhuman manner in which they were persecuted
anciently, makes all men of feeling admire them. That
person is never of a great character who laughs at the *hill-
fowk*; there is less patriotic blood in the veins of such than
would fill a nut-shell, and the heart is as rotten as a
yellow puddock stool. They are called the *hill-fowk*, from
their love of the primitive plan of worshipping the Creator,
as his son did, amongst the hills and mountains in the
open air, under the cerulean canopy. Of all the sects of
Christians in the world, these and the Quakers for me;
because the last say little, and wrangle less, respecting
religious matters, but venerate the whole with solemn and
silent awe, moving, about on this sinful planet, an honor
to the human race; and the first for why, they do speak
but in a natural and manly manner. I have felt myself
frequently very much refreshed with hearing a *hill-preach-
ing*, and once was foolish enough to scrawl a little pam-

phlet respecting *hill-preachers*, which was published in Galloway, intitled *Osborn and Syminton on the Weigh-beam.* The *Hill-fowk* are the *fowk* to whom the kirk of Scotland owes all her beauty; for this they paid dearly with their blood at *Drumclog, Bothwell Brigg,* and else-where—scenes never to be forgotten.

HILT NOR HAIR—When any thing is lost, and cannot be found, we say, that we " canna see *hilt* nor *hair* o't," not the slightest vestige. To English the phrase closely, we may say, " Top nor tail."

HINGING-LUGGED—A person is said to be *hinging-lugged* when having an ill-will at any one, and apparently sulky. " Such a one has a *hinging-lugg* at me," means that that one is not well disposed towards me. For my own part, I am in love with all mankind; I never had a very great outcast with any, and at present have not a *hinging lugg* at a living soul. The kicks and thousand rebuffs of this world, thank God, I can take with pleasure, and give none. This phrase comes from the way dogs, and some other brutes, have, of letting their ears—*luggs,* droop when on the eve of battle.

HINGINS—Bed curtains.

HIN-HAN-PLAYERS—For common, the best players at the game of curling of their party; they play after all the others have played, and their throw is always much depended on. Some argue that the best players should not play last, as then the *rink* is made so foul with stones they have no chance to do any thing. However, the nature of man is always for having something good to rest his hopes on at the *last*; so good players must always finish the *splore.*

HIN-HARREST-TIME—That time of the year between harvest and winter. The same with *Back-en,* which see.

HINNERLITHS—The hind parts.

HINNIE-PIGS—A school game; also pots to hold honey. The boys who try this sport sit down in rows, hands locked beneath their hams. Round comes one of them, the *honey-merchant*, who feels those who are sweet or sour, by lifting them by the arm-pits, and giving them three shakes; if they stand these without the hands unlocking below, they are then *sweet* and saleable, fit for being *office-bearers* of other ploys. As to the *pigs*, real honey-pots, an old bee-man once had a very bad boy for a son, who longed to get at his father's *hinnie-pigs*, which were kept secure in a strong chest. Long the boy attempted to get a *lick* of the treasure, but in vain. At last he hit on the infernal plan of loading the lid of the *bunker* so with stones, that it gave way, and *smashed* the hale o' the *hinnie-pigs*. His father, hearing the crash, hunted him through the *clauchan*, bawling out, " I never saw the like o' him, ye never saw the like o' him, nor mortal man ever saw the like o' him."

HINTINGS—The furrows which ploughmen finish their ridges with. These furrows are not like the others; they are lifted out of the bottom of the main " *furr*," and are soil of a different nature.

The greatest difficulty young ploughmen have to surmount when learning the tilth trade, is the proper way to " *lift hintins.*" This is the key-stone of the business, and ploughing-matches are always decided by the way in which this is done. I may here add, that it is never those who gain prizes at the art of Cain who are the most useful ploughmen to the farmer; they are too conceited, always running to the forge with their *airns*, and still flattering and fattening their horses; a common hand is always worth any two of these.

HIPLOCHS—The coarse wool which grows about the hips of sheep.

HIRPLE—To walk in a lame-like manner.

HIRR—The call to a dog to make him hunt.

HIRSLE—A flock of animals ; also, to slide softly on our bottom.

HITCH—A noose, a knot, a turn of a rope round any thing.

HIVING-SOUGH—A singular sound bees are heard to make before they *hive* or *cast*, or leave their parents. Only *Bee-fowk* who understand the nature of the insect well, know any thing about this *sough* or sound. It is commonly heard the evening before their departure. The *bee's bonello* probably it may be. It is a continued buzzing hum, full of melancholy-like cadences. While on bees, I may note a few of the many curiosities respecting them, unspoke of by *Virgil* in his *Georgics*; *Bonar*, or any one else. When a swarm intends to have a long flight, they gather close together into the space of a few yards square, or, as the peasantry say, into the *breath o' a gude grey plaid.* When they assume this figure, it is vanity to follow them. This is the method they take of *easing their flight*, a plan Poet Milton discovered, respecting wild-geese, and other migrating birds. And what is singular, bees, in this state, always wing their way right against the wind ; now, know they where they intend to journey to before they start, or fly they at random ? If they know the place, then they must look out for a *fair wind*, though with us that is a *head* one, in present maritime law ; but methinks, at these times they know not where they wander, as frequently they alight on a spot open to the elements, and so perish, whereas they might have easily found a snug place. Bees, taken to the torrid zone, do well the first year, but learning there is no winter, but summer for ever, they soon turn lazy, as when brought from the Moorlands to the Dale. Some fancy we may take the honey from them without killing, but this cannot be done. Let *Bonar* reason as he will. Mine original *Mossie Cloon* would once turn a *Bee-*

man, so followed one through the country awhile, to learn the trade of *taking* and *leaving* a part. At last he thought himself fit for the trick, so a friend would let him try; a crowd gathered round, and *Mossie* began operations. The bees became crusty; out they rushed in legions, vowing revenge. The mob of spectators fled; friend *James* was indeed the last to *fly*, but had to do it, and to take his bed for some time after, being so stinged, and never more would he profess to be a *Bee-man*.

HOAST—To cough; to have the " *Hoast*;" to have the cold.

HOBBLE—To make a rocking motion.

HOBBLE-TE-HOY—An unfeeling lad towards the ladies—

> " A *hobble-to-hoy*,
> " Neither a man nor a boy."

They are indeed " *senseless asses, O,*" who do not love the sweetest work in all creation.

HOCH—The back of the leg.

HOCH ANEE!—An exclamation of grief.

> O! what's come owre my Sawnie,
>   Wha ance was sae blythe and free,
> And what's befa'en Nanny,
>   Wha lo'ed the blink o' his e'e;
> Alas puir cheel, he sank in a wave,
>   Awa i'the foaming sea,
> And she broke her heart, and's now in her grave,
>   Sad, sad news—*Hoch Anee*!
>
> Whan thegether they ay war funny,
>   It was nice to see them sae free,
> And they ran on the braes sae sunny,
>   That haud in the river Dee;
> But sinner'd they were I kenna how,
>   And meikle grief they did dree,
> Till they war ta'en to whar they're now,
>   Sad, sad news—*Hoch Anee*!
>
> And sae we are left a sobbing,
>   The tears blob in the e'e,
> The heart wi' grief is throbbing,
>   For them nae mair we'll see;
> O! they're fled awa and left our shore,
>   In the gude place may they be,
> Tho' the twasome's fate we'll lang deplore,
>   Sad, sad news—*Hoch Anee*!

HOCH-BAN'—A band which confines one of the legs of a restless animal; it passes round the neck and one of the legs.

HOCHLE—To tumble lewdly with women in open day.

HODDAN—To have a kind of jog when either walking or riding.

HOG-MA-NAY, or HUG-ME-NAY—The last day of the year. Dr. Jamieson, with a research that would have frightened even a Murray or a Scalinger to engage in, has at last owned, like a worthy honest man as he is, that the origin of this term is quite uncertain; and so should I say also, did I not like to be throwing out a hint now and then on various things, even suppose I be laughed at for doing so.

Then here I give, like myself, who am a being of small scholarcraft, a few *hindish* speculations respecting this mystic phrase; to be plain, I think *hog-ma-nay* means *hug-me-now—Hawse and ney*, the old nurse term, meaning, " kiss me, and I'm pleased," runs somewhat near it : *ney* or *nay*, may be a variation that time has made on *now*. Kissing, long ago, was a thing much more common than at present. People, in the days gone by, saluted other in churches, according to Scripture, with *holy kisses;* and this *smacking* system was only laid aside when priests began to see that it was not *holiness* alone prompted their congregations to hold up their *gabs* to one another like *Amous dishes*, as Burns says. And in " ane compendious buik o' *Godly* and *Spiritual Sangs*, for the avoiding of *Sinne* and *Harlotree*," printed in the old black letter, by *Andro Hart*, at Edinburgh, in 1590, the song of " *John, come kiss me now*," made its appearance as a suitable one to be sung in the *kirk*—

" John, come kiss me now,
" John, come kiss me now ;
" John, come kiss me by and by,
" And mak nae mair ado," &c.

S

At weddings too, what a kissing there was; and even to this day, at these occasions much of it goes on : and on the happy nights of *hog-ma-nay*, the kissing trade is extremely brisk, particularly in *Auld Reekie*; then the lasses must kiss with all the stranger lads they meet, while phrases not unlike to—

" John, come kiss me now,

or

" John, come *hug me now*,"

are frequently heard.　From such causes, methinks, *hog-ma-nay* has started.　The *hugging day*, the time to *hug-me-now*.

HOG-SCORES—Distance-lines in the game of curling.　They are made in the form of a wave, and are placed one-fifth part of the whole *rink* from either *witter* ; that is to say, if the *rink* be fifty yards long, from *tee* to *tee*, the *hog-scores* of that *rink* are thirty yards distant from other.

If the bottom of a stone gets over this " *score*," and its upper bulb not, still that stone is no " *hogg*."　If the stones come not over this line, they are flung out of the game. Sweeping is not allowed until the stone comes over the *hogg*, unless by the person who played it.

HOLIN WI' HUNGER—Those a-gnawing with hunger, are said to be " *holing wi' hunger*," or that the worms are eating up their empty " *ingangs*," and *holing* their bodies.

HOOCH—A shout of joy.　" *Hooch, its a' like a wadding*," shout the peasantry, when dancing, making their heels crack on other at same time.——*Hooch* is sure to inspire glee while *tribbling Bob Major*, or *cutting double quick time*.　This *call* is considered extremely *vulgar* by the genteel, but what the devil cares the honest rustic about the *genteel*. One of his terms, warm from the heart of nature, is worth a million of artful *gentilities*; it carries a strong *sough* always.

HOODICRAWS—Carrion, or *grey-crows*, called *hoodicraws*, for when they get old, they become white in colour all but the feathers of the head; these keep black, and look as if the bird had on a cowl or *hud*. About wild sea-shores, these fowls mark the outgoing of the tide, so to get at the shell-fish called wilk, or periwinkle, a kind of sea-snail, cased in a strong castle, but not impregnable to the hoodicraw; he lifts them into the air thirty or forty yards, then entrusts them to the care of gravity, which brings them crashing down on the rocks, followed close by the voracious bird, who picks up the uncastled gentry as dainty food for the *gizzeron*.

The whut-throat or weazle, and the *hoodie*, have often bloody wars with other about a piece of food they both relish, such as the egg of a hen. Once, Squire Weazle seemed rather too many for his hudded lordship, who flew up into the air, thinking to get rid in that element of his vicious opponent; but no, the weazle would keep his hold, fly as he would, and as high as he pleased. At length, when they had almost got above the clouds, poor *hoodie* was beheld coming *owre the body* and *owre the body* to the earth; and, on going up to where they fell, there was the crow lying with spread wings, quite dead, the weazle, with its sharp teeth, having *nicked the wizen*, and pumped the blood from his heart.

HOOLOCH, or HURLOCH—A burl of stones, an avalanche. Boys go to the *heughs* whiles to tumble down *hoolochs*, receiving much pleasure from seeing them roll and *clanter* down the steeps. It is dangerous sport though, for some-

s 2

times they miss the balance, and make part of the *hooloch* themselves.

HOSHENS—Hose without feet.

HOTTER—A person over-run with vermin, who *hotches*.

HOTTER-BONNET—A person much the same as above.

HOTTLE—Any thing which has not a firm base of itself, such as a young child, when beginning to walk; the same with *tottle*.

HOWDER—To hide; also a game at *scull-duddery*.

HOWDIE—A midwife. Midwives shine respectable in history from the days of Moses downward to the present day. Anciently in Scotland, the superstitious made some observes respecting them—

" For, Wattie's mare stood still, and swat wi' fright,
" Whan she brought east the ' *howdie*' un'ernight,"

says Allan Ramsey.

HOWK—To dig.

HOWM—Flat pieces of land by a river or burn-side.

HOW's A'?—A common salutation.

HOWSPEAKING — Speaking like ventriloquists, from the belly, as it were. Burns has Death speaking this way. " He spak right *how* my name is Death," &c. Country folks say of those who speak this way, " that they speak as if the soun' cam out o' a *hogyet*."

HOWTS—Huts. The word which sometimes prefaces one thing, sometimes another; such as, *howts*—nonsense; *howts*—ay; and so *howts* means a something between yes and no, which is not easy to express.

HOW-WECHTS—Circular implements, of sheep-skin stretched on a hoop, used about barns and mills to lift grain and such things with. See *Wechts*.

HUAM.—The moan of the owl in the warm days of summer; it retires to the darkest recesses of woods, and continues repeating, with a moaning air, "*huam.*" I had some work before I found the sound proceeded from the owl; the people about me said, as their ancestors had no doubt done, that the sound " was the humming o' boggles i'the dark green wud." But I discovered the " *boggles.*"

HUDD.—A builder's implement for bearing mortar on the shoulder.

HUDDERON.—A dirty, ragged person.

HUGGER MUGGERIN.—Doing business not openly, quibbling about trifles, and raising misunderstandings.

HULDIE.—A night-cap; see *Pirnie.*

HULE.—Some will have *hule* to be a demon of some kind or other, but I am inclined to think that "*hule*" is little else but another way of mouthing *hell.* " *He's* a terrible *hule.*" " He's a *hule's* boy," and " saw ye the *hule ?*" these phrases, for instance, may all be explained by using *hell* instead of *hule.* *Hule* therefore, does not express any kind of creature, unless that creature be a moving *hell,* of itself.

HUM-DRUM.—A person of careless habits; one who pays attention to nothing under the sun; who has no business, and no *hobbies,* and who keeps the intellects in a " *strait-jacket.*"

HUMMEL'D.—Chew'd in a careless manner.

HUMMOCK.—The fingers of the hand, put so together by themselves, that the tops of them are all on a level with one another; when the hand is cold, it is impossible to fling the fingers into this form. People in frosty weather try who stands cold best, by the way the *hummock* can be made. This word and *tomack* are connected, they both mean little hillocks.

HUMPH'D.—Food of any kind, but particularly flesh meat, is said to be *humph'd*, when it has a putrid taste and smell.

HUMS.—Mouthfuls of chewed matter.

HUNKER-SLIDE.—To slide, sitting on the hams or *hunkers*, down *shuttles o' ice*, or *braes* made sleek by a basking sun; young people slide on their *hunkers*.

HURDON.—A big-hipped woman.

HURROO—A holloa. A noisy hurry started, a *hurly-burly*, a *hurlubrelu*, as the French call it; and the Hottentots, *hurrocks*; a murmuring noise, as the *sea surge* on a peebly shore. How wonderful it is to see strange tribes of man-kind, laying hold of the universal language of nature!

HURSON.—A whoreson, a name of reproach.

HUSHIE-BAW-BABY.—The cradle-song to babes.

HUSHOCK.—A loose quantity of any thing.

HUSSOCK.—A lump of hair.

HUZZY.—A woman's purse.

HYKE.—To move the body suddenly, by the back joint.

HYVES.—Rushes which come out at times on the skin of infants; the most dangerous hives are those which come out in the interior.—See " *Bowell-hyve*."

I.

ICKER.—An ear of corn.

IDLESET.—A turn of idleness.

ILL-E'E.—Some people are yet suspected of having an *ill-e'e*, otherwise, having an eye hurtful to every thing it looks on. Blacksmiths pretend to know of many this way, and will not allow them to stand in their forges, when joining or welding pieces of iron together, as they are sure of loosing the *wauling heat*, if such be present.

ILL-GATED.—To be bad inclined.

ILL-JAW.—Bad tongue, or bad things spoken with the tongue.

ILL-WILLY.—Of a bad disposition. " Ill-willy kye sud hae nae borns," as the Scotch proverb goes ; and which means " that people of a bad disposition should have no hellish weapons to work with."

IMRIE.—The scent of roasted meat.

INCH.—Any small island, such as the " *Inch o' the Isle*," well known to wild ducks ; and " *Inch Keith*," as well known to the natives about the *Firth o' Forth*.

INGLEBERRIES.—Fleshy wens, which grow on the tender parts of oxen ; they are of a firey nature, which may be the cause of them being named as they are ; when cut they bleed profusely, and must always be seared off with a red hot iron.

INJINE—Genius. We say of any with a dungeon of a head, that that person is a " *great injine*." Burns has the *Bauld Lapraik o' Muirkirk*, an *injine*, because he was a *deacon* at song making ; and I hold his son *Geordy Lapraik*, in London, a *worthy man*, if not an *injine* ; he is quite a *chip of the old black*, whereas the *eldest son* of *Burns*, I am sorry to say is, —— no, I will not say what. Our Scotch songs are all immense flights of genius, all composed by persons having *injine* ; they are mostly of a melancholy nature, and this lives much longer than mirth ; indeed, a tinge of melancholy gilds every thing that lives long. The *Duncan Grey*, and *Tam Glen*, of Burns, are just humourous touches of melancholy, the same as Shakspeare's comedies are ; this melancholy then, is the foundation of a poet's genius, this is his *injine*. " But why seek to know, (as the Swiss philosopher says), what is genius ? if thou hast it, thy feelings will tell what it is ; if thou hast it not, thou never canst know it. If thou art calm

and tranquil, amid the works of nature, and transports
of music; if thou feelest no delirium, no extacy; if thou
art only moved with pleasure, at what should transport
thee with rapture; dost thou dare to ask what genius is?
profane not, vulgar man, that name sublime, what im-
ports thee to know what thou canst never feel."—
Russeau—sur le mot genie, on the word genius. O! that
I knew what it was. O! that I had *injine*; but alas!
poor me!

INKS.—On muddy, level shores, there are pieces of land
overflowed with high spring tides, and not touched by
common ones, according to the laws of nature; on these
grow a coarse kind of grass, good for sheep threatened
with the rot; this saline food sometimes cures them.
When there comes a roaring spring tide before a storm,
its whirling motion washes out circular holes in the
sludge; these are left filled with water, which soon stag-
nates, and becomes of an inky colour, but I do not think
that it is from *ink* the word *inks* arises, for all that; such
land is called *links*, in various districts of Scotland, and
I am inclined to fancy the word derives its origin from
some ancient tongue.

INLEAK.—A coming in of measure.

INNERLY HEARTED.—Of a feeling disposition.

INNS.—Those places in many school games which the
gaining side hold; to obtain the *inns*, is the object of
these games.

INRING.—That segment of the surface of a channlestone
which is nearest the "*tee*."

INWICK.—This term is somewhat different from *inring*;
to *inwick a stone*, is to *come* up a *port* or *wick*, and strike
the inring of a stone seen through that *wick*; now this is
different from a common open *inring*—the two are often
confounded with other, but they are quite different; to

take an *inwick,* is considered by all curlers, the *finest trick* in the game.

IRKED.—Teased, forced to become a foe.

IRR.—To call, to hunt a *curr.*

ISH-WISH.—The call on the cat to her food.

IS-KISS.—The call on a curr-dog to his food.

J.

JABBLE.—A slight agitation of the waters of the sea, with the wind; small irregular waves, and running in all directions: such a state of the ocean makes open boat navigation sometimes more dangerous than if the swells of the sea were larger.

JABBLOCH.—Weak, watery, spirituous liquors.

JAFFLED.—Fatigued looking, down in body and clothes.

JAG.—To prick ; *jagging,* pricking.

JAMP.—Did leap.

JANNERER.—A person who ever talks, and all he says in the course of a year is not worth a *gowkspittle.*

JARBLE.—An old tattered garment.

JAW.—Insulting language.

JAWCKED.—Baffled in some attempt, deceived with *hope.*

JAWHOLE.—A hole out of kitchens, where all refuse is poured.

JAWPED.—Bespattered.

JAWS.—The waves of the sea, when they rush with fury against the rocks of the shore. "Jaw," in some of the ancient tongues, means "pour;" we use it yet for that in ours ; so *jaws* may mean a pouring out, or a wasting of the wrath of the ocean.

JEAMIE'S HOLE.—A very singular hole at the *Borrowhead*; it goes right through and through a reef of rocks: the tide runs a little way into it.

JEEGETS or SHIEGETS.—Little sounding boards, pegs and wheels in a piece of machinery, such as a mill. I heard an original say once, That the head of any party was like a *mill-dam*, grasping, as it were, all the little streams that flow into it, and by lifting the *sluich* board when any emergency appeared, it flowed down on the *meikle wheel,* the next head, the which set all the *jeegets* in motion. The same worthy once made a remark that I could never forget; he said, that the old Scottish proverb, " *what's gude to gie is gude to keep*," was not only true; but " *what was gien was sometimes not worth the taking,*"— though thought otherways by the giver; this was " casting an *auld coat* to a *puir body,* but afore doing sae, to set to, and cut the *buttons* out o't," which rendered the present indeed, not worth the taking.

But 'tis not right, as the old Roman distich says,

——————————— " anditaque lingua,
" Auget, & ex humili tumulo producit olympum,"

Englished, thus—

" Add not our what to what we hear,
" And of a mole-hill do a mountain rear."

JENNIE SPINNER.—A toy; also, a fly with long legs; a *spinner,* as the bard of Avon calls it.

JERKINS.—Meetings or gatherings of people for a certain purpose; these are not ancient, they have been introduced by the Irish intruders some time ago; they are called whiles *drinkings* and whiles *tea drinkings,* about Dumfries; a poor woman, such as a widow, gets some tea and whisky; she then awakens the country to her meaning; some fling in the mite to her *jerkins,* but go not thither, as *jerkins* are truly meetings of the *low vulgar*; a real Scot won't look near one of them; they are commonly attended by full bred and mongrel Irish.

JIBB.—To milk closely.

JIBBINGS.—The last milk that can be drawn out of a cow's udder.

JICKERING.—A female is said to be *jickering* when she is rather better dressed than she should; " mair braw than she is fine."

JINGLE.—To ring, or the sound that metals make when moved together.

JINK.—To make quick motions.

JINKING'S HEN.—A hen that never knew the cock; metaphorically used for an old maid—" she pined awa like *Jinkin's hen*,"—saith Nicholson; the old maids are great favourites of mine, but not so bachelors; listen to a maiden's tongue, in the Gallovidian way, of

HAUD AWA FRAE ME, DONALD.

Haud awa, bide awa,
  Haud awa frae me, Donald,
Keep your hands to yoursell,
  *Wha can suffer theè, Donald.—*Chorus.

Ye hae cheated mony a dear,
  But ye shall ne'er cheat me, Donald;
Ye hae drawn the sobbing tear,
  Frae mony a downcast e'e, Donald.

The lasses they are sairly blamed,
  For being fause a wee, Donald;
But that ane was never named,
  Could lee sae base as thee, Donald.

Afore I'd be a wratch like thee,
  I'd fling mysell i'e sea, Donald,
Or tak a rape and hing me hie,
  On yon auld scruntet tree, Donald.

And after thou had graned thy last,
  Nae Corbie wad paik thee, Donald;
The hoodicraw gude faith wad fast,
  Or thy curst flesh she'd prie, Donald.

To live and die an auld grey maid,
  Be naught to heeding thee, Donald;
Was I a man, I'd be a man,
  Sae there's the last o' me, Donald.

JIRGING.—The noise *too* dry shoes make when walked with.

JIRT.—To squirt.

JISP.—A stain, or a piece decayed in a web of cloth.

JOCK.—John, also a name for the bull.

JOCKIE FAW, the GIPSIE LADDIE.—A celebrated gypsie who flourished about two hundred years ago, in the
south of Scotland. Mention is made of him in various
traditions; and in the old song of the *Annandale Thieves,*
honorable notice is taken. However, he himself is im-
mortalized in an ancient ballad, in which he is the hero;
which informs us of his enticing away the lady of *Lord*
Cassle in Ayrshire; the tale says he gave her a certain kind
of *ginger,* which *cuist* such a *glaumry* over her, that she
followed the gypsie through thick and thin; whether this
ginger was the *dodgell reepan* already spoken of, is not
known, but it had had a similar effect to it. I have heard
of an herb of the *daffie-down-dilly* stamp, which, if got
into a lady's shoe, that lady will follow the herbalist every
where; and that on its being put so once, when the lady
had to take off her shoes for the purpose of wading a
river, she changed her notion in the middle of the stream,
returned to the bank, extremely vexed with herself that she
had been so foolish, but the moment she put on her shoes
again, the *tid* took her, and made her wade and return,
and wade again, until she was quite exhausted. But to my
subject—Many editions of the song of the *Gypsie Laddie*
have now been given the world, but was ever this one of
mine given? Never—And I believe it to be as genuine
as any that have ever appeared :—

> The gypsies they came to Lord Cassle's yet,
>   And o but they sang ready,
> They sang sae sweet and sae complete,
>   That down came the lord's fair lady.
>
> O she came tripping down the stair,
>   Wi' a' her maids afore her,
> And as soon as they saw her weelfared face,
>   They cuist their glaumry owre her.

She gaed to them the gude white bread,
   And they gaed to her the *ginger*,
Then she gaed to them a far brawer thing,
   The gowd rings af her finger.

(Quo' she) to her maids, " there's my gay mantle,
   " And bring to me my plaidy,
" And tell my lord whan he comes hame,
   " I'm awa wi' a gypsie laddie."

For her lord he had to the hounting gane,
   Awa in the wild green wuddie,
And Jockie Faw the gypsie king,
   Saw him there wi' his cheeks sae ruddy.

On they mounted and af they rade,
   Ilk gypsie had a cuddy,
And whan through the *stincher* they did prance,
   They made the water muddy.

(Quo' she) " aft times this water I hae rade,
   " Wi' many a lord and lady,
" But never afore did I it wade,
   " To follow a gypsie laddie."

" Aft hae I lain, in a saft feather bed,
   " Wi' my gude lord aside me,
" But now I maun sleep in an auld reeky kill,
   " Alang wi' a gypsie laddie."

Sae whan that the yirl he came hame,
   His servants a' stood ready,
Some took his horse, and some drew his boots,
   But gane was his fair lady.

And whan he came ben to the parlour door,
   He asked for his fair lady,
But some denied, and ithers some replied,
   " She's awa wi' a gypsie laddie."

" Then saddle" (quoth he) " my gude black naig,
   " For the brown is never sae speedy,
" As I will neither eat nor drink,
   " Till I see my fair lady."

" I met wi' a cheel as I rade hame,
   " And thae queer stories said he,
" Sir, I saw this day a fairy queen,
   " Fu' pack wi' a gypsie laddie."

" I hae been east and I hae been west,
   " And in the lang town o' Kircadie,
" But the bonniest lass that ever I saw,
   " Was following a gypsie laddie."

Sae his lordship has rade owre hills and dales,
   And owre mony a wild hie mountain,
Until that he heard his ain lady say,
   " Now my lord will be hame frae the hounting."

" Than will you come hame my hinnie and my love,
  (Quoth he) to his charming dearie,
" And I'll keep ye ay in a braw close room,
  " Where the gypsies will never can steer ye."
(Said she) " I can swear by the sun and the stars,
  " And the moon whilk shines sae clearie,
" That I am as chaste for the gypsie Jockie Faw,
  " As the day my minnie did bear me."
" Gif ye wad swear by the sun,"(said he)
  " And the moon till ye wad deave me,
" Ay and tho' ye wad take a far bigger aith,
  " My dear I wadna believe ye."
" I'll tak ye hame, and the gypsies I'll hang,
  " Ay I'll make them girn in a wuddie,
" And afterwards I'll burn Jockie Faw,
  " Wha fashed himself wi' my fair lady."
(Quoth the gypsies) " we're fifteen weel made men,
  " Tho' the maist o' us be ill bred ay,
" Yet it wad be a pity we should a' hang for ane,
  " Wha fashed himself wi' your fair lady."
Quoth the lady, " my lord forgive them a',
  " For they nae ill e'er did ye,
" And gie ten guineas to the chief Jockie Faw,
  " For he is a worthy laddie."
The lord he hearkened to his fair dame,
  And o' but the gypsies war glad ay,
They danced round and round their merry Jockie Faw,
  And roosed the gypsie laddie.
Sae the lord rade hame wi' his charming spouse,
  Owre the hills and the haughs sae whunnie,
And the gypsies slade down by yon bonny burn side,
  To beek themsells there sae sunnie.

JOCK MULLDROCH.—A fellow who lived at *Craigwaggie,*
Galloway, once, perhaps about 150 years ago. Tradition
says that he *laid eggs,* ay eggs, larger than *goose eggs,* and
strangely spreckled black and yellow; he used to *cackle*
too after he laid them, which was on a *truff laft amang a
wheen breckans*; sometimes he was called *Craigwaggie's
meikle chuckie*; once a fortnight he is said to have produced
an egg, and his mother, after having sold a few of them as
bonny goose eggs, she set a couple of them beneath a *braw
tappend hen to clock.* Long and *dreich* did the favourite
chucky of *Lucky Mulldroch* sit on them before they were
hatched; at length they *chipped,* and out came two little

lads clad in green, and under the *gudewife's* care they *thrave*, and were well known long over the south of Scotland by the title of the *Birlies*. *Willie* and *Wattie Birly* were well liked by every body; they were something in the nature of *brownies*, or rather *mangrell fairies*. They vanished away though, and after the year *forty*, the year of the *lang storm*, they never were heard of; some think they sank in a *snaw wride*, and afterwards into a *Qua.*—See *Quaking Qua*.

Jock-tae-Leg.—Jock with *the one leg*; a large knife for kitchen use.

Jollock.—Jolly, fat, healthy, and hearty.

Jorgle.—The noise of broken bones.

Jorinker.—A bird of the tit-mouse species; its name is its cry.

Jottrell.—Any thing about to fall in pieces.

Jouk.—To avoid a blow by an active turn; also to conceal on a sudden.

Jow.—A driving sound as it were; a *swing* attended with a *sound*; it is hard to express the full meaning of *jow*. After the sad battle for Scotland of *Flodden Field*, when the "*flowers of the forest war a wed away*," fought 9th September, 1513, on the news coming to Edinburgh next day of the disaster, the magistrates gave out a proclamation, that the inhabitants were to get ready their "fensabill geir and wapponis for weir," and appear before them at the *jowing* of the common Tolbooth-*bell*. This is about the first time *jowing* appears in print. Burns has the bells in his Holy Fair "began to *jow* and croon," swing and sound. *Jow* and *show*, I dare say, are twins; and *show* and *shove* are one. *Shuggie show*, a "shaking shove."— We say of the sea, whiles in a stormy day, that the *jaws* of it are coming *jowing* in, rolling on the rocks and roaring.

JUGGLE.—To shake.

JUGGS.—Little decanters.

JUMM.—A noise of a singular nature; it is a deep hollow sound, which comes from the wild rocks of a sea-shore in the time of a storm, when the ocean is highly agitated; it forms as it were the bass to a sounding surf, and is heard by a keen naturalist to be a sound distinct by itself; it is not the sound of the *troubled waters,* nor the sound of the *hurling peebles,* but the sound that these combined draw out of the rocks by striking them; it is one of the wildest and most awful sounds in nature; it is just *jumm, jumm,* on a high and tremendous key.

JUMMLIE.—Sediment of ale.

JUMPERS.—Little maggots, which leap; common in hams.

JUNDIE.—A blow.

JUNRELLS.—Large irregular masses of stone, or other hard matter.

JUNT.—A large quantity of liquid of any kind, but how *large* is not yet determined. *Gowdie,* the cow, gives a *junt* of milk, but we know not how much that is, though we are aware it is a considerable deal. *Junt,* too, is understood to be more than expected.

JURR.—The noise a small water-fall makes, when it falls amongst loose stones and gravel.

JUTE.—Sourish ale.

JUTTLE.—To shake liquids.

JYBE.—To taunt.

JYPLE.—A person with clothes badly made.

K.

KAIL.—Colewort; also broth.

KAIL-BROSE.—A mixture of the oily scum which gathers on the *lee side of the broth pot*, and oatmeal.

KAILGULLY.—A large knife for cutting vegetables.

KAILRUNT.—The stalk of a colewort; a full-grown colewort.

KAIM-CLEANERS.—In old houses, by the side of the fireplace, horse-hair is found stuck in the holes of the *" standards"* of wood which support the old walls; this hair was used for cleaning combs. A person once told me, " that there was a bunch of hair for this purpose drilled into the hole of an oak beam, in an old house he lived in; and that this hair, though frequently cut with a knife close to the wood, soon grew out again as long as ever." From this, one may think that oak will give life to hair: the same person said, " that if one be buried in an oak coffin, the hair won't decay like the other matters belonging to the body, but continue to grow." These things must be better investigated, though I have heard that the nature of hair has puzzled able heads.

KAIMS.—Honey-combs.

KAIN.—Tithe-money, or money that seems to be needful to pay.

KAUCH.—To be in a *kauch*, to be in an extreme flutter, not knowing which way to turn; over head and ears in business.

KAVE.—To clean; to *kave* the corn, to separate the straw from the corn; there is much art in *kaving* grain.

KEB.—A blow.

KEB-EWES.—Ewes that have lost their lambs, so fattened for butchers.

T

KECHT.—A consumptive cough.

KECKLIN.—Making a foolish noise.

KEEK-BOO.—Bo-peep, toying, &c.

KEEL.—A reddish earthy stone, good for marking sheep.

KEELROW.—A Gallovidian country-dance; the song of the " *Keelrow*" is in " Cromek's Nithsdale and Galloway song."

KEEP-WHITE-ICE.—One of the many orders at curling. It is always given to the one about to play, and means, that he is to throw his stone, if possible, up the middle of the run, and not throw it to a side.

KELL's-RANGE.—A range of wild rocky moors, to the north of Galloway, covered with snow the greater part of the year.

KELPIES, or WATER-KELPIES.—Evil-disposed beings of the supernatural stamp, thought by the superstitious to haunt fords, and be the cause of people getting themselves drowned in crossing such places; it is said that they are kind to *maidens*, as generally all beings are; the following strange dialogue looks something like this:—

THE WATER-KELPIES AND THE MAIDEN.

The first kelpie—

> Look, behold the waning moon,
> Wading in her snow shoon,
> Through the whirling wild drift,
> Far amid the gloomy lift;
> Round her body pale a ring,
> Come, invoke the blast and sing.

Second kelpie—

> Ay' ye gloomy clouds, form
> Watery round Madam Storm;
> Croak away, thou freckled frog,
> Amongst the rushes of the bog.
> Now the tempest south is howling,
> Grumbling waves in anger rolling:
> Lash, dash, snow and hail,
> Ye mountain torrents never fail,

Sweep down the snoring herd,
Down with the flowery swaird ;
Sheep and goats all there,
Pour away, never fear.

Third kelpie—

Hallo ! On it pours,
Rain first, then sleety showers ;
The wind whistles while it blows,
Nipping hail, smooring snows ;
Rash, splash, it feels the charm,
For man's woe, full of harm.

Fourth kelpie—

Now our eddy madly boils,
Foams upon the ford, and toils ;
Burnbeckers neath the brow,
Flutter out, or smother'd now
You will be ; listen me,
Wing away, see, see
The water-rat, obliged to swim
For rest to the grassy brim.
Get ye into water deep
Ye hirrlings, and therein sleep ;
Now the froth, now the bubbles
Gather in behind the cobles,
Now the moon I cannot see,
That's the pleasant sight for me.

First kelpie—

Brother stand there and watch,
While I remain here and catch.
What is this, a craig o'heron ?
Hah, lad, you've got your fairing.
Here again, what are you ?
Rotten sheep, bow, wow.
Go, avaunt, float to hell,
What a most infernal smell.

Second kelpie—

So, brother, what is this,
Something surely not amiss ;
Garments like the azure swimming,
Border'd round with silver trimming,
A woman, oh ! perhaps a maid,
See her hair is out of braid ;
Poor heavenly, earthly creature,
Far the loveliest work of nature—
Dead are ye, or alive,
Speak can ye, strive, strive ?

Third kelpie—

> Alive she is, I heard her sigh,
> Bear her up in air high,
> If she be a virgin blooming,
> Free from art, unassuming,
> Surely to her we will give
> The fluid whereupon to live;
> But if she be not so,
> Down the torrent she shall go,
> Like the rotten sheep to hell,
> None but maids can break our spell.

Fourth kelpie—

> How loving is she, fair, fair,
> What locks of yellow hair;
> These are eyes none but a maid,
> Ever had, ever had.
> We will guard her from the storm,
> We shall save her gay form,
> We shall nurse her in the sun,
> And round about her radiance run;
> We all know how she came
> To us so devoid of shame.
> Cease storms, calm your blowing,
> Silence, hail, give over snowing;
> Peace be to the roaring ford,
> Until again we give the word.

KELTON-HILL-FAIR.—This is one of the largest meetings or gatherings of Gallovidians that are to be met with. This fair is held on a day about Midsummer, every year, on rising ground beside the *clauchan of Rhonhouse,* in the parish of Kelton. At this fair one is gratified with a sight of the peasantry of both Scotland and Ireland; and here may sometimes be *lifted* a tolerable idea of the *Donnybrook* of Erin, or *Ballinasloe*; at one time in danger of having the scull bared with a cudgel; at other times hemmed in, as it were, with *rowly-powly men, fling sticks,* and *sweetie-wives.* Then the ears get charmed with the hoarse throats of ballad singers, and not unfrequently nearly rode over with *horse-jockies.* And all this humbug and justling combined form the best of fun; one gets delighted. *Tennants Anster* rather seems flatter than the reality, though sometimes we see with the drollish poet. While the scenes thicken, the *tents* get crowded ; whisky is skilted over like whey ; bonny lasses are to be met with, who cling round one like binwud ; and who would not cling to them in return, sweet souls ? For an hour or two of bustling nonsense, then. I know of few places where it is to be had in greater perfection than at Kelton-hill-fair.

KEND GRUN.—Land we are acquainted with ; yet sometimes we wander on *kend grun* in misty nights, and walk fast until we entirely bewilder ourselves ; in such trying times, it is the best plan to sit down in some *dry beil,* until more light be flung on the subject. Writers, too, when they leave *kend grun,* are apt to go wrong, if they have not a genius of a vast nature to bring them back ; they are like navigators having lost all reckoning in the midst of a dreary ocean. Small wits, like myself, should never launch largely out to sea, but keep dabbling about the shores ; for if we try to flash with witches and ghosts beyond the cloud, like Shakspeare, or soar, like Milton, into regions far beyond our knowledge, we are apt to rue the day we ever left *kend grun.* But, as I said when I began this subject, we may wander even on *kend grun* ; so I may run myself wrong in *Gallowa,* a land I *weel ken.*

KENK.—To cough, having a severe cough. *Kenkhoast,* the chin-cough. To cure this, the mothers put their children through the *happers* of mills, when they fancy it leaves them.

KENT.—A large long staff; also a tall person.

KEP.—To intercept, so as to catch ; but the word does not go so far as some will have it, of absolute catching ; kepping is nothing more than " opposing and *wearing* ;" " he *kepped* the ball" means, he so weared in the ball with his hands, that he got hold of it.

KERMONT, the TANNER—A good composer of songs,
and a Gallovidian born and bred I believe. He is a tanner
by trade, and wrought sometime at Mr. Grayson's tan-
neree, Kirkcudbright, but has removed from thence some
years ago, and gone to Newtonstewart. His songs are
very natural, and contain some good strokes of humour.
I could name twenty persons and more in the south of
Scotland who write songs, but then their effusions are so
made up of art, that I refrain from speaking of them.
Kermont, though, methinks is an exception. His " *Lammas Fair*," is a good song, but his " *Laury o' Broom, Sir*,"
is famous. Some say he got help to compose it, but I
do not think so. I shall give it here as a curiosity. The
song of " *Cankerd King Cowan*," written by an Irishman,
for a *Gallovidian lay*, and this song of *Laury o' Broom*,
done in the *Irish style*, by a Gallovidian, are things very
amusing—

LAURY O' BROOM, SIR.

I am, do ye hear me, a weaver to trade,
   And my name it is Laury o' Broom, Sir,
My father he died, left me all that he had,
   Hoch! a good breeding sow and a loom, Sir.
I lived quite happy a very short space,
Then I married a wife who soon altered the case,
She black'd both my eyes, and she spat in my face,
   It was tight times for Laury o' Broom, Sir.

I thought to myself, that this would not long do,
   My passion I could not well smother,
So I instantly sold off my loom and my sow,
   And I pack'd the wife home to her mother.
Being thus, then, set free, I for Scotland did steer,
I left the sweet place that was once to me dear,
Whilst grief in my bosom was like to go tear
   The heart of poor Laury O'Broom, Sir.

On a staff o'er my shoulder my bundle I slung,
   My figure was one of the oddest,
I did not know which was the right road or wrong,
   But I stuck to the one that was broadest.
And at length I arrived at Donachadie,
Where I found to my grief I was stopp'd by the sea,
Then I wish'd I'd had wings, like the swallow, to flee,
   What a bird would be Laury O'Broom, Sir.

But I got aboard of a tight little smack,
  Just afraid's I'd been bound for the gallows,
Yet to keep up my spirits, I sang " Paddywhack,"
  As she toss'd o'er the turbulent billows.
At length I grew sick, and was like to go die,
My belly of meat it was empty, quite dry,
Hoch! I lay all besmear'd, like a pig in a sty,
  And " A Doctor," cried Laury O'Broom, Sir.

But the winds and the waters gave over to roar,
  And I mended, and jumped on deck, Sir,
Then went up the mast-ladder, to view Ireland once more,
  To the danger and risk of my neck, Sir.
Tho', alas! dear Hibernia was hid from my view,
I was damn'd to come down by the captain and crew,
Then I thought on my wife, and my loom and my sow ;
  But far distant was Laury O'Broom, Sir.

Then I found out the place where the " ship's clock" it lay,
  But 'twas too much for my comprehending,
I asked at the " skipper" the time of the day,
  But he, smiling, replied, she was standing.
The " sea-travel" seem'd very lonesome to me,
Because not a mile-stone I ever could see,
Nor an ale-house to call at from Donachadie,
  To cheer up poor Laury o' Broom, Sir.

At the quay of the port, then, we got to at last,
  And our big flying sheets we did lower, Sir,
I thought all my perilous dangers were past,
  When I got with my brogues to the shore, Sir,
A " tenpennie" paid for my passage, and then
I shoulder'd my bundle and cudgell again,
Ha, honey, farewel, said the captain and men,
  I'm your servant, quoth Laury O'Broom, Sir.

So the smack then I left, as you easily guess,
  And took a walk looking about me,
A man he gives two or three peeps at my dress,
  And thus he began to salute me :—
Do you know what the " croppies" in Ireland do now,
Or whether their numbers be many, or how ?
By my soul, neither croppies nor Ireland I know,
  I'm a Scotchman, says Laury O'Broom, Sir.

But quoth he, your a croppie, by the " cut of your hair ;"
  This struck me with terror and wonder,
So I instantly flung up his heels in the air,
  Hoch! I laid him as flat as a flounder.
Then off I did run, till I came to Glenluce,
As frightened's a crow, and as dizzy's a goose,
And whenever a person peep'd out of a house,
  I'm a madman, cried Laury O'Broom, Sir.

Being wearied at last tho', I stopp'd at an inn,
  The head public-house in the place, Sir,
I pop'd into the parlour, and called for some gin,
  The people stood all in amaze, Sir.
So I told I was a nobleman's son in disguise,
But the landlady told me my story was lies,
Sweet Paddie for ever, the landlord he cries,
  And out he kick'd Laury O'Broom, Sir.

From that hell of a shop, then, I soon did dismiss,
  And thought on my loom and my sow, Sir,
My wife, tho' the devil, was nothing to this,
  And a sigh from my bosom she drew, Sir.
The scenes of my youth then came fresh in my mind,
My little turf hut, where once happiness reigned,
Hoch ! Fortune thou'rt fickler far than the wind,
  How ye change with poor Laury O'Broom, Sir.

My spirits, however, I keeped up still,
  And pass'd o'er the wild Corse o' Slakes, Sir,
A fellow came up and cried " clean Kelton-hill,"
  We went into a "tent," soon, of stakes, Sir.
The whisky came round, there I drank and I sang,
The boxing began, and the cudgels they rang,
And right in the stomach I got such a bang,
  That hearted poor Laury O'Broom, Sir.

But soon I came to, and my mother o' the sloc,
  I whacked about with my might, Sir,
And or I knew rightly a friend from a foe,
  My wrists were in the *figure eight*, Sir.
So some then did kick me, and some did me trail,
I wished that my coat had been a coat of mail,
So snugly just here in Kircubrie's old jail,
  At last they've got Laury O'Broom, Sir.

Hoh, Fortune, you've blown me a damnable blast,
  And my folly you near make me rue, Sir,
I wish I was o'er the " long bridge o' Belfast,"
  Again to my loom and my sow, Sir.
For hunger at home and a day whiles of strife,
Between a poor boy and a hell of a wife,
Are innocent things to a rambling life,
  What a witness is Laury O'Broom, Sir.

So much then, and perhaps too much, of Laury
O'Broom, Sir. I never could catch a very correct copy
of this stave, so was compelled to add words and lines of
verses as I went on, to keep the sense together; and at
the last I was obliged to ask my own wayward muse for
three full verses.

KIBBLING—A rude stick or rung. Some put great value
on a favourite staff; listen to the *Irishman's Address to
his Cudgel*—

> Sweet mother of the sloe,
> Hoch! where did ye grow?
>   On the banks of the lovely Ban-water;
> By the hoakey, the like of thee never was carried,
> Six years have I with ye now thumped and barried,
> A dozen, sometimes, in a fair I have scared
>   With thee, just as hard's I could batter.
>
> In Dublin's big town
> You were very well known,
>   Some sculls I have there with ye cracked;
> From morning to night, I've taken delight,
> In joining and bruizing away at a fight,
> Hoh, Barney, the boy, was up to the slight
>   Of wielding thee well, he saved, he smacked.
>
> With thee in my hand,
> Not a wench in the land,
>   But I durst go catch in a twinkle;
> Where was the bulley could keep her from me,
> When determined was I that with me she should be?
> Who the devil could stand many downers from thee?
>   You play'd hell with a chap's periwinkle.
>
> Few matches for thee,
> In Erin there be,
>   But, for my countrie's sake, be there many;
> Give an Irishman whisky; O! rare Inishone,
> That would warm and would soften the heart of a stone,
> And a cudgel, like thee, then let him alone,
>   For, few dare oppose him, if any.

KILCH—A side blow; a catch; a stroke got unawares.

KILLICK—The flue of an anchor; the mouth of a pick-
axe.

KILLMAN—The man who attends to the kiln in a mill.
These are commonly very honest men, well liked by the
lasses. Mark the song—

> Weel, uncle, I shall never wed
>   The Cameronian Hill-man,
> But I'll rin haffers wi' the bed
>   O''Wattie Broom, the kill-man.
>
> For Wattie is a worthy lad,
>   And fu' o' warly skill, man,
> The ither prays and swaur than mad,
>   He's naething like the kill-man.

Nae gate an erran' I wad gang
  Mair soon than owre tae mill man,
For than I'd see or it was lang,
  My blythsome lad, the kill-man.
In the killogie, wi' his arms
  He clasps me till I thrill, man,
His seedie ingle finely warms,
  Whanere he steers't the kill-man.

In love he rows me ay about,
  I let him kiss his fill, man;
His goodness ay I never doubt,
  He's nae take-in, the kill-man,
And tho' he towsles me right aft,
  He never means nae ill, man;
He's daft about me, and I'm daft,
  About my darling kill-man.

Yestreen, I met him, blyth and gay,
  He splat a whusky gill, man;
And spak about the wadding-day,
  Right seriously the kill-man.

KILLOGGIE—The fire-place of the kiln.

KILLRAVAGE, OR CULLRAVAGE—A mob of disorderly
persons, either engaged in scenes of savage and actual
devilry, or intending to be so.

KILT—Proper method, right way, or right thing. We say of
such a one that is not properly up to his trade, that he has
not the *kilt* of it, and of those who well understand what
they are doing, that they have the *kilt o't*.   Can this word,
and *kilt*, a loose garment, be one? I know not: probably,
the Highland clans long ago used the phrase, " ye have
the *kilt o't*," to those of the same tribe or dress with
themselves, and those who were not, of course had not
the *kilt* of it.   The following tolerable verses were composed in a church, on seeing a countryman asleep while
a priest, (who had not the *kilt* of preaching), was holding
forth.   Probably *kilt* and *kent*—to know, are one:—

Whae'er ye be that taks y'er nap,
  Aside the pulpit bink,
Maun surely be a happy chap,
  Maun surely rightly think.
O! could I fa' asleep like thee
  I wad be unco glad,
Or, were my lugs but stuff'd awee,
  I wad na be sae bad,

For, o! I'm tortur'd wi' a gomf,
　Wha's gampin like a half-hang'd dog,
He weel deserves i'the arse a yomf,
　Or some as ill-far'd shog.

I, true, he has mista'en his trade,
　To learn to preach and pray,
To be a priest he ne'er was made,
　Nor ne'er will ony day.

O! this is really sad sad wark,
　For Godsake, say nae mair,
Ha, yet ye bow and maunt and bark,
　What hearer is na sair.

I see *frien Willie's* gude *red wig*
　Has an uneasy seat;
The *Duke o' Kent* doth yawning lig,
　And burn with wrathfu' heat.

Ay, a' wha are dear nature's frien's
　Are wearied to the bane,
Ilk way they sit, their flesh complains,
　And sauls within it grane.

We're no a squad that's ill to please,
　A silly cheel is fit,
A wee hotch heavenward will us ease,
　To meikle we'll submit.

But wull awuns! what can we say,
　'Bout thee, thou awsome gow,
A mass thou art o' saulless clay,
　A boss croon'd foozie frow.

A pity 'tis that we should be
　Sae troubled wi' the hash,
And that we dare get nane but he,
　And his slim senseless trash.

O! patronage, this is thy crime,
　Sae sorrowful to tell,
Cam ye frae regions high, sublime?
　Nay, ye cam out o' hell.

And there the sooner ye win back,
　For Christians 'twill be best,
Then, cheels wha ought to wear the black,
　Will come and gie us rest.

Snore on, snore on, my happy saul,
　Just like a stocking-loom,
And see to deave this dranting drawl,
　Which comes frae haurns sae toom.

Was ance I out o' this kirk door,
　They'll see weel, sees me back,
For this place I cannot endure
　Wi' patience on the rack.

I'll read my buik upon the hill
Ilk Sabbath-day that's clear,
And try mysell wi' heaven to fill,
And never mair come here.
Now Lord be thanked that his gab
Is fairly closed for ance,
Up come alang, my snorkin *Rab*,
And let us down the trance.

KILTED—Clothes furled up on the body are said to be
"*kilted*."

KILTIE—A spawned salmon ; they are then very lean.

KIMMER—A gude-wife.

KIMMERINS—The feasts at births. These, the "*Kimmers*,"
or gude-wives, have to themselves ; no men are allowed
to partake along with them.

KING AND QUEEN O' CANTELON—A chief school game.
Two of the swiftest of the boys are placed between two
doons, or places of safety; these, perhaps, two hundred
yards distant. All the other boys stand in one of these places
or *doons,* when the two fleet youths come forward, and
address them with this rhyme—

" King and Queen o' Cantelon,
" How mony mile to Babylon ;
" Six or seven, or a lang eight,
" Try to win there wi' candle-light."

When out, they run in hopes to get to Babylon, or the
other *doon,* but many of them get not near that place
before they are caught by the runners. Who *taens* them,
that is, lay their hands upon their heads, when they are
not allowed to run any more in that game, that is, until
they all be *taend* or taken. This sport has something,
methinks, of antiquity in it ; it seemeth to be a pantomime
of some scenes played off in the time of the Crusades.
King and Queen o' Cantelon evidently must be *King and
Queen o' Caledon,* but slightly changed by time. Then,
Babylon in the rhyme, the *way* they had to wander, and
hazard the being *caught* by the Infidels, all speak as to the
foundation of the game.

KING GALDERS—On the farm of *Cairnholly,* in the parish
of Kirkmabreck, stands a rarity, the large stone coffin

which held the body of a king, which tradition calls
" *King Galders*." It is at the present day, just as it has
been all along ; such a weighty concern has preserved it
from being removed. Around the tomb are many stones
of various lengths standing on end.

Murray, in his history, refers to the account of a *King
Galdus*, by a person named *Sympson*, and that his tomb is
beside the *Blednoch water*. The two kings must be one,
and how it comes he has two tombs, 1 cannot say ; the two
places are many miles distant. *Galders* was probably a
Dane, and the conjecture that Galloway derived her name
from him, is not unlikely.

KINTRA-CLASH.—The bad news with the few good astir
in the country.

KINTRA-COOSER.—A human stallion ; a fellow who de-
bauches many country girls.

KINTRA-SIDE.—That part of the country any one lives in,
is his kintra-side.

KIP CAIRNS.—An original of a very rare cast, and I am
sorry that I have not got enough about him, to enable me
to have a dash at his character. He was laird of a farm
called *Kip*, but the law and smuggling brought him to sell
it ; he died in indigence, and his death was lamented all
over the land of Galloway ; he is not yet forgotten by a
great many. And if any who knew him well would take
the trouble to publish, in a little book,

" *The Anecdotes o' Kip Cairns*,"

That book, I may prophecy, would repay them ten per
cent.

Come friend " *Morrison o' Fellen*," put thy " *bunch*"
through the *press*, or send them to me, for thou alone
canst do justice to *Kip Cairns*.

KIRKCORMOCK.—An ancient Gallovidian parish, like *Dunroddan, Gatah, Senwick, Kirkandros*, and others. The

names of such only remain now, and their *kirk-yards*, with perhaps the ruins of the *auld kirk*. At Dunroddan, the *fount*, which held the *holy water*, is yet to be seen in a fine state of perfection ; a blacksmith lately thought it might answer him for a *troch*, so introduced it into his *smiddy* ; but a worthy *kirk-yard antiquary*, whom I and many others could name, restored it to its ancient situation ; the *kirk-yard* of *Kirkcormock* is worthy of remark, on account of an old *troch stane*, three feet by two therein ; to translate its inscription was no small trouble, the characters being of old runic stamp, and the language Latin. " Honorabilis Sir Patricius Maclellana qui obit anno M.DXXXIV. anno XVIII. Ætatis." This gentleman seems to have been one of Maclellans of *Auchlane*, by a daughter of Herries, the second Lord Herries, who died (the lady) in the same year ; had the stone not been broke through at the middle, and otherways mutilated, more of its inscription might have been gathered. In this *kirk-yard* there is also a little tumulus, but lately much injured by a planting of young trees. O ! ye moderns, have mercy on the memory of your ancestors.

KIRKCUBRIE—Kirkcudbright. Not only the metropolis of Galloway, but a curiosity of itself, so it therefore lays double claim to my attention, though I am not going to say much about it. That it is ancient ; that its name comes from St. Cuthbert ; that it now is a place containing from two to three thousand inhabitants ; that though on a fine navigable river, it has little trade ; these, and other things are all in print already, and I print nothing over again if I know it. But few, perhaps, are aware, that *Willie Wallace* used to ship from this place to the court of France. South of the town is his camp ; this royal borough has many bonny *lasses* in it ; shall I name a few ? No, names are odious ; though, were I to do so, they would get husbands in a handclap ; there are also some very

social men in it, with whom I have spent some happy
hours, but there are foolish men in it also, and many very
fond of drink, termed tipplers; and, like all little places,
it is full of scandal, what not; but on the whole I have
never loved any small town so well as *Kirkcubrie.*

KIRKING.—That ceremony of attending the *kirk* the first
Sabbath after marriage; to the modest this is the most
trying concern in the matter, and commonly the man
blushes deeper than the woman; she seems quite uplifted,
having caught a husband, but not so *he*, because he has
got a wife; a number of friends and relatives generally
attend the *young fowk* on these occasions; the bride
comes forward *linked* or *huiked*, in the bridegroom's *best
man's arm*, and to this party are directed all eyes in the
church. What a nonsense in truth is to be borne with,
before an honest man can enter the matrimonial state. I
could wager, that in the space of twenty or thirty years,
gieing up the names, crying, kirking, &c. will be all dead
and damned, like the *cutty stool*; as so they should, for
where is their use? and the evil attending them is great;
in this age of light, the church laws in Scotland keep
many from marriage, for what is worse to endure than
foolish ceremonies? they do well enough when the eyes
of the mind are glazed with ignorance, but now they will
not do at all. I would not go through with them, as they
exist at present in my native *kirk*, were I sure to gain the
loveliest and richest female in Britain.

KIRK-LADDLES—The *laddles* or implements elders use in
rustic kirks, to gather the *bawbees* the congregations bring
with them for the *poor fowk.*

KIRK-STILES—The stepping stones people walk over
church-yard dykes on. At these places, of course, the
greatest crowd generally stands, on Sabbath days; there
the bonny lasses shew themselves with their best braws on
to the *young cheels*, and they in return flash before them
their *watch seals, braid claith, neat baws*, what not, which

is returning love for love; by degrees the flames burn
brisker, so that many have cause to both bless and rue the
day, they ever met *wi ither* at *kirk-stiles.*

KIRNIE.—A little pert impudent boy, who would wish to
be considered a man.

KIRNING—Churning. The art of making butter; the
upstaning kirn, is but little used now for that purpose,
only those who have little cream make use of it; the
barrle and *box kirns* have quite displaced it. But still the
doughty wife of Auchtermuchties will be well understood; yes, even though we adopt the South American's
method of churning. About Buenos Ayres, says my
famous wanderer, *Sawnie the Sailor,* green hides are
sewed together in the form of a large bag; the cream, or
ratherly the whole of the milk, is then poured in, for there
is no cream on the milk in warm countries; this bag, when
about full, is tied with a rope to a horse's tail, which drags
it scampering through the streets, until by agitation it
becomes coagulated.

KIRNS.—Harvest sports, after harvest is concluded; also,
the last hookful of grain that is to be cut, is called a *kirn ;*
who to cut this is a great matter; the *rip* left is three
plaited, the reapers range back a few yards, and fling at it
with their hooks, and he or she who flings, and cuts it, is
accounted the cleverest in the *boon* or *banwun.* That, at
the dancing *ateen,* he or she wears in the hat or bonnet
like a soldier's feather, the whole of the night, beautifully
busked with ribbons of various hues. Afterwards it is
hung up in a conspicuous part of the house, and given to
Bill Jock, the *king o' the Byre,* on *Auld Candlemas-day,*
so that none of the kye, the incoming year may be guilty
of *picking-cauve.* *Ranting kirns* are now bid farewel to
Galloway almost; refinement and the inroads of low Irish
reapers, are the cause; anciently the famous *laird o' Senwick* used to send for a fiddler out of Dumfries, to give

music to his *kirns,* a distance of thirty miles; this was running the matter to a high pitch.

KIRNSTAFF.—That long staff with a circular frame on the head of it, used anciently, when " upstanding *kirns*" were fashionable.

KIRR.—Blythe, cheerful, &c.: a person so inclined is said to be a *kirr* body.

KIRSENING or CRISENING.—Christening, the ceremony of baptism ; to these, large parties are invited, and feasting and fun are the result ; the sketch of a curious scene, seen at one of these meetings, runneth thus—

At a kirsening yesterday down in the glen,
War assembled a possey o' crouse honest men,
Wha cracket their jokes, and discussed the wather,
For a frost some wad wish, for a thow some wad rather.
Whan the job was got owre, the grave ceremony,
The tea was set down on the table sae bonny,
The faurls and the kebbuck, the butter and ham,
The binnie, the short-bread on ither did cram.
The cups round the trays in their orbits war placed,
A couple o' trackpots the system weel graced,
What-a glorious sight, see the kettle a reeking,
The winsome gude wife a' the needfu's a seeking.
Wi' his kindness the gude man is ay in the gate,
He fain wad assist but the body is blate,
He canna weel sit, and he canna gae rise,
What a portrait is his, between doubt and surprise.
Draw in now's the word, while ilk mou' ran wi' water,
Come draw round the table, clean changed the clatter,
The priest meikle swankie declined the chair,
Sae 'twas a gye bout to get ony else there.
His seat it should be on the lid o' a chest,
Pretending to act like the humblest guest,
But watch how he'd look'd had ony neglected,
To hand him alike wi' their comrades respected.
Mair wark about him there maun be than 'bout fifty,
Wi' flethering and serving to keep him in ti.t ay,
His jokes maun be laugh'd at, tho' not worth a doit,
And ilk tale he tells is an unco exploit.
At last every gossip has got to its station,
A grace is a drawling to grace the occasion,
Whilk ended, adown sunk the *black-garbed boss,*
On the lid o' the worm-eaten chest wi' a soss.

U

But it proving frail for his corpus sae gravid,
Down, down it did crash, and his feet ill behaved,
Up aloft quick they drave, causing sic an erruction,
Owrewhelming the truckery a' wi' destruction.
The tea cups in air were like pearies a turning,
The *scau:* they contain'd was the company burning,
What waistcoats and breeks were a screeding and ripping,
Some down and some up, near the na'el were a stripping.
The blushiony blisters on briskets and thees,
Soon started and spread by alarming degrees,
The priest was haurl'd out wi' a gye deal o' trouble,
 Frae whar he lay jam't, like a sack in the double.
The gude wife kend hardly what way she should look,
Her husband thought ance faith on " taking the book,"
But bottles o' whusky and some o' gude gin,
War turn'd into toddy and brought raeming in,
Whilk welcomer company, soon grew to be,
Than a fat foolish priest and a spoutroch o' tea.

KITH.—Acquaintance.

KITTIE.—A common name, or rather an universal one, for
all cows ; witness the strange old rhyme—

> There was an auld man stood on a stane,
> Awa i'the craft his leefu' lane,
> And cried on his bonny sleek kye to him hame.
> " Kitty my Mailly, Kitty her mither,
> " Kitty my Do, and Kitty Billswither,
> " Rangletie, Spangletie, Crook, and Cowd rye,
> " And thae war the names o' the auld man's kye"—
> > *Legendary Wallet.*

KITTLE.—To tickle ; also, to bring forth kittens.

KITTS.—Vessels for holding water.

KIVAN.—A covey, such as of partridges.

KNACKUZ.—A person who talks quick, snappish, and ever
chattering.

KNAPING.—The talk of a *knackuz* ; one ever on the catch,
whutthroat fuffing, confab of weazles.

KNAP O' THE KNEE.—The lid of the knee.

KYTHE.—To look like ourselves. To seem just what we
are, without any guile or hypocrisy; to do so is honesty.
And " An honest man's the noblest work of God."

L.

LAB.—To be intoxicated.

LABB.—The sound of the waves of a summer sea, as they sweetly kiss the rocky strand.

LADE.—Load; also the stream which drives a mill.

LADY O' THE MEADOW.—A sweet smelling plant, with a cream-coloured flower, which grows in meadows.

LAE.—Leave.

LAGGAN.—Fatiguing, beginning to weary.

LAGGANS.—Dresses for the legs.

LAGGIES.—A name for geese; *laggie! laggie!* is the call on geese.

LAGGIN.—That part of a wooden vessel, in which the bottom rests.

LAGGIN-GIRD.—That gird round the " *laggin,*" or " *staps*" which compose the sides of the bottom of any vessel ; this *gird* is always considered the chief one about wooden vessels.

LAIGH-FIEL.—Low lands, the reverse of the moor lands ; thus we say a *Laigh-fiel farm,* a *Laigh fiel lass,* &c.

LAIRD.—The lord of a manor; some of these are the best, and others the worst characters in Scotland ; who has not heard of *Laird Wiggiewussock* ? his lands lay on the Solway shore. Greedy as the grave was he, his gourmand imagination saw an island off his shore a little way, once in seven years. Thus would he describe it :—" O ! it was a bonny big isle ; I saw gran swankies o' nowt on't, feeding on rough claver fiels ; rare corn growing too, every stalk o't as thick as my wee finger, and ilka head wad hae filled my gowpins. Apple trees I saw there, wi' apples hinging swagging on them like warping clues, the haleware o't seemed to be gran plowable lan. I cud hae made sillar on't, like sclate stanes." (Then would he add)—" O ! if I had got a spunk o' kennelling on't, it a' wad hae become my ain ; the Manxmen's Isle was ance enchanted the same way, but a spark o' fire lighted on't ance frae out a sailor's pipe, broke the charm, whilk has hinner'd it to sink mair ; but war a' the fires at ony time to gang out, it wad just gae whar it was again ; ance they went a' out but ae wee bit gleed in *Laxy*, and faith, the Isle o' Man was begun to shog and quake."

Mine reverend original, *Nathan M'Kie*, was once obliged to leave his rural abode, the *Manse o' Baulmagie*, and go to London on some important business ; his friends in the mighty metropolis were glad to see him, and introduced the worthy eccentric every where, as a piece of great curiosity. A young *German lady*, hearing of *Nathan*, in some of her gay circles, wished very much to be some evening where he was, to see the rare Scotch clergyman, the which wish she was soon gratified with ; after chatting with the strange man, in rather a saucy way, she asked at him if he knew " what kind of an *animal* a *Scottish laird* was ?" adding, at the same time, that she had " read Buffon, Linnæus, and other naturalists, without finding any satisfaction." Nathan turned his queer phiz towards her, and quoth—(giving himself a *hursle or twa* at the same time)—" Wi' faith, madam, I'm nae great naturalist either, but I believe the *Scottish laird* to be an animal unco like your petty *German prince* ahame, in being baith damned *poor*, and as *proud*."

Lair'd.—Stuck in mire. The Moorlands in particular are full of dangerous places for animals to sink in ; these seem green and inviting, but no sooner are they entered upon than they are found to be all a deception.

" I set af tae Moors ance (quoth a Lowland farmer), to buy a wheen *fogging ewes*; I had the *Mall mare* aneath me, the best stump o' a beast ever I had ; owre ae hag after anither I rade, and crossed mony a garry, till every bane in my body was sair."

" My chief moor house was Drummruck ; there was 1
steering, when down sunk the Mall mare wi' a snore, in
ane o' thae green flow bogs ; 1 gaed on tae tap o' a hie
hill, and *wow'd* wi' my hat, and in less than a quarter of an
hour ten herds, wi' twice as mony dogs, gathered to me :
we gaed down tae mare, pull'd, and better pull'd ; I dare
say we had to draw her near hauf a mile, afore we cam
to steave grun.

" The poor brute was a' racked to pieces, and never was
like the same beast after. I gaed the lads shillings a-
piece, and ane I gaed hauf-a-crown to, to guide me to
the road that led hame. Sae I gat back again, but if ever
I ride sic anither fool erran, it will be de'ils queer to
me."

LAIRD COWTART—Or the obstinate man. His proper
name was *James Coltart* ; he was a labouring man, as I am
told, the greater part of his life ; and whether he became
heir to a little house and garden in the suburbs of Kirkcudbright, or obtained it by his own honest industry, I
know not ; however, a little *laird* he was, and went the
most of his days under the name of *Laird Cowtart.* He
was the most attentive man to his word ever known in
Galloway. What he at any time said, that he would have
abided by to the last. For a trifling wager, he sat the
length of a summer day once on the *"rigging of a barn,"*
with his face to the wind, not flinching an inch from Boreas ; at another time, for a similar bet, he sat upon a
brow for a whole day, and gazed directly at the *sun* ; no
eagle ever looked Sol so boldly in the face. There was a
merchant in Kirkcudbright, of the name of *Harris,* who
sold groceries ; this person and the laird once disputed
about something, and our obstinate man said "he would
purchase nothing out of his shop more, nor allow himself
to taste of any of his wares." The laird's wife, however,
who knew nothing of her husband's determination, bought
some candles from Harris ; on their being used for lighting

up the house, the good man inquired of her, " where she had bought them ?" on being told from Harris, he spread his *grey plaid* between the candle and him, in order to keep himself out of its hateful light. Another time the mistress purchased from this merchant some barley for the broth, the laird knew not of the matter, till he had dined on the said broth ; so in his stomach they should not remain, he raged about, and there was no peace in the house, until the laird had disgorged what of them he had swallowed, every "*groat.*" He used to make "*beeskeps,*" in the evenings, when his day's work was over, that's to say, his " *day's work*" with those with whom he was employed ; once while so engaged, out before his door in the open air, the wife came and called him to supper; he said "he would come if she did not call him again," the wife forgot though, came out after a little, and called James to come iu to his "*champed potatoes ;*"—" ay, ay, gude wife," he exclaimed, " ye hae done for me now ;" as usual he held by his word, and amused himself sitting out all night. Being challenged once, coming through a field, by its tenant, that he had no right to come that way, the laird said, "his feet should never touch the grass of that field more ;" some of the laird's fellow-labourers heard of his determination, and bore him into the field by force ; there he lay on his back with his feet up in the air, and roared and cried so mightily, that they were obliged to bear him out of it again. I could multiply specimens of obstinacy, this way, for a long time, and give many of his singular sayings, but these may suffice ; he drove a mule in a little cart long, and many thought he and the *mule* were a " dead match ;" he was always considered to be rigidly honest, was well liked, and the good family of Selkirk was all along very kind to him.

LAIRD O' COOL'S GHAIST.—We have not a more popular tale or pamphlet in Galloway, than the one bearing the title of this article. The *Laird o' Cool* flourished about one hundred years ago, in the parish of Buittle; he was proprietor of a farm therein, called *Cool,* and how he became so was never rightly known; it is the belief of all, however, that there was *foul play* in the matter, either by getting wills and deeds signed by *dead mens' hands,* or some such way. When this laird left the world, as other men do, his *ghaist* or *ghost,* returned soon after; was seen by many *stegging* about the estate, like a thing in trouble, to the terror of the people about; it was frequently seen sitting down on a stone, termed a *cool stane;* at length the priest of the parish would *lay him,* a thing of the most serious nature in those days; the *ghaist* gave him the reasons why it could not remain in darkness for the deeds it had done when in the flesh; all of which crimes the priest promised to remedy, if it would trouble the land of light no more; so, by praying and circumscribing circles with *cauk* and *keel,* the terrific task was accomplished, the *laird's ghaist* sank into the earth, and has never more burst the cerements of the tomb.

LAIRING STAFF.—A staff used by herd boys to drive the flocks to their *lair;* sometimes it is termed the *lairer.*

LAMETER—A cripple. The dialogue of two beggars, who met once on a country-cross road, ran thus:—"What's come o' daughter Mary, now?" quoth the one to other; " Mary? she's married," was the reply; and " wha has Mary gotten?" added the inquirer; " a braw *horsecripple,*" answered the *mither.* " Weel done Mary! (said the other) we maun hae a blaw o' the pipe owre that thegether."

LAMMAS SPATES.—Those heavy falls of rain, common about *Lammas* or Midsummer. Farmers who live by the banks of *waters,* prepare themselves against the falling of these *spates* or *spouts,* by removing every thing out of the river's way; that though it swells, and comes foaming down, it can do them no injury; not rob them of their *wunter's fodder.*

LAMPER EELS.—Eels, common in spring wells during summer; they are so much like horse-hair, that the folks think it is hair alive; they even put *hair* in the water to see if it will become *lamper eels*, but I have never known the trial to succeed. It is wonderful to examine these *lampreys*, to see they are things of life, and seemingly without either *head* or *tail*; cut them in twenty pieces, each piece is just a little *eel*, having the same motions, be it one inch, or be it ten in length.

LAN-EN'.—The end of ridges.

LANDIN—Landing. Ending with a "*set*," at shearing, cutting through from one side of the field to the other.

LANGLES—Manacles. Home-made fetters.

LANG MEGS.—A name for a species of long apple.

LANG-NEBBED.—Having a long beak, bill, or nib; " Gude preserve us frae a' witches, warlocks, and *lang-nebbed* things ;" this is one of the greatest wishes of the country people ; they consider that some of the beings of the nocturnal world have *sonsy snouts*, like *powder-horns*. Words too, in the English tongue, difficult to be understood, are said to be *lang-nebbed* or *double-breasted*; sometime ago at country schools, when the scholars were learning to read the *buik*, whenever they came to a cramp word to pronounce, the *Dominies* bade them call that a *passover*, and " *syne skelp awa.*" It may be added too, that some of those windy terms in the nomenclatures of our modern sciences, are truly *lang-nebbed*, and may be made passovers by sensible men.

LAPPELS.—The folds on the front of a coat.

LAPPER.—Snow in the act of melting. Lapper'd, curdled. " The milk sits *lapper'd* in the dirty coags," saith poor Bob Fergusson, as bright a young genius as ever sang on the earth. " The *lapper'd* cluds conglobe and roll," saith another author—perhaps myself.

LAW.—A high hill.

Laying Ghaists.—When ghosts showed their pale faces in the days of yore, the ministers of the word *laid* them by praying; that is to say, they described circles, stood within them (for over the circumference of a circle no *ghaist* durst pass), and there they addressed the foul spirit, until it sunk into the earth; they then crossed the place with lines, which hindered them from rising any more.

> Awa, awa, thou fearfu' ghaist,
> Flee hence and ne'er return,
> In thy dark chaumer there gae rest,
> Lae us and boggle burn—
>
> *Auld sang.*

Laying Sheep.—The art of putting greasy matters on sheep, so that they may be kept warmer through winter. See the article *Sheep-smearing.*

Lead o' the Ice.—A curler's phrase, and means the bias of ice. Many, however, when they do not play well, ascribe their bad success to the unevenness of the ice; man, generally speaking, being loath to take a fault to himself.

Lead the Ice.—Another curler's term, being the order given to the first player, when about to play; also to any player, when stones are in the direct way to the "*tee.*"

Lee.—The ashes of green weeds, such as *breckans*; when burned, *gude wives* use it in bleaching; also, *lee*, to lie, to tell fibs or untruths; and also, *lee*, a place surrounded by hills, an open space, yet sheltered from almost every blast. What for a song, is

THE SHEPHERD OWRE THE LEE.

> Awa frae me now Sawnie lad,
> And dinna fash me mair,
> We a' ken weel your purse has gowd,
> And that your head has lair;
> But for your sillar and your lair,
> I dinna care a flee,
> My love is Tam the shepherd boy,
> Wha whistles owre the lee.

Pair cheel he canna gab like you,
  Nor's cled in sic braw claise,
But what he says is sweeter far,
  And ay his dress does please ;
He is the darling o' my heart,
  And ever mair will be,
My bonny, merry, shepherd boy,
  Wha whistles owre the lee.

The morning whan he climbs the hill,
  The laverocks to him sing,
And round him do the paitrics trip,
  And mawkins skip and spring ;
They a' luik blyth at my dear Tam,
  But no sae blyth as me,
For he is my lovely shepherd lad,
  And whistles owre the lee.

O ! happy is the sailor lad,
  Whan he comes aff the sea,
And wi' his bonny lassie meets,
  To kiss and crack awee ;
But wha can happier be than me,
  Aneath the hawthorn tree,
Wi' my cheerfu', harmless, shepherd lad,
  Wha whistles owre the lee.

LEEMERS.—Nuts which leave their husks easily.

LEESE.—To arrange, to trim, to sort, &c.

LEESH.—A piece of tough string.

LEESH-FALLOWS.—Tough strong fellows.

LET ON.—A phrase, meaning " the giving a hint of any thing ;" never " let-on," we say to those whom we wish to keep secret some little thing we have told them ; that is to say, not to hint the matter to any other.

LETTERED-CRAIGS.—In various places of Galloway, large crags are to be met with, having very ancient writings on them, some of which the antiquary deciphers, but others not ; one of these, in the farm of Knockiebay in the *Shire*, has cut deep on the upper side—

  " Lift me up, and I'll tell ye more."

Many people have, in separate years, as time rolls on, gathered to this rock, and after much labour, have succeeded in lifting it up, with the hopes, no doubt, of being well repaid for their trouble with the treasure beneath ; but how must they have been deceived, when, instead of finding any gold, they find wrote on its ground side,

> " Lay me down as I was before."

It must have been no small wag in the days away, who invented this. On another, in a neighbouring parish, this strange inscription is found cut—

> " This stane lies on auld Robbin's wame,
> " His purse and his staff are aside the same,
> " If thou thinks this wrang, tak the stane af my wame,
> " And lay it on thine to preserve thy name."

Sawners M'Clurg, the old innkeeper, at *Blednoch Brig,* about eighty years ago, allowed almost every kind of *wildness* to go on in his house, except fighting ; and whenever any rustics started a *collieshangie,* Sawners reached for a *thick stick,* he kept up in the brace, and being a very strong man, stood up and gave the ground one *thump* with it, saying, *quietness is best* ; when quietness instantly took place. At last, when he went the way of all men, a friend laid a rude rock on him, with this epitaph deeply engraved on it—

> " Beneath lies Sawners M'Clurg,
> " Enjoying his quiet rest,
> " When he was alive he ay said,
> " Quietness was best."

This inscription nearly pleases me as well as that one a fellow blabbed carelessly out, on his master, who offered fifty pounds, to him who should write the best thing on his grave-stone :—

> " Here lies Billy Knox,
> " Wha lived and died like ither folks."

So he cheated many a learned poet.

LEUG.—A tall, ill-looking man.

LEW—A heat. Stacks of corn are said to take a *"lew,"* when they are built, not being dry, when they heat.

LEWRE.—A long pole, a lever.

LEZIE.—The name for Elizabeth.

LICHTS.—The lungs of an animal.

LIDDERIE.—Feeble and lazy.

LIDED.—Mixed, thickened, &c.

LIFT.—A term much in use at rustic funerals ; *let us lift,* say those people at these occasions, when they have had five or six *services* ; which means, let us *lift* the corpse and be going, for we have had enough, though it is well known not to be come to that time yet, and that all they want by repeating often, *let us lift, boys,* is to have another *service,* or round of bread, cheese, and whisky, so that when lifting time comes, some of those drunken and gormandizing mourners can scarcely *lift* themselves, never speaking of being able to *lift* others. To *lift a brae,* is to ascend a brow. *Lift,* also means the whole of the sky, that can be seen at once ; anciently, says tradition, the people fancied that there were some mighty persons far above the firmament, who had always in *lift,* as it were, the whole of the celestial regions, and who hindered the clouds and heavenly bodies from absolutely falling on them, and that they carried the clouds from place to place, as they thought fit ; hence the word *carry* ; these were the times when " spirits came on the blast," and ruled the whirlwind and the storm.

LIGGETT.—A reclining gate—from *lig,* to recline, and *gate* ; they must recline, or they would not close of themselves ; they are hung on what is termed a *hangrell* ; in the hold-stone at the foot is a *bot* to turn on, called a *bot-stane* ; the long bar which crosses the others obliquely, is the *sord.*

LINCLUDEN.—A venerable old college in ruins, standing on the lovely banks of Nith, a little above Dumfries.—Francis Grose, in his antiquities of Scotland, takes notice of it, but as he has not spoke about matters to be met

with at this place, respecting Galloway, it becomes me to
do so. On entering the chancel, one is struck with awe
and wonder, at seeing the remains of ancient grandeur,
of the most beautiful workmanship and decoration ; what
first attracts notice, is the tomb of Margaret, eldest
daughter of King Robert the Third, sister of the gallant
King James the First, (who was cruelly murdered at Perth,
by his uncle, cousin, and others, who were his confidants)
and wife of Archibald, fourth Earl of Douglass, and first
Duke of Touraine in France, (who was slain at the battle
of Vernuil, 17th August, 1424, and lies buried in the
church of St. Gratian, in Tours, the capital of his duchy).
Margaret was alive May, 1426 ; over the tomb is inscribed, in Gothic characters—

Ꭿ l'aïde de ꭍíeu.

" Hic jacet, Ana Margaretta, regis Scocie,
filia quoda comitissa de Douglas Ana
Galwidie et vallis Anadie."

Her tomb-stone, which has no inscription, is lying
broken in the grave. This tomb is beautifully decorated
all round and over the top ; in the midst of the decora-
tions is the representation of three large chalices or cups,
intermixed with a heart and three stars, the arms of the
Douglasses ; the former from the *heart* of Robert Bruce,
entrusted to the *good Sir James* ; and the *stars*, by marriage
with the heiress of Bothwell, in the person of Archibald,
the third earl, commonly called the *grim*. On the left of
this beautiful tomb, which should be told, is on the north
wall of the chancel, is a door much ornamented ; over
it is cut out the *heart, stars,* and *lion rampant* ; the
latter, the *arms of Galloway*, of which the Douglasses were
lords. On both sides of the wall in the chancel are many
shields, some with arms, some plain ; but in those having
arms, the *lion, heart,* and *stars*, prevail ; over one of the
shields, and cut out on the south wall, (supposed to belong

to *Stewart of Bonkill,*) is a scroll, with a few words in
the Gothic or Saxon character. but which stands *so high*
that it is impossible to decipher the inscription with
a *common ladder*; on the whole, this college is a noble
old pile, and worthy of walking a long summer day to
see. What holy emblems and inscriptions there are
about it!—the Three in one, surrounded by a glory, viz.
The Father, Son, and Holy Ghost, with the words *Jesu
Christi*, frequently appear; also Mary and the Child,
with the seven wise men kneeling before them; and, according to the *Golden Legend*, the two first figures of this
group seem armed. I may add, that Margaret, mentioned
already, daughter of King Robert the Third, whose husband
was Archibald, the fourth Earl of Douglass, was nicknamed *Tyne Man*, from the many battles he *tyned* or lost,
and his general unsuccess; he was wounded at Hamilton,
and taken prisoner by Hotspur Percy; refused to be delivered up to King Henry the Fourth. This and other bad
blood was the pretence for the Percy rebelling, where
defeat attended them, and where Douglass was made prisoner by Henry the Fourth, 1403. It seems, the inscription was made before either *Maggie*, or her *grim* husband died; as he had the gift of the duchy of Touraine,
April, 1424, and fell in battle, August the same year.
Now, the wife was alive May, 1426, for at this date she
had a charter—" To Margaret, Duchess of Touraine,
Countess of Douglass, Lady of Galloway and Annandale,
of the lordship of Galloway, as possessed by Archibald,
Duke of Touraine, and Archibald de Douglass his father,"
according to *Wood's Peerage*, page 427. But I am sick of
dates and learned antiquity, as I can extract no fun out of
them; however, I am the devil's own drudge when I set
fairly to.

Lingle-back.—Having a long weak back.

Linked.—Persons walking arm-in-arm, are said to be linked
or *huiked*.

LINKS O' PEATS.—Each division of a *peat-stack*, is called a *link*; so the stack is made up of *links*.

LINGED.—Lashed, beaten, &c.

LINTIE.—A linnet; also, a sweet young child.

LINTSTRAIK.—A head or handful of new-dressed flax.

LIPPIN-FU'.—Brimming full to the lips.

LIRK.—A wrinkle, a crevice.

LITCH.—To strike over.

LITH.—A joint; also, one of those divisions of an orange, or onion, of which they are composed.

LOANING.—A road which has a dyke on either side.

LOCHINBRACK-WELL.—A loch scarcely worth the speaking about, was it not for the famous mineral fountain beside it; the waters of which are of a strong chalybeate nature, good for removing pains in the stomach, and other complaints, which causes it in the proper season to be well attended by invalids; and if there were more houses about it than are, the larger, doubtless, would be the company. The *loch* answers well for the waterers to fish in, while the moors around are inhabited by grouse, and other moor fowl.

LOCH SKEROCH.—A large, wild, loch, to the north of Galloway, famous for its *scythe sand*. This is found on the beach of the lake, and is wrought of grey-stones, in the lake by the waters; it is sold in shops during the mowing season, at about twopence the Scotch pint.

LODDANS.—Small pools of standing water.

LOGGIE.—A fire in a snug place, or a snug place for a fire.

LOGGWATER.—Luke-warm water.

LOITS.—Those liquid drops, which leap out of pots when they are boiling, and *scaud* those persons seated round the *ingle*.

Lonkor.—A hole built through dykes, to allow sheep to pass. I have no idea where this word is derived from; probably from the same source as *loan*.

Loof-bane.—The centre of the palm of the hand.

Loofie Channlestanes.—When curling first began, it was played by flat stones, or *loofies*; these are yet to be found in old lochs.

Loofies.—Plain mittens for the hands.

Loot-down.—To stoop down.

Loup the Bullocks.—A very rustic sort of amusement. Young men go out to a green meadow, and there, on *" all fours,"* plant themselves in a row about two yards distant from each other. Then he who is stationed farthest back in the *" bullock rank"* starts up, and leaps over the other *bullocks* before him, by laying his hands on each of their backs; and when he gets over the last one, leans down himself as before, whilst all the others, in rotation, follow his example; then he starts and leaps again.

But what makes this fun of a *bullock* or brutish description, is the severe tumbles the leapers often meet with; for that *bullock* is considered the most famous of the *" herd"* that can heave up the *" rump"* highest and smartest, when the leaper is going over, and can launch him on his nose, to the effusion of his blood on the meadow; yes, much *" claret,"* to use the slang of pugilists has been spilt, and many wrists sprained at this work.

I have sometimes thought that we have borrowed this *" recreation"* from our neighbours of the *" green isle,"* as, at their *" wakes"* they have a *" play"* much of the same kind, which they seem to enjoy, called *" Riding Father Doud."* One of the *" wakers"* takes a stool in his hand, another mounts that one's back; then, *" Father Doud"* begins a rearing and plunging, and if he unhorses his rider with a dash, he does well. These Irish wakes must surely be very singular frolics. There is another " play" at them called " *kicking the brogue,*" which is even ruder than "*Riding Father Doud* ;" and a third too, behind neither of them in rustic madness, called " *Scuddieloof.*" These rough concerns originate from a hatred they have at too much melancholy ; for, when the parents, or other friends of the deceased, see a person at the " wake" dull, and sitting sorry-like, they get displeased, and will say, " Why came ye here to mourn, for one that's in Heaven ?" At these meetings all are made welcome, and a *Scotch stranger* is adored. Much whisky is drank at them, and plenty of tobacco smoked. Amongst the lower orders of the people there is no scene like a " wake." And to see the relations of the defunct Papist retiring, one by one, now and then, and talking and asking questions at the cold corpse, really bespeaks a terrible ignorance and gross superstition. If the deceased has left behind a wife, then will she lean over her breathless husband, and go on with her tongue in the following manner, rocking her body to the words she utters :—" And o' *Barnie,* why are ye gaen to lave me ? what harm did I to ye, *Barnie?* I never struck ye, nor slighted ye ; the loom will stand toom now, for the want o' ye, *Barnie*; and how will I get out the *web* ? and how shall I get turf for the fire, *Barnie* ? O ! why man did ye lave me," and so on. Then the *daughter Bridget,* or the *son Morgan,* will go and make their wail, perhaps, in a similar manner. But this wailing gets into howling on the day of the funeral : like the natives of some savage nations, they follow the bier, giving out shrieks and howls that are heard miles off. " *Oho*" is sounded on a thousand different keys. The priests generally attend the funerals of those who die in their parishes, and this attention is for the sake of their purses, as all their " *attentions*" are.

x

When they come to a " cross-road," or any thing like a
" *cross*," the corpse is laid down on the ground by the
bearers, and set up at " *aunction*" by the priest. " And
who will give me most for the sake of this man's *soul* ?"
will he say.   Then one will bid three-pence, another
perhaps five-pence, and a third may probably give a penny
more, which six-pence his reverence pockets, and tells his
poor infatuated followers " that this will help the deceased
through *purgatory.*"   A corpse has been known to have
been " set up" by a priest ten different times on its way to
the grave.   When the interment of the body is over, the
priest returns to the " *Burial house,*" and scares by his
words the " *spirit*" of the deceased away, which is
thought to linger behind about the " *eazles o' the house,*"
and other strange places.   He then regulates the " *beads*"
of the family, puts all the " *saints*" in order; and if, as
before fancied, it has been a man that death has taken
away, the priest, for common, passes the night with the
widow woman, and trims her " *beads*" in secret.   But, I
am falling into my wandering system, digressing a little, to
expose strange truths; truths that I have fallen in with
while dipping into the manners of the rustic world, and
may be firmly depended on to be strictly true.   To give
the rude manners of Erin fair play, I may some day soon
put through the *press* a small treatise, written about them
entirely.

LOVEANENDIE!—An exclamation, " O ! strange."

LOWE, the Poet—A person about whom a great deal has
    been written and said, and for what reason I have never
    rightly known.   He is held up as being the best poet that
    ever sang in Galloway.   Far be it from me to take any
    thing from his character; yet I cannot help saying that I
    think more notice has been taken of him than he deserves.
    His whole fame as a poet, rests on the song of " Mary,
    weep no more for me ;" and it is doubtful whether ever he

composed a line of it. I met with an honest man once, who told me " that he knew an old woman who sang it long before *Lowe* was born." Lowe had the merit, however, of singing and making it popular at his *singing schools*; and let him be the author or not, still the song has nothing very original about it. There are ten times better songs, the productions of Galloway bards, and not a word about them. However, Fame trump away; stop not one of thy blasts for Lowe, for a wretch like me.

Lowne.—Calm, not windy; *be lowne,* speak in a low voice.

Lowping-on Stanes — Stones common about country inns for getting into carts, or mounting horses from.

Lowsness—A laxness, purging, &c.; " to be fashed wi' a lowsness," means not to be costive. 1 have heard of priests preaching themselves into a lowsness, for the sake of saving sinners. Poets, too, rhyme themselves whiles into this state; really men of genius should be *wary.*

Luce—A blue matter which is scraped off the face in shaving.

Luchter—An handful of corn in the straw; some reapers are better than others at rowing *luchters*; that is to say, better at rolling a neat handful of grain when they cut it.

Luckie—A canty old woman, neither young, nor dead old.

YOUR SERVANT BIRKBUSH.

My dear Lucky Clink, come now alter thy plan,
　Ye know what I mean, you're beginning to blush,
Come be clapped and squeez'd by anither bit man,
　The bachelor body, Your Servant Birkbush.

Long have I courted thee, Lucky, my love,
　Long have I made a most desperate push,
And a honeyblob ay, unto me ye doth prove,
　Then clasp to thy bosom, Your Servant Birkbush.

Tho' mine hair now be grey, Lucky, yet I am young,
　As supplè as whalebone, as straight as a rush,
Mine nerves like a youth's about twenty are strung,
　He's as merry's a mautman, Your Servant Birkbush.

O ! but your heart, my kind deary, is warm,
   How lovely ye talk, and can sing like a thrush,
Was I made of ice, thou hast beauty could charm,
   And make him run mad, Your Servant Birkbush.

I never yet found ye, sweet Lucky, inclined
   To give me a sneer, mine affections to crush ;
But I always observed, that you fully designed
   To wed sometime soon, Your Servant Birkbush.

Now ye sit by my side, this is pleasure indeed,
   Now ye give me a kiss, I am all in a flush,
My pulse moveth now at a cantering speed,
   What enjoyment is this, to Your Servant Birkbush!

I'm o'erpower'd, scarce another bit thing can I say,
   Lie still then, my tongue, all my gabbling hush,
To morrow, I'm told, will be my wedding-day,
   Then hooh, cockabendie, Your Servant Birkbush.

LUCKPENNY—The cash which the seller gives back to the buyer, after the latter has paid him ; it is given back with the hope that it may prove a lucky bargain:

LUCKRASS—The name of a cross-grained, cankered, gude-wife.

LUGGIE—The horned owl.

LUIKING the GRUN—When a farmer starts inthe morning, staff in hand, and *collie* at his foot, then clambers up one hill and down another, seeing how his cattle are faring, how his labourers are going on, how his crop looks, and how the weather appears—this job is called *luiking the grun.* If he has taken too much whisky on the market-night, he throws the *spring-wells* in his range, while *luiking the grun.* And though he should leave his wife, sweet soul, by the *skreech o' day,* she rather out of good humour, and he with a confounded *sair head,* proceeding from the effects of taking the *wee drap* ; yet after this de-lightful exercise, he will return full of health and spirits, and meet with his spouse up and bustling amongst the af-fairs of the household, as busy as a bee, and as happy as the day is long. What wonderful scenes have nature opened up to me whiles, when *luiking the grun !*

LUMMING—The weather is said to be *lumming* when raining thick; *a lum o' a day,* a very wet day; the rain is just coming *lumming* down, when it rains fast. This word and *loom,* a mist or fog, are of kindred.

LUNIESHOTT—The loin bone gone out of its socket.

LUNTING—Walking and smoking a pipe.

LURDAN—An extremely lazy woman; an abominable female.

LUSCAN—A sturdy beggar, and a thief. A *luscan* was lodged once in a farm-house in the parish of Minniegaff, and thought proper to walk off in the morning with the bed-clothes, which had been given him to sleep in during the night; but he had not long made off with his booty, before he was bewildered in a misty day; so our *luscan* wandered, and knew not where he was going; he still kept walking on, however, and when evening came, a house appeared in view, so he would go in and seek *quarters*; but what house was this but the very one he had left in the morning? and what gudewife did he meet but the one he had robbed? The scene *dumfounder'd* the wretch, and *swarf'd* him so, that he could not utter a word.

LYE—Pasture land about to be tilled; ploughmen talk about the *lifting of a tuich lye* with as much concern as statesmen do about nations, or astronomers about other worlds.

LYSE-HAY—Hay mowed off pasture land, and not off meadows; this hay is more difficult to mow than any other kind, for it has what *mawsters* call a *matted sole,* which racks the *showther-blades* in cutting it, and makes the *boutings* short to a *sharp.*

M.

MACDIARMID—John M'Diarmid, Esq. Editor of the " Dumfries and Galloway Courier," a gentleman well

worthy a place in my never-failing Encyclopædia; for ever
since he became connected with the *south*, as a journalist,
he has behaved himself like a man of honest genius. He
has reported many good original things, and his ears have
never been shut to the calls of real merit, for which he is
and long will be well liked all over Galloway. The rustic poets around have ever found him leaving a *corner* to
their service, and many have availed themselves of sporting
the muse on that *esplanade*. The most prominent of these
have been the Reverend Mr. Gillespy, of Kells, a gentleman surely a very good poet, but just rather too refined
for my taste (I am fond of hearing the rude *sough* of nature). Mr. Malcomson, of Kirkcudbright, has also given
us some good verses on *Tears* and *Snawdrops*; while
Mr. Millar has sung " *Mamma, Mamma*," very prettily,
and the scenery seen from the *tap o' Criffle*. But the hero
of this article is a better poet himself than any of these.
Behold his talents directed this way in the early numbers of
Blackwood, when he was allowed to be the first orator,
except the *Ettrick Shepherd*, in the *forum of Auld
Reekie*. His *Scrap Book*, too, evinces that its author
knows good composition from bad; while his *Life of
Cowper*, the darling English poet, is a biographical sketch
rarely gone beyond, and could not have been written by
any but a person of similar taste : such is the honest
fact, as felt by me; the world, though, may speak for
itself. In dressing up an account of a *Rood Fair*, a *Swollen Nith*, a *Burns' Anniversary*, and such things, our author has great merit; he gives them that natural touch
which mightier pencils could not pourtray. He has also
been the means of helping forward to notice a merchant
in Dumfries, a Mr. M'Vittey, the same person, I suspect,
who sang the battle of *Dryfe Sands*, and who published
Tales for the *ingle-cheek*, a little while ago, which are
thought by me to be *fair wark*. So much then for Mac-

diarmid, and this much will often be read when he and
me are no more.

> O ! the pleasures poets feel,
>   When they do ride a sound Pegasus,
> With daring front and nimble heel,
>   What hobby-horseman them surpasses?
>
> A brave Pegasus, that doth scorn
>   To tramp the path ere trod by any,
> Even tho' its own should seem forlorn,
>   Devoid of sweets and beauties many.
>
> And will not yield for deserts drear,
>   With whirling sand and thorny bramble,
> Will snore through stormy seas 'thout fear,
>   And o'er the hugest mountains scramble.
>
> Nor turn aside for tempests black,
>   For savage gales, unpiteous howling,
> Nor for the forest grim put back,
>   Tho' bloody tigers round be growling.
>
> But bear along its rider strange,
>   Through worlds where curious tribes are swarming,
> Where scenes delight to hourly change,
>   From something wild to something charming.
>
> Fly, where balloons can never fly,
>   Sail, where no ship can sail, nor shallop,
> Fling far behind both earth and sky,
>   And through celestial regions gallop.
>
> So may he sing the glowing song,
>   The song that sets the heart a weeping,
> That manly song by nature strong,
>   Which never falls a nodding, sleeping.
>
> But groweth like the summer rose,
>   The root being in the human bosom,
> How can it wither? still it blows,
>   And bloometh in eternal blossom.

MACTAGGART—This is no less a personage than myself,
born some twenty-five years ago, at Plunton, in the parish
of Borgue, quite beside the *auld castle o' Plunton.* The
Friday night before *Kelton-hill fair* was the night in
which I, *gomerall Johnie,* first opened my mouth in this
wicked world. My father is a farmer, and throughout my
pilgrimage on earth, from the cradle till this moment, I
have never met with any whom I considered had so much
native strength of intellect. Let no man say of me, that
I am a creature of ability, for such would be wrong ; but

that my worthy parent is, and to a great degree, is right ;
his father was also a farmer, and my grandfather's grandfather got his head cloven at the *brack o' Dunbar*, fighting in the Highland army against Oliver Cromwell. The
name *Mactaggart* comes directly from the Gaelic, as all
names beginning with *Mac* do. *Mac*, a son, and *tachart*,
a priest; signifying, the son of a priest. God knows if
there be much of a priest about me. My father rented
the farm of Plunton from Murray of Broughton, and this
being at the outskirt of the parish, my lot was cast three
miles from the parish school. A half-grown boy was
therefore brought into the house to teach my sisters and
me the A, B, C, for I had then two sisters older than myself; though I was the oldest of the boys. There were
eleven of us altogether once, six boys and five girls ; but
I have lost two dear sisters. Well, this boy taught and
lashed us occasionally. I mind of being happy when the
harrowing came on, as my father required him to *harrow*
the ploughed land in the sowing season, and not us. A
neibouring farmer became partner with my father in this
dominie, so one part of the year my sisters and me went
to this farmer's house, and were taught along with his family, and they came to us in return. While at this work,
coming home one night I tumbled into a *peat-hole,* and
should have been drowned, had not my sisters been with
me ; they *haurl'd* me out, and so saved a *valuable* life
from perishing in *glaur.* At length my sisters were thought
strong enough to go to *Borgue academy*; the teaching boy
was set adrift, and I being only six years of age, was allowed to remain happy at home, as not thought able to
accompany them. So I ran about and hunted butterflies,
built little houses on *brae sides,* and adorned them with
bleached periwinkle shells, brought to me from the shore ;
I also waded in a *burn* that ran by beside the house, and
neived *beardocks.* I had no companion but a *hoolet*; this

was brought me when young from the *auld castle*; I fed it
with mice, but it found the way to an old *sooty truff laft*,
and there caught plenty of mice for itself; one day it came
down from its *reeky* habitation, to wash itself, having need
enough of that; and while doing so, in a tub by the door-
cheek, a cock came the way, and sank his deadly spurs into
the scull of my poor *hoolet*; I mourned about this many
a day. At last I was thought fit to go with my sisters
to school, and then again began my woes; nothing could
I learn. I was begun to the *Latin* long before I knew any
thing almost of *English*; as the order ran in these days,
"one could not be put to the Latin too young." Of a
truth then I was put young enough to it, but could learn
nothing about it. I was lashed upstairs and downstairs,
and was saved, I believe, from dying an unnatural death,
by my parents *flitting* from *Lennox Plunton*, to the farm
of *Torrs*, in the parish of Kirkcudbright. A country
school lay just beside us, we had only a hill to go over to
it; the master taught the scholars no Latin; this was a
great thing to me; he was quite an easy, soothing teacher,
a good *counter*, and could *read* and *write* pretty well.
With him I began to learn somewhat. I begat an affection for arithmetic, and was soon the best hand amongst
figures in the school, going through all the *count-books*
that came before me, like smoke. In truth, *Mr. Caig* is
an excellent teacher; he gives nature fair play; he lets the
scholars pursue their own inclination, be that what it will.
If I have any learning, or any genius about me, to this man
am I indebted for their improvement. Had he been a
dominie who gave out *tasks*, who obliged the scholars to
learn this, and then that, who made a slave of the mind,
when in its tender state, and who valued the feelings nothing, I, *Mac*, would never have been heard of. I
should have crawled about, a mean artificial worm of man's
formation, without one spark of nature's fire about me.

Whenever a *fox-hunt*, a *shipwreck*, a *bonspeil*, or such thing happened in the neighbourhood, the school was flung open to all who wished to run and see; and I, for one, seldom stayed behind. Indeed I was looked on as rather a careless boy of my *book, speiled heuchs* for *gull-eggs*, and trees for *young craws;* went a fishing frequently; attended all raffles, tea-drinkings, fairs, and what not. Wherever there were any curious sights to be seen, there was I; nothing would have kept me from them : but as I got older I met with fewer novelties. My father, thinking from my habits I was learning but little at the country school, (being fond of reading nothing but ballads and histories, as they came to the house in the wallet of the hawker), sent me to the academy at Kirkcudbright, a distance of four miles; this I had to go and come every day. During winter I could not get to it very regularly, with bad weather; and in spring and harvest, when a *throng* was about the farm, I had to stay, or rather I was fond to stay, and lend a hand. For all, when the *examination* came on, I laid all the school below me with the mathematics, and so obtained the premium. Being nothing, however, but a mathematician, the rest of the boys laughed at me; so I would go and learn French. I attended this an hour every day, but could not learn it, because *tasks* were laid out. I now, in my thirteenth year, took a huff at schools and schoolmasters altogether, leaving them both with disgust. At this my parents were displeased; however, they let me take my own mind of it, and as I now had to work at little jobs about the farm, I soon relished this life not very well either; so I would learn a *trade* : a *mill-wright* was thought a good one, and a *ship-carpenter,* but I would go and *bind* myself to neither; that of a *book-printer* pleased me best of any; I wrote to the firm of Oliver and Boyd, Edinburgh, stating the matter, and my wish to become an apprentice. My letter was never answered. I wrote again to Fairbairn and

Co, in the same city, and to Mr. Jackson, Dumfries, but never received any answer from either, which caused me to grow very dull. It was about this time that I began to feel a melancholy working in on me, which I will never get rid of. I may here mention though, that ever since that night on which my mother told me that there would come a day on which I should *die,* and be covered up with cold mould in a grave, I have been rather haunted with thought; it gives the young mind a dreadful shock on being first made acquainted with this awful truth. Finding, therefore, myself worsted in getting to be a printer, I consoled myself with my lot, and became extremely *bookish* inclined; and, as the old song goes—

> " I bought and borrowed every where,
> " I studied night and day,
> " Ne'er miss'd what Dean nor Doctor wrote,
> " That happen'd in my way."

I began to the French again by myself, and soon could translate it, and the Latin too. I got hold of a dictionary and Virgil, and pondered away the long *fore-nights.* A friend who lived in the neighbourhood had an Encyclopædia Britannica; this I was given whenever I wanted a volume; and I must own I have received no small benefit from this kindness. I gathered ten times more out of that book than I did at the College of Edinburgh; a place to which I started on foot, staff in hand, when in my nineteenth year. Before this time I had taken a ramble through England, had been often in love, had wrote poetry, and the devil knows what. I have rhymed since ever I remember, but I keeped dark. After passing a hard winter in Edinburgh, attending my favourite natural classes, reading from libraries, writing for magazines, and what not, I returned to the rural world in the spring; and the next winter I went back to Edinburgh, but not to attend the College, though that was the apparent motive. I never received any good from attending the University. I was

there told nothing but what I had before gathered. But
I am running this sketch too far; let my Edinburgh adventures, my wanderings through Scotland, my learning the
engineering, my trip to London, my rebuffs from Fortune, and my receiving them kindly, my finding an independent way of making an honest livelihood with industry, &c. &c. form the subject of another foolish discourse
at some future period.

When I reached my twenty-first year, the following
poetic coin my muse cast forth from her mint, inscribed—

MAC IS MAJOR.

Now *Mac*, upon the Soloway shore,
Whar seamaws skirl and pellocks snore,
　　And whilks and muscles cheep ;
Whar puffins on the billows ride,
And dive adown the foaming tide,
　　For sillar-fry sae deep.
Puir cheil his ane-and-twentieth year,
　　He entereth upon,
My merry days are past, I fear,
　　And sad anes coming on—
　　　　Nae matter, I'll batter
　　　　As weel's I can through life,
　　　Ay dash on, and brash on,
　　　　Throughout this wardly strife.

Thanks to thee, Death, wi' a' my heart,
For hauding back thy wutter'd dart
　　Sae lang frae stanging me ;
The smapox, meazles, and a fever,
Ye let me through 'thout seeming ever,
　　To wuss that I sud dee.

I hope ye'll let me yet awhile,
　　Wild nature's warks admire,
And up Parnassus twa'r three mile,
　　Clim' till I lag and tire—
　　　　For thinking, and clinking,
　　　　Hae ay been a' my joy,
　　　And stringing, and singing,
　　　　The foolish laddies toy.

To danner by the craigie fells,
Amang brown fog and heather bells,
　　Or roun the lanely shore ;
And there to croon the feeling sang,
Warm frae the heart no unco lang,
　　I dearly do adore.

Whiles glowring at the azure sky,
  And loomy oceans ure,
Which Phœbus makes whan he is dry,
  Thrang sooking waters pure—
      Contented, and scented
        By blooming flowers around,
      What pleasures, and treasures,
        I thus hae aften found.

There's mony a wanton minor laird,
Wi' frothy haurns and goarling baird,
  Wha langs to be my age ;
Sae that he just might hae a fill,
Without being curbed o' his free will,
  His passions wild that rage.

That he might ope the sillar stores,
  Collected aff the grounds,
And flash the same mang winking whores,
  Trig flonkies, horses, hounds—
      Ay lashing, and dashing,
        As fast as he cud ca,
      Ne'er thinking—but drinking,
        And florying awa.

But Hoch-ance, to humble me,
Nae gowden hordes collected be,
  That I may smack about ;
And see the warl and a' its games,
To lewdly lie wi' Paris dames,
  And blaw a rotten snout.

Or in the parliament to gab,
  A futty, feckless story,
Fu' fit to gie the yaws or scab,
  To either whig or tory—
      Unpestered, sequestered,
        Deep hidden I remain,
      Whiles sawing, whiles mawing,
        As seasons come again.

O, endless is the farmer's toil,
To rake the rent frae aff the soil,
  Else twig the mealpowks string ;
A harvest's never snodly shorn,
Unless the shearers every morn,
  Are early on the wing.

Through ilka turning o' the year,
  I moil and brose awa,
E'en out in winter I appear,
  Amang the frost and sna—
      Cauld ploddering, and foddering,
        The nowt amang the biels,
      Then curling, and hurling,
        The channlestane at spiels.

A lanely melancholy lad,
Ane quarter wise, three quarters mad,
   Wi' gloomy brow a burning ;
Whiles merry too, and looking gay,
Enjoying then a sunny day,
   Before rude storms returning—

Is wh :t I am, and in this breast
   I find wild creatures working,
A throbbing pulse that will not rest,
   Strong independence lurking—
       Nae cringing, nae whinging,
         Shall ever come frae me,
       Nor fawning, nor yawning,
         My stars have born me free;

Gang and be slaves ye fools wha will,
And get wharwith your kytes to fill,
   Frae ither bigger knaves ;
I envy not your fu' broth pot,
Your beefy, bursen, rifting lot,
   And roomy howket graves.

Rather aneath yon binwud brae,
   Amang the yellow broom,
I'd on the bonny e'ening stray,
   Wi' belly rather toom—
       What's jinking, and slinking,
         And crouching night and day,
       To grandeurs, and splendours,
         Which nature doth display.

I'll never hae a poet's name,
Nor in the gaudy house of fame,
   Enjoy a wee bit garret ;
The clinking I may hit, hooh, hoo,
As also could the cockatoo,
   Or green Brazilian parrot.

I want that potent pithy nerve,
   Which Bardies ought to hae,
Frae nature too, I owre far swerve,
   And her sweet melody—

       The muse whiles, refuse whiles,
         To lend poor Mac a lift,
       She'll sneer me, and jeer me,
         And winna come in tift.

The lasses tho' are glad o' me,
Sweet dearies wi' the blythesome e'e,
   And I lo'e them as weel ;
They are the soul of this dull earth,
Whaever hates them damns his birth,
   And lives a canker'd cheil.

O ! if I had her in my arms,
My fair, my blooming queen,
She wha my heart for ever warms,
And ay my love has been—
I'd kiss her, and bliss her,
And praise her to the skies,
I'd clap her, and hap her,
Frae every blast that flies.

For a' sae shortly's I hae been
Upon this warl' what hae I seen,
Big hubbles never ending ;
How mony millions ither nosing,
How mony thousands peace proposing,
Yet the de'ils ne'er mending.
Broils wi' pens, and broils wi' swords,
And graves wi' bouks a cramming,
Gloomy plots, and lofty words,
Silly man a shamming—
But brattle, and rattle,
My slavering gomfs, awa,
I'm fearless, and careless,
O' you baith ane and a'.

I'll ramble down my rural hows,
And jump amang the clints and knows,
And rant my sangs fu' cheery ;
And roose auld Scotland a' I can,
Like ony ither honest man,
For o' her I'm ne'er weary,
She yet has been fu' kind to me,
A mither true and faithfu',
To glunch at her I'd sorry be,
Ay most confounded laithfu'—
But here then, I'll speer then,
Gif it be time to quat,
The de'il man, can tell man,
'Tis fully time for that.

Some of my readers may probably think me a bit of a poet, by the spouting I hold, but 'tis nonsense; when I publish my poem of the *Rustic Madman,* which I have past me in *Six Tornadoes,* then will appear what I am as a poet :—

Suppose I was the richest man,
That ever strode upon the globe,
Suppose I rode in gold sedan,
And wore a weighty diamond robe.

Had shoals of slaves both he and she,
    Had sporting ladies, many a score,
Had grandeur quite done out with me,
    And luxury exhausted sore.

An independant man with sense,
    Would be a greater man by far,
Even though his purse contain'd but pence—
    A noble soul's without a par.

Then scratch your dross from every shore,
    Ye greedy, bustling, grubbing men,
Sum up at last, what's in the store,
    And 'twill amount to nothing then.

MADES.—The larvae, or seed of *mawks,* maggots ; as laid by the *blue douped mawking flee,* or maggot fly, on *humph'd* or putrid flesh.

MAHERS.—A tract of low, wet lying land, of a marshy and moory nature ; *Mahermore* or *Mahermere,* is a specimen.

MAIDEN.—An ancient instrument, for holding the *broaches* of pirns until the pirns be wound off.

MAIDEN-HAIR.—The muscles of oxen, when boiled, termed *fix faux,* towards the border ; it is called maidenhair, from its resembling in colour the hair of a maiden ; the *gowden-fair,* sometimes too it is ycleped *yellow hair.*

MAIDEN-KIMMER.—The maid who attends the *kimmer ;* or matron who has the charge of the infant at *kimmerings* and baptisms ; who lifts the babe into the arms of its father, to receive the sprinkling of salvation.

MAILLIES.—An affectionate name for sheep ; from *mae,* the bleat of a sheep.

MAISTER.—A dominie ; a school-master.

MALE-A-FORREN.—A meal of meat, over and above what is consumed ; a meal before hand.

MALL.—Moll ; *Mally*—Molly. *Mall Trott* was a character well known over Galloway. Perhaps as well as Hudibras's *Mall Cutpurse,* or Defoe's *Moll Flanders,* are

to the curious reader; hear the song of *Mally Whur-
lie* :—

> O, wha i'st ye like best,
> Ye like best, ye like best,
> O, wha i'st ye like best,
> > My merry *Mally Whurlie.*
>
> There's nane amang the hills and hows,
> Nor yet amang the Fumart knows,
> Wha I can every inch gae roose,
> > But jolly *Wully Gurlie.*
>
> And what's Wullie but a gow?
> But a gow, but a gow,
> And what's Wullie but a gow?
> > My merry *Mallie Whurlie.*
>
> He's worth a hunner gows and ten,
> I wat he is the king o' men,
> Tho' laird but o' a clocking hen,
> > My jolly *Wullie Gurlie.*
>
> Ay atweel he's poor enough,
> Poor enough, poor enough,
> Ay atweel he's poor enough,
> > My merry *Mally Whurlie.*
>
> But what's his poverty to me,
> For riches care I no a flee,
> He's ay worth ony ten o' thee,
> > My jolly *Wullie Gurlie.*

MANITOODLIE—An affectionate term which nurses give to
male children.

MANKIE—An ancient kind of worsted stuff, much glazed,
worn by females; where it was manufactured I have not
gathered; it could not have been in the *Isle of Man.*

MAPSIE—A pet-sheep, called so from its *map, mapping*
with its lips; young hares are also *mapsies.*

MARK nor BURN—The same with *hilt* nor *hair*; when
one loses any thing and finds it not again, we are said to
never see *mark* nor *burn* of it again; it is a shepherd's
phrase, as he burns the sheep with a red hot iron on
the horns and nose, to enable him to know them.

MARK O' MOUTH—A mark in the mouth, whereby horse,
sheep, and other cattle-dealers, know the age of the animal by opening its lips. I believe the mark respects the

number of teeth, as these animals, for a certain number of years, get two new teeth annually ; but, when they live beyond a certain period, they lose the *mark o' mouth*; old maidens are said sometimes to have lost the *mark o' mouth,* when the rose leaves the cheek, and the snowy breasts, which once seemed like little hills, have melted or shrunk away.

MARKSTANES—Stones set up on end for marks in the days of yore, that farmers might know the marches of their farms, and lairds the boundaries of their lands; these stones are most common in the moors.

MAUNT—To speak thick and fast ; to have a *marr* in the speech.

MAUTMAN—A man who makes malt.   Sometime ago, *maltmen* had always good ale about them, so were merry ; hence arose the phrase, " as *merry's a mautman."*

MAWSTER—A mower; a wielder of the scythe.

MAW-WAW—A tom-cat's cry when he goes a-courting.

MAYNE—John Mayne, Esq. part editor and owner of the newspaper called " The Star," a London paper, published every evening.   This gentleman is a Gallovidian, and a poet; he is the author of that well-known poem the *Sillar Gun,* a poem Walter Scott says, is beyond the might of *Robert Fergusson,* and approaches nearer to *Burns* than any thing in the Scotch language; this says much for Mr. Mayne's muse.   In my opinion, the *Sillar Gun* is a good rustic poem, though I think the young bard before mentioned the greater poet of the two.   He also wrote the sweet song of *Logan Braes,* a poem named *Glasgow* ; another way of *Kirkconnel-lee,* different from that of *Stewart Luis,* the author of *Owre the Muir amang the Heather.*   Mr. M. was bred a printer, is now an old respectable man, with much of the Scotchman's warmth about him, with the soul of genius still *glinting* in his eye.

It refreshes me very much to get a shake of the hand and a *crack* from Mr. Mayne, for there is more goodness and originality about him than I can express.

MEAL-HOGYETT—A barrel for holding oatmeal.

MEALOMS—Very dry potatoes, when boiled.

MEALPOWK and the STRING—Begging accoutrements.

MEALSTANES—Rude stones of seventeen and a half pounds weight, used in weighing oatmeal.

MEG O' MONY FEET—A black hard worm, with many hundred feet, and two feelers before : it is quite common between the stones of old dykes, and suspicious places; its length is generally about three inches, and the bite of it poisonous. Hence it is dreaded by youths ; indeed, children have a natural instinct to dread it. For all the number of feet it has, and which has given rise to its name, the motions of it are not quick, and when any way interrupted it coils itself up. There is another sort of worm found in the same kind of places with this, and has a number of feet also, though not so many as the other, yet its movements are much quicker ; the colour of this one is grass-green ; it has no name, but may be termed, with propriety methinks, the *Scotch centipee,* as it is of the same genera with the centipee of the torrid zone.

MELLGRAVE—A break in a highway ; a place requiring the genius of *M'Adam,* the celebrated *roadman,* to repair it. In roads which pass through soft countries, *mellgraves* most prevail ; it is said that a horse with its rider once sank in a *mellgrave* somewhere in Ayrshire, and were never more heard of.

MELL I'THE SHAFT—A phrase, literally meaning a *mell,* or maul, or mallet in shaft, but used allegorically thus :— when a person's worldly affairs get disordered, it is said the *mell* cannot be keeped in the *shaft* ; now, unless the *mell* be keeped in the *shaft,* no work can be done. Bills become immoveable, the *day* and the *way* cannot be keeped clear; and when, by struggling, a man is not overset, he is said to have keeped the *mell* in the *shaft,* or the soul and body in partnership.

MERLIE—Sandy and sweet; when honey is in this state, it is said to be *merlie*; when it is beginning to grow this way, it *merles*; and when it is let go on, it is *merling.*

MERMAID'S PURSE—A beautiful kind of sea-weed box, which is found driven in on the shores, of an oblong shape, that is to say, longer than broad, being about two inches and a half one way, and three the other, with a long *spraing* or talon stretching out from each corner, as long as the box; it is of a raven-black colour on the outside and sea green within, hoven up in the middle, and open at one end; and, unlike other sea-weed, never found connected together.

MERRICK—Five large hills or mountains in Galloway; they lay beside one another, and gradually rise, the one a little higher above the other; in the morning and evening the shadows of these hills on the level moors below seem like the fingers of an awful hand; hence the name *Merrick,* which, in the Gaelic, signifies *fingers.* How expressive that language must be. O! that I were master of it.

MERRY-MEAT—The same with *kimmering*; the feast at a birth.

MERVADIE—Any fine sweet brittle cake is said to be *mervadie*; this word and *merlie* are someway connected; but as I am such a slim linguist, I cannot see the relationship.

MICELED—Did eat, somewhat after the way of mice.

MID-KIPPLE—That piece of hide which keeps the two *sticks* of a flail in partnership.

MIDSE-DAY—Middle of the day; *mid-room,* a little room between the kitchen and parlor; *mids, middle.* " There's a gude *mids* in a' things;" which means, extremes should be avoided.

MILKER—A cow that gives much milk. A cow with a large udder is not always a good *milker*; it is said that it is by the *head* that the cow gives the milk ; which means, that if a cow be a great eater, she is also a great *milker*.

MILLAE—The loftiest mountain in the south of Scotland, away by four thousand feet above the level of the sea; seldom doth it doff its cowl of snow in honour of the sun.

MILLBANNOCK—A circular cake of oatmeal, with a hole in the centre; it is generally a foot in diameter, and an inch in thickness ; it is baked at mills, and *haurned* or toasted on the burning seeds of shelled oats, which makes it as brittle as if it had been baked with butter ; of course, then, the *millbannock* is allowed to be the chief of all *bannocks*. A miller in Wigtonshire once made an enormous one of a *boll of meal*, as a present to his laird the Earl of Galloway, in hopes that the Earl would give him a *down-come* of the rent; but instead of doing so, he raised it on him fifty pounds per annum, saying, "that if he could afford to make sic *millbannocks* to his friends, he could be no way distressed." Poor *Dusty* then had no other shift than to return to his old shop, with his finger in his mouth, and curse confound the *plot* o' the *millbannock*.

MILL-CLOOSE—The same with *mill-trowse*. The boxed wood-work which conducts the water into mill wheels.

MILLER o' MINNIEIVE—Somewhere in the south of Scotland, a traveller may fall in with (by searching every nook) a village, or, more properly, a *clauchan* termed *Minnieive*. Its latitude and longitude have never yet been properly ascertained ; a thing, by the bye, much wanted now, as the place is every day getting farther into vogue. It will soon eclipse *Ambleside* on the lakes, as a hamlet of celebrity ; for there is the abode of a miller, with whom, for poetry and a thousand other fine things, no *laker* can be compared. Respecting this personage, none but poets can see or have any dealings, but to them, he keeps not in utter darkness; so I shall just give my readers a peep of him from behind the cloud: and firstly then, his

COMPARISONS.

Those bergs of ice which do arise
In arctic worlds to such a size,
Surprising travellers so bold,
Who wander through these realms so cold;
Remind me, by their strange narration,
Of this vast debt which damns our nation;
Like it, they higher, wilder rear
Their awful heads from year to year.
Each winter's frost and fall of snow
Do make them swell, and larger grow,
Just as the interest doth the sum,
And foolish broils with sword and drum.

Till now 'tis got so mighty big,
It frights the tory and the whig;
Few find their souls sufficient bold,
As can the monster huge behold;
None but philosophers must dare,
And poets, who are free of care.
No taxes that reduce are felt,
No suns the dreadful mount will melt;
'Twill tower away yet for awhile,
Ascend yet farther two, three mile,
Then down 'twill tumble with a dash,
And who, good God, will stand the crash?

So much then for the Miller; his *comparisons* are worth the looking at. Mark another :—

Squire *Kirtle's* worth ten thousand pounds,
    And more than that the squire's a *villain*,
Bob *Keel* has neither cash nor grounds,
    And yet the lad is worth a *million*.

How comes this, let's see the plan?
    'Tis very plain, you need not doubt it,
Bob Keel is just an honest man,
    So that is all there is about it.

At this, Squire Kirtle now may itch,
    May roup his farmers, try stock-jobbing,
Do all he can to be as rich,
    And yet he'll ne'er come up wi' Robbin.

Squire Kirtle with his hounds and whores,
    And all the luxuries of folly,
Are smother'd quite by Robbin's stores,
    And what are they?—a kent and collie.

Squire Kirtle lolls on sofas soft,
  When he with wine gets swell'd and groggy,
But poor Bob Keel reposeth oft
  By cauller springs on banks sae foggy.
Which now, is the better man?
  The one is hemlock—t'other myrtle,
We need not guess, we see the plan,
  Bob Keel is far before Squire Kirtle.
An honest man's the king of men;
  If heaven hath *good* and *better* places,
The best place there some yet may ken,
  Is, where the soul that's honest graces.

For the sake of fun I may give another, and the most singular of the three :—

Whar yon burn frae Kirrbride
  Tummles into the sea,
Twa hizzies abide,
  Thus admired by me :

The tane for her dourness,
  The 'tither for sweetness;
The first for her sourness,
  The second for neatness.

They are baith in ae house,
  They are baith named *Jeanie,*
The tane's never crouse,
  And her hide's like a guinea :

O lord! she is yellow,
  And yawps like a peany,
But the tither is mellow,
  O, she is my *Jeanie.*

Sweet heaven, what an eye,
  O, how she loves kissing,
In my arms she will lie,
  And receive my best blessing :

But the ither may go,
  The auld scraighton sae din,
To the regions below,
  And display her tan'd skin.

O, sweet is the pear,
  O, sweeter is hinnie,
But sweeter's my dear,
  My ain melting Jeanie :

Sour is the crab,
  And wrinkled's my grannie,
O, where is the drab
  A match for this Jeanie ?

The first is a blossom,
Befitting my bosom ;
The second's infernal,
External, internal.

A singular poet is this Miller of Minnieive in truth ;
see how he paints himself to a friend :—

I'm but ane humble dusty miller,
No unco fond of grubbing siller,
Nor steering wi' a steady tiller,
  Through life's queer sea;
But tak my dram wi' a care-killer,
  My Jock like thee.

For why should I mysell immure
Eternally, mang powks and stowre ?
I like a breath o' air that's pure,
  As weel as ony ;
A buik, a bumper, to be sure,
  And hizzies bonny.

My killman, cheerfu' soul, and me,
To ithers hands do work wi' glee,
And weel I wat we've mony a spree,
  In the killogie ;
Nae twasome thou didst ever see,
  Sae blythe and vogie.

The miller's muse, tho', is unfit
To praise thee, Johnie, for thy wit,
But, like a wise man, ye'll submit
  To glimmer owre me ;
The tod he kens a halesome bit,
  Sae won't devour me.

Will. Shakspur and the ploughman Robbie,
Wad baith be beat too wi' the jobbie,
Tho' they cud dance in nature's lobbie,
  Wi' meikle glee ;
Then how can I, a dusty dobbie,
  Do aught wi' thee?

The warl at large may join and thank ye,
And 'mang the first o' moderns rank ye,
Auld Scotland in her plaid may fank ye,
  Fu' bein and warm ;
For e'en the sauls o' *Killiemanky*,
  Yeve powers to charm.

Behold yet, what a songster the Miller is; hear to his
Wild roaring Sea.

Where, think'st thou, Mary thy lover is,
 Where now does he doat on thee ?
O ! far away from the land of bliss,
 And my darling far from me ;

I'm on the black wide rolling deep,
  Where pleasures never be,
O Mary, my love, here do I weep,
  On the wild roaring sea.

I weep for thee, Mary, my lovely dear,
  But the surges care not for me,
The billows do not my wailing hear,
  My soul is in sorrow for thee ;
My poverty did force us to part,
  Our parents did not agree,
So I am flung with a broken heart,
  On the wild roaring sea.

Come down, ye dark clouds, that lower above,
  Come dashing down on me,
For since I cannot get with my love,
  From this life I long to be free ;
O, was I sure that beyond the grave,
  My Mary I would meet with thee,
I would plunge myself beneath that wave,
  In the wild roaring sea.

   So poetry and poverty,
    Are ne'er a kin to ither,
   The tane the sister is I see,
    The tither is the brither.

Then ye whose haurns, are cram'd with wit,
  So as to keep the world alive,
May make a friend if ye think fit,
  Of the *Miller o' Minnieive.*

MILL-LADE.—The drain or *lead,* as it were, which conveys the water from *mill-dams* to the *mill-wheel* ; sometimes called *mill-race.*

MILL-SHILLING.—The shelled grain, which runs out of the *mill-e'e.* When we see a person vomiting, from the effects of drinking spirits, we say he was " 'sendin' the drink frae him like a mill-shilling."

MILTS AND ROWNS.—The seed of fish, such as herrings ; those with *milts,* are said to be the *male herring,* the other with *rowns,* the *female.*

MIM-MOU'D.—Having an affected way of speaking.

MINNIEGAFF.—One of the wildest Moorland parishes in Galloway; some of the natives of it live fifteen miles from church ; this was the parish wherein was born and bred, our celebrated linguist Murray. The following love song, respecting this bleak tract, somewhat pleases me—

My Mary dear's awa'
My sweet love's awa',
And left me in this weary warl,
Where I hae nae joy ava'.—Chorus.

I saw her laid in her cauld bed,
   And happed wi' a green sod,
My e'en fill'd fu', my heart it bled,
   O! I hope she's wi' her God.

At the school we war fu' pack,
   We sat ay upon the ae bink,
O! I liked to luik at her e'en sae black,
   For lovely she could blink.

Whan she bade wi' her auntie Jane,
   'Mang the Moors o' Minniegaff,
To see my love I hae aften gane,
   And thought it nae way aff.

I hae waded the waters deep,
   I hae clam the mountains hie,
To see my Mary, but now I maun weep,
   'Neath the auld bowrock tree.

O! Mary was a sweet, sweet lass,
   The joy o' a' my heart,
To me the like o' her never was,
   And yet we're forced to part.

Naething but death the bluidy knave,
   Cud hae sinner'd my love and me,
O! wad he lay me aside her i'e grave,
   Kind, kind to me he'd be.

How strongly too is this parish hinted at in the *Fareweel o' Meg Bohells.*

Ha Minniegaff thou Moorland clout,
Wi' thee I hae had an unco bout,
But faith, at last thou'st beat me out,
          Without a cheel;
Maybe to tak a better rout,
          Sae fare thee weel.

Sax years, and something mair are gane,
Since I cam to the stanning-stane,
And twa three lads too, there I've haen,
          At least I thought sae;
But now I'm left without a 'ane,
          My fortune wrought sae.

Tam o' the Todholes lo'ed me best,
And I thought mair o'm than the rest,
He was ay better bred and dress't,
           And bonnier far;
But some confound, else I'd been blest,
           My luck did mar.

He gaed to Ayr, some sheep to sell,
(Sae neebours roun' the tale do tell),
And there wi' some queer jades befel,
           Wha' trounce the street;
They shab'd puir Tamous aff to hell,
           Wi' nimble feet.

Rab Gurnell too, wha had a farm,
Did tell me I had mony a charm,
And that his heart grew unco warm,
           Whan he was wi' me;
Guess what a laughable alarm,
           The cheel did gie me.

I lived wi' my maiden auntie,
Wha was fu' puist and unco canty,
Rab wad come in, and seem to want me,
           But mark the hash;
'Twas my auld friend he did gallant ay,
           Or else her cash.

He'd speak to her and then to me,
Play wink at her his scoundrel e'e,
He did na think that I wad see,
           His tricks sae mean;
Tho' them I saw fu' bonnily,
           Wi' my twa e'en.

And Patie Plumrock whiles cam owre,
The black moss hags at me to glowre,
Ay on't the Hogyet he wad cour,
           And seem fu' blate;
But weel kend I what kin' o' wo'er,
           I had o' Pate.

He was ane o' the hoolet class,
Wha nightly flee frae lass to lass,
A bleer-e'ed, hirpling, silly ass,
           An' oozly tyke;
I'm sure nae woman ever was,
           This gomf cud like.

Sic and sic like, my lads hae been,
A waufer squad sure few hae seen,
I wad been mad had I been keen,
           O' ony ane o'm;
My fortune I may thank I ween,
           For getting nane o'm.

They'd hing about the auld kirk-stile,
On Sundays wi' a sneering smile,
Whan I'd be coming owre the while,
              Wi' my white frock on;
'Bout me they stories wad compile,
              And jibe and joke on.

O ! there stood gaping mony a loon,
Frae clinty moors wi' muggart croon,
Boss a' gates but whar the horn-spoon,
              Its lades did coup ;
Lifted at morn, mid-day, and noon,
              Frae Goan and stoup.

I bid them fareweel, ane and a',
They ne'er again shall see me braw,
Out owre the seas I'm for awa,
              Ere this day week ;
To Boston, in America,
              A man to seek.

I'm on the right side thratty yet,
Has twa' red cheeks and gyly neat,
Can put on gowns that are fu' feat,
              Sae Minniegaff;
Farewel for ay, I shan't be beat,
              Adieu, I'm aff.

MINSHOCH.—A female goat two years old. *Barniewater*
said, he shot a *witch* once, wi' a *crooked saxpence*; she
was in the form o' a hare, but whan he drew *maur* her,
she was as big as a *minshoch*.

MISERTISH.—Having the manners of a miser; being
avaricious.

MISSLIE.—We say such a one is *misslie*, when his presence
is missed any where, and thought to be a wanting.

MITELED.—Eaten away, as if with *mites*. When *siller* is
chynged, it is said to be soon *mote* or *mitle* away.

MITHERS-PET.—The youngest child of a family; the mother's greatest favourite; the *Tony Lumpkin* of the house.

MOCHY.—We say of the weather, when it is warm and
moist, that it is *mochy* weather; and of every thing else
in a similar way, that it is *mochy*.

MOEMS.—Scraps of any thing, such as *moems* o' curiosity. Perhaps the English word *moiety* and it are one.

> Than moems, o' poems,
> I will sing unto thee,
> Sae laughing, and kauching,
> Thou fain would follow me.—
> *Auld sang.*

MOIDERT.—One whose intellects are rendered useless, by being in the habit of taking spirituous liquors to excess, is said to be *moidert*.

MOLLAN.—A long straight pole, such as fishermen use at their *fish-yards*.

MOOLLIE-HEELS.—A kind of chilblain, troublesome to the heels in frosty weather.

MOOLLIE PUDDING.—The game of *deadelie*; one has to run with the hands locked, and *taen* the others.

MOONOG.—A name for the *cranberry* or crawberry.

MOORLANDERS.—The natives of the moors. The manners of these people differ decidedly from those of the vale; there is more of nature in her primitive state about them, even the very priests become tinged; behold the portrait of one drawn the other day—

THE MOOR MINISTER.

> Weel do I like to see that worthy man,
> He has nae art, he's led by nature's plan,
> Nae pride o' laire, but modest, calm, and free,
> Nae fluent gab, and yet he pleases me;
> His neives ne'er lifted like a sledging mill,
> As if 'twad dash his harmless flock to hell,
> Nae gown has he upon his body laid,
> But his braid showthers fanked in a plaid;
> While on his feet he has a pair o' clogs,
> For plunging mang the saft and spouty bogs,
> Nor does he wi' them gie a clamping clink,
> Whan he wad wish his curious flock to think,
> But lets them see the lovely road fu' even,
> Owre the blue mountains to the Father's heaven.
> He dis na rant and seek for meikle words,
> Whatere he wants the bible soon affords,
> For sterling facts he never seeks for proof,
> But skelps the truth directly aff his loof;

He never writes, and makes a fuss and caper,
Out owre a lengthened sermon-scrabbled paper,
Fu' weel he tells his modest tale without it,
A downright text, and little mair about it ;
Lugs out his mull, and aft his neb will prime,
Lets out his fowk or it be dinner time,
While his queer hearers ane and a' agree,
A noble han' for *backing out* is he.

At christnings he taks a cheerfu' glass,
And on the ice his like sure never was,
He's fu' o' glee has a' around him sae,
They pingle meikle on his side to play ;
And aft a party he'll hae at the manse,
Some farmer's sin can fiddle, sae they dance,
While aft is seen upon the braw deal floor,
My worthy cheel—The *Minister i'e Moor*.

MORGOZ'D.—Made a confusion of ; any thing put into disorder, so that it cannot be righted, is said to be *morgozd*.

MORN-I'E-MORNING.—The morn after light dawns forth. Morning begins when twelve o'clock at night is run ; but the *morn-i'e-morning*, in the dead of winter, begins not until near eight o'clock. It is a singularly expressive phrase, the *morn* on the *morn*, and far from being the same with the morrow-morning ; *that* is the morning of another day spoken of, whereas *this* relates to one and the same morning.

MORROCH.—To soil any thing. When any thing is trampled in a gutter, we say it is *morroch'd* ; probably this and *gorroch*, is one and the same word as to derivation, but different as to meaning.

MORTH O' CAULD.—Those who receive a severe cold, get what is termed their *morth o' cauld* ; which means, their death from cold, (from Latin *mors*, death ; or *mort*, deadly.)

MOSHIN-HOLE.—The touch-hole of a piece of ordnance ; "*pike the moshin-hole*," say we, to those who are for firing a gun, when, on being *snap'd*, it *burns priming* ; which means, to clean out the touch-hole.

MOSS-BOILS.—Large moorland fountains, the sources of rivers.

MOSS-HAGGS.—Any break in black-looking, wild, mossy moors, is called a *hagg*.

MOWDIE-HILLANS.—Mole-hills; in the large ones, the animals have their nests, there they breed the young *mow-diewarts*.

MOWDIEMEN.—Mole catchers, from *mowdie*, a mole. These men are generally all from Westmorland, and commonly very singular characters. My *friend John Rook* is the most celebrated in this way. John is truly a wonderful, shrewd, good-natured fellow; his observations are all original, and his tales, jokes, &c. with the manner in which he tells them, have made me laugh a thousand times.

MOYLIE.—A mild, good-natured person; an *auld moylie*, a tame person, even to sillyness; a *moylie*, is also a bullock wanting horns.

MOZIE.—A *moidert-looking* person; a being with silly intellects.

MUCKLE-CHAIR.—The large *arm-chair*, common in all houses, whose inmates revere the memory of their forefathers; for farther knowledge respecting this rustic throne, peep at the following poem :—

Sae there ye sit, my worthy, snug,
In nuik aside the chimla-lug,
                    Whar there is nae frost air;
'Bout sofas let the gentles craik,
Of velvet cushions raise a fraik,
They canna' match the black moss-aik,
                    My muckle auld arm-chair.

Nae worm nor clock can break thy skin,
To hand a ticking din within,
                    And crump and hole thee sair;
Thy airny joints what time can fade,
That wricht kend surely weel his trade,
Whan thee sae strongly a' he made,
                    My darling auld arm-chair.

Faith, ablins true is that remark,
That thou wert ance in Noah's Ark,
       Some plank or timmer there ;
For every sage is at a loss,
To tell whan plonks lay down in moss,
I wat this is a question cross,
       My gruesome auld arm-chair.

But fancy we'll nae mair bout that,
In thee my douce fore-fathers sat,
       Three hundred years and mair ;
They sat in thee wi' honest pride,
The hazle clicky by their side,
And ruled around them far and wide,
       Their throne, the auld arm-chair.

There ploughmen's tales about their socks,
And what the herds kend o' the flocks,
       War laid afore them fair ;
There brye women too, wad ask,
What wark outby composed their task,
While round the ingle tykes wad bask,
       And neath the auld arm-chair.

And through the wunter lang forenights,
Mine Gutchers auld douce farming wights,
       O' clatters warna' spare ;
They'd crack 'bout things o' ither years,
Or take a turn at wads and wears,
Whilk ay the heart sae blithly cheers,
       My noble auld arm-chair.

And aften too, wi' serious luik,
They sat in thee and *tuik the buik,*
       Then read and gaed a prayer ;
While a' aroun' wi' a'e accord,
Wad listen to the sacred word,
They too wi' psalms wad praise the Lord,
       Frae thee, thou auld arm-chair.

Whan gurly norlan' blasts wad blaw,
And swurl in sneep white wrides the snaw,
       While lochs wi' frost wad rair ;
And burdies frae the wuds grew tame,
And curlers trimmled at their game,
I wat they'd fin' themsells ahame,
       Whan in the auld arm-chair.

O ! how my ancient seat I luve ye,
Nae plenishen in a' our Cruevie,
       Can wi' thee ava' compare ;
The glorious days o' Auld Lang Syne,
Ye lay afore the fancy fine,
While some ane o' the tunefu' nine,
       Ay haunts the auld arm-chair.

Whan I grow auld wi' blinkers hazy,
Wi' banes a shiegling and crazy,
            To thee I will wi' joy repair;
Forsake my craigs aside the shore,
Whar whiles I sit whan surges roar,
And nature's howfs whilk I adore,
            For thee my auld arm-chair.

There will I wear out life's frail trum,
Just clotching canny on my bum,
            We'll be a curious pair ;
My sma cauld spawls the gleed will beek,
And should my e'en whiles rin wi' reek,
Thou'lt gie me a' the ease I'll seek,
            My gracious auld arm-chair.

And should fate, like a shark gae chace,
Frae here the hale Maotaggart race,
            (Thou famous relique rare);
I hope the warl will thee regard,
And never reel ye unco hard,
But let some honest rustic bard,
            Enjoy the auld arm-chair.

Tho' ne'er will your brade bodden bear,
A man sae excellent, sae dear,
            And fu' o' nature's lair ;
As he wha now possesses thee,
And lang may he possessor be,
I mean my father, kind and free,
            Now in the auld arm-chair.

MUGG.—To strike or *buck* a ball out from a wall, as is done in the game of the *wa'baw*.

MUGG-SHEEP.—Sheep all white-coloured ; lowland sheep.

MUGGART.—The *mugwort*; out of these boys make *blowch-tons*.

MULDERT.—Mouldered, rotted, &c.

MUMPLE.—To seem as if going to vomit.

MUNN.—An old person with a very little face ; see *Cutty-mun*, and since writing that article, *Cultymuns and three Laddles*, have come into my head ; so this phrase may seem to say, that *Cuttymun* is a short-shanked spoon.

MUNNONDAY.—The ancient way of naming Monday.

MUREBURN.—The way they have in the moorlands of burning down the old heather, so that grass may arise to feed cattle and sheep. The heather is never allowed by

z

good farmers to grow more than four or five years. The work of *mureburn* goes on in the dry weather of spring, and blazes away with a rapid wildness, frightning hares and grouse from its neighbourhood. When viewed from the Lowlands on a fine night, it makes one fancy of the devastations of war, spreading so quickly when lighted, and encircling the wild mountains in red flaming curves. It must also somewhat resemble that scene seen by some travellers in foreign countries, of forests set in flames by the natives to destroy serpents, and scare away wild beasts. When any thing like bad news spreads fast, we say, " it goes like *mureburn*."

MURE-ILL.—A disorder common among cattle, and thought to proceed from the animals eating poisonous herbs; it is somewhat cured with doses of salts and saltpetre. *Nowt taen to a new gang*, or *nowt*, after a *spate*, are apt to take the *mure-ill* or *red-water*; it also prevails much with cattle which graze on a moor pasture; hence the name *mure-ill*, or the *ill* of the *moor*.

MURRAY, the Historian.—Mr. Murray, a gentleman who lately published the Literary History of Galloway, a work he has certainly done much justice to ; and I only think it a pity, that he paid so much attention to a subject, not surely worth the paying *attention* to. For instance, what was the use of rummaging ancient libraries, to know whether a certain priest once lived in a certain parish, and a *priest* who, when all is known of him that can be or *could* be, is worth nothing, he turns out to be a mere common *priest* ? Mr. M. is also too in an error, when he thinks that there are, or have been, no literary characters in Galloway but *priests*; however, the industry of this author I laud, and long to see directed to something of more consequence; perhaps I may take this home to myself.

MURRAY, the Linguist.—Dr. Murray, the celebrated linguist, and author, born in Minniegaff, died in Edinburgh, &c. &c. I have only one remark to make on him, and I have done. Why has he not given the world something respecting his native language, his mother tongue? did he look down on, and despise it? this I cannot think, for he was a lover of his country: yet I cannot help thinking that the Gallovidians are as good a tribe of human beings as any in the neighbourhood of *Gondar,* and as much worthy attention. It will be some time, in my opinion, ere a native of *Senaar,* returns the compliment to the Doctor's country which he has done to his. Had he clubbed his skill in the Scotch language to that of Dr. Jamieson, how much would Scotland have praised his name! What he has done, however, is well enough, and had his life been spared, we might have expected more. He has travelled with *Bruce* to the source of *Nilus,* as arduous a task as his name-sake *Bruce* had in establishing the independence of Scotland. Murray has shewn himself to be a creature of strong intellect, and unabating perseverance; view him in any light we will, we discover a wonderful prodigy.

MURRLIN.—A very froward child, ever whining and ill-natured.

MUSH.—A vast of matters tossed together, such as straw, grain, hay, chaff, &c.

MUSHOCH.—A heap of grain, thrashed out and laid aside in a corner for seed; this grain is confined into as small a bulk as possible, by surrounding it with *mushoch-rapes,* thick ropes twisted on purpose.

MUSSLE-BROSE.—A *brose* made from muscles. These shell-fish are boiled in their own *sap,* and this juice, when warm, is mingled with oatmeal; so a strong *brose* indeed is made, perhaps the strongest that can be; for it is

> A dish by Jove might feast a king,
> And paint his cheeks the rose,
> Make dulberts laugh, and poets sing,
> The sparkling Mussle-brose.

MULTER or MUTTER.—The miller's fee for his *melders*; if the *melder* be six bolls, the *mutter* is about the fortieth part.

MUTTYOCH'D or MOTTYOCH'D.—Matted; when sheaves of corn grow together, after being cut in moist weather, we say they are *muttyoch'd*, or matted together.

N.

NAB—A blow on the head.

NABBLE—A narrow-minded, greedy, laborious person.

NACKIE—A person expert at any art is said to be *nacky*.

NACKUZ — One who tells a tale pretty sharply; sometimes *naxie* is the word.

NAELSTRING—The umbilical cord.

NAGGS—Large pegs for hanging things out of the way on.

NAIL'D—Knocked over. Thus we say when we see a hare shot, that she's *nail'd*; also a villain caught at his tricks, is *nail'd*; and a girl when she gets pregnant of a spurious child, is said to be *nail'd* : the term is applied various ways, and may literally mean *fixed* as with a nail.

NAMES O' GRUNS—Names of farms. Our names for farms, like our names for various other things, are somewhat strange; a few of the derivations of them may be traced by good Celtic scholars to that ancient language, others to tongues of a like nature. Thus all those beginning with *Auchen, Drum, Nock,* &c. we may easily expound; but it would require a dab, methinks, in the Gaelic, to know the true meaning of *Orhars, Mollock, Killiemingie, Nabeny,* and so on. *Airds,* we know, stands for rocks; *Torrs,* for wet rocky land; *Senwicks,* for sandwicks, or sandy bays; *Granges,* for garnels or barns, &c. In every parish there are generally two farms, the

one named *Boreland*, the other *Ingleston* ; how these are
so named, antiquarians differ ; but as to those which have
burn, glen, cleuch, or any such natural objects in their
names, we see through them at once. Moorland farms,
too, differ much from those of the dale, with respect to
the character of their names ; they seem to be of a wilder
and outlandish nature. In Wigtonshire a cluster of moor-
farms lie together, unable amongst them all to grow a boll
of corn. I never hear their names mentioned but they
make me laugh—*Pultidee, Dirniemow, Glenkitten, Glen-
whully, Muirdow, Craigbirnoch,* the *Quarter* and the
Close. There are many in the stewartry of Kirkcudbright,
too, which amuse the ear, such as *Clauchendolly, Cull-
keggerie, Barrcheskie,* &c. People fond of flinging every
thing into rhyme, often fling the names of a number of
farms so for fun, but none of these I have heard comes
up with the Ayrshire one on this subject :—

     " Doughtie, Auchengairn, Dawine, and Dahairn,
     " Clasgalloch, the Balloch, the Challoch,
     " The Chang, and the Cairn."

These farms are all lying round the celebrated *Steps o'
Styncher,* on the way from Maybole to Newtonstewart,
by the famous *Nick o' the Balloch* way from Ayrshire to
Galloway—(not by the way of the famed *Laird o' the
Knows.*) The *Chang* is the Gaelic, I believe, for a
tongue, and the *Nick o' the Balloch,* means a *nick,* a hollow pass through moors, from which a great *balloch* or
moor view is to be had ; indeed, a great part of both Ayrshire and Galloway is seen from this place. It is not
long since some families lived in Galloway, who spoke
Gaelic ; so it will be found, the greater part of the names
of farms, *waters, parishes,* &c. come from that language ; thus, *Cree* is a march, a boundary, &c. ; *Ken,* the
chief ; *Kenmore,* the chief head. But why treat of this
farther ?

NANSE—The name for *Agnes*, or *Nannie*, or *Nancy*; a lovely lass of this name gave cause for the following song :—

NANCY GREENWOOD.

Farewell, say I, to learning
   To dungeon studies, dark and deep,
My heart is set a-yearning,
   I'm out of trim, I cannot sleep;
And all for Nancy Greenwood,
   Charming cheeked rosy queen,
I ne'er thought to've been this way,
   A fool with love so madly keen.

My mathematic brain now
   Is whirling all as wild's the wind,
Algebra gives me pain now,
   And nought with Fluxions I can find ;
But lovely Nancy Greenwood,
   Standing fair within my sight,
Sweet soul, she's all I now see,
   And all I care for in the light.

With rapture oft I've gazed
   Upon the sun, the moon, and stars,
But now my eyes are glazed,
   My passions all run to the wars ;
'Bout smiling Nancy Greenwood,
   Eclipsing deary, fair and free,
Shut up thy treasures, nature,
   I want no other gem from thee.

And let me climb that hill there,
   Or rove along the roaring shore,
My heart finds Nancy still there,
   And will, I fear, for evermore ;
'Tis full of Nancy Greenwood,
   The pain is heaven to endure;
Disorders are delightful,
   When love is both the cause and cure.

So sweet she comes before me,
   Shining like the solar beam,
That phantom would restore me,
   But ah ! that phantom is a dream ;
My darling Nancy Greenwood,
   Cares nothing for the rural boy,
As Nancy is a lady,
   So I must love, but ne'er enjoy.

NAPPLEROOT—The black knotty root of an herb, diligently digged for and greedily chewed by boys; its taste being rather pleasant.

NAPPS—Small vessels made of wood, for holding milk; little tubs termed *boynes*, in some places of Scotland, and coags in other.

NAPSIE—A fat little animal, such as a sheep.

NATHAN MACKIE—A very celebrated original Gallovidian priest and poet; his song of "*Jeamie, the glory and pride o' Dee*," is very natural, and sweetly sung; he was a most eccentric character, went about home very roughly clad; his hair, which was black, stood right on end; and in an old song wrote on him, a verse hints at this :—

> He gat na't frae his minnie, O !
> Nor yet frae his daddie,
> Some craddle fright, or some auld wight,
> Did swarf the young *Mackie* laddie.

He was a great fisher, and extremely charitable. In the *water* of Dee he would wade for days together, and fish for *geds*; few beggars ever came the way of his manse, but he gave them *quarters*. An old *carle* called on him one evening, and seeing the reverend gentleman in the *nuik*, and not very *divinely* clad, the beggar fancied that this was a personage like himself, but who had been more fortunate in getting the snug birth before him; so he turned on his heel, and walked away, saying "*hech how*, my room's taen up!" when the priest spoke out, and bade him "come away and reestle himself at the *ingle-cheek*;" which the *card* gladly obeyed. The anecdotes of Nathan are many, some of which will appear in the course of this work. A few specimens of his poetry I may give, thought to be his :—

> O ! I shall follow no man's way,
> Nor shall I imitate a manner,
> The best may often go astray,
> Tho' marching under virtue's banner.

> Would some kind spirit let me know
> This curious mystic, I'd like well,
> Which are the creatures here below
> Will go to Heaven, and which to Hell?

Then I'd be sensible which best
'Twould be for me to follow close,
To shun the damned, and love the blest,
Tho' they were hedged by many foes.
But none will this me e'er inform,
Yet Christ has pointed out the way,
Which I shall walk, and fear no storm,
With hopes to hail the eternal day.

BACK AND BELLY.

Confound ye for a cursed twa,
For you we grub and toil awa,
   And yet ye're ever yurning;
I wunner what wad really please,
And set ye truly at your ease,
   Your yammering and mourning.

Until ye're shot aneath the mools,
 Ye winna be at rest;
For here while living, just like fools,
 Ye're an unceasing pest.
  Nae claise there to lease there,
   Ye'll fin Sir Jolly Back,
  Nor Squire Belly, nought to fill ye,
   There ye'll sleep fu' pack.

O! had our bonny mither Eve
Ne'er dune that crime to make us grieve,
   Nae claes we now had needed;
And we'd hae had the best o' meat,
Whane'er we'd been inclined to eat,
   How happy we'd hae feeded.

But sae it is, we maun hae duds,
 Or else we canna do;
Toil we maun to co'er our fuds,
 And toil to meat us too.
  Ay rive on and strive on,
   And peck away and yisk,
  Till bitches o' stitches,
   Will catch us by the lisk.
Yirth's fu' o' wae, and mony a cheel will tell ye,
It maistly a' proceeds frae Back and Belly.

Nathan was really not a bad song composer; witness what follows:—

  O! I wish I had a bonny wee wife,
   To lie wi' me ate'en, O!
  Altho' she whiles might vex me sair,
   And keep my sorrows green, O!

For, curse me, I'm wearied lying my lane,
  I turn, I tumble, and gaunt, O!
I sweat and fret, and burning feels
  A gnawing, vexatious want, O!

Had I but Kate frae the Claverhown,
  Or Jeanie frae out Glen-nap, O!
Or Mary frae aff Barngaber hill,
  How I'd kiss, and cuddle, and clap, O!

But, damn me, I hae nae scun ava,
  And's ay for counting my purse, O!
The women I do lo'e devilish weel,
  Ise hae ane, tho' she plays the curse, O!

NATURALLS—Human beings who want a part of the mind that seemingly they ought to have; who move about, as it were, purely by the dictates of nature; such creatures are common in all countries, and attract the attention of men by their wild and out-of-the-way eccentricities. In Galloway there are and have been not a few of them; and I have often pleased myself in admiring their ways. *Davie Eddie* is one of the chiefs of this band; he *hotters* about the *clauchans,* and a troop of boys in his train, dancing to wandering fiddlers, and street bagpipe players. *Wull Gourlay* runs about the country, plays tunes on his nose, by making sound come through it, and touching the sides with his finger, so produces *sneeling* notes. He is also fond of eating *sclaters*; he puts the insects on his tongue, and, like the Ant-bear, lets them travel down his red gullet. *Sawny Clarnoch,* the *doil'd New Galloway herd*; there is something poetical in this *naturall*; he wanders by lonely shores, wild woods, and the tops of mountains, standing frequently and pondering; he is extremely modest, and would die, I dare say, before he would beg a bit; he runs barefoot, and attends country kirks on Sundays. *Jamie Neilson* is a droll soul, and every thing with him is either the *plan* or not the *plan*. Thus *peelocks* and *buttermilk's* the plan; *porridge* in a *barn* is not the plan.　*Girzey Whay*, a strange female, thus drawn by the poetic *howlate* :—

> In auld Kirkcubrie's borough town,
> Aboon her pillars o' renown,
> In ane bit garret hole sae high,
> Wi' lozzen keeking at the sky,
> Alane, half crackit, day by day,
> Wons shunner gatherer, Girzey Whay.
> 'Tis said she was o' extract good,
> And that her veins had gentle blood,
> But that some tyke betrayed the hizzie,
> Which left her mind, ay after, dizzie.
> Puir Girzey, wi' her upset chin,
> A nedeum gnaws her ay within;
> For ay she's gleboring to hersell,
> And cursing some to gang to hell.
> Whane'er rejoicing bells do sound,
> And flags are flapping a' around,
> The patriot, then, dis Girzey play,
> Frae her wee lozen waves awa;
> Ane pocket napkin on a staff,
> Which makes the burgess bodies laugh.—&c. &c.

Many act the *naturall* who are not so; they play the character for the sake of deception. *Johnie Girr*, of *Auchencairn*, was famous at this; in his young days, he was one of the greatest smugglers on the shores of the Solway, and outwitted the most sagacious *kingsmen*. Once while driving from the Isle of Man, with his little wherry pretty full of contraband goods, he was seen by a revenue cutter, who gave him chase. When Johnie saw this, he hove his barrels overside, fixed to a thick rope, and sank them; afterwards he took his seat at the helm, and bade the boy who sailed with him "go into the fore-scuttle and lie down." The cutter came snoring and firing, but our smuggler sat still in his *auld sea coat*, and never seemed to mind her; at length the revenue tars brought their row barge alongside, and damn'd our hero, saying, what "hindered to haul his wind and lie to, when he saw them playing away upon him?" "Gude guide us, (quoth Johnie, with a great deal of seeming ignorance) if I had ken'd it was me ye war firing at, I wad hae been *terrible fleyd*;" which

answer, and seeing nothing but a stupid looking old man
aboard, convinced the *kingsmen* that John was doing, or
could do nothing in the smuggling trade. *Gude guide us!*
was always his favourite exclamation, and he gave it with
such a mystic gravity of face, that the most serious could
not help laughing at him.

NEB O' THE MORNING—That part of the day between
day-light and sun-rising, or sun-light; the *neb* or nose of
an animal being its front member, so this part of the day,
being its front part, is termed the neb also; now the *neb*
of any animal is commonly its coldest member, the beak
of the morning is the coldest space of the day. And there
are few who do not love to keep the bed until the *neb
gangs aff the morning*; the coldest time, in cold weather, is always this time before sun-rise; it is when the *neb
is on the morning* that the hoar-frost is produced.

NEDEUM—A gnawing pain; when a corn is biting a toe
grievously, that toe is said to be *nedeuming*; when a person considers himself injured by the world, and is seen
to shun society, foster melancholy and misanthropic
feelings, that being is said to have a *nedeum* gnawing his
inwards; when he is heard to curse and utter wicked im-
precations to himself, he is then *nedeuming*.

NEERS—The kidneys of animals; *neer-strings*, those strings
which are connected with the kidneys.

NEETS—Young lice, or the eggs of lice. *Powlie*, the
muirkirk name for a louse.

NEETY-CUD—A low-lifed fellow who commits mean actions.

NEIVEIE-NICK-NACK—A fireside game; a person puts a
little trifle, such as a button, into one hand, shuts it close,
the other hand is also shut; then they both are whirled
round and round one another as fast as they can, before
the nose of the one who intends to guess what hand the
prize is in; and if the guesser be so fortunate as to guess

the hand the prize is in, it becomes his property; the whirling of the fists is attended with the following rhyme :—

> " Neiveie, Neiveie, nick, nack,
> " What ane will ye take?
> " The right or the wrang;
> " Guess or it be lang,
> " Plot awa and plan,
> " I'll cheat ye gif I can."

NIDDER—The second shoot grain makes when growing; in dry seasons it never bursts the *nidder*; this and *niddering*, to pine and fret, to seem in a withering state, are the same.

NIDDLE—To overcome; *he niddled her*, that is to say, he overcame and robbed her.

NIDGELL—A fat, froward young man; a stiff lover, one whom no rival will displace.

NIG-MA-NIES—Unnecessary ornaments.

NITTERS—A greedy, grubbing, impudent, withered female.

NITWUDS—Woods of natural hazel, where *nuts* are found.

NOCKET—A mid-day lunch.

NOCKS—Little beautiful hills; *Nockshinnie* and *Nocktannie* used to be favourite *nocks* of mine; to these places I would steal sometimes, when melancholy set sore upon upon me, and so get ease.

> Whan mirky cluds in the south-wast,
> Are masking up a blashy blast,
> The welkin blae to overcast,
>   And hide the starns;
> How like they're to the brewings vast,
>   Whiles o' my haurns.
>
> Wild, gloomy, melancholy, mad,
> Detesting beauty, sick, and sad,
> Wi' passions boiling furious bad,
>   May nane e'er be,
> As I hae been, weak, simple lad,
>   Born as ye see.
>
> In vain I try my brain to cool,
> 'Twad burn within the cauldest pool,
> I ramble downcast, like a fool,
>   By thought opprest;
> Wi' fancy a' flown out o' rule,
>   And winna rest,

It winna wi' me here abide,
But darts athwart the ocean's tide,
And flashes through creation wide,
                    The flighty wight ;
Nor halts where marches do divide
                    The day and night.

If Nature had na been a charm,
If had my heart been no sae warm,
Owre keen to burst and take alarm
                    Frae nought ava,
I might then live 'thout feeling harm,
                    And grub awa.

My days wad then be ne'er alike,
Nae feelings than wad make me fike,
Then might I, like a young doaf tike,
                    Bough at the moon ;
Or crazed Billjock ayont the dike,
                    Play boo and croon.

Pain and remorse, sweet fun and glee,
Wad than be ne'er unken'd to me,
In vain might Tibbie's heavenly e'e,
                    Wink fu' o' love ;
For than nae mair I'd stewed be,
                    In Cupid's stove.

O! wad my passions row mair queem,
My sunless saul delight to gleam,
How happy wad I down life's stream
                    Gae soom awa ;
Without a restless, hellish dream,
                    My saul to thraw.

Then, like the south-wast, whan 'tis urey,
Divested of its wrath and fury,
Wi' sun-beams sooking blue and pure, ay,
                    The saut green wave ;
I'd be dear, oh ! wi' nought to hurry,
                    Or gar me rave.

But, thanks to God, wha ne'er forgot
An humble craving sinner's lot,
Thou't pouring forth the antidote
                    For its relief ;
A cure for this vile nether spot,
                    And a' its grief.

On every sorrowfu' occasion
I flee to him for consolation,
No wi' a lang and canld narration
                    O' ills to mend ;
But shortly, simply, my sad station,
                    Sae makes an end.

Whan meikle's asked for, little's gien,
Ane lang petitions ay, ill ta'en,
The thing is natural, I ween,
  Sae wants nae proof;
There's nought like skelping a' things clean,
  And warm aff loof.

Religion sooths my weary saul,
By it alane on yirth I crawl,
And fronteth ilka bitter brawl,
  'Thou't dread or fear;
Ay hoping broyliments will quall
  Frae year to year.

Indeed, now I am not near so much troubled with this distemper as I once was. When in my teens, I often thought it was going to overset my mind altogether.

NOGGAN—Walking steadily, and regularly nodding the head.

NOGGINS—Little wooden dishes.

NOGGS—The handles of a *scythe-sned,* or scythe-shank.

NOITLED—Intoxicated with spirits.

NOITS—Little rocky hills; also any little rocky rise.

NOOF—Snug; sheltered from the blast.

NOOLS—Small horns, which are not connected with the scull-bone.

NOOPING—Walking with eyes on the ground, and head nodding.

NORART—When the wind blows any way out of a northerly *airt,* or direction, it is said to be blowing from the *Norart.*

NORWASTERT—A bitter blast; any thing of a rude cold nature is said to be a *Norwastert.*

NOUDS—Little fish, about the size of herrings, with a horny skin, common in the Galloway seas.

NUBBIE—An unsocial person, worldly, yet lazy.

NUIST—A blow. When two are boxing, and one gets the other's head beneath his arm, he is said to *nuist* him with the other hand: also *nuist* means a greedy, ill-disposed, ignorant person.

NURGLE or NURG—A short-squat, little, savage man.

NURLING—A person of a *nurring*, or cat disposition.

NYAPH—The female nymphæ, Clytoris, Pubes, &c.

NYARGLE—A person fond of disputation, yet reasons like a fool. *Nyargling*—wrangling ; *threaping*—nonsense. That being is a *nyargle*, who—

> " Whenever there gets up dispute
> " Will still change sides, and try confute ;"

as was the plan of Doughty Hudibras, who, like the *Dominie*—

> " That even tho' vanquished, he would argue still."

NYATTERIN.—To keep chattering when others are speaking ; a person who wants not to hear any thing, but wants a *hearing*; a pest to society. All should obey the natural orders of Allan Ramsey—" Learn to steek the gab awee, and think afare we speak."

O.

O! AY!—O yes.

OBERING.—A hint; an inkling of something important, yet thought a secret. " I gat the *obering* o' a wadding that's to happen soon ;" means, I got hint of such like, in a crafty way.

OHO!—An exclamation of joy, or rather a joyous assent to the truth of a tale a telling ; thus, if it is said that such a one has got haud o' a rich hizzie for a wife, " *Oho!* faith, that cheel has done weel," is the answer.

OOZLIE.—A person is said to be *oozlie* looking, when he has on a long beard, unbrushed clothes, and dirty shoes, as is the case with those who love the " late debauch.'

ORISHEN.—A term of reproach, for a savage-behaved individual ; probably this word is from the French *ourson*, a bear's cub.

ORPIE-LEAVES.—The leaves of a plant called Orpy ; good for healing cuts.

ORTS.—Food for horses ; the seed of hay and corn mingled together.

OSHEN.—A mean person ; from the French *oison*, a ninny.

OUNCLE-WEIGHTS.—A general sweeping name for all the *weights* that are used about farm-houses, for the purposes of weighing ; these weights are generally sea-stones of various sizes, regulated to some standard. And the Galloway folks have been long famed for giving *down-weights*, or something more than enough, of any thing they either sell by weight or measure. I once heard a tolerable joke respecting this. A person came to an honest *gude wife*, and wanted a *pun* o' butter, but, as bad luck would have it, the *punstane* was lost, so she did not know how in all the world she should serve her customer ; the *ouncle-weights* were rummaged over and over, and none less than the *mealstone quarter* could be found, and with this she saw it was impossible to weigh a pound ; while pondering the matter as a gude wife ponders, the *tangs* (tongs) struck her fancy. " O ! (quo she) I ken how we'll manage now ; the gude man brought hame a pair o' new tangs the ither night, which weighed in the smiddy just twapun ; sae stand by and I'll soon weigh ye wi' them your butter." She then opened the legs of the tongs, put one leg in the scale against the butter, and let the other hang out. The beam got its fair swing, and so weighed a douce Galloway pound of butter.

OUTCA.—A wedding feast given by the master to a favourite servant ; also a small inclosure to drive *housed* cattle a while of the day to, so that they may snuff the *cauller air*.

OUTINS.—Tours from home ; young people are all fond of this, too fond whiles, seeing the truth of the old proverb, that a " Rolling stane will never gather fog."

OUTLERS.—Cattle which are wintered in the fields.—See *Yellnowt.*

OUTRING.—A channlestone term, the reverse of *Inring*, (which see). To *take* an *outring*, is generally allowed to be more difficult than *taking* an *inring*.

OUTSHOT.—Any thing shoved or *shot* out of its place farther than it should be ; a bilge in a wall.

OWLING.—Looking like an owl.

OWRE BOGGIE.—People are said to be married in an *owre boggie* manner, or to have an *owrie boggie wedding* when they do not go through the regular forms prescribed by the national kirk. There is some sweetness, I should think, and gallantry felt in weddings of this kind ; there is something glorious in a trip to *Gretna Green* with a lovely lady : staying and getting quietly noosed at home is no work— I relish the *owre boggie* system. Those who plot in secret are called *auld boggie fowk* ; and displaced priests, who used to bind people contrary to the canon laws, though agreeably to nature's, were designated *auld boggies*. There was an ancient song, I believe, of the name of *Owre Boggie*, burned at Edinburgh in the turbulent times ; this song is lost, so think the antiquaries.

OWRGAUN RAPES.—Ropes put over stacks to hold down the thatch ; the vertical ropes into which are wove the *bridlers*, or those which run horizontal.

OWRIM AND OWRIM.—When a *bandwun o' shearers* meet with a *flat* of growing grain, not portioned out to them by *riggs*, the shearing of this is termed an *owrim and owrim shear*, or over-him and over-him. It is a bad plan of reaping, as when the reapers have not equal shares, some will work and some not ; some take more than they should, others not so much. A fellow from Green Erin thus exclaimed once against this mode—" Hoh ! botheration, rigim and rigim was a pleasant shear, but *owrim* and *owrim* was the devil ; but *Barney* can do any thing sweet and azy. What's the use of a fellow, if he is not a hell of a fellow, and has driv a hearse through all *County Down*, with his hair close *tied?*"

OWRTER.—Farther over. *Lye owrter*, lie farther over.

OWRWALES.—The refuse of any thing selected; the goats, when the sheep are taken away.

OXTER.—The arm-pit; also to walk arm in arm. *Oxtering alang*, walking away arm in arm.

OXTERLEE.—An old fellow of an extremely *crabbit* nature, who once lived at this place in Galloway; he unluckily was a weaver, a trade that by no means agrees with a bad temper; when a thread would have at any time broke, he would leap down through the web with his feet. The wretch also loved drink, and to beat his wife when he was intoxicated; while going home from the alehouse once, he was heard saying to himself, " If she's gane lye I'll lick her; and if she be up, I'll lick her," viz. his poor wife. Mercy on us, this was giving her no chance for life!

OYEZ!—Hear ye! The word is from the French *oyez*; old imperative of the verb *ouir*, to hear. It is used in France as a call to attention, before proclamations are read in public places; anciently it was used in our country for the same purpose. *Oyez*, and sometimes *a-oyez*, was heard sounding at fairs, as common as " Roll away, sport away, and be handy," is at this day by *Irish fling-sticks* and *wheel o' fortune sharpers*; at present, old men use it after mentioning things of consequence, as " my son gat a rich wife, *oyze*."—" The fallow's worth siller, *oyze*."—" It's a gude farm, *oyze*," and so forth.

P.

PADDERT—Padded. Thus a road through the snow is *padderd*, when it has been often trod.

PADDLED ROUNALL.—In large fields where great flocks of oxen graze together, they have places where they often assemble and seem to amuse themselves, following each other round and round, like boyant bodies in an aquatic vortex. The cause for these animals thus employing themselves at intervals, I have never learned; it proceeds neither from heat, nor from troublesome insects. The brute creation often astonishes man with scenes which seem full of sense ; this is instinct : but what I have been here speaking about surprises him with a mystical something he cannot describe. These circular spots then shorn of grass are termed *paddled rounalls.*

PADDOCK.—A small farm ; also a machine shaped like a frog, for carrying large stones.

PADD-SADDLE.—A soft seat for females to ride on horseback behind their husbands.

PADJELL.—An old veteran pedestrian ; one who has often beat at foot races—these races were once very common in Galloway. A servant of Lord Kenmore beat the whole country at running for years. The night previous to a New Galloway fair, his lordship sent his man away to Edinburgh on an errand, that he might be out of the way, and not shame the fair for a season with his swiftness ; off went the fellow, but returned in time to run and gain the prize as usual, though he had run 180 miles in twenty-four hours just before it. Prior to the invention of post offices, all lords and barons had their couriers, and this fellow must have been a fleet one.

PAINCHES.—The paunches of animals—the guts.

PAISING.—Weighing any thing by the feel of the hand— poising.

PALACE-TREE.—The place in Galloway, near the village of Gatehouse, whereon stood a *palace* in the days of yore ; a deep ditch surrounds a level space containing about two acres—on this stands the ruined edifice ; over this ditch, which is about thirty feet, and filled with water, a draw bridge yet remains in perfection. This palace is thought to have belonged to our olden Scotch kings; and suited them for a *Holyrood,* when in the southern parts of the dominion.

PAP.—To let any thing fall lightly, is to let it *pap.*

PAPPLE.—A noxious seed which grows amongst wheat: extremely prolific.

PAPPLE, THE SPEAVER.—On my life, I cannot pass this original in silence, for few men would I rather spend an hour with than Mr. Papple, the *speaver*; he personally knows almost every one in the south of Scotland, and is deeply acquainted with the manners of his native country; he seems as if he had gone up and down the interior of the bosoms of men with a lantern and candle, and seen all the hidden springs of the mysterious mind. He goes regularly round the country, castrating and keeping the brute creation in order; all news hears he, and what he hears never forgets: methinks he has all by heart that he has heard these fifty years; ask him of any particular respecting his country, either of one thing or another, and if he knows nothing about it, it is strange. When at home, he is to be found at New Galloway; but he has a home every where in the country, and had I a house, that should also be one of his homes; there might he dawner in on an evening, 'lay by *clicky* on the press head, throw off his *laggans,* draw into the *ingle,* take tea, toddy, what not, with the utmost comfort; then to the pipe, and crack how folk in *moor countries* were doing, and how the famous and worthy *Provost o' New Galloway* was coming on; how sheep *smear'd* and sold; how *Shiel,* honest man, did; and my friend Dr. *Trotter,* if writing any good tales, or if *Barbour* had any thing ready for the *press*; how *Kenmore* was doing, and how the Miss *Dayells* were looking; if the *Lammas spate* made the *brig totter*; or if the *tip premium* was good, and whether *Manson* had any old *brandy*; such and such things would be through hands, before Mr. P. and me would part; aye, and five hundred things more, which have not been dreamt of.

PARTONS—Crab fish; for more particulars, see the article *Roddock.*

PASPER—Samphire. When taken and eat green from the *heuchs,* makes persons as hungry as a hawk, consequently a healthy herb; it is not easily obtained in some places, no more than it is on *Dover Cliffs.*

PAT AND PLAIN.—A downright honest way of speaking.

PAUL JONES, the Pirate.—The late celebrated sea robber; a Gallovidian, I am rather sorry to say, but he was a clever devil, had strong talents of the infernal stamp; he was a short thick little fellow, about five feet eight in height, of a dark swarthy complexion. Now I am going to say somewhat of this fellow, and all I say I think is truth, for I have it from the lips of many who personally knew him, and all about his singular ways. He was a common sailor for several years, out of the port of Kirkcudbright, and was allowed to be unmatched on that coast for skill in sea matters; he was a pilot of the first kind, was quick at conception, and a prophet at foretelling the coming of storms; and when tempests might catch the bark he was in, he dreaded them not, but, like Falconer's Rodmand, was

> " First in action—in retreat the last."

Yet, though a famous seaman, his mess-mates generally disliked him; he was of a quick, fiery temper, and of a mad, ambitious, aspiring nature; and when roused, he cared not what he did, but would have knocked down all who came in his way, with the first weapon he fell in with; a *capstern-bar* was his favourite cudjell, and once being beset with a *press-gang*, in Liverpool, he laid three dead

on the deck, and dashed the rest overside his sloop, into
the *Salthouse Dock.* Having got the command of a pretty
large vessel belonging to Kircudbright, he set sail with
her to America, for a cargo of tobacco; while crossing the wide Atlantic, one of the crew, a young lad of
fair promise, having some how or other irritated him, the
devilish monster ran to a pot of pitch boiling on the deck,
and flang a ladle-full of the horrid fluid about the youth,
who, in desperation with the pain, leaped overboard,
into the gulf stream, and was seen no more. The Earl
of Selkirk, hearing of this diabolical act of Paul Jones,
threatened, that if ever he came back to the country, he
should receive his reward in punishment for the same.
Such news reaching the horrid captain, as he lay with
his ship off Long Island, New York, gave him the first
hint of changing his mode of life; having got a crew he
could depend on in every infernal enterprize, and having
turned such as did not suit him adrift, he steered out a
pirate, bent on bloody deeds, scouring the ocean in all
directions, and taking prizes and property to great amount;
it was now neck or nothing with him, so he brought his
mighty talents fairly into action. Ships of all nations
dreaded him; the name of Paul Jones struck terror into
thousands, and he was frequently thought, like *Crumwhull's*
gib cat, to be where he was not. Having captured, at
one time and another, a large fleet, he became quite a
piratic Commodore, and was more severe on Britain than
on any other nation, and most favourable to the French;
the latter soon becoming acquainted with this kindness,
offered him one of their highest naval situations, which
was channel pilot, the which he accepted, and became
a great favourite at the court of France. It was just
about this stage of his career, that he made his attack
upon *Auld Scotland,* to be revenged on the Earl of
Selkirk, for his threat towards him. He brought his
fine ship of war, the Serapis, to an anchor, at the mouth

of his native river Dee, one beautiful summer morning, about forty-five years ago, and sent his barge, manned and armed, to *St. Mary's Isle,* for the purpose of catching his Lordship, who luckily was not at home that day. After surrounding the mansion, and making search, the pirates came off disappointed, but took the family silver plate with them, the which they, after a time, returned, accompanying the same with a singular letter, in which was notified, that if his lordship had been with him, after he left the Dee, he would have witnessed a fine sea-fight between him and the Ranger, British frigate: this was a severe bout; the pirates beat her off, but did not follow up their capture. What he would have done with his lordship had he caught him, has been a question; it is thought that he would ransomed him for the value of his estate, and so caused his utter ruin. Before arriving at the Dee, he had called at *Whitehaven,* a town that had once huffed him, and having spiked the cannons on the battery there, he attempted to set the place on fire, but the houses being all of free-stone, he could not get it to blaze so well as he wished; such traits, in the character of Paul Jones, prove him a being of an hellish disposition ; for those men of a revengeful nature, are evidently the most horrid wretches on earth. Having rounded Scotland, and visited the Firth of Forth, he returned to Brest—attended on the French navy, and had them frequently on the point almost of starting to the invasion of Britain ; falling sick, however, he retired to Paris, or somewhere in its neighbourhood, where he died, a young man rather, not fifty years of age ; he died very rich, and all his gold went to the French treasury ; whether any of his heirs in Galloway, could come at any of this, I know not. He was the father of a natural son, by a married lady, the which son yet lives, but is ratherly a *doyloch.* Paul Jones seems to be unrivalled as a pirate; his undaunted courage, his penetrating judgment, and his savage temper, befitted him in an extraordinary manner for the damnable trade. It is laughable to look back at the sensation he caused amongst the rural bodies of Galloway, when he brought his ship upon their lonely shores; some armed themselves with scythes, some with pitch-forks, old guns too were looked at, while many fled and hid themselves in *Rossens o' whuns,* caves, and wild mosses. A row-boat went down the river heavily armed, the evening he stood out to sea, for the purpose of *intercepting* him with their tale of it, if he dared to return; when this boat came in sight of the *Oyster Craig,* it was thought to be *Paul Jones's armed barge,* so a heavy firing was opened on it, and as the tide was filling, the rock in time became covered with water, so the fluttering fancies of the borough-bravadoes conceiving that the barge was down, they returned in a joyous flight home; next day they went back, and on examining the rock, found it battered *blue* with the leaden bullets, since which time it has been termed the *Frenchman's Rock.*

PAWCHLE.—A frail old body, seeming, as it were, to *paw* for assistance; also, a person of low stature, rather silly.

PAWMIE.—A name for the Knave at Cards; oftener *Jack.*

PAWT.—To paw with the feet; she never gaed a *pawt,* she never moved her feet.

PEANER.—A cold-looking, naked, trembling being—small of size.

PEANERFLEE.—A light-looking, *craw o' a body;* one like *Auld Ned,* who looks like *taking the air.* Ned is really a wonderful soul, and singular enough in his way; an honest body, full of life, and takes a glass of good *whisky* with any man; his *intimmers* are of the best kind, he can be drunk and sober three times in a day; can drink as much as would fill three strong men full; *tarr ar a, tantra bubus, big bull waggie, bow, wow, wow,* is Ned's song, which he gives with a *scraigh* when *fou;* indeed, he is the finest *scraigher* I ever heard; he has no care, and as for the kicks of the world and fortune, he values them nothing.

PEANIES.—Female turkeys.

PEATCLAIG.—A place built with stones to hold peats.

PEATNUIK.—A nook to hold peats, generally a dark corner; it is the prison in country schools for culprits and dunces, and is the first gaol of many that bad boys are frequently put into. In a worthy *dominie's diary*, the following funny day's work appears:—" 24th May—A little restive the greater part of the night, was often lying on my right side, often on my left: started at six, said prayers, washed face, and mounted hill to look about me; a fine breeze S. S. W. thin clouds over the sun's face. Saw the fox steal into the wood with a hen between his jaws; thought at first it was my white duck, was agreeably surprised on finding it was not she. Found a lark's nest, and four young ones in it; put up my *mark*, so that I might see it again; thought about taming a lark, then thought again there might be despotism in me if I did so, laughed at the idea; took breakfast, eat three eggs, wife a little sulky; opened school at ten, looked the key to Hutton's Arithmetic, found the boys riotous, put three to the *peatnuik*; opened a new Latin class, saw a beauty in Horace I had not seen before. Boys still riotous, put two more to the *peatnuik*; plied my cane freely, broke it o'er a young rascal's head, had a sorry day's teaching; let the school out an hour sooner then usual, looked at my lancets, went and bled a female friend; met at her house a young man from Edinburgh, a doctor, found much medical knowledge in him; came home, wife in better humour, planted some cabbages, took the cow to the bull;" so ends that day's principal transactions.

PECHAN.—The belly; *peching*, blowing; *pech*, to blow.

PEDRALL.—A child beginning to walk; *paidle*.

Peelaflee.—A light person, and not heavily clothed.

Peelaneets.—Potatoes, boiled with their skins on.

Peeling.—Travelling in a windy, wild day, with light clothes on.

Peelocks.—The same as *Peelaneets*; *murphies* needing *peeling*.

Peg.—The ball *shinie players* play with.

Pegpie—The magpie; *pees-weep*, the lapwing.

Peg Puff.—A young woman resembling an old one in her manners.

Pellocks.—Porpoises; seen before a storm

Pen.—An old saucy man, with a sharp nose.

Penn.—A sewer; see *Rummling Sire*.

Penpunt.—*Waefu' cheel*, as he used to term himself, when running the country. For *Penpunt* was a beggar of strange character, and because he belonged to the *clauchen o' Penpunt*, from it had he is name, and well was known for long all over the country. Though pretty well liked by folks as a poor man, he was a greedy wretch, and outwalked all other vagrants that crossed his path; could walk between fifty and sixty miles every day, and call at all houses that came in his way; on entering a house he used always to sing out—" Here comes Auld Penpunt, waefu' cheel, gie him his *awmous*, and let him rin again!" He understood the art of begging well, could tell a tolerable tale, and sing a smutty Galloway snatch, such as the *Bonny Muirhen*; and also shew that he knew more than one would have thought. A *brade blue bonnet* wore he, ane bonnet like a *winnowing wecht*; a plaid was always fanked round his shoulders, so with a large *rung* or *bourdoun* in hand, rambled *Penpunt*; his wife and family would never eat any of his *awmous* meal. On a brother of his who had a small farm, he often insisted to take the mealpowk by the string, and follow him, as his trade was much better than farming; he would often say, " that begging was not worthy the following gin, ane cudna turn a crown a day at it." He departed this life, *waefu' man*, about two or three years since, and was honoured with some notice, in the obituary of a Dumfries newspaper—

> Tho' his tongue was na blunt,
> Tho' he bore a strong runt,
> Death dang to the de'il, the queer shaver Penpunt.
> Sae he's taen frae his trade,
> And his bonnet sae brade,
> And lies here 'neath the swade,
> Waefu' body Penpunt.—
>
> *Penpunt's Epitaph.*

PETER A DICK'S PEATSTACK.—A favourite dancing *step* with the peasantry, performed by giving three *flegs* with the feet, and two stamps with the heel alternately; such is the simple dance, the movement of the feet correspond to these words when said at the same time; indeed, the noise the feet makes, seems to speak them—*Peter a Dick, Peter a Dick, Peter a Dick's Peatstack.* It is commonly the first *step* dancing masters teach their pupils; the A, B, C, &c. of dancing science, when the scholars become tolerable at *beetling it*; they are next taught to *fleup* through the *side-step*; then *Jack on the Green, Shawin-trewse*, and other *hornpipes*, with the *Highland Fling*, mayhap; these dances are all got pretty well by the feet in the *first month*, with sketches of *foursome*, eightsome reels, and some country dances; but if the scholars attend the *fortnight* again of another *month*, they proceed at great length into the labyrinths of the art. A *light heel'd sooter* is generally the dancing dominie; he fixes on a barn in some *clauchan* to show forth in; he can both fiddle and dance, at the same time; can cut double quick time, and *trible Bob Major*; he fixes on, and publishes abroad when his *trial night* is to come on, so the young folks in the neighbourhood doff their *clogs*, and put on

their *kirk-shoon*, these being their *dancing pumps*; off
they go to the *trial*, which, if it be a good turn-out, he
tries no more, but begins teaching directly; if not, he has
a *second*, and even a *third* trial; well, in the first month,
as has been stated, such dances are taught; in the second,
The "Flowers of Edinburgh," mayhap; *Sweden* and
Belile's Marches, with other hornpipes, and country dances
many; such as the *Yillwife and her Barrles—Mary Grey—
The wun that shook the barley*, &c. with the famous
Bumpkin Brawley; yes, and they will even dare, sometimes, to imitate our Continental neighbours over the
water, in their *waltzing, alimanging*, and *Cotillion trade*;
ay, and be up with the Spaniards too, in their *quadrills,
borellos*, and *falderalloes* of nonsense; so out-taught, they
become fit to attend *house-heatings, volunteer, and mason-
nic balls*, what not. *Partners* are taken to the *practeez-
ings* and *balls*; these girls, whom boys choose thus to
partner them, are commonly beloved by them for ever
afterwards; indeed, *love* is first felt by thousands at danc-
ing-schools; to those sweet dears, *ribbons, lockets, and
strings o' beads*, are brought, adorn their fair bodies.
Now, after all, I am not meaning to laugh at this art,
nor do I intend to praise it. Dancing is a famous
amusement, but, like every art, I have known some better
at it who were never taught than those who were; who
could give a *hooh* and a *crack* with their heels, in a wonderful funny original manner.

PETER'S PLEUGH.—The constellation Ursa Major, or the
big bear; the *twa big stars o' the soam*, point to the
Pole star.

> "Lang Peter's Pleugh lift hintings round the Pole."
> *Wallet Poem.*

PETT-DAYS.—Good days, among foul weather. A *pet* is
always a dangerous creature; thus a child, *petted* by its
parents, plays the devil some day or other in the world;

a sheep *petted*, is apt to turn a *duncher*; and a friend, *dawted* too much, is likely to become an adder.

PEYAY.—The call milk-maids make for calves to come to their mothers.

PEYVEE.—A strange nonsensical bustle, for no end; a ceremonious fluster; some people are always in a *peyvee* throng, seemingly to the last degree, yet doing little; still in a breathless state, without a moment's time to spare to speak to an honest man, who *bicker* quick along the streets, and have brains *full* of emptiness.

PICK and CHUSE.—Select, and stand by the selected; to find a wife, in the wide world of women, then keep by her.

PICKING-CAUVE.—Cows are said to *pick-cauve*, when they have *miscarriages*; that is to say, bring forth their young before the proper period; when one *cow* in a flock takes this, *gee* generally more of them do. Farmers, to prevent this, take good care not to irritate their cows, by bringing dogs amongst them, or shedding blood of oxen on their pasture.

PICKTHANK.—A talepyet; one who bites behind backs.

PIEING.—Looking steadfastly at some object; like a dog, when he sees ground a stirring by a mole in it; how he looks, making his head move from side to side, before he pounces.

PIEPHER.—An extremely useless creature, probably a *cypher*; a nothing in a common wealth, such is a *piepher-ing monkey*.

PIGGS.—Porcelain ware. *Piggs and whustles*, a man's foolish furniture, *nick nacks*, which are always in the way. *Pigg-wives*, females who trudge the country with *trackpot ware, bowls*, plates, &c. they are only one remove from common beggars, and mostly more disliked.

PIKET-BODIES.—People narrowly disposed, who grub and *pick pikings*, food left after a feast. " Dogs are flung banes to *pike*." A beggar man once got a bone from a miser to pick, and was observed on the sunny side of a dyke, *piking* it with his *specks* on, which bespoke the charitable *donor*.

PILLION—A sack filled with soft matter for people to ride on; also *pillions* are sacks and budgets full of soft stuffs.

PINGLE—To strive, to *kemp*, to compete; *pingle-pans*, little pans for preparing food for babes in.

PINKERTON—A person beneath expectation, one with a small mind, with only a *pink*, or small gleam of light in it, such as Sawnie Corbie, who, being at a parish kirk once, with a " *split new* suit o' claes on," after the *preaching was owre*, a *wat day* came on; Sawnie, loath to have his clothes *steeped*, flung them off his back, bundled them in his plaid, and *skelped* home mither naked; such is a *pinkerton*, or *pinkie*.

PINKLE-PANKLE—The sound of liquid in a bottle.

PIPER'S Co' o' COWEND—A very celebrated Gallovidian cave in the parish of Colvend; it is situated on a lonely shore, and frequently is heard the sound of the *bagpipe* therein; whiles the wild pibroch is a merry, but oftener a melancholy air; some think the *piper the devil*, others fancy the musician to be some kind *carline*, who reveres the memory of departed Highlanders, who were anciently smothered in the cave; there is also a bottomless well in it, at least one which lead and cord hath not yet sounded.

PIRNIES—Night-caps, woven of various coloured threads, such as those bearing the name of *Killmarnock*. The Laird o' Broomcleuch was a bachelor, and for many years was troubled with a swelling in the breast, so that the old gentleman could scarcely bestir himself any where; so his friends gathered about him like *corby-craws*, and one took away this part of his property, another that, until the laird's house became almost entirely empty, or, as he said

himself, " they herried me." One day while he was
sitting alone in his mansion, reflecting about its emptiness, a monkey which he kept, and which his relations
did not think worthy to carry away, came frisking about
him, leaped on to his shoulder, and plucked off his *pirnie*,
making off with the booty as fast as it could *spang*. The
laird, at this, fell into a tremendous fit of laughter, which
so much agitated the swollen breast, that it burst in the
interior with an awful gush, the which bilious matter he
vomited up, and in a short time was able to move about
amongst his friends, and thank them for the kindness and
attention they had shewn him during his illness, by desir-
ing them, in not a very pleasant tone, to return him every
article which they had forcibly purloined ; afterwards he
made a will, in which, I believe, there was no mention
made of those who so kindly attended his sick bed ; such
is always the fate of the over-greedy—

> For if they glie and grasp at a'
> The devil ha'et they'll get ava'.

PIRR—Blood is said to *pirr* from the wound made by a
lancet; a girl is said to look *pirr* when gaily dressed. *Pirr*
is also a sea-fowl with a long tail and black head, its feet
are not webbed ; it flies above the bosom of the calm sea,
and whenever it sees any small fish or fry, dives down
through the air on them, crying *"pirr!"* It lays five eggs,
somewhat like *tewhit* eggs in size and colour.

PIRKUZ—Any kind of perquisite.

PISHMINNIES—Ants; *pish* means piss ; *pishminnie tam-
mocks*, or *hillans*, ant-hills ; *pish* also means a heavy fall
of rain.

PISK—A dry-looking, saucy girl ; *pisket-grass*, dried, shri-
velled grass ; any thing withering dry is *pisky* ; to behave
dryly to a friend is to behave *pisket*.

PITTER-PATTER—All in a flatter ; sometimes *pittie-pattie*,
the movements of a perturbed heart.

PLODDERAN—Toiling night and day almost; the first thing that disgusted me with a farmer's life, and what disgusts thousands at it, is the not having a moment of time that can be said to be our own.

PLOTTED—Boiled, or ratherly plunged in boiling water.

PLUMB—The noise a stone makes when plunged into a deep pool of water; people guess as to a pool's depth by this *plumb*.

PLUMROCKS—Primroses; in some places *pimroses*.

POCKIAWRD—Marked with the small-pox.

POCKSHAKINGS—The youngest children of families.

PODDS—The boxes wherein nature preserves the seeds of various plants; a *bean podd*, that holds five beans, and a *pea podd*, which contains nine peas, are considered to be *sonsy*, and put up above the lintle of the door by maidens, and the first male that enters after they are so placed will either be their husband, or like him.

PORR—To stab; the noise a sharp instrument makes, darting into the flesh.

PORTUALE—A singular song, commonly sung about Christ mas. See *White boys*.

POSS—To squeeze wet clothes in a tub, to wash by squeezing.

POSSEY—A large party of people all of a mind.

POUCHING—The trick of pocketing; if a lady shows us her garden, and we fall to the plucking of fruit and eating it, before she grants permission, do we not behave rudely? and if we pull and *pocket*, our manners become abominable. In truth, *pouching* is a gentle method of stealing, and I would as soon become a real thief at once as a petty *poucher*. Some people, though, have a natural propensity this way, and others can look at every thing, but touch nothing; but those who *pouch* at funerals are the most hateful race of *pouchers*. One in particular, which I will not trouble myself to write his detestable name, whenever the *service* came round to him, he looked for the largest piece of *short-bread* or *plumb-cake* on the *servet*, seized on it with a sharkish manner, took a bite of one corner, and *pouched* the rest. The wine or drink with which he was served to, baffled him to play the same trick with it; but he pouched, or *painched* it every drop, another way. Once some wags espied my gentleman very throng at a wealthy funeral, and as the burial folk had to come down a strait stair after they *lifted*, they made up a plan to there jostle him, and ease his large wallets of their contents, which they accomplished very handsomely, by some going before and others behind, the upper pushing, the under *stelling*, while an expert hand brought out the cargo, consisting, no doubt, of sundries, all of which were never missed by him until he came home; but on his there discovering that the treasure was extracted, he got such a shock of remorse, as never allowed him to *pouch* any more.

POULLIE-HENS—Plucked-looking hens; *poullie*, to look plucked like; *poul*, a *mollan*, a pole.

POUT—To start up on a sudden, as something from under the water; to *pow up*, to shew the head, *pow* being the head; *pout-worm*, the worm with the head, the grub.

POUTREY—Poultry; *pouts*, young game birds.

POW—The head; *pow-heads*, young frogs.

> There's little wit in the *pow*,
> That hauds the cannle to the lowe.
> *Auld Say.*

PREEN-CUDS—Pin-cushions, places to hold *preens*, and *corking-preens*.

PREEST-CAT—An ingleside game; a piece of stick is made red in the fire; one hands it to another, saying

> " About wi' that, about wi' that,
> " Keep alive the preest-cat."

Then round is handed the stick, and whomsoever's hand it goes out in, that is in a *wad*, and must kiss the *crook*, the *cleps,* and what not, ere he gets out of it ; anciently, when the *priest's cat* departed this life, wailing began on the country side, as it was thought it became some supernatural being, a witch, perhaps, of hideous form ; so to keep it alive was a great matter.

> " Lilly Cuckoo, Lilly Cuckoo,
> " Sticks and stanes, lie at thy weary banes,
> " If thou fa', for a' I blaw,
> " Lilly Cuckoo, Lilly Cuckoo."

This rhyme is common in the *priest-cat* sport toward the border.

PREEST-DRIDDER—Dread of priests. Not long ago people in the country were very much in awe of their priests ; they considered them creatures supernaturally endowed, fit to *lay ghaists,* talk with *boggles* and *spreets,* shake hands with death, and do many other such wonders. Them and their *sessions,* their *cutty-stools,* and full *bottom'd wigs, hollow granes,* and *dranting prayers,* made the fowk at times almost *swarf* with a *dridder* or dread. But *Burns,* and other clear-brained fellows arose in time, and after stripping them to the buff, let the *bleer-e'ed* see that the priests were like *ither fowk,* and many of them even worse. I give the clergymen of Scotland no claim at all to the better *light* now beaming in the country, for they wished to keep all in darkness, rather than otherwise, " brutes being easier managed than men ;" but in spite of their clouds we got suns, whose rays penetrated them. I am no foe at all to them, as they are now-a-days; but am far from obeying the old proverb, " that *corbies* and *clergy* are a shot right *kittle.*" I feel no *quams* of conscience in speaking about them what I think, whenever they chance to come in my way. Though a *greedy* enough *squad,* yet still I take some pleasure in going to church to hear them preach now and then; but for *dread* they give me none, nor can they give any to a manly person ; a black coat and a blue one causing the same sensations of *dridder.*

PRIGGING.—Higgling in *market-making*; some merchants alter not the price of their goods, let the buyer *prigg* as he may. I think, however, there is something natural in a seller to fall a little in the first value he lays on to the purchaser.

PRODDS.—Pricks; *proddled*, pricked; the same nearly with *proitled*.

PROITLED.—To stir after a pushing manner, as we do when we wish to rouse *burntrouts* out of *water-rat holes*; we *proitle* them out from beneath the overhanging brows with the *but-end o' the fish-wan*.

PROKER.—Poker, for stirring fires.

PROO.—Cry, at horses when they are wanted to stand still, or, at least, not to gallop.

PROOP.—The *still small voice* of a certain *wind-pipe*; one of the children of that strange animal which *flies wingless*. We hear of animals *broken wund*, what are these? viz. those which breathe quick, which have a kind of asthmatic wheezle; horses are sometimes this way, so think that *respectable class* of men, horse-jockies, who are themselves oftener *broken wund*. " I hate *stane naigs*," quoth one the other day, " but waur I hate them wha lead them." *Broken wun* and *braking wun* are different though, *hech how*.

PSALM-SINGING BODIES.—Religious folk, of an austere disposition. When those sacred pieces of poetry, termed paraphrases, were first introduced into the public worship of our maker—An old woman, one of these *rigid righteous*, said " They did na taste sae weel in her gab as the *auld p'salms* o' Davie;" and to make another trivial remark, an Irishman who had been engaged with a farmer during harvest, was astonished one evening with his master when he started the psalm, to be sung as a thing preparatory to the *taking the buik*. The poor fellow, who had probably never heard of such a thing, or of the psalms either, exclaimed, after the family had *lilted* a verse or two, probably with all the *swing* of old *Coleshill*, or the *Martyrs*, " Hoch! botheration, what kind of singing is that? stop, and I'll give ye a barr or two of the *bleaching pin.*" To please these holy folk, these *psalm-singing bodies*, I may give a few verses, written by a *Galloway bard, guess who*—

THE SOUL OF SORROW.

O! my God, why was I born?
　Why am I tantalized so sore?
Why do I wander wild, forlorn,
　Along this rocky, roaring shore?
Grief and woe come every morrow,
And load my humble soul with sorrow.

No friends have I to take my part,
　No man will take me in to toil;
Cold famine's ice begirds that heart
　Which once with genuine love did boil;
I want that brazen face to borrow;
Nor can I beg for bursting sorrow.

O! lend an ear to what I crave,
　To me indulgence once be given;
I long to be within my grave,
　My heart in dust, my soul in Heaven;
Then surely I would meet a morrow,
Fraught with no melancholy sorrow.

I never injured mortal man,
　So far's I know, so far's I think;
Nor scoff'd fair Nature's lovely plan,
　Yet bitter drugs I'm doom'd to drink:—
The sun of Fortune shines no morrow
On *Orrles*' bewilder'd soul of sorrow.

Was I on some far savage isle
　Amid the sea, besouth the line,
There would my gloomy visage smile,
　My heart to joy and mirth incline;
For there I'd hail no murky morrow,
There death would free my soul of sorrow.

With these, my hands, to ope this jail
　And set the growling culprit free,
I shall not dare—but wretched trail
　Along this path of misery;
Far better bear life's scowling morrow,
Than an eternity of sorrow.

PUDDOCKS.—Frogs. *Puddock-pipes,* a moss herb. *Puddock-stools,* a kind of long-shanked conical and comical mushroom. *Puddock-reed,* the spawn or *rid* of frogs ; what says the *auld stave*—

> Puddock-reed is fu' o' e'en,
> And ev'ry e'e's a pow head ;
> But Nelly's twa beats them clean,
> She is a charming pow-head.

PUE O' REEK.—A little smoke, or, ratherly the manner smoke ascends. " The reek's *pueing* up." " There's no a *pue* o' reek in a' the house." " Whar comes the reek *pueing* frae ?" are phrases I need not explain.

PUIST-BODIES.—People in a comfortable way in this world, or ratherly having the wherewithal to make them so. Some are *puist,* though not contented ; but we cannot be *puist* unless we are competently rich ; we ought to be pretty contented, though not rich. For my own part, I have been as happy without a *bawbee* in my *pouch,* as I ever was with *gowd* in it.

PULING, or PEULING.—The way of a sick animal ; it leaves its comrades, and gaes *peuling* about alone—commonly applied to cattle. *Peuls,* small bites which sick oxen eat. For these bites *nowt* seek mosses in the spring, where *peuls* of green grass first appear ; to get at them, they frequently lose their life, and are drowned ; also at this season, they tumble down heughs while ranging for these *peuls.* A Herd must keep a sharp look out in the *waur time.*

PUNSE.—To push and strike, as with a stick, to *punse* a *brock* in his lair ; to push, or ratherly striking push, a badger in his den.

PUTT-GUDE.—A man is said to have made his *putt-gude,* when he obtains what his ambition panted for ; thus I have got my *putt* made *good* respecting this book, for all the thousand *barrs* flung in its way. This compliment to the land of my home, I intend, perhaps, on some not very far distant day, to give, in one large quarto volume, " The

Scotch Encyclopædia, or the *natural, original,* and *anti-quated* curiosities of Scotland." I have much matter gathered for it; and hope every true Scotsman who loves his own wonderful country, will help me with it, as they think best, by giving me *hints,* and singular out-of-the-way *whusherings;* so, this work is only the harbinger of one of the same stamp, but on a larger scale; and I hope Heaven will permit me to make my *putt-gude.*

PYARDIE.—One of the many names for the bird Magpie.

PYDLES.—Cones made sometimes of rushes to catch fish with; they are set, " whar burns out owre the lynns come pouring," so the trouts, in coming down the stream, run into them, and cannot make a retreat.

Q.

QUAK.—To speak like a duck.

QUAKINQUAWS—or *Quaws,* or moving quagmire bogs; some fancy that *Jack and the Lantern,* alias *Will o' the Wisp,* has his habitation in the *Quakingquaw,* from his being generally seen in the neighbourhood of such places, and from his desire to conduct the midnight wanderers therein; it is also imagined, too, that they are entrances, as it were, to other strange worlds, where are ever myriads of fowk, such as were seen in the *Carlines o' Cairnsmoor.* When the method of boring through the soil of a wet bog was tried, so that the water might sink, and find vent away in the rocky stratas beneath, a poor superstitious mortal was standing by once, observing attentively how operations went on, and when he beheld what every one present did, that the plan would not answer, he went up to the borers, and insisted on them, (*through wit*) to go through with the borer into the world below, and then the waters would follow. He was not like a certain gentleman, who loved good liquor, as many do, and who went into an agricultural society once, when draining land was the order of the day; there stood the laird, and listened to one speech after another, on the benefits which would *no doubt* result from such and such sure grounded modes as were proposed; at length, getting weary, he exclaimed, " For God's sake, gentlemen, leave as much water with all your drainings as will mix a glass o' grog ;" which *satire* rendered all plans useless for that day at least. My worthy original, well known in Galloway by the phrase, " *For faith ye see am saying*," knew, amongst many other things, like the late mentioned gentleman, where all the *spring wauls* of note were in the country, and their names—the which information he gave me in the *kindest* manner, for which I here, according to the custom of authors, publicly thank him.

QUALL.—Quell, settle, &c.

QUAT.—Quit, let alone.

> " Whan the rain draps off the bat
> " 'Tis fully time for folk to quat,
> " Wha on the harrest rig do shear
> " Barley, wheat, peas, rye, or beer."
>
> *Auld say.*

QUAZIE—Disordered somehow ; squeamish, such as after being intoxicated.

QUEEM—Calm. *Queemly*, calmly. " The gled glides *queemly* alang ;" the kite glides smoothly along.

> " Dream, dream, that the Ocean's *queem* ;
> " Dream, dream, that the moon did beam ;
> " And the morning will hear the waves roar,
> " And the sun through the cluds will not find a bore."
>
> *Auld say.*

This old concern always brings that lovely verse of Miss Baillie's into my head, who, by the bye, is ratherly a Galloway lady ; as also Miss Paton, the sweetest *stage-singer* I ever heard—

> " Up lady fair, and braid thy hair,
> " And rouse thee in the breezy air;
> " The lulling stream, will aid thy dream,
> " That glitters in the sunny beam."

QUINTON RUMMLEKIRN—A pretty fair Galloway philosopher and poet, who flourished, according to the book of
Doomsday, kept by *Scoot Hutchie*, in the *time come never*,
three months ago. He was a *cronnie* while he lived with
the *Miller o' Minnieive*, and, I believe, married his *kill-
man's* third daughter—the one with the *buck-teeth*. He
was fond of drinking filthy fluids, and his belly gave birth
to some *asks* and *man-keepers*. I do not know that I have
explained *man-keepers*: they are a kind of nimble lizard,
and run about quarry-holes, in warm weather. It is said,
that like the *robin-breestie*, they are in love with man,
hence their name, and like that bird, no man will harm
them. They are serpent-looking creatures, which he *keeps*
as it were. Well, this *Quinton* flashed about *Tibby Sharpers* for a few months, but kicked up his heels at last in
Auld Ned's anti-chamber, after quaffing *vitriolic mountain
dew*. He gave me, when living, the meanings of a few
rare words, though I differ with him, in some respects, as
to their import. Thus *peelaflee*, he said, was a creature
out of its element; a *dandy* attempting to play with men
at the *channelstane*, for the *dandy* looks as if the wind had
him *peeled*, and that he looked as if going to *fly*. A
being much liker a warm room, sitting by the hip of a
lisping lady, and a simmering *trackpot*. Peelaflees are
all those who look better on a *street* than they do in the
country. It is a strange thing that, termed *optics*; how
full is it of deception. I wonder those Brewsters, and other
chaps who study it, cannot give us something to prevent
our *e'en* being misled. Thus, some ladies look well in
candle-light, and they all look their best in frosty weather.
Let no man marry a wife in the time of *frost,* for when a
thaw comes, she may disgust him. Bullocks look best in
snow : when cattle are transported from " heathy fells to
flowery dells," they have quite a different appearance ; ay,
ay. " *Brocks* look best catching *bumclocks* ;" situation is

every thing. On the *fore ground* of a Scotch dinner, the *haggis* should show his *hurdies*; and on the *back* the *whusky grey-beardy*." But to Quinton, as a philosopher, he said *I* was a fool, and he would prove it as fair as ever a mathematician proved Euclid's *fifth* in *first* to be *Pons Assinorum*, or the Asses Bridge ; but I said it was needless o prove what all my acquaintance knew to be a *fib*; and that the world would say some day *I was a damned clever fallow*, one who would do what Archimedes could not do, make this very earth tremble in her orbit. The old *mill-wright*, and *speckglass-grinder* said, if he had a *fulcrum* he could do this, as he had a *lever* ready. Now, I have found the *fulcrum*, which is my mighty—I was just going to add, *genius,* when Quinton struck me beneath the *lug*, with a *hazle-rung*, cut in *Plunton wud*, and laid me sprawl-ing on Kirkcubries auld *causey*, just at *Christal's Corner.* So farewel to him and his philosophy. Let us view him as a poet, and firstly then—

MAGARLAA, THE INDIAN CHIEF, TO HIS TORTURING FOES.

At last you've, by a crafty turn,
  Magarlaa clutched all alone;
Then fire teed, his nerves come burn,
  And roast the flesh from off the bone.
Why be so long with your death-song,
Come, set you to, your tortures strong.

Then have you got your pinchers hot,
  So, where then will ye go begin,
My tongue is cold, 'twill answer not,
  Fix on the tendons—peel the skin ;
Fix on, and burn, my eyes out turn,
Your worst of torments I do spurn.

Now you begin, take time, take time,
  And do not let me go too soon ;
Keep me down from the cloudy clime,
  For soon I'll fly beyond the moon :
Then back again, tho' you were fain,
I will not come to bear again.

The other leg and arm then take,
 For these you burn I do not feel ;
Come, bite me like a rattle-snake,
 And prick my heart with burning steel.
Now, now I go, yes, bravely so,
And back I shall not come—no, no.

I may give one of his many strange songs, by way of concluding—

My dearest Marget, I hae been
 A tod to thee, a sad deceiver ;
And this, my Marget, ye hae seen,
 Yet thou art kind to me as ever.
I drank and courted ither queens,
 My fortune sweil'd down pleasure's river,
Yet, tho' I squander'd sae my means,
 Thou ay wer't kind to me as ever.
Thou never sald'st, O ! Willie, lad,
 Thou art an unco' gypsy shaver ;
But, ay wi' me wad seem fu' glad,
 And ay wer't kind to me as ever.
As kind's that day when by the burn
 We sat and saw the sun-beams quiver,
And up the glen did take a turn,
 Thou'rt ay as kind to me as ever.
Now, we hae met, nor will we part,
 O ! Marget, we will never, never,
Our hearts, now counteth, ae warm heart,
 That wi' true love will beat for ever.

QUIRKLUMS—Little arithmetic puzzles, where the matter hinges on a quirk. The peasantry are madly fond to have their great minds always employed, either at one thing or another ; so they propose *quirklums*, as they do *riddlums*, and set one another a thinking upon them. *Quirklums* make them *lay at the thinking*, perhaps, as much as any thing ; and those of a mathematic turn, like my friends *Geordy Wishart* and *Jeamie Caig*, are the best at solving them. These *quirklums* are generally told in rhyme, and many of them are not unamusing. For fun, I may give one or two of them—

" Three cats in a wunnock sat,
 " And every cat had aside her twa ;
" How mony cats, now, to a cat,
 " On that wunnock sole sat and nyurd awa?"

       Answer—*three.*

" There are four weights, which can be found,
" Which ought will weigh from one to forty pound;
" What these weights are, to me declare,
" And I shall say thou art a genius rare ?"

Answer—1, 3, 9, 27.

Being a wonderful *Oriental scholar,* and quite up to the idioms of all the languages spoken in Asia, from Kamschatca to the Straits of Bablemandel ; as also quite a *proficient* in the slang spoken at the courts of the *Grand Turk* and *Great Mogul,* quite as much so as of that spoken in a *London Badger Den,* by *coves, corks,* and other " unhang'd blackguards." I met with the other day, while reading the works of *Hallagree,* the famed Persian poet, the *Walter Scott* of the east, an arithmetical *quirkle,* so set about the translation instantly, for the benefit of the curious ; but though *Van Bluffberg,* the celebrated Dutch linguist was at my elbow, we found it no easy matter to hold strictly by the original. Thus, however, we made it—

Had our first Parents, when in Eden,
Not tasted of that fruit forbidden ;
Death likely, they would ne'er have met,
But would been living happy yet :
Suppose this to have been the case,
Alive yet all the human race,
And that each year (if not too wild),
Eve unto Adam bore a child,
Alternately a son and daughter,
(Come, Fancy, be not beat with laughter),
And that those children did again
Sweet beings free from grief and pain,
Remorse, so grim, and fractious rage,
When they were twenty years of age
Bred, like their parents, happy creatures,
Love smiling fine through all their features,
These bred again, contented souls,
And filled the earth between the Poles ;
Say ye, my friends, who are expert
At calculation's mystic art,
That art which has the darling tongue
For telling what is right from wrong.

> How many of us, to a man,
> Would here been now, and such the plan,
> I know there are can say in *learn'd Ishpahan?*

The answer to this, for the present, I keep to myself.

> The unassuming do the job,
> The assuming take the praise,
> By what they do from merit rob,
> Themselves to fame they raise.
>
> *Hint by mysell.*

R.

RACKET—A disorder in an assembly of persons. " A *racket rase,* and wha to get out soonest." The sooner out of a smoky house the better. " I heard an unco *racket* ;" " I heard the sound of a *row*." Some are good at raising a *racket* amongst social friends; such (as the great *preacher* saith,) should be " kicked over the walls of creation into infinite space."

RAELINGS—Ravelings. " Boys rael out auld hoshens to make hand baws."

RAEM—Cream. *Raeming caup,* a wooden milk-skimmer ; *raem-jug,* a cream-mug. Some girls in the country, in order to keep youth in the face as long as possible, have a mixture of sour cream and the sap of *bogbean,* or trefoil, made up in a mug, to wash their faces with, in dark times convenient. This *raem-jug* they keep in the most secret *nuik* of the house, on the *back skelf* of some *auld aumry,* for they consider, were it found they would be *blown* for ever, and never get a man ; but, as the poet finely says, *Darwin,* I think—

> In vain, poor nymph, to please our youthful sight,
> You sleep in *cream* and frontlets all the night ;
> Perfume with roses, and with paint repair,
> Dress with gay gowns, and shade with foreign hair.
> If truth, in spite of manners, must be told,
> Why, really fifty-five, is something old.

And *Matthew Prior* too, the son of *Adam* and of *Eve*,
on this subject poetizes beautifully—

> How old may Phillis be, you ask
>   Whose beauty thus all hearts engages ;
> To answer is no easy task,
>   For she has really *two ages*.
>
> Stiff in brocade, and pinched in stays,
>   Her patches, paint, and jewels on ;
> All day let envy view her face,
>   And Phillis is but *twenty-one*.
>
> Paint, patches, jewels laid aside,
>   At night *astronomers* agree,
> The evening has the day belied,
>   And Phillis is some *forty-three*.

RAENS—Ravens. *Raen-nest-heugh*, the steepest precipice
generally among precipices. Then the *carrgate*, the way
or road on steep rocks. Ravens, like eagles, build not
only on cliffs, but on the *crag* of the *cliff* as the book of
Job hath it. Here may follow an oddity, struck off many a
year ago. ELEGY *on the* DEATH O' *a puir* PET CORBIE—
He wandered from home one day away by the *Netherlaw*,
and having fallen in with the *coat* of mine auld crusty herd,
Davie Maben, he turned inside out the pockets of the
same ; and while in the act of making off with *Dawvid's*
spleuchan, he was set upon by the herd's *collie-dog*, and
the attack being followed by the herd himself with a stick,
they succeeded in ending the life of my *pet corbie*—

> Ha! low puir fallow now ye be
> Wi' striffan white drawn owre thy e'e,
> Food for the mawk and mawking-flee,
>   Death can out-trick ye ;
> Auld Dawvid end'd thee o' thy glee
>   Wi's dog and clicky.
>
> What notion gard ye croak awa
> Sae far's the rosseny Netherlaw ;
> I'm sure your errand there was sma',
>   We mann ye blame ;
> Thou'st been, I doubt, like mony a wha,
>   Owre het ahame.

My glossy cheil, I'm wae to think
Thou now can'st only rot and stink,
For weel I lo'ed to see thee jink
        And hap about me ;
O ! tho' ye were an unco slink,
        I'm sad without ye.

Whan I was e're through passion, folly
Borne down wi' wretched melancholy,
He'd catch the whusking tail o' collie,
        And queerly swung;
Sae than I soon was laughing jolly,
        And blythly sung.

Whanere I gaed to count the sheep
Amang the hills and hags sae steep,
A swooming then he gaed to peep
        About the farm ;
And or I kend adown wad sweep
        Upon my arm.

There wad he sit, and cok fu' snug,
There rike his neb up to my lug,
And talk awa his *urum ugg*,
        To me unknown ;
Then, maybe, gi'en my hair a tug,
        Syne aff wad flown.

In wunter or a storm o' snaw,
Or rain down on the yird wad fa',
Afore the wun began to blaw,
        Or tempest blatter,
Upon the hill he it wad jaw
        Wi' potent clatter.

And whan it just was gaen to flog
Our naked land, and houses shog,
How angry did he hotch and stog,
        And croak about,
Owreturning stanes, and riving fog
        Wi' his strong snout.

Yea, at the warst, whan it bid dash,
And pinging brutes without, did lash,
While meikle trees fell wi' a crash,
        Mine hardy cheel
To seek a shelter ne'er wad fash,
        He scorn'd a beel.

Wi' some wild spirit o' the blast
He seem'd to janner thick and fast,
Yet shrinked not, nor stood aghast
        Wi' tottering spawls ;
But, like a chieftain, to the last
        Withstood its brawls.

In every clime the Ra'en is seen,
On every shore where man hath been,
On mountains, be they white or green,
  Ice, or black rock,
There he can find a hame, I ween,
  And cheerfu' croak.

Tho' Arctic wanderers do crack
Whan they frae Baffin's Bay come back,
That there he doffs his doolfu' black
  For robes o' white ;
To look mair like that dismal track,
  He fills his kyte.

Nae doubts the Pole he aft hath seen,
Through Beehring's Straits hath aften been,
And flung our navigators clean
  To leeward, o ;
Ay, dawner'd too, wi' Bedoween
  To Tombuctoo.

The eagle's ca'd the burd o' Jove
Because he hie in lift doth rove ;
The dove, dear Cupid's, for its love
  And happy cooing,
'Mang sillar-firs, in sunny grove,
  Sae sweetly wooing.

But the corbie, and 'tis odd,
Belanged to nae Heathen god,
The de'il a ane gaed him a nod
  While passing by ;
As he sat on his blighted sod,
  Or peak sae high.

Altho' a burd as bonny's ony,
Wi' pranks baith tragical and funny,
Belike my grave and merry cronnie,
  Alas! no more ;
Wha tummling-flew, whan it was sunny,
  Roun' heugh and shore.

Indeed, o' a' the burds that lide
The air, or ocean's jabbling tide,
There's nane seems to enjoy the ride
  On wings like he,
But only mark wi' what a pride
  He whiles will flee.

The dark brown tap o' some big hill
He centers, then around will sweill,
And after he has ta'en his fill
  O' this high pleasure,
Away he scents, wi' mighty skill,
  Some cabroch treasure.

And whan he fin's a sheep fa'en aval,
Her trolly-bags he can unravel ;
The corby-craws and him will caval,
       Ay, worry owre her;
The e'en out o' her head they'll naval,
       And sae devour her.

But ah ! my pet will never more
Flee curving roun' the hill or shore,
Nor see again his weel stuff'd store,
       Whar mony a button
And spleuchan lies, wi' joints galore
       O' beef and mutton.

His horde frae me gat mony a knife,
For a' I never hurt his life ;
O' robberies his days war rife,
       Yet what the matter ;
I ne'er at him did boil wi' strife,
       Clod stanes and batter.

Tho' I ha'e seen my mither whiles
Pay strict attention to his wiles,
About the barn, the stacks, and styles,
       Wi' chicken burdies,
And treating him wi' nae sweet smiles,
       Nor bonny wordies.

I saw his nature joyd doing ill,
His glory was, to rive and kill ;
Pu' puddings out, and warm blude spill,
       Completely savage ;
O ! but he join'd wi' right gude will,
       A wild culravage.

At ev'ry stack we meand to house,
There wi' the currs he happed crouse ;
And whan outspouted e'er a mouse
       Frae 'mang the grain,
Despite o' tykes or fuffing puss,
       That was his ain.

He made its tender ribs play crack,
His horny lips round it wad smack ;
Sae gullied her a dainty chack
       Without a glutt ;
Then glowr'd and glented round the stack
       For mair tae gutt.

Whan boys rave out, the sparrow's nest
Wi' young goits therein gorling drest,
He soon did set their tongues at rest,
       The chirping choked ;
Then leas'd them in his stamock's chest,
       And never boked.

The beggar bairns wi' naked feet
He aften caus'd to sab and greet,
Whan him and them wad chance to meet;
   He gard them squeel;
Wi' him it was a noble treat
   To nip the heel.

How mony chuckies brawly tappit
He turn'd a corner on and snappit;
What yellow gaizlings heads he crappit
   About the dub;
And even auld ducks he roughly graipet,
   The pawkie scrub.

But yet, altho' the hellish knave
Did thus sae aften ill behave,
When a' condemn'd him, I wad save
   Wi' great ado.
Strong oratory I had to brave
   To bring him through.

Like Barrington, and Captain Blood,
My noble culprit bravely stood
Owre high in crime for gallows food
   The famous loon;
Wi' me he had a life fu' good,
   For mony a moon.

O, bards may sing, and priests may pray,
True de'ils will wi' their daddy stay;
Frae hell they scorn to steer their way.
   Wi' vice they anchor,
And prie the smirking lady gay
   And faeming tankor.

Upon the braid claise-drying thorn,
What sarks war by the Corby torn,
How aft the lasses on a morn
   Wi' him had scuffles;
And oh, how some o'em wad hae sworn
   About their ruffles.

" My cambric mutch I mean'd to crimp,
" That was trimm'd bonnily wi' gimp:
" My spencer, too, whilk make me jimp,
   " (Loud ane o'em souns)
" Is by that *curse* which there doth limp
   " Torn a' in roens."

" And here's my tippet," Meg wad rair,
" Wi' whilk I mean'd to gang tae fair,
" Just like your braws, a' here and there,
   " In swatches scatter'd;
" See to them lying every where,
   " A ri'en and tatter'd."

C C

My father maistly did incline
To join his voice for him wi' mine ;
" Some things," he said, " there were divine,
            " And high about him ;
" Ye, tho' he whiles on lammies dine,
                " I will not shoot him."

" They war his ancestors, wha took
" Food to Elijah by the brook,
" As mention'd in the holy book ;
                " By orders gi'en,
" For whilk the prophet blythe did look,
                " Baith morn and e'en."

" And Noah, too, whan in the ark,
" That unco meikle floating bark,
" Sent out a corby, to remark
            " Dry land again ;
" Wha glowr'd lang for a tree or park,
                " Or he faun ane."

" Sae agents o' Heaven's mighty king,
" We maunna by the thrapple swing,
" Nor lift a stane, and giet a fling
                " At them wi' might,
" For fear we may oursells gae sling
                " To hell's grim knight."

" Its lang since Scotchmen heard the note
" Or proverb, ne'er to be forgot,
" That corbies are a *kittle shot*,
                " Like clergymen ;
" Misfortune gets that meddling sot
                " Wha disna ken."

But, pooh !—What flummery's this I blaw,
About the auld daez'd corby craw ?
It is na like mysell ava,
                A mighty poet !
To fyke wi' sic a theme sae sma',
                Right owrboard throw it.

A mighty poet ! hear him, hear him,
A mighty blockhead, Heaven be near him,
Some critic worricow, come fear him ;
            And whan he flinches,
Damnation, like the Ra'en, gae tear him
                Ay, a' in inches.

O, wee, wee men, mind trivial things,
The silly bardy silly sings,
He'll vaunt about his fancies wings,
                And how they flutter ;
But when on them he upward springs,
                He lights i'e gutter.

The welkins high aboon our head,
And higher far souls o' the dead ;
What is this earth, we're doom'd to tread ?
   And what are we?
Bewilder'd cormorants indeed,
   In a wild sea.

Our deepest thoughts are shallows slim,
The brightest eye is woefu' dim ;
Our logic sound—perhaps a whim—
   For who can tell
When that we dive we only swim
   Like corkwud speall ?

Then let the sage gae brownly think,
And courtiers at crimes gae wink ;
Let rustic bards sing on and drink
   'Bout Joan and Dorby,
I'll lean me owre, and mourn a blink
   About my Corbie.

RAFFING FALLOWS—Ranting, roaring, drinking fellows.

RAGABASH—A ragged crew of unmannerly people.

RAGGING—Corn is said to be a *ragging* when it is a putting
the first time through the *fans*, or winnowing machine.
When this is done it is *ragged*, cleaned of its *rags* and
roughness ; also corn is said to be beginning to *ragg* when
the grain-head first appears out of the *shotblade* ; corn first
rags which grows on the sides of *riggs*, by the *furbrow*,
and if none *ragged* be seen before *Kelton-hill Fair*, it is a
symptom there is going to be a *late harrest* that year.

RAIRDING—Ice is said to be *rairding*, when it is cracking
from some cause ; in the time of a very hard frost, *lochs*
are heard to *rair* of their own accord.

RAIS'D—An animal looks *raised* when its temper is up.
To *raise* any one, is to stir or rouse the passions.

RAM-HORN SPOONS—Large spoons, made of the horns
of rams.

RAMP—A creature is *ramp* that is rompish inclined : a *ramp
smell*, a strong smell, the smell of a *he-goat*. *Ramps*,
wild leeks, common on shores.

RANNLE-TREE—A bar of wood or iron fixed in chimnies,
to fix the *crook* to, for the purpose of suspending pots

over the fire : amongst the many amusements of the *ingle ring,* one is, who shall say a certain saying quickest, without going wrong. In one of these, mention is made of the *rannle-tree.* " The cat ran up the *rannle-tree* wi' a lump o' raw red liver in its teeth." For fun, I may give more of these sayings. The peasant's cottage is indeed a den of curiosity. " Briskly reeks Rab Logan's lum," and retrograde again, " Rab Logan's lum reeks briskly ;" another, " I can count the cuts, and the cuts count me ;" then to the *sieve* and the *thissels,* and who shall say *criffles clear* oftenest, without drawing breath.

RAP and STOW—A phrase meaning root and branch.

RASHES—Rushes; " as straught's a *rash*"—straight as a rush. Straight people are likened to a *rush* commonly. *Rash-buss,* a bush of rushes; *rash-whups, rash-bonnets, rash-pyddles,* are whips, caps, and fish-wears, made of rushes: *rash* also means a fall of rain, attended with wind ; " hear to the rain rashing," hear to it dashing. " The spuings came *rashing* frae him," means, he vomited freely.

RATTON—A rat. *Ratton-fa',* a rat-trap ; *ratton-flitting,* a flitting of rats. Sometimes these animals, for causes known to themselves, leave one haunt where they have fed well a long time, and go to another. Many have met them thus removing, and leading the *old blind ones* with a straw, which passed between mouths like a *kissing-string.* What instinct is this ? Those *Percy Anecdote folks* should have heard of the matter. People do not like the rats to disappear thus on a sudden, as the thing is thought to portend nothing good, and sailors will leave their ships if they observe the rats quit them.

RATTRUM—A confused mass of words, the language of a rattle-scull, as it flows from them the words " in dizzens and raws."

RAUCKED—Marked as with a nail. *Raucking,* the noise a nail makes writing on a slate ; it touches the nerves. " A

cat *raucking* on a beden," was one of three things mine
obstinate *Laird Coutart* could not endure; the other two
were, a " *priest preaching wi' specks on,*" and a " *wee
boat drawing a big ane.*"

RAULLION, or RULLION—A rough ill-made animal.

RAULTREE, or RAELTREE—A long piece of strong wood,
which is placed across *byres*, to put the ends of *cow-stakes*
in. The one the foot of the *stake* rests in, is the *raeltreefit*,
the other the *raeltree head.*

RAWLY—Not ripe. *Rawly cheel*, a young lad.

RAW-WEATHER—Cold wet weather; this is much disliked
by rural hinds.

> There's mony a thing we dinna like,
>   But we maun wi' them just put up ;
> For, wha the de'il cares what we like,
>   Or how we feel, or how we sup ?
>
> We dinna like the weather raw,
>   The dawding win', the blashing rain,
> Nor sleety showers frae the nor-wast,
>   And o' the snaw we are na fain.
>
> Weel aff are they aneath the mools,
>   They never fin' the caul ava,
> But in their lanely narrow beds
>   Do snugly doze and rot awa.
>
> The frost may bite, the hail may nip,
>   The rain may steep us to the skin,
> But thae aneath the auld green truffs
>   The waes o' weather never fin'.

" *Raw-dawds make strong lads,* as the saying is; that
is, *pieces*, viz. whangs o' bread and cheese ; or *a piece* spread
wi' the gude-wife's *thumb*, of the *kirnbannock*, tastes ay
weel in the gabs o' stirrahs," quoth *Meg Murdoch.*

REDEARLY.—Grain that has got a *heat on* sometime or
other, either whan the " stack took a wee lue," or in the
mushoch.

REE.—A round sheep-fold, where sheep are put into on
snowy nights, to hinder the snow to *ree*, or wreath them up ;

as the wind, by whirling round this circle, lets the snow
not wreath in it. *Ree*, is often confounded with *bught*,
but a *sheep-ree* and a *sheep-bught*, are different; a *bught*
is a little *bight* to catch sheep in, no matter what be its
figure. To *ree* grain, is to whirl it through a riddle, so
that the *tares* in it may be seen; this *ree* then, and the
other *ree*, are one; we say *rees o' snaw*, for wreaths of
snow, and whiles *wrides*; let this word *ree* then, be properly understood; but there is another *ree*, with which
it seems to claim no kindred.   When a man is *rammaged*,
that is, *rais'd*, *craz'd*, or damaged with *drink*, we say that
man looks *ree*; he looks mad and flushed. A poet too, in
a wild phrenzy, with fancy flashing from earth to heaven,
and from thence to hell, looketh *ree*. Poets are generally drawn this way, by artists. In truth, Byron always
looks in a print shop as if he saw the devil; why, ye
draughtsmen, make all the sons of genius look like fools?
it is nonsense,

> For Bob, I will invert your rule,
>   And so by proving plainly show it,
> That if a poet be a fool,
>   Sure every fool is not a poet.
>   *Prior.*

REEPAN.—A low-made wretch, a talepyet.

REESTIE.—A horse is *reestie* when it stands fast, and will
not move for the whip, but is rather inclined to go backwards; *rested*, to be arrested.

REEZIE.—A horse is *reezie* when he is inclined to whisk
his tail, so that the hair thereof, in swiftly going through
the air, causeth a whistling sound, and plunge, so that a
a bad horseman like myself, sits in jeopardy.

RHEUMATIZ.—Rheumatics.

RICKETY.—Dickety. A toy made of wood, for children.

RICKLE.—A piece of bad building; a cairn of stones. A
rickle o' banes, a skeleton, a lean man; a bad stone
builder, is called a *rickler*.

RIDDLUMS.—Riddles, sometimes called guesses; some of the riddles of the peasantry are worth a laugh, so I will not pass them over; they have a peculiar nature of their own, and a rural riddle is at once known from one of foreign manufacture. *Riddlums* and *quirklums* are in some instances like other.   As a farmer asked another " how many shearers he had in his *banwun* ?" the other answered, " I hae one hundred and twenty bansmen, sae ye may guess frae that ;" well, as a *bandsman* generally binds to five shearers, the inquirer began his calculation, by multiplying the 120 by 5 ; when he had done, " bless me, (quoth he) hae ye *sax hunner* shearers ?"—" Na, na, (said the other) ye hae counted yourself out of it ; I have just what I said, one hundred *shearers*, and twenty bandsmen ; but because I didna make a wee *stop*, after saying the *hunner*, ye took me up wrang." This one is just like that ball, with the three-score-and-three fiddlers at it, each fiddler having twenty dancers, how many dancers were there ?—

> " Bonny Kittie Brawnie she stands at the wa,
> " Gie her meikle, gie her little, she licks up a'
> " Gie her stanes, she'll no eat them, and water she'll dee,
> " Come tell me that bonny riddlum to me."

This is a favourite Scotch riddle, meaning the *fire*.

> As I cam owre Lonon Brig,
> I met wi' *Geordy Caning*,
> I took aff his head, and drank his bluid,
> And left his body staning.
> > *A bottle of ale.*

> Come tell me wha was that sannie,
> Wha was got afore his father,
> Wha was born afore his mither,
> And wha took the maidenhead o' his grannie.

Answer—*Abel* ; for his *father* was not *begot*, nor his *mother born* ; his grand-mother was the earth, he was the first who was bedded in it ; as Eve was his mother, a piece of frail *earth* also.

" As I stood cn yon castle wa'
" I saw the dead carrying the quick awa."

Answer—a *boat*.

" What *gangs* through the wood what it can flee,
" And never touches a single tree?"

Answer—a *cry*.

The expression in this riddle, of *going* what it can *fly,*
belongs purely to Galloway. " If I *gang* tae town the
day I'll *ride*," is a phrase often flung in the teeth of the
natives, by those of other districts, as extremely *vulgar,*
but it is not so; for you may *go*, which is *ganging* any
way you will; you may either *riding go*, *flying go*, or
swimming go, the grammar is good: when " heard ye any
news?" is asked, the answer is frequently—" No, I heard
na as meikle as ae auld wife dinging owre anither;" and
when to alarm a party, with saying to them, " did ye hear
you awfu' news the day?" when *no* is replied, with much
trepidation; the answer is made, "why I heard to-day
that a man had ta'en the levelling o' *Cairnhattie,* and that
twaul mile square o' the sea has been brunt ayont the
Isle o' Man." But where do I ramble? Was I to note
down all the sports I have heard in my native country, a
book as large as *Noah's Ark* would hardly hold them;
of *riddlums* then, I take my leave, by proposing a popular one, which may be answered as thought best :—

" What is it, that is skinless born,
" And whilk doth wingless fly,
" To death a rairing it doth go,
" Perfuming earth and sky?"

RIDING FOR THE BROESE.—This scene has been somewhat touched by other rustic writers, so I briefly say,
" That it is a ride on horseback by the *wadding fowk* attending a bridegroom to the bride's house; he who has
the swiftest horse wins the *broese,* or a cog of good broth
made for the occasion." It may well be fancied then, that
this is a horse-race, worth all those, for good fun, that
ever were run at Newmarket. A gourmand Moor-farmer
once gained the *broese,* so long before his rivals came, that

he had the whole *cog-full* lapped into his *kyte*; when they came up, he was just *at the heels o't*, after which he gave it to his *collie* to *lick the lagging*.

RIDING the BEETLE.—Those who are on foot, or *shanks naigie*, with a party on horseback, are said to be *riding the beetle*.

> " War ye at the fair, saw ye mony people,
> " Saw ye our gude man *riding* on the *beetle* ?"
> *Auld sang.*

RIDING the STANG.—A public punishment, inflicted on adulterers and fornicators. A large pole is got, and passed between the culprit's legs; he is then carried and *cudgelled* through *clauchans*, to the laugh and scorn of the mob. If the guilty man is married, and hath been leaving his wife and debauching young girls, he is then carried by men, the ends of the pole are manned with males; but if he hath been caught with another man's wife, females bear him forth; if he be unmarried, and hath been toying with men's wives, young men carry him, and so forth; it is a very severe punishment, but perhaps not so bad as the crime.

RIG-ADOWN DAISY.—At weddings, anciently the *waddin fowk* danced a great deal on the grass, before they went into barns; this fun was termed *rig-adown daisy*.

RIGG and FURR.—Land is said to be divided into *rig and fur*, when parcelled into ridges, by furrows; some kinds of hoze are called *rig and furr*.

RIGLING.—A ram with one stone in the scrotum, the other is about the parts of the back, and sometimes not at all; this is an animal between the *tip* and *dumchaser*.

RHYNE.—Hoar frost.

RINGING BLACK FROST.—A very severe frost when the ground keeps *black*, and seems to *ring* when struck; this is the season for *channling* or playing at the channlestone; few stars stud the lift at this season; the moon has a brass face on, and a dark-brown haze hangs round the horizon.

RINNER.—A little brook; also, butter melted with tar, for *sheep-smearing.*

RINNINGS.—Ulcers, which are the fountains of running matter.

RINS O' GALLOWA.—The borders, *roons*, or selvages of Galloway. The *rilings* or ravelings, or ruggid margins of the country.

RIPPET.—A bitter-tempered, chattering creature.

RIPPLEGIRSE.—A broad-leaved herb, which labourers put on cuts.

RISKISH LAN'.—Land of a wet and boggy nature; the plough *rairs* and *risks* in it when ploughing.

RIZZLES.—A species of berry; sometimes they are called *russles.*

RIZZLING.—Any thing such as straw, is said to be *rizzling*, when it is free of moisture, quite dry, rustling.

ROBBIN-A-REE.—A game of the *ingle-nuik*, much like the *preest-cat*; only in passing the *brunt-stick* round the ring, the following rhyme is said :—

> " Robin-a-Ree, ye'll no dee wi' me,
> " Tho' I birl ye roun' a three-times and three,
> " O Robin-a-Ree, O Robin-a-Ree,
> " O dinna let Robin-a-Reerie dee."

I have been somewhat pestered to know who or what this *Robin-a-Ree* was. The old song here brings him before us in another shape.

> I dinna like the Meg o' mony feet,
>   Nor the brawnet Conochworm,
> Quoth Mary Lee, as she sat and did greet,
>   A dawding wi' the storm ;
> Nowther like I the yallow-wym'd-ask,
>   'Neath the root o' yon aik tree,
> Nor the hairy adders on the fog that bask,
>   But waur I like Robin-a-Ree.

O! hatefu' its to hear the whut-throat chark,
   Frae out the auld Taffdyke,
And wha likes the e'ening singing lark,
   And the auld moon boughing tyke;
O! I hate them, and the ghaist ateen,
   Ne'er the den o' puir Mary Lee,
But ten times waur loe I, I ween,
   That vile cheel Robin-a-Ree.

O! sourer than the green bullister,
   Is a kiss o' Robin-a-Ree,
And the milk on the tade's back I wad prefer,
   To the poison on his lips that be;
He has ruin'd me the de'ils-needle,
   He has kill'd puir Mary Lee,
Whan my heart awa, he did weedle,
   Nae mair saw I, Robin-a-Ree.

'Ere that my lum did bonnily reek,
   Fu' bien and clean was my ha',
At my ain ingle than my spawls I cud beek,
   Whan that sw aul'd the wridy snaw;
O! ance I liv'd happy by yon bonny burn,
   The warl was in love wi' me,
But now I maun sit 'neath the cauld drift and mourn,
   And curse black Robin-a-Ree.

Then whudder awa thou bitter biting blast,
   And sough through the scruntie tree,
And smoor me up i'the snaw fu' fast,
   And ne'er let the sun me see;
O! never melt awa thou wride o' snaw,
   That's sae kind in graving me,
But hide me ay frae the scorn and gafaw,
   O! villain's like Robin-a-Ree.

There are two other *Robbins*, celebrated in an out-of-the-way kind of song, which I feel inclined also to give—

Twa lads at *Clauchendolly* bide,
   Wha I lo'e weel, they're baith sae spree,
I'd be the tane or t'ither's bride,
   Dear *Robbin Bell*—sweet *Robbin Bee*.

But what's the odds wha I do like,
   There's nane o'm cares a doit for me,
Which makes me lie, and sab, and byke,
   For *Robbin Bell* and *Robbin Bee*.

The tane o'm shaws his buckskin brecks,
   And cordivans sae nice to see;
The tither has the dress bespeaks,
   Trig *Robbin Bell*—tight *Robbin Bee*.

And nane o' them can ither beat,
   At putting-stane, and doure sweartree,
Then to the kirk they baith come neat,
   Braw *Robbin Bell*—brisk *Robbin Bee.*

O, but they baith are funny cheels,
   I never saw them wanting glee,
And wi' the lasses, too, they're de'ils,
   Mark *Robbin Bell*—match *Robbin Bee.*

The tane has bastard bairnies twa,
   The tither he has twa or three,
But O, they're darling boys for a',
   My *Robbin Bell*—and *Robbin Bee.*

At sock or scythe they hae nae match,
   They ay do get the biggest fee,
And baith o' them do wear a watch,
   O, *Robbin Bell's*—like *Robbin Bee.*

'Bout them rin mony a lizzie daft,
   Ay waur than me, puir Girzle Gee,
For O, their tongues make hearties saft,
   Blythe *Robbin Bell*—brave *Robbin Bee.*

O, wha can stand their squeezes warm?
   And whan they cadge us on the knee,
We clean forget there's ony harm
   In *Robbin Bell*—and *Robbin Bee.*

Robbin Breestie—The Robin Redbreast; in Germany, *Tommy Linden.* The following poem, termed the *Twa Burdies,* I give, for why, it hath very little poetic merit, but treats of the *Robbin Breestie,* and the *Willie Wagtail,* and has a tolerable moral:—

Whan a wunter storm was ance taking its breath,
   And the snaw did cease to drift,
And the sun peeped through a straight blue bore,
   Laigh, laigh, i'the southeron lift.

Twa burdies 'neath the easle o' an auld house,
   Sat chirpling out their wail,
The tane o' them was the Robbin Breestie,
   And the tither the Wullie Wagtail.

Puir Robbin's wings war hinging unco side,
   And his shankies seem'd truly sma',
While Wullie's tail wi' its white and blae feathers,
   Cud hardly gie a wag ava.

The twasome pied down on the cauld sneep snaw,
   Wi' the sorry hauf striffen'd e'e,
A wee teat o' gool was no to be seen,
   Nor ane spawl'drochy lang-legged flee.

Then follow me, quoth the Robbin Breestie,
  To his comrade the Wullie Wagtail,
Let us bauldly enter yon bielie gill-ha',
  And for food we winna fail.

Sae into the bonny ha' they did hap,
  And the bairnies them daigh did mool,
Wee Mary ran out to the wnnnowing the corn,
  And brought them in plenty o' gool.

Then on to the lip o' the meal-girnel,
  Lap Robbin and sang his sang ;
But Wullie the lad look wullyart and blate,
  And was wagging his tail fu' thrang.

Ane bawdrons wha had kitlins under a bed,
  Whan she heard Robbin's sang,
Came sprauchlin in a hurry out,
  And at Wullie Wagtail did spang.

He flew against a lozen wi' a thud,
  Glass light deceived the cheil,
Back fluttering he was dung, and cudna be saved,
  To bawdrons he did reel.

She nyarr'd whan she gat him, as he had been a mouse,
  Or some lang-snouted, cheeping strow,
Robbin sat still, and keep'd a calm sough,
  Than happ'd out whan he was fu'.

A lesson is this to a' mankind,
  Whan we're strangers ony gate never fail
To mark them that's *nane*, like the Robbin Breestie,
  Or we're worried like the *Wullie Wagtail*.

ROBBIN-RIN-THE-HEDGE—A trailing kind of weed, which *runs* along *hedges*, a *robbin net* ; its seed sticks to woollen cloth.

RONNET BAGS—The rennets for coagulating milk.

ROON-SHOON—Shoes made of the *roons*, or selvages of cloth.

ROOSING—Praising, with a little flattery. The Gallovidians are not much given to this fault ; when the merchant asked *auld Ned* about the *cow* he intended to sell, what were her properties, and so forth, Ned, who knew nothing about *roosing*, or lying, said, " Why the cow has very little *milk*, and no *butter* at all ;" Ned, indeed, did not butter up his property. Another man said of his friend's whisky, " that it was de'ils swear to gang down, nor wad it stay whan it was *down*." And a third, whom a neighbour was buying *seed corn* from, the latter said that he doubted it wad not grow, as it was a wee thing o' the *red early cast* ; "that's a queer thought of your's," (quoth the former) "for I'm sure it was de'ils fond to grow in the *harrest-time* ;" but grain, when once it hath budded, and is checked, will not *bud* again. Such are swatches of the flattery of the peasantry.

Roov'd—Rivetted. Two persons once tried who would tell the largest lie ; the first said, " he knew a fellow who made a ladder, and went up on it to the moon, and there drove a *spike nail* right through her face ;" " O, but (says the other,) my fellow went up and *roov'd* that nail on the other side." " Well," (cried a third) " I think you are about equal ; you may try again."

Roped-een—Sore eyes ; the rheumy matter hardened on the eye-lashes.

Rossens—Bramble covers, sometimes termed *rons*, clumps of thorns and briers ; same with French *ronceroi*, a wild, thorny place ; a king, or *roi*, of rustling brushwood places. A fox was once sadly beset in one of these *rossens o' whuns* ; the hounds could not uncover him, so the *ron* was set in flames about his *lugs* ; out he came with his tail a-blaze, like one of Sampson's, and was shot by one of the sentinels.

Rouchton—A rough, strong fellow ; *rouch*, rough.

Rounall—Any circular thing, such as the moon.

Rouse-away !—A call of a fresh-water boatswain ! *haul away.*

Rout—A heavy blow with a stick.

Roving-Sleep—When one talks while sleeping, we are said to be *roving* in our *sleep.*

Rowings—Wool made up in long rolls, with *cards*, before it is spun.

Royating—Feasting well ; *rioting* on the sweets of the earth.

Rug—A bed-cover; " as *snug's* a *bug* in a *rug*."—Old say.

Rule o' Thumm—Rule of thumb, the king of all rules. The *rule of three*, and Pythagoras's *golden rule* are nothing to this ; it is that rule whereby a person does something which no other can. Thus *Burns* wrote *Tam o' Shanter* by the *rule o' thumm* ; this is the *rule of genius*, or the *rule of nature*, which surpasses all the rules of art ; every soul knows less or more of this rule, and yet no two know exactly the same. Thus, who could compose this *book* like me?—None. Many might be found to do it better, and few worse; but none could do it exactly as I do; of course, then, I am making use of this valuable *rule*, and so doth every one; without book or *dominie* we all become acquainted with the *rule o' thumm* ; we even gain the affections of the lasses by it—the only thing worthy of gain in this world.

Rules o' Contrary—A female school game, much like *Allicomgreenzie*, which see.

Rummlekirns—Gullets on wild rocky shores, scooped out by the hand of nature ; when the tide flows into them in a storm, they make an awful rumbling noise ; in them are the surges *churned*.

Rummlinsires—Small sewers filled with little stones.

Runches—White roots, common among ploughed land ; swine are fond of them, but farmers not.

Runge—To rummage, to search with avidity.

Runse—The noise a sharp instrument makes, piercing flesh.

Runt—A short thick stick, a *rung* ; also a short person, *runted tailed*.

Run-wull—A person is said to be *run-wull*, when run out of the reach of the law ; with wildness.

Ruralach—A native of the rural world.

> Whan I came hame frae my weary travels,
> My bonny lassy I thought to see,
> My lovely dearie, wha aften wander'd,
> In sunny blinks roun' the shores wi' me.

But whar was she, O, whar was my sweetheart?
   But in her grave 'neath the truff sae green,
There she doth sleep, and I bitter weep,
   For my only true love, my Rural Queen.
Whate'er she said, I did joy to hear her,
   Howe'er she look'd, she was heaven to see,
In my arms I press'd her, and sweetly kiss'd her,
   Her feeling heart quickly moved me.
What caused me then not to wed my darling?
   'Twas reason blighted my love sae keen,
For Poverty he did frighten me,
   Sae I bade fareweel to my Rural Queen.
I bade fareweel to the blooming creature,
   Until a fairer day I'd see,
But Death came forward while I delayed,
   And a doolfu' wretch he has made o' me.
Thus always cowards by the world are treated,
   It is the way, and has ever been ;
For fate grows cross, and their loves they loss,
   As has been my luck wi' my Rural Queen.

S.

S—An iron hook of the shape of this letter, used by *har-rowers* and ploughmen to join the *treadwuddie* to the *buck* in harrowing, and to the *soum* in ploughing ; also to the *swingletrees* in each.

SACKIE—A person somewhat like a sack when full.

SADDEN'D—Made solid, by tramping or otherwise.

SADDLE-TAE-SIDE—The way females sit on the saddle, to the one side.

SADDLER HALLIDAY—A well known Gallovidian original, of the Christian name James, but being bred a saddler, and becoming notorious, he is known by no other name than *Saddler Halliday* ; when young he was the best-person'd man any where to be seen ; when at his apprenticeship, dukes and lords, in passing through Dumfries, stopped their carriages to observe the young *saddler*. Having served out his time, he married his master's daughter, but she proving not to be a very good woman, and he none of the very best of men, they soon dissolved

partnership. He said of her, " that had he fished the
loch o' hell wi' a *tade* on for a *bait,* he could not have
drawn up a worse wife." After this, he took a ramble
away through England, as far as London, and drunk and
was merry wherever he went, dipping at the same time
deep into the knowledge of the ways of mankind, the
most extensive science of any. But what may seem strange,
he would not walk a mile undernight, no, not for all the
world ; here then do we behold a young strong man,
nearly seven feet high, so afraid of *boggles,* that he could
not move alone, when gloaming set in. He used to say,
" that though very timorous he was this way, he was not
so bad as the auld *priest Nathan Mackie,* who durst not
gang to the door ate'en to ————, unless ane of the
servants gaed wi' him, and held him by the coat tail."
The boggles have quite the upper hand of the *saddler* ;
once the cloud involved him in darkness on some of the
roads of Galloway, so he would proceed no farther, and
bolted into a *barn* by the way-side, and covered himself
among some straw ; about midnight he heard something
like the moans and groans of some being in the same
barn, and his fears squared, the sounds of distress in-
creased, and at last a vomiting noise was heard ; the smell
of the disgorged matter told in the saddler's nose, that the
being was nothing of the supernatural order ; he sought it
out, and who was this but his own worthy wife, hopeful
woman ? Next morning they parted again, and never, as
I have heard, have had the happiness to pass a night with
each other again. It is long now since the Saddler became
a wandering tradesman ; he wanders from one friend's house
in the country to another, and "fettles the naig graith."
Bachelor's *haws* are his favourites ; there he goes through
his tales, and makes his pointed remarks; he is ratherly
given to Scotch satire, which assists in making him the
famous character he is ; he has the manners of the best

bred gentleman at hand, whenever he needs to use them; his abilities wont to shine with brilliancy over a bottle, and the *cock* of all parties wherein was he, was always allowed to be Saddler Halliday.

SADJELL—A lazy unwieldy animal.

SAEGED-TEETH—Teeth set on edge by eating unripe fruit.

SAEL'D—Sealed.

SAIP-SAPPLES, or SAIP-SUDDS—Water that clothes has been washed with.

SAND-TRIPPER—The sand-piper, common on shores.

SAUGHWAND-CREELS—Wicker baskets.

SAVING-TREE—A shrub common in gardens, of a medical nature; given (the leaves of it, when decocted), to horses having the *botts*; also, it is said to kill the fœtus in the womb, though I doubt if there be much truth in this. It takes its name from this though, as being able to *save* a young woman from *shame,* by her committing *murder,* a pretty way indeed. This is what makes gardeners and others wary about giving it to females. Burns fancies *Hornbuik* knew this tree. " She trust hersell to hide the shame in Hornbuke's care."

SAWING SHEET—A sheet out of which grain is sown. To *saw braid-cast,* to scatter grain with the hand. *Saw,* salve for wounds.

SAWNIE, the SAILOR—No original is more worthy a place in this book than *Sawnie Brown,* or *Sawnie the Sailor*— Born in Borgue, bred a farmer, ran off, and became a sailor when about twenty years of age. Sailed in the slave-trade; was impressed on board a man o' war; was at the taking the Cape of Good Hope, and at Monte Video, in South America. After serving his Majesty ten years against his will, he returned to his native country, and, like his ancestor, *Sinbad the Sailor,* recounted his wonderful adventures, and really wonderful they are; entirely true, as Sawnie never lied in his life. It is not

exactly the many brunts and strange scenes he has been in
that make them so, but it is the strange observations he
made in these brunts and *broiliments,* and the way he tells
them ; for what is singular, all the while he was away from
friends, amidst foreigners in distant lands, his native
tongue and native manners changed nothing ; he came
home a greater *Borguenite* than when he went away, and
talked *brader Scotch* than any in the country; to hear
him in this language telling of one of his *shirramuirs,* how
laughable it is.   I shall give the account of the battle of
the *Cape,* as taken from his lips ; all his other adventures
I have also by me, and will give them to the world some
day or other, for indeed they are as original things as I
have met with.   " Weel, the fleet started ; I kend na whar
the devil they war for.   We had sogers without end
aboard, wi' Sir David Baird and his *white naig,* and mair
care was ta'en o' this *white naig* than o' ony human creature
we had wi' us.   Our Commodore, Sir H——— P———,
was a damned lang yellow leug, wi' buckteeth ; he never
gaed lie hardly, but wad hae lain wi' his claise on 'twar-
three minutes whiles *aboon the blankets* ; he ay look'd
oozilie, his hat a' in clours, and his coat covered wi' woo
and stoure ; he feared neither God nor the Devil, and his
oaths made the auldest sailor aboard trimmle.   After we
had plunged at it for twar-three weeks, we saw the loom of
the Cape, and soon landed the sogers on't, at a place three
miles frae Cape Town, round the shore.   The Dutch and
French forces war to be fought next day ; the sailors o' the
fleet war to man the big guns ; and I was ane amang the
rest picked out to push and draw the meikle cannon on the
fiel o' battle.   Lord, I ken'd na now what to think, I had
never been at a battle ; a kind o' shilpetness cam owre me ;
wine was dealt roun' ; I skilted at it, but had I drank at it
till yet, it wad na hae doitered me, a noggin fu' has nae
effect in a time o' that kind.   The marching began about
sunrise, and soon we cam in sight o' the enemy : how

the sun did dazzle on the sillar-laced claise o' the French troops; I looked at them whan I had time, but the haurling the guns keeped ane thrang. Soon we gat near them, and they began to burn powther first. I hated to hear the balls soughing by me, and thought on my Father's auld prayer, some o' which I said quitly to mysell. At length the faught began in earnest; gude Lord! what a tirrivee and stramash! We had twa Highland regiments; some o' the sogers in them being shot, the rest gat mad on the instant the moment they saw blood. Donald cudna be hadden in; they flew in on the fae with their bagonets, and sent the enemy in confusion. Now was the time for us; we pointed the guns to the greatest *cludders*, and they being loaded wi' grape, we just cutted roads through them, and fain war they to lay down their arms at our feet in a wee time, and ask for quarters; but the devil's o' Highland bodies seemed anxious for mair o't, and seemed vexed the dust was owre; mony a ane they necked after the battle was at an end. Then marched we into Cape Town, and stack up the flag. I was as black as the Ace o' Spades wi' gunpowther; but whan washed and dressed, faith I was as weel as ever; the de'il the scart I had got, though I had morroch'd through the mids o't. I was glad at this, and gaed away, and saw the *bonny lasses* o' the Cape." So goeth *Sawnie* on, and who would not be pleased to listen? but I shall let him rest at this time until I bring out the strange " *Adventures of Sawnie, the Sailor.*" The following is two verses of his

WELCOME TO GALLOWA.

The whusky pig we'll fill fu', the best things i'the house
Faith, we shall set afore ye; gude Lord, man! we'se be crouse;
And owre the ills o' Fortune, like glorious souls shall craw
Thou'rt welcome hame, dear Sawnie man, to bonny Gallowa.

At the Cape there wi' Sir Davie, and eke Mount Video,
What awfu' broiliments ye had wi' the mighty foe;
Ye drave the French and Spaniards as rain drives aff the sna,
O! but ye're welcome, Sawnie man, to bonny Gallowa.

SAXES AND SEVENS.—To have all rid, a clear plan laid out; is to have it all portioned in *saxes and sevens.*

SCADES O' LICHT.—Flares, or flashes of light; *coloured light,* as it were.

SCAFFY SHOWERS.—Showers which soon blow by; " a baul *scuff* o' a shower," a pretty severe shower.

" A sun-shiny shower, last's not half an hour."
Auld say.

SCAIL.—To separate; *to scail the kivvan,* to separate the party.

SCALBERT.—A low-lifed, *scabby-minded* individual.

SCARCEMENT.—A shelf amongst rocks; a shelf leaning out from the main face of a rock; on *scarcements,* build sea-fowl.

SCARROW.—The shadow. The *scarrow* o' a hill, the shadow of that hill; the *scarrow* o' a *craw,* the shadow of a crow or other bird, on the earth, while it flies in the air; this is one of our poetical words; it means too something more; than mere shadow, but I cannot express the idea. To translate Scottish into English, is no easy matter.

SCART.—To scrape; *scartings,* the scrapings of a pot.

SCAUM O' THE SKY.—The scum of the sky; the thin white vapours of the atmosphere; *a scaumy day,* a day when the sun's face is behind white thin clouds; there is *red scaum, white scaum,* and many others. By the colour, or hue of the *scaum,* do Watherwiseakers guess about coming weather. *Scaum,* like *scarrow,* is also a poetical word.

SCAUP.—The scalp; a *bare scaup,* a bald head; *scaupy land,* bare land, thin of soil.

SCAURTS.—A name for the black cormorant; for why, this bird hath its nest on *scaurs* or wild rocky places; its common name is *douker,* because it is a great diver; also,

Mochrum lairds, because they have been, as it were, pro-
prietors there of a piece of wild shore, for an *unknown*
length of time ; and also, they are called *Elders o'Cowend,*
from their black, grave, and greedy appearance, and being
common on Colvend shores.

SCAWD or SCAUD.—A disrespectful name for tea.

SCLATERS.—A species of ear-wig; also slaters. *Sclater's
eggs,* little white eggs like beads, found amongst *red land.*
Sclateband, a strata of slate amongst bands of rock.

SCLIFFANS.—Useless thin shoes ; the same with *scloits.*

SCLOY.—To slide; *scloying,* sliding; the same with *scly-
ing* ; a *scloy* or *scly,* a slide.

SCODGING.—Looking sly. *Scodgie,* a suspicious person ;
scodge, to pilfer, to *half thief.*

SCONES.—Soft bread; cakes baked with flower.

SCOOL.—To scowl; *scool o' herring,* a herring *tack* or
shoal ; *scool,* a disorder with horses.

SCOOT.—To squirt water through a hollow tube ; *scoot-gun,*
a syringe ; *scoot a scout,* a person on the look-out.
Coblers are termed *scouts,* being always on the prowl.
Scoot, a wooden drinking *caup,* sometimes *scoop,* being
wood scooped out. *Scootifu'* the full of a *scoot* ; *scootikins,*
drams of whisky ; also *scootle,* to spill any thing when a
carrying.

SCOWBS.—Bended sticks for holding thatch down on houses;
scowbed, bended ; *scowb and scraw,* a *snug* phrase.

SCOY.—Any thing badly made ; *scoyloch,* an animal which
plaits its legs past others in walking.

SCRAFFLE or SCRAMMLE.—When any one, such as a
bridegroom, or an electioneerer, flings loose coin among
the mob, the rabble is the said to *scraffle* or *scrammle* for
it, or that the scene is a scrammle.

SCRAICH or SCRAIGH.—A shriek; *scraighton,* a person
fond of screaming.

SCRANNIE.—An old, ill-natured, wrinkled, bell-dame.

SCRATT.—A rit, as with a bier; *to be scratted*, to be torn by females.

SCRAWS.—Thin turfs, pared with flaughter spades, to cover houses.

SCREAH, SKREEH or SCRACH o' DAY.—The morning dawn; probably this word and *scarrow*, a shadow, are connected; the shadow of the morning, the first appearance of light; or is it allied to *scraigh*, shriek, at this time, when the cock crows or shrieks, hie the nocturnal wanderers to their confine. Jamieson has it from *creek o' day*, or crack or break, in this I do not just agree with him.

SCREED.—To rive; the noise cloth makes in tearing.

SCREEL.—A large rocky hill nigh the sea; a haunt for the fox.

SCROGGS.—Low bushes; *scroggie, scrunted*.

SCROW.—A large quantity of people; no fixed number, though.

SCRUBBERS.—Articles made of heather, for *scrynging naps*, for washing " ony scrubbers the day mystress." *Sawnie Ragg's* well known salutation to the *gude wives o' Galloway*.

SCUDS.—Lashes; the same with *sculls*.

SCUFF.—To touch, to graze, the scuff is the wind, as it were; the *scuff of a cannon ball*, blows a man to pieces.

SCULLDUDDERY.—Fornication. The following is the concluding clause of an Antiburger's sermon:—" The time of the Peatmosses is now at hand, *my friens*, when the lasses will fling bits o' clods at the lads, *my friens*, and than they'll seem to rin awa ye see, and the lads they'll follow them; whan heels owre gowdie will they gae as if something had whurl'd them, *my friens*; the lads gae out owre them, and sae begins *Sculldudderie, my friens* which is the beginning o' a evil, *my friens,* and which sends mony a worthy cheel to hell, *my friens,* there to lie on a bed o' brimstone *lowing blue* for ever mair. Amen, *my friens.*"

SCUN.—Plan, craft.   A scunge, a sly fellow; a maid seducer.

SCURR.—A low blackguard; from Latin, *scurra,* a scoundrel; *scurr,* any thing low; *scurrie-thorns,* low dwarf thorns, in moorland glens.

SCUTCH.—To beat; *scutching spurkle,* a stick to beat flax; *scutchintow,* rough flax, the refuse of the *scutching.*

SEALCH.—The seal, the phoca; also *a shillcorn* or small *bunyion.*

SEEDIE INGLES.—Fires made with the husks of grain.

SEEPING.—Filtrating, circling slowly; *seeking* vent; *seeps,* sypes or sykes, trivial springs.

SELLIE.—Self; *sellie's ay sellie,* self is still for self.

SERVICE.—The funeral treat; the *dredgy,* now much done away with, a wise thing, for it was a custom hurtful to the poor. *Servets* are the little trays the *service* was served round to the gossips on; it has been remarked, and with truth, that those who take a dram most free of any, on other occasions, are modest at funerals as *drinkers*; so much then to their honour; and it is only those unsociable wretches who will not pay for a *gill* in a *public-house,* who are voracious at them, who ought (confound their *monyplies*) to be shipped to Iceland, and pitched down the crater of Heckla.

SEY or SAE.—A shallow tub, used in cheese making.

SHA.—What is said to a dog, when ordered to hunt; *sha-awa,* run you dog!

SHABB.—To smuggle; to send any thing away privately.

SHACK.—A word used in encouraging a *curr-dog* to worry a fox; *shack him!* is the cry—from *shake,* probably.

SHACHLE.—A weak animal, all *shachled* or *shaken.*

SHAIRD.—A piece of furniture ill-put together; a *shieging* concern.

SHALLOCHY LAND.—Land of a shallow nature.

SHANGAN.—A split stick put on a dog's tail; when *collie* comes snuffing and snoaking about *unco* houses, this is put on his tail, and so he lies *gowling hame.*

SHANG O' BREAD AND CHEESE.—A *piece,* a *cull,* a bite between meals.

SHAWP.—An useless creature; the stalk, as it were, without the root.

SHED.—To separate; to separate the calves from the cows, we *shed* them.

SHEEP-SMEARING.—The art of smearing sheep with oily matters, so that they may better withstand the winter's cold, termed *laying*; whiles for the wool is laid aside, and the *tare* poured into the *lay* by the *Herd's* hand, like *sheep-clipping,* this a throng spell with Moor-farmers, and those who wish to dip into moorland manners, should attend a *sheep-smearing* bout; there will the ear hear very astonishing curiosities. I would much rather be at one of these meetings than to see a Play performed at Drury Lane. *Sheep-tade* or *sheep-tick,* an insect which feeds on the blood of sheep; *sheep-faws* retreats beneath the moors for sheep in winter; *sheep-tathing,* confining sheep on a piece of land until they *tathe* or manure it.

SHILLINGS.—Shelled oats; *shilling hills,* before the invention of *fans*; the seeds of corn had to be sifted from it; on a hill, in the wind, such hills, were so called.

SHILPIE.—A person trembling always, a sycophant; a poet who dreads critics, a being whom independence knows nothing about; a *shilped,* a *shelled wretch,* a heart stript of manliness.

SHINNIE.—A game described by Scottish writers by the name of *shintie*; the *shins,* or under parts of the legs are in danger, during the game, of being struck; hence the name from *shin*. *Shinans*, sinews of the body.

SHITTLE.—Any thing good for nothing.

SHIVELAVAT's HEN.—A hen which hath given over laying; used allegorically for females having done with child-bearing; the term is from Ireland, so ought to become obsolete.

SHOING THE AULD MARE.—A dangerous kind of sport; a beam of wood is slung between two ropes, a person gets on to this, and contrives to steady himself, until he goes through a number of antics; if he can do this he *shoes the auld mare*, if he cannot do it, he generally tumbles to the ground, and gets hurt with the fall.

SHOING THE MOSS.—When moss is *stripped* for *peatcasting*, the upper turf is thrown into where peats have been taken out, this preserves the soil of the moss; this *shoes* it as it were.

SHUGGIE SHOW.—The amusement of boys on the *slack-rope*, riding and shoving one another in the curve of the rope; they recite this to the swings—

> " Shuggie Show, Druggie Draw,
> " Haud the grup, ye canna fa',
> " Haud the grup, or down ye come,
> " And danceth on your braid bum."

SHUTTLE O' ICE.—The Scotch Glacier. A brook which runs down a mountain's side is frozen, but the fountain which supplies this brook keeps springing away; new water runs over the old, which is now ice, and there freezes too; in this way it continues with the frosty season, and or the thaw comes it is got to a great thickness, and is always our last ice in thawing. School-boys slide in rows down these shuttles, reminding travellers of the Alpine hunters, descending with their goats to the valley of Chaumonie.

SHYLING.—Not looking directly at an object, but out at a side; the leer of a *shell-faced* vagabond.

SIDIE FOR SIDIE.—Side-by-side.

SILLAR SAWNIES.—Periwinkles, common shells on shores.

SILLAR SHAKLE.—Silver shakle plant.

> " The sillar shakle wags its pow,
> " Upon the brae my deary,
> " The zephyr round the wunnelstrae,
> " Is whistling never weary."
>
> *Auld sang.*

SIMIE or SYMIE.—When there are two things quite like one another, we say they are like *simie* or *symie*, either of which will answer for the name Simeon.

SINN.—To wash; to make clean. Probably, this and *shane*, that which breaks witchcraft, are one; red-hot irons are sometimes thrown into a churn, so that it may *get*, or that the cream therein may become butter; this is termed *shaning*.

SINNIE.—The medical plant senna.

SIRSE.—Sirrahs.

SKELLIE.—To look with one eye—to squint—to go astray.

SKEMMLING.—Going astray; a foolish way of throwing the legs.

SKEPPING BEES.—The art of putting bees into their houses when they hive.

SKERIE.—Somewhat restive. *Ramskerie*, very restive and lustful; of the nature of a ram.

SKILTS.—Drinks of any thing. *Skilting*, drinking deeply.

SKIN-FLINT.—A hard person; a grub, who would try to take the skin of a flint stone.

SKINKLE.—To sprinkle, to sow thin. *Skinks*, bad pieces of flesh.

SKYB.—A worthless fellow. *Skyball*, the same.

SLAGGIE.—The land, or *ice* after a thaw, is said to be *slaggie*. A *slag-day* with *curlers*, is a day on which the ice is thawing; from *clog*, comes this word.

SLAP.—A gap in a fence. *Milking-slap*, the place where cows are milked at.

SLARGIE-STUFF.—Matter of a gluey nature.

SLAWK,—A slimy plant, which grows in *burns* and springs.

SLEEKET.—A person of a sly disposition; smooth and deep.

SLEETCH.—A kind of fat mud, taken from shores to manure land.

SLEUG.—An ill-behaved man; also, one not good looking.

SLEW.—To lean any thing to a side; off the perpendicular.

SLINK.—A greedy person; a young calf before it is calved.

SLOCHER.—A person careless in dress, particularly about the feet.

SLOMIE.—An ox is said to be *slomie* when it has on a false appearance of flesh.

SLONK or SLONKING.—The noise our feet make when sinking in a miry bog; also, when walking with shoes full of water. *Slouching*, a wetting. *Slouched*, drenched.

SLOUGH.—A fat harmless man. *A fine slough o' a cheel*, a harmless contented man.

SLUNEOCH.—A person of a brutish disposition, who would do all the harm he could, if he had the ability to project; much the same with *Slunge*.

SLYPE.—To peel the skin off the flesh; also a fellow who runs much after the female creation, yet has not the boldness, (though the willingness) to seduce any of them.

SMA FAMILY.—A family of young children. *Smattery*, a quantity of small articles.

SMEEK.—Smoke. *Smeeked*, smoked.

SMEERIKIN.—The sweetest of all kisses; the kiss one lover gives another, when they are quivering in one another's arms : few joys on earth exceed a *smeerikin*.

SMIDDIE SPARKS.—The sparks which fly off red iron when beat.

SMIOK.—A dish of good food; to *smiok*, to feast on the best.

SMOIT.—A person who chatters *silly-bawdy* matters,

SMUDDOCH.—A bad burning fire—more smoke than blaze.

SMUDGE—To smile when we should not, such as in a church. To *smudge*, to try to suppress smiles, or laughter.

SMUIST.—Disagreeable smoke. *Smuisted*, smoked.

SMURR.—Light rain, rather heavier than dew.

SNAGGER-SNEE.—A large knife, first introduced from Germany.

SNAM.—To snap at any thing greedily.

SNAPPER.—An unforeseen accident; a misfortune. *Snap*, a little cake. *Snap*, a sharp noise. A veteran soldier once told me, that he would not be afraid to *take* a whole corps of *Gentlemen Yeomanry Cavalry* prisoners with a *Snap-candlestick*.

SNASTRY.—Low chat. *Snash*, converse hurtful to the feelings.

SNAWBROE.—Melted snow. *Snaw o' the rink*, the snow round the sides of a *rink*, or channlestone run.

SNAWBURDS.—Birds which visit us in winter. *Snawbrack*, a thaw, which frequently raises rivers, and does great damage. *Snaw-powther*, fine snow ; when this begins to fall first in a snow storm, its depth may be dreaded. *Snaw-wrides*, wreaths of snow.

> " Whan ere the wun began to shift,
> " We dreaded faith some mair snaw,
> " The sulky sonth began to rift,
> " And on it fell a sair snaw.
> " The cluds came banking up fu' swift,
> " The night did bring a fair snaw,
> " For or the morning, frae the lift
> " There fell an awfu' lair snaw,
> " And smoor'd the sheep."
>
> *Auld poem.*

SNED.—The long pole a scythe is fitted, into for the purpose of mowing with it ; the *runt* must be *siccard* in the *den*, so that the blade may have a *snanging* sound. *Bow'd Sneds* are preferred by mowers to straight ones, because they enable them to keep their backs more upright when working, and are not so apt to raise *stitches*.

SNEEL.—To snivel ; to speak through the nose.

SNEEP.—The glitter or dazzling of a white colour, such as snow.

SNEGG.—To interrupt ; to invite a broil ; to check, &c.

SNELL.—Any thing, whether animate or not, which biteth hard.

SNIBBLE.—A small piece of wood put through the end of a rope, so that-it may be fixed into an eye in the other end.

SNIFFLIN.—Apparently throng, yet doing nothing.

SNIRK.—To give the nose a smart draw up with the membranes of itself.

SNOIT.—A young conceited person who speaks little, thought to be the beginning of some genius ; but alas! it generally remains a *snoit* all its days.

SNORK.—The snort of an affrighted horse.

SNOTTERS.—Snotts. The mucous, viscous matter of the nose.

SOAM.—The iron of the head of a plough. *Herring soam,* the fat of herrings.—Young girls throw this against a wall, and if it adheres to it in an upright manner, then the husband they will get will also be so ; if crooked, he will be crooked.

SOBERSIDES.—A creature of sober habits. *Sobering,* growing sober.

SOCY.—A person who walks with a manly air, *sockieng.*

SONKIE.—A man like a *sonk,* or sackfull of straw.

SOOPER—A bunch of feathers for sweeping. *Soopet,* cleaned. *De'il soopet,* means cleaned neatly out. "The de'il soopets there," there is nothing there. *Sooping,* sweeping. *Soople,* the half of the flail, the half which sweeps round the head.

SOOTIPILLIES.—A moss plant, which grows on a thick stalk, like a willow wand—the head is about half a foot long, and of a *sootie colour.*

Soss.—To fall with a *soss* ; to fall with all our weight. *Soss,* a mixture of various things for feeding dogs with.

Sotter.—To saturate ; the noise of flesh roasting. The damned are said to be set a *sottering* in hell.

Sough o' the Sea. — The sound of the sea. Those skilled in the weather, understand by this sound if any storms be brewing, as the sea begins to speak before the sky. When the sea thus doth growl, farewell to fair wea_ ther for a while ; when the *dumb swaul* comes heaving over the sand bank, and its bottom rubs the bar, then the surge curves and curls with indignation a-top, spreading its wrath in a white sheet of foam, which, for a while, re_ mains together on the billows, like flower lime spread on *red land.* The black rock looking out of the sulky deep, seems to have a white ruff round its neck ; the gloomy bank appears over the southern horizon ; the ships come tilting over the waves to places of shelter, when turning down the swell of the billow, the rudder waves in air, and then swing they round, lurching in the hollow of the sea, while the *maws* fly *skying* by the sounding shore, and the raven seems to rejoice in the coming storm :—

> Let me gang whar I will, o'er the hills smoor'd in snaw,
> Or the black boiling ocean, to lands far awa' ;
> A day ne'er flees o'er me but it brings to my mind,
> The dear rural scenes which I hae left behind ;
> Ahame wi' my friends, whom I'll ever adore,
> Wha pleasantly dwell on the Soloway shore.
>
> O ! the days I hae run on the warm shelly beach,
> And gather'd the beauties the waters do bleach,
> Wi' my dear youthfu' cronnies, now far, far frae me,
> Will we ne'er meet again, and there frolic sae free ;
> O, this makes me sorrow, and often deplore,
> For we'll ne'er trip again on the Soloway shore.
>
> Was the garden o' Eden yet flourishing grand,
> Wi' its roses and sweets, all around on each hand,
> Was a fair Arab dame, blushing joyous with love,
> To invite me to live in her gay spicey grove,
> I'd fling them aside, and go where the waves roar
> Round the Land of my Home, on the Soloway shore.

SOUROCKS—Sorrel; *sour scone*, literally sour bread, but used to represent something disagreeable; as when a person without cause lashes the character of another, he is said to be making himself a *sour scone*.

SOUTER'D—We say a card-player is *souter'd*, when he loses all.

SOW BY THE LUG—When a fellow wishes to play away upon another, so that he may show his own ability, and lower the other's in the eyes of the world, and if this one deceives him, and has greater talents than he was aware of, we say he has taken the wrong *sow by the lug*; one whom he can neither "hap nor win by the ear," according to Hudibras.

SOWDIE—A dirty woman, partaking much of the nature of a sow.

SOWLOCHING—Wallowing in mire, like a sow.

SOWP—A washer-woman's term; when washing, she gives the clothes her *first sowp*, and then again her *second sowp :* which means, first and secod washes.

SOWSE—A swinging heavy blow; sometimes a load.

SPAIG—A person with long, ill-shaped legs.

SPAIN, or SPEAN—To wean; to take a young animal from sucking its mother.

SPAIVERS—Persons who *libb* and *spaive* cattle; *to libb*, is to castrate a male animal; *to spaive*, to do a female; the former is an easy matter to do, in comparison with the latter. A young cow with calf, that is to say, an *apen quey*, will not *speave*; neither will a cow that has had a calf, nor twin female calves. All castrated females are marked in the ear; to mark them so, is to *heifer* them.

SPALES—Chips; *spales o' the cannle*, little curls of tallow, which sometimes appear on a burning candle, paid some attention to by the superstitious.

SPANG—To leap, to spring; *spang-tade*, a deadly trick played on the poor toad; a small board is laid over a stone, on the one end of which is put the reptile; the other end is then struck by a hard blow, which drives the toad into the air, and when it falls it is generally quite dead. *Spang-new,* any thing quite new; *spang-fire-new,* the same; *spanging,* leaping; *spangie,* an animal fond of leaping.

SPANKER—A tall, well-made woman; *spankering hizzie,* a tall nimble girl.

SPARRABLES—Hob-nails for shoes.

SPARTLE—To kick with the feet, to *paw.*

SPATE—A large fall of rain, a spout.

SPAWLS—Legs; *spawldrochie,* long-legged.

SPEDDART—A tough old creature, tight as a wire; *spee-dart,* the spider.

SPEIL—To climb; also, any sort of play or game; thus a *boor* who takes his meat well is said to play a good *speil* at the *porridge coag.*

SPELKS—Sharp *speals* or points of iron, starting off from the mass it belongs to; *spelked,* ragged wood.

SPELL AND SPELL—Turn by turn; working so at labour.

SPINDRIFT—The spume of the sea; the spray.

BEN SPINDRIFT, THE OLD PILOT.

Ay, yonder is Ben Spindrift,
   Launching his little boat,
Adown the beach beneath the clift,
   Now he has it afloat.

Off he shoves a sculling,
   Where does he mean to steer?
Now he strips and's pulling,
   The good old Timoneer.

His bonnet, too, he's doffing,
   He means to have a trip,
Away out to the offing,
   To meet a foreign ship.

And safely in he'll bring her,
   O'er sand-bank and bar,
And on the cables swing her,
   Were she a man of war.

A cannon is heard roaring
  A little to the lee;
Ay, yonder cometh snoring,
  A vessel from the sea.

The pilot's flags down hauling,
  For Ben has got aboard,
And's on his trumpet bawling
  To watchful tars the word.

The captain's minding nothing,
  Good Ben's the captain now;
See how the brine is frothing,
  And rising o'er the bow.

Up in the breeze they heave her,
  The anchor's 'neath the tide,
Now old Ben doth leave her,
  The captain by his side.

O was my little reason
  As good a pilot's Ben,
Through the most stormy season,
  I right could steer me then.

On rocks I'd ne'er be crashing,
  And weeping with despair,
But merrily on be dashing,
  So trig and debonair.

Sleep soundly on my pillow,
  My conscience would not sting,
And on each surging billow
  Of life I'd sit and sing.

None like me for a steerer,
  Then moralists would see;
For no jiber nor no jeerer,
  Would then e'er pester me.

Through mankind ever mobbing,
  How would I jog along,
My heart most softly throbbing,
  My fancy ever strong.

Earth would delight to have me,
  I'd then be no outcast,
Heaven with joy would save me,
  And lead me home at last.

SPINNLESHANKS—A creature with small legs.

SPINNLING—Grain is said to be *spinnling*, when it is shooting.

SPIRG—As much liquid as will moisten one's lips.

SPIRLINGS—Small burntrouts.

SPIRRAN—An old female of the nature of a spider.

SPLAE-FEET—Feet which are rather inclined to let their sides appear foremost; *splenner*, to stride.

SPLATCH—A patch of dirt; *sploit*, a little liquid filth.

SPLINTER-NEW—Any thing quite new.

SPLUNTING—The same with *sproaging*, running after girls undernight. This work ran high with the higher ranks in Galloway once, but these days are away.

SPOUTROCH—Weak thin drink, bad whisky.

SPRAWCHLED—Sprawled; *sprawchling*, sprawling.

SPROOZLE—To struggle, sometimes *stroozle*.

SPRUCE—Very neat and well-looking; a young fellow is said to *spruce himsell up*, when he sets forward to see his *lass*, or only darling.

SPY-ANN—A game of hide and seek, with this difference, that when those are found who are hid, the finder cries *spyann*; and if the one discovered can catch the discoverer, he has a ride upon his back to the *dools*.

SQUACH—The noise a hare makes when a killing.

SQUEEF—A blackguard; one who rails against women, and yet is fain to seduce them. I hope all my readers are perfectly aware, that I am quite on the *women's side* always. I have no sins on my head, thank God, for injuring innocent woman, and I hope never shall. He is no *man*, say I, who triumphs over female frailty.

SQUIRR—To skim a thin stone along the water.

STAGGIE—Grain is said to grow *staggie*, when it grows thin; *stallyoch*, a thick stalk of grain standing by itself; *staggrell*, a person who staggers in walking.

STANE-CHACKER—The bird stone-chatter, for why, it keeps chattering about rocks, and old stone walls. This bird is much detested in the country, because it is said to be " hatched by the toad." *The tade clocks the stane-chacker's eggs*, is the phrase, which may be partly true, as the toad is often found in its nest, for they make their nests both in one hole. It is singular such a beautiful bird should be naturally fond of the toad's dirty mansion ; but so it is. I have seen a fair and good-looking young man toy with one lovely female after another, until his gay season fled, and espousing at last an old harridan, verifying the adage, " that he wha is ill to please will land in the dirt at last." Now, though the toad may be often found in this bird's nest, yet its body is of too cold a nature to hatch its eggs. In the country they look at this bird with the same sensations, almost, that they do at a female prostitute ; they imagine it chatters the following rhyme, and its injunctions are obeyed :—

    " Stane Chack, devil tak'
    " They wha herrie my nest,
    " Will never rest, will meet the pest,
    " De'il brak' their lang back,
    " Wha my eggs would tak, tak."

STANEGRAZE—A bruise from a stone.

STANERAW—A yellow-coloured moss which grows on rocks, and is used in dyeing.

STANK-LOCHENS—Dead lakes, covered with grass; *duck-haunts, stank-hens, water-hens.*

STAMMAGER — A *busk* : a slip of stay-wood, used by females.

STAPPLES—Thatch made in handfuls, for thatching.

STARN.—A small quantity of any thing; same with *syne.*

STAR O' DUNGYLE.—A few years ago, the most beautiful woman in Galloway was a Miss H———; her father was a laird. *Keltonhill fair* was often by her laid in dust and ashes, for no girl was looked at or admired in all the fair but Miss H———. The celebrated Maggy Lauder never so much attracted the attention of the crowds in *Anster Loan,* whatever *Tennant* may say to the contrary. Many and many a *Rob the Ranter* had she; her features ran exactly in the curve of exquisite beauty, and were always kept in the most enchanting animation ; her eyes, her hair,

her lips, were the most charming objects man could behold—they set the most callous a burning with love! every
movement she made was of the most attracting and en-
gaging nature. The Irishmen from *Ballinasloe* would
have left both their horses and oxen, and joined the crowd
that followed Miss H——, bawling out *" By Japers,
she's the game*; O! honey, if I had thee but at the sweet
town of *Limavadie*;" another, " By the *Long bridge of
Belfast,* Barney's eyes never saw such a girl; I'd fight for
her with my mother of the sloe, till all the bones in my
body were bettled to mummy." The sons of *John Bull*
beyond the Tweed, got also enamoured of Miss H——;
but the good boxer or bruiser were the only persons who
could get to speak to her, and she was always fonder
of that class, than of well-bred rich-dressed gentlemen.
In short, for all her beauty and elegance, the low and
mean were her associates, and she cared not what length
she went with them almost; would lay in barns with them
at night, put on beggar weeds, and bade farewell to virtue
altogether, and bore to some of them bastard children:
yet, for all this, wherever she appeared in proper array,
all Galloway was charmed with the lovely Miss H——.
Beauty of the very first order, in defiance of vice, brought
her always crowds of admirers, who obeyed every nod of
her head, every wave of her hand: her sway was truly
despotic in the world of gallantry. A *strong blacksmith,*
who could not get her entirely to himself, got so mortified,
that he would off, and perish in the wilderness of Canada
for her sake; away he went to the banks of *Lake Huron,*
but was not there long before a letter followed him from
Miss H——, inviting to return again to Galloway, and
she would assuredly marry him. Back over the Atlantic
the son of Vulcan came, true to her mandate; but alas!
how must he have been deceived when the dear Miss H—
disdained to look or to speak to him? Thus she wielded

the sceptre of love! He afterwards became a game-keeper, and she really married an *old cattle dealer,* who had weeped about her many years ; to him she acted the part of not a bad wife—had a family—is yet living ; but, like the celebrated *Mary of Buttermere,* the beauty of *Cumberland,* her beauty hath entirely fled her ; she will be remembered in Galloway not only by the songs of her *Laureates,* but by hundreds of others, years unseen yet ; her popular name was, " *The Star of Dungyle.*"

The following verses were supposed to have been sung by her lover, the blacksmith, when coming back over the ocean.—

> For thee, my dear Miss H——,
>   I'll ride out owre the roaring sea ;
> O ! happy will be Gerron
>   When he does kiss and cuddle thee.
>
> I wad come to thee, Miss H——,
>   Far, far ayont America ;
> Thou's a' and a' to Gerron
>   O ! to see thee and Galloway.
>
> My bonny love, Miss H——,
>   For thee my heart does melt awa !
> O ! were ye as fond o' Gerron,
>   Wad ever there be sic a twa ?

STAVERALL.—A bad walking foolish person.

STAWD.—To be *stawd;* to be satiated ; to feel a loathing.

STED.—A trace. *Fit-sted,* a foot-track, such as *Crusoe* startled at on the sand. *Stedding o' houses,* the ground on which an *onset* is built.

STEEKERS.—Shoe-ties. *Steek your een,* shut your eyes.

STEGG.—The gander goose. *Stegging,* to walk like a *Steg.*

STELL.—A prop ; a support. *Stell your feet,* fix your feet so as not to fall. The *stell o' the stack,* the stick which props the stack.

STICKET.—Any job is said to be *sticket* when it is broke off in the middle, like the tale of the *Bear and the Fiddle.* A speech is *sticket* when the speaker is unable to proceed.

The captain of a volunteer body once *sticked*, or stuck up with a speech he had framed with great pains for a galaday; then looked he into his hat, where it lay wrote on paper; but alas! the confusion of his mind ere this time had blinded him; he could not read a word, but retreated in a lamentable situation.

STILCH.—A young, fat, unwieldy man.

STIVERON.—Any very fat food, such as that of a *haggis*.

STOG.—One with a stupid kind of gait—*stogging*.

STORG.—A large pin. *Storging*, the noise a pin makes rushing into flesh.

STOTTS.—Castrated oxen; the *stotts* mean the black cattle. A *cattle jobber* once told me, that he would rather see a good *stott stirk* as Buonaparte! all men to their fancy.

STOWL or STOLE.—A scion from a root. Thin-sown corn on good land is said to spread by *stowling*.

STOWRE.—Dust. A person at a *diet o' examine* once, was asked by the priest, " What he was made of ?" he forgot the English term *dust*, and gave the Scotch, *stowre*, which made the *diet* burst into laughter.

STRAGG.—A thin growing crop, the stalks straggling.

STRAMASH.—A battle; a broil; a battering and mashing concern; the same with *stram yulloch*.

STRANG.—Old urine, kept in the *strang pig*, and used in washing.

STRAPPS.—Bands for binding grain with. *Strapping Hizzies*, tight-bound girls; females of a strong, well-knit frame.

STRAVAGERS.—Wanderers; beggars; idle people.

STREEN.—An abridgment of *yestreen*, or yester evening. The *streen's milk*, the milk of yester evening.

STRIBBED.—Milked neatly. *Stribbings*, the last milk that can be drawn out of the udder.

STRIFE RIGGS.—Debateable ground; patches of land common to all; land which none is laird of.

STRIFFAN.—Film, thin skin. *Striffan o' an egg*, that white film inside an egg-shell.

STRING O' WULLGEESE.—A string of wild geese; these birds come to us from the Norlan nations in strings.

Frae Baltic's lided sea o' sna',
Or frozen loch i'e north awa,
Ye cackling come fu' merry a',
            For some lee shore,
Whar flysome icebergs dinna bla,
            Nor monsters snore.

Ye come, led by your chosen king,
Some champion *steg* wha heads your string;
For whan ye do in figure fling
            Your core, I see
Him, always on the foremost wing,
            Point-angle he.

The Firth wharin he once did dabble,
Or benty flow, he used to gabble,
And after paddocks rais'd a jabble,
            Wi' swattering cheer;
Without a compass he is able,
            There straight to steer.

I see ye yet, far south, south-west,
Ye mean to flee, or ye will rest;
Your guide kens weil what place is best
            To pass the night;
Now *motes* ye seem, now clouds molest,
            Ye lae my sight.

Again, tho' may be in the spring,
Whan ye return on Norlan wing,
I'll see your joyous cackling *string*;
            Sae happy a',
By me, poor soul, wha here doth sing
            My griefs awa.

I'm no like you, can flee before
The wintry hurricanes that roar,
The nipping hail that galls me sore,
            The frosts and snaws;
But here I maun on a cauld shore,
            Endure what blaws.

Nor can I, (like ye) whan the heat
Begins to make me strip and sweat,
To caller climates fast retreat,
            Whare sol's returning;
But pant below his beams, that beat
            In summer burning.

It's queer indeed to think o' man,
For a' we plot, for a' we plan;
And toil dreigh wi' the head and han,
                    To bide the weather;
The wild geese (let's do a' we can)
                    Are snugger rather.

Like them, we canna change our clime
Whan we think fit, at any time
To riot on the best sublime
                    That suits our maw;
We're villains, chained for a crime,
                    To fret and thraw.

But, tho' that be our wretched state,
Let us enjoy'd at any rate,
And whinge not 'neath the lash of fate,
                    Wi' sobbing moans;
God surely ne'er did us create,
                    To hear our groans.

Then grim November round me scowl,
Ye lapperd clouds conglobe and roll,
Ye gurly blasts remorseless howl
                    O'er land and sea;
I hope Heaven has gaen me a soul
                    To manly dree.

STROODS.—Very old shoes.

STRUM.—The first draw of a fiddle-bow over the fiddle-strings.

> " Dirdum, drum,
> " Three threads and a thrum."
>   *Cat's song.*

STRYNE.—To strain. *Strynd legs*, sprained legs.

STUMPIE.—A little, good-natured creature.

STUNCH.—A lump of food, such as of beef and bread.

STUNNER.—A big foolish man. *Stunner o' a gowk*, a mighty fool.

STURDY.—A disorder with sheep; also a plant which grows amongst corn, which, when eaten, causes giddiness and torpidity to come on.

STURNILL.—An ill turn; a back-set.

STYME.—A little light; a gleam. *I canna see a styme*, I cannot see the least glimmer of light.

SUGGAN.—A thick bed-coverlid. *Tawted rug*, the same.

SUGGIE LAN.—Wet land. *Sump,* a great fall of rain. *Sumped,* to be wet :—

> Since the hour of my birth, on this wearisome earth,
> I've been tumbled and toss'd to and fro ;
> But now with the dead, I must lay down my head,
> On this *bluid sumped* field—Waterloo.
> > *The veteran's farewell.*

SUPPIE MAE.—The name for a pet sheep.

SWACK.—Plenty and good. *Swacking nowt,* fat large animals.

SWAG.—To swing. *Swagging,* swinging.

SWAMPED.—An animal is said to be *swamped* when it seems *clung,* or *clinket,* or thin in the belly.

SWATTER.—To swim close together in the water, like young ducks.

SWATTROCH.—Strong soup ; excellent food.

SWAUL.—A large swell. *Swaulings,* swellings. *Swaultie,* a fat animal.

SWEER TREE.—A trial of strength. Two persons sit down feet to feet, and catch a stick with their hands ; then, whoever lifteth the other is the strongest.

SWEIL.—Any thing which hath a circular motion.

SWINGE.—To lash.

SWINGLE TREES.—The wood beams by which horses draw ploughs and harrows.

SYLING.—Sieving milk through a *syle*; a fluid sieve.

SYPLE.—A saucy, big-bellied person.

SYMION-BRODIE.—A toy for children ; a cross stick.

SYZZIE.—To shake. *He never syzzied me,* he never shook me :—

> Misfortune, fire away, ye bitch !
> > Come level well, and vizzie me ;
> For fear o' thee I shall not flitch,
> > The de'il e'en cudna syzzie me.
>
> Yestreen I met a gruesome witch,
> > She wi' her breath did whizzie me ;
> Then 'neath the lug lent me a litch,
> > Gude faith, the whap did dizzie me.
> > > *Warlock's Wadding.*

T.

TACKING—A taking, a prize. *Herring-tack*, a herring shoal.

TA'END—When schoolboys catch one another in their games, they lay their hands on the heads of the one caught; this ceremony is termed *taening* or taking : a *catcher* has often more trouble in doing this, than in *catching*. After a *runner* is *ta'end*, he is not allowed to run any more in that game.

TAFF-DYKE—A fence made of turf.

TAHIE—Moist ; *tahie*, or *dahie* day, a warm misty day.

TAILILL—A distemper common with cows. The *tail* is sometimes cut quite away, ere a cure be effected.

TALLOW-LEAF—That *leaf* of fat which envelopes the inwards of animals. When an ox or a sheep has a *gude tallow-leaf*, it is considered to have *fed weel*, and to be *deep on the rib*. *Tallow-powk*, a bag through which melted tallow is strained when refining ; this *powk* is much used on the *day* o' the *canle-making*, formerly a great day in household matters. I may give a list of the other celebrated days. " The day o' *sauting the beef*, the day o' *brewing*, the *washing* day, and the one in which the cheese is made, termed the *sweetmilker*"—

" Her *tallo-powk* hide, she scryng'd in the tide."

People with tanny skins are said " to hae hides as din as the *tallow-powk*."

TAMOUS KINNIGHAM—Mr. Thomas Cunninham, brother of Allan, a writer from his youth, well known in the Scottish Magazine, signing himself there *Thomas Killigrew*. His chief article is the *Bride o' Balauchan*, full of excellent humour. This gentleman is a native of Galloway, but has long been one of the *Londoneers* ; still the affection for the land of *blue heather* is strong, and the scenes of his youth flash brightly before the fancy. Like his brother, he is a poet, and one too of considerable pith ; his strain is ratherly comic, that of Allan's melancholy. Mr. T. could write a famous comedy would he try it, but like the great writers of the age, he detests the stage. It is to be hoped that he will give us another " *She stoops to Conquer* ;" no present writer, perhaps, could do this much better, he having at command such a fund of contented humour, and an extent of information respecting the ways of the world which is endless.

TAM-O'-TAE-END—The prince of the *pudding tribe*, the *haggis* being king. It hath but one open end, hence the name *Tam of the one end*.

TANTRUMS—Foolish fancies ; the same with *Daldrums*.

TAPLOCH—Tawploch, or tawpie, a giddy-brain girl.

TAP O' TOW—A head of flax ; any thing of firey nature ; a quick-tempered person, like flax, easily kindled.

TATHING—Manuring land, by confining cattle on it.

TED—To toss ; *tedding hay*, tossing hay ; *tedding alang*, tossing along.

TEE—A mark to be played for. *Teedling*, singing a tune, without accompanying it with the words ; *tee-hee*, a fool's laugh. The goaf was *tee-heeing*, the fool was at his merriment.

TEEVOO—A young man who flashes about with ladies, but has no great affection for them ; one who learns the rules of affectation, who *sweetheart's* with warmness seemingly ; who goes a *larking* as others do, but never feels the genuine throbs of love : with him it is as the play actors say, " All my eye and Betty Martin."

TEMPER-PIN—A pin which tempereth machinery.

TENNRILLS—Dry twigs ; tender or *tenner* matters, tendrils.

TETUZ—Any thing tender ; a delicate person.

TEYPARD—Taper'd ; a high frail building is said to be a *teypard biggin.*

THACKING SPURKLE—A broad-mouthed stick for thatch-ing with.

THARTY—Thirty, the number, sometimes *thratty* ; Irish, *thurty.*

THIGGERS—People who *thigg,* are those who beg in a gen-teel way ; who have their *houses* they call at in certain seasons, and get corn, and other little things.

THIRLAGE—A species of slavery. Many farmers are yet *thirled* to certain mills, being obliged to have their corn ground in these, and in no other, or else to pay the millers of such a certain annual sum in money. They were brought under this bondage first when mills in the country were rare, when a few *lairds* subscribed to build and uphold a mill. In this way many mills were built, and all erected by such compactions are *thirling mills.*

THOUM—Thumb. *Thoum-syme,* an instrument for twist-ing ropes, a *thrawcrook* ; *thoum-rapes,* ropes twisted on the thumb—

> They wha canna make a *thoum-rape*
> O' *thratty thraws* and *three* ;
> Isna worth their mett, I wot,
> Nor yet their penny fee.
>
> *Auld say.*

THOW—Thaw. *Thow-hole,* a name for the south, for the wind generally blows out of the south in the time of a thaw—

> The mermaids can ought thole,
> But *frost* out o' the *thow-hole.*
>
> *Auld superstitious say.*

Indeed, frost, when the wind blows from the south, is most severe with cold of any from any other quarter ; it is an unnatural cold.

THRAWEN-DAYS—Name for a petted child; sometimes, *auld thrawen-days.*

THREAD O' BLUE—Any little smutty touch in song-singing, chatting, or piece of writing; perhaps there may be a few in this book, but if modesty is not absolutely insulted, these, if not too gross, are not fraught with much harm: all works which stand the test of ages are not free of these *threads,* even the *Bible* itself is not clear.   When nature is followed close, it is almost impossible to avoid them—

> O ! they who feel the pith and flame
> Of manly strength, obtaineth fame,
> Who look to neither left nor right,
> But dash on forward, full of might ;
> Who scorn to take a hint, a plan,
> From humble creature—mortal man,
> Feel those delights felt by the brave,
> Who scorn like hell the sorry slave,
> Who for themselves will ever think,
> And do the will in prose or clink,
> Which still shall be the way with me,
> Though poor or rich, I shall be free.

THRIDD—Third.   " Twa part and *thridd,*" the two-thirds of any thing ; anciently, the quarter-staff was held " twa-part and thridd," one-third part of it beneath hand, the other two-*thirds* above.   Thus the way, when—

> " Robin Hood, in the greenwood stood,
> " Amang his merry men all."

THRIST—Thirst.   *Thristy thrapple,* thirsty throat—

> " Thy thristy thrapple nought can sloken,
> " Nae imp in hell thy visage gloken."
>   *Cock-o'-leary-lay.*

THROCH-STANES—Those oblong stones which stand horizontally above graves, not the vertical ones; the *head-stanes.*

THROUGH-BANDS—The long stones which bind dykes. *Through-gaun,* one who reflects little, but dashes away, is a *through-gaun* person. *Through-the-wud, laddie,* a phrase much the same with *craw-plucking.*   *Throok* the *wyle,* the *thrawcrook,* the *twister.*

THRYST—A promise to do any thing, a kind of vow; to set a *thryst*, to make a promise to perform something at a certain place and time : a young man and an old maid once *set a thryst* to meet one evening, and have some private confab with other in a glen ; she was punctual to the hour, and so he, but his intentions were different from her's ; he kept himself concealed, to observe her motions, while she longed to behold him ; at length, despairing of his appearance, she uttered the following, in great wrath—

> " O ! Rab, O ! Rab, shal't thou make me sab,
> " Thou beardless boy, sae slee ;
> " Na down my face, for thy cunning race,
> " A tear shanna flow frae me.
> " Nettles be thy bed, on soot be ye fed,
> " And may thy bonny gillpie, Nell,
> " Entice ye advise, till Nickie Ben will prize ye,
> " And yomf ye head foremost to hell."

THROWING the HOSHEN—At weddings, when the time of *bedding* comes on, the *young fowk* are surrounded by the people at the wedding, to witness the ceremony ; one part of which is, that the *bride* takes the stocking off her left leg, and flings it at random amongst the crowd, and whoever it happens to hit will be the first of them who will get married. This custom prevails too in Ireland ; see the song of *Paddy's Wedding, O.* While on this subject, I may mention a thing connected with wedlock, which is not very well known in the middle parts of Galloway, but common away by the *border.* When a young woman gets a husband before her sister, who is older, this sister, at her wedding, must dance without shoes on her feet. In a lovely little original poem, termed *Mallie's Wadding Day,* by an Annandale lady of native poetic genius, the following verses hit this affair—

> " O ! how can I be blythe and gay,
> " Whan this is *Mallie's* wadding day,
> " For I should *first* ha'e been away?
>   " O ! she has beat me clean."

" Alas! puir me, what will I do,
" This day maun *dance* without a *shoe*
" Maun thole the scorn o' a' fowk too?
    " And lie my lane ateen, O!"

Of all the songs and poems belonging to the south of
Scotland which have come through my rummaging hand,
(and many a worthy *bunch* have), not any of female composition have taken my taste half so much as those of the
young lady lately mentioned; and though modesty holds
my tongue from telling her name, I cannot refrain from
letting the world have a little peep at her poetic talents,
which, if cultivated perhaps a little more, bid fair for giving Scotland another Miss Bailly, or one with power equal
to her, though directed in quite a different way.   In her
farewell to *Kinmount* witness the tenderness, feel the
feeling—

Dear frien's, I now maun bid adieu
To a' my native scenes and you,
My sunny haunts, whan life was new,
    O! I maun gang and leave ye.

Dear Annandale, a garland's due,
Fain wad I wreath it fair for you,
For aft your vale I've wander'd through,
    Now I maun gang and leave ye.

Fair *Kinmount* woods, where aft I stray'd
And seen the leaves aft bud and fade;
Farweel now to your rustic shade,
    For I maun gang and leave thee.

Nae mair maun Criffle I descry,
And Skidda through the hazy sky,
Nae mair the Firth glide smoothly by,
    O! wae am I to leave ye.

Wae am I to gang away,
But while my fancy it can stray,
Thy image never will decay
    Tho' I maun gang and leave ye.

Fareweel, I lea my calm retreats
For dusky domes, and crowded streets,
My heart with throbbing sorrow beats,
    O! maun I gang an' leave ye?

THUDD—A blow; "to fa' wi' a *thudd*," to fall, and cause a noise like *thudd*, to start.

THUNNER—Thunder; *thunner-plump*, a *thunder-shower*; *thunner-speal*, a board with a string in end ; when whirled round in the air, it causes a thundering sound. *Thunnery weather*, weather pregnant with thunder.

TICHERS—Little firey pimples, young whisky tackets, *girrons*.

TICK—A sheep-louse; *ticking*, the noise of a watch.

TID—Inclination; the inspiration, of small duration.

TIFT—Any thing as it ought to be. A poet's muse is in *tift* when she sings well ; corn also is in *tift* when it is dry, viz. in *tift to lead*.

TIGG-TOW—To touch and go, to be off and on, neither serious nor merry ; *to tigg-tow wi' a lass*, to seem inclined to marry her, yet to hang off; it is a shame to use females so ; to run *lengths* with them, and then come retrograde. To *tigg-tow* with talents, to show the world a part and keep a part, to seem to range through the regions of genius, and all of a sudden to dart into a *brock-hole*. " To show the fins of the dolphin," to flash whiles in silk, then *hotter* about in *hodden grey*.

TILLIE-CLAY—Cold clay, unproductive soil; the heart that never felt love, is said to be a piece of *tillie-clay*; *tillie-licks*, taunts and sneers.

TIMMERIN—A beating with a stick.

TINKLER'S-TIPPENCE—Useless cash, money full of harm.

TIRLIES—Little circular stoppages in pathways which turn round.

TIRRAN—A tyrant; a *tirrivee* ; a painful bustle; a commotion of strife. *Tissle*, a struggle ; same with *dissle*.

TOD-TYKES—Dogs half foxes, half common dogs ; shepherds *tether* their *het bitches* about fox-haunts, and so this breed of dogs is acquired ; they are said to be excellent hunters. *Tod-tracks*, the traces of the fox's feet in snow ;

he is such a regular walking animal, that by the marks of his feet he seems to have but *two*, for why, he sets his hind feet exactly in the tracks of the fore ones. *Tod-touzing*, the Scottish method of hunting the fox, by *shooting*, *bustling*, *guarding*, *halloaing*, &c. famous fun, without a regular plan.

TOMERALL—A horse two years old; a young *cout* or *staig*.

TOOM-SKIN'D—Hungry; a person so is said to be *toom-skin'd*; *toom*, empty; *tommacks*, little hillocks; to *toom* out, to pour out, to make empty.

TOORRIN—Hay is said to be *toorrin*, when it rises on the rake in raking; a fire is also said to be so when blazing freely. *Torrish*, a *dairy-maid's* term to the cows when she wishes them to stand still.

TOOT—To drink; to *toot* over, to drink over; *toot*, to sound a horn, or the sound of a horn.

TOOTIN-HORN—A bullock's horn, with the heart out of it, used for blowing or "tootin" through, about some farm-houses; these horns are much in use in the harvest-time, such as about meal-times, and create some hilarity. Two Scotch soldiers having got a month's furlough from their regiment, quartered somewhere in England, to go and see their friends beyond the Tweed, set off from the barracks in high spirits; but alas! poor fellows, before they had journied far to the north, poverty beset them, "and the devil and all his witches danced in their poor pouches." No manner of relief then could they find, but to sing undernight for "*bawbees*" in the large towns on their way; and it was all they were able this way to procure as much cash as keeped in the life; for one of them could sing little or none, and the other was not good at it. However, the one who could not sing was a trumpeter, and by good luck had his "*tootin-horn*" with him, which often got them a dinner, when sharply beset with hunger. One night, though, as they were reposing themselves in a barn in the neighbourhood of Kendal, they felt their stomachs a-biting confoundedly, and were just on the point of starting and catching the first thing of food kind they would meet with, exclaiming, " they wha winna ficht for their meat, winna ficht for their king;" when the barn-door was flung open, and a large party of people entered, who instantly struck up lights, and loaded a long table they brought in with various viands of luscious dainties, the " *imry*" of which went up the noses of the red-coated lads like electricity. This was a religious sect, somewhat of the epicurean order, who mingled eating, drinking, and other good cheer with their holy concerns. The lads lay in the straw as quiet as mice in a mill, and observed their movements; one of the club got on his legs, and harangued at no small rate, with a loud voice, rounding his sentences always with these words, " When the archangel shall sound the last and awful trumpet :" our soldiers hearing this, the singer of them muttered to his comrade, the trumpeter, " gie them a toot man, Tam, whan he says that again." Tam agreed, and just as the preacher was concluding one of his long breaths as before, the trumpeter sounded one of his marches, in its highest key, when out of the house rolled the congregation, in the utmost disorder, leaving behind them the whole of the untasted feast to the famished soldiers, who leaped from the straw, welcoming the same in the most gracious manner. And after they had bounded their sides for once with the fat of the land, they crammed full their knapsacks, and went whistling away, rejoicing, " Blue Bonnets owre the Border;" not forgetting, for many a long day afterwards, the good turn of the *tootin-horn*.

TOSHOCH—A comfortable looking young person, from *tosh*, happy.

TOVIE—The same with *tozie*, warm and comfortable; blowzie-looking, with drinking warm drink.

TOWK—A bustle, a set-to. I had an unco *towk* wi' a de'ils bairn; *towk*, a take up in ladies' clothing; *towlie*, a toll-keeper.

TOWTS—The same with *howts*; *tootlie*, unsteady; *toothfu' o' drink*, a quantity of drink for the drinking.

TRACKPOT—The teapot; sometimes *trackie*, a disrespectful name for the teapot.

TRADWUDDIES—The pieces of linked iron which are fixed to harrows, and with which they are drawn.

TRAE—Stubborn; a boy who is *trae* to learn, is stiff to learn, and will teach himself; the majority of mankind are the better to be taught; but there are others who cannot be taught, and some who learn of themselves.

TRAIK—To decay; to look *traiket*, to look in a consumptive state. *Trailie*, one who trails about in shabby clothes. *Trailoch*, the same, also *trallop*.

TRANCE—A passage, an entrance, an area, &c.

TRANTLES—Bits of broken iron; odd things of hardware about a farm-house, same with *trantlums*; there are generally *boles* or holes about, where broken *horse-shoon*, *iron nits*, *auld spikes*, and clicks be thrown; these are termed *trantle-boles*.

TRAPP—To trip, to catch another reading wrong.

TRAVISH—To carry after a trailing manner.

TROGG—Old clothes; *troggers*, persons who gather old clothes, Gallovidian *Jews*. It is somewhat strange there are none of the children of Israel crying " *Auld cloe! cloe!*" through any town in Britain but London.

TROLLIEBAGS.—The inwards of animals.

TRONE.—A trowle, a masonic instrument; *tronnie*, a boy who plays the truant.

TROTTER O' NEW GALLOWA.—Mr. Trotter, son of Dr. Trotter, the famous *muir doctor* in his day, and brother of Miss Trotter, author of her worthy father's life. Lately Mr. T. published some rustic Gallovidian tales, the which I am very far from disliking, though I have

Ireard them railed against; they are homely, told in a half poetic, half Ossianic strain, and contain contented feelings. So far as I think, Mr. T. is a gentleman, whom the world's cares sit lightly on, and I am glad to think so; his little book will be more relished sometime after this than it is at present. Rusticity is of slow but steady growth; as to his sister, I hope she will not lay aside her pen; wherever I be she may rely on me, a steady, though unknown friend; the book on *Heraldry*, I do not know how it may do, but success to trade. There is some gentleman too, besides Mr. Trotter, in the Moorlands, who publishes books, but without his name. I believe that is *Barbour of Bogue*; what is he afraid about? Is it in the nature of *Hillmen* to shrink? no, no. There is no occasion, now-a-days, Mr. B. to skulk; come boldly forward, fool or no fool; this is not the season of *time* to slumber' in a corner and wait for *patrons*, for the days of *patrons* are over, and it is as well. " Let us trust in our own strength ;" when a man lays his shoulder to the work, he is seldom overcome; then the glory of buffeting the ocean of adversity, single-handed industry is before all interest, the very essence of independence. The tales of his are tolerable, though methinks, not just so much as Mr. Trotter's, the one has more fancy than the other.

TRUCKERY.—The porcelain stuff attending the tea-table.

TRUFF.—A turf; *trumf*, trump, at cards.

TUE.—Fatigued; *tued*, fatigued out; *tueg*, to tug.

TURN THE WULLCAT.—The art of grasping the bough of a tree with the hands, and turning the body through between it and the bough. *Turze*, a truss.

TUSKY.—A person with large tusks or teeth. An old man had lost all his teeth but one large one in the under jaw; had moreover been a gourmand all his life, and was one day observed at a large dinner, *mumbling* and bolting away as fast as he was able, until a large bite or pellet of half chewed beef stuck in his throat; frightfully his eyes stood in his head, one ran behind and struck him a smart blow between the shoulders, (the best way thought to be on these choaking occasions) out bounded the beef; but alas! a thread of it had been wound round the solitary tusk, which was the cause of it sticking in the gullet, and was also the cause of dragging the long fang from a station it had graced many years, to the secret smiles of the party.

TWAFAUL.—Twofold; *twa hand crack,* a familiar discourse between two.

TWELLIE.—A dispute, a *tulzie*; *tweezars,* hair curlers; *tweest,* to twist.

TWOLT.—A coverlid for a bed.

TYSDAY.—Tuesday.

U.

UGG.—To vomit; *uggsome,* loathsome.

UNCOES.—Things uncommon.

UNDERTHOUM.—A little trick projected in secret, is said to be done *under thoum, underfit peats.* Peat turf, digged beneath the foot, not in the common way of cutting them of a *breest.*

UPPLAN SHOWERS.—Moorland rains; much more rain always falls on the moors than in the dale; mountains attract clouds, then their tops like daggers stab them, and down foam the black torrents.

UPPLE.—When the weather at any time has been wet, and ceases to be so, we say it is *uppled*; now this is from *upheld,* or it is the same; the sky is held up, here do we see *lift, carry,* and *upple,* all connected together, all proceeding from one cause, the which I have already explained, in articles *Lift* and *Carry*.

URE.—A kind of coloured haze, which the sun-beams make in the summer time, in passing through; that moisture which the sun exhales from the land and ocean; the appearance is most obvious on the sea, and when very dry weather, on the moors; when such is seen, it is called the *dry ure* :—

> " The east was blae, *dry ure* bespread the hills,
> " And gizzend hang on charule pins, the mills."
>
> *Gallowa yearly Report.*

V.

VEEM.—A person is said to be in a *veem*, when inspired looking, when exalted in spirits; this word, and *vehement*, may probably be allied.

VENTERS.—Any thing which the wind or tide drive in from the ocean upon a shore; they are termed so from " venture," because people have often to *venture*, or risk their lives in obtaining them; for when a junk of shipwreck, or other drift wood, gets into the surf of a rock-bound shore, the rude *"venterers"* catch hold when the prey comes within reach, and are dragged by the rebounding waves into the deep, and so left to perish in the turbulent brine. This is often the case; and those who are so unfortunate, never cause many tears to be shed by the living for their sake, they are never lamented for; as it was a greedy and savage disposition which hurried them to destruction, else they would never have taken such a death-grasp of (very often) a poor prize. Persons living by shores who happen to get rich, are always suspected to have " made themselves up," by gaining rich *venters*, such as trunks full of cash, pipes of wine, or casks of brandy, but this, when sounded to the bottom, is often not

true, and that their weighty purses have been filled some
other more honorable way. There are many who make a
practice indeed of *"rinning the shores"* of the south of
Scotland : but where will we find one of these who is not
a poverty-struck looking creature ?   By a time perhaps, a
windlass-barr, or a deal of some kind or other, may be
caught, but for once any thing is found, twenty times nothing is got ; and they would find themselves and their
families much better off were they to stay at home and
look after more sure matters, though this advice will seldom be taken.   An old fellow who lived about the shore,
once said " that he wad rather rin roun the craigs, and
look out for something, wi' a north wun blawin, than stay
ahame wi' *Mall* the wife ;" his luck indeed, might have
been a little " snell wi' the tongue," as some others are ;
yet, had he run the shore less, and been thronger some
other way, he would, maybe, have met with a fuller hut
than he once had, and a quieter spouse—"ateen."   But
what signifies all the trade of *renters,* which goes on
about the south shores of Scotland, compared to that
of other places, and chiefly the west of Ireland ? There
the gulf stream disgorges what it takes into its maw in
its retrograde range athwart the broad Atlantic. And there,
as the darling poet Falconer says—" Hell hounds prowl
along the shore."   No savages on earth are worse than
these.   No New Zealanders, nor Africans, are so bloody
and base.   When a ship in distress is driven about that infernal strand, as many are, it is not the bark the sailors try
to save, but their lives, and often are they stripped naked,
and inhumanly murdered by these detestable wretches.
O ! Erin, I weep for this, of thee.   O ! rulers, why are
ye thus blind ? Plant on these inhospitable shores, a
power to protect our brave seamen, the guards of our
liberties, and the foundation of our nation's riches and
honour.

VIRGUS.—Some fancied liquid, considered to be the sourest of any; "it's as sour as *virgus*," this is the phrase of comparison; what this *virgus* may be I do not see, unless it be sour vinegar.

> Man, without a wife,
>   Is only half a man,
> And wanting half the joys of life,
>   Which Providence did plan.
>
> A pity there's for maidens grey,
>   But none for bachelors at all,
> For why, the moving cause are they,
>   So should not let the others fall.
>
> That heart so cold's the frosty fell,
>   With feelings all like *virgus* sour,
> Will only thaw away in hell,
>   And be alive to demons power.
>   *Verses by the way.*
>
> Awa wi' a' your German *Vons*,
> Your flashie, gabbie, Frenchie *Mons*,
> Your lazy, *virgus* Spanish *Dons*,
>   They're no for me;
> Give me my Scotias darling sons,
>   Sae kind and free.
>
> O ! but I loe their hamely tweils,
> Their auld sweet sangs, and foursome reels,
> Their heathery hills, their glens and beils,
>   Sae snug and warm ;
> Rare honest, independent chiels,
>   Wha dread nae harm.
>   *Verses by chance.*

VIZZIE DRAP.—The little mark stuck up at the mouth of a gun-barrel to guide the sportsman's view. " To take a *vizzie*," to take a steady aim ; some raw hands, when *vizzying* first at the *nail* in the *bull's eye* of the *target* with loaded ball, feel *dooms queer*. Poet *Main*, in the *Sillar Gun*, catches at this, and makes a good deal of it. One of those who were *shooting*, he tells us, was so afraid, that he *misbehaved*; an expressive term.

VOUTS.—Vaults; burial places of the rich—" where those above the vulgar born do rot in state ;" also any arched roof place under ground. One of these, at the *auld Abbey of Glenluce*, contains the famous library of *Michael Scott*, the *Warlock.* Here are thousands of old *witch songs* and incantations, books of the *Black Art* and *Necromancy, Philosophy of the Devil, Satan's Almanacks,* the *Fire Spangs* of *Faustus,* the *Soothsayer's Creed,* the *Witch Chronicle,* and the *Black Cluds wyme laid open,* with many more valuable volumes. None but priests above *four-score* are admitted entrance to this sacred archive; and if they take down a volume from one side of the library and set it on the other, when they return, it is found brought back to its place, planted exactly on its own *skelf.* Moreover, when they find a book they would wish to take home with them, and peruse quietly by the fire side, if it is put in the pocket, or under the *oxter,* when they get back to the *Manse* the book is vanished; the invisible librarian, like those impudent ones in the Edinburgh *College* Library, will allow no book of worth to be read in *private,* not for any *deposit.* A priest went once to it, as some go to that of the *British Museum,* with the intention to *copy,* alias *cabbage;* and after he had spent a whole day noting down some of the dark *mystics* of *Masonry,* he hied him home, called the wife to read her the *treat,* but alas! when he opened the copy, there lay the paper as *white* as if pen had never been laid on it, which much enraged the reverend *Cowan.*

VOWL.—People playing at cards have their terms; and this *vowl* is one of them. When one of the parties playing gets nothing, not so much as a *trick,* then they are said to be *vowl'd*—this and *sutter'd* are one; and a *vowl* is said to be worth *nine games.* This is something like that saying, or *taylor's skit*—that it takes nineteen taylors, a bull-dog, and a *tippeny brick,* to make a man. The chief Galloway games at cards are, *Catch the Ten,* or *Catch Honours, Lent* for *Beans, Brag* and *Pairs* for *Slaes, Beggar my Neebour, Birkie, Love after Supper,* and *Wha to be married first.* These are the genuine rustic games; but lately

Whist, Cribbage, and other genteel nonsense, hath been introduced. To hear a party playing the auld harmless favourite *Catch the Ten,* the word *renunce* often strikes the ear, renounce, reject, &c.

Come deal the carts, spit on your thoum,
　And fling us roun' a han ;
Their *cutten* Jock, and shuffled too,
　Sax players are the plan.

Now, what's the *cut ?* The *Jack,* by jing ;
　O, if they hae the Ten,
The game we lose, tho' in *dirt's hole*
　We be, as a' do ken.

Come, let na Johnie get the lead,
　O trumf about they go ;
'Twas shameless Tam, ha sma' anes haith,
　The *Ten*—the *Ten,* no, no.

Now, Clubs they lead—the first time roun,
　That's a *renunce* fu' clean ;
Down goes the Ten—'twill run, 'twill run,
　No, down on't sweeps the Queen.

Ten and eleven is twenty-one,
　The Queen, anither twa ;
O ! there's the Ace—it gets the King ;
　We're beat—we're cowl'd, and a'.
　　　　　　Sang o' the Cartes.

W.

WAD.—Would. *Wad,* wadger. *I wad a crown,* I wadger a crown.

WADDINGS.—Weddings. These ceremonies are not so largely attended as in the days of yore ; auld wives tell me, that the *Spirit o' Waddings* is left the country ; now sic a thing is *slippet* by in a *prevet* way, and a body never gets the *thrapple watted* owre them. *Wadding-baws,* money tossed among mobs by wedding people. *Wadding-braws,* dresses for marriage ; the buying of these *braws* is a serious matter, for this is the first time the *young fowk* appear in public. *Wadding sarks,* the bride, previous to marriage, makes the bridegroom a shirt, these shirts are termed *wadding sarks.* A peasant once told me, " That he ance did na intend to take Meg for a wife, but the cutty saw this, flew to my neck, and measured the *sark,* and than I was *obliged* to tak her." *Waddings o' Craws,* large flocks of rooks, particularly when in " blackened train," they fly at eve to " their repose."

> " A *fiddler*, a *fifer*, and three *castlekaws*,
> " Ay gie the music to a *wadding o' craws.*"
>   *Auld say.*

WADDS AND THE WEARS.—One of the most celebrated amusements of the *ingle-ring.* I believe Mr. Cromek has touched at it slightly in his Nithsdale and Galloway song; yet ample room is left for a description of it by me, without being called a plagiarist. To begin then, one in the ring speaks as follows :—

> " I hae been awa at the *wadds and the wears*
> " These seven lang years;
> " And's come hame a puir broken ploughman ;
> " What will ye gie me to help me to my trade ?"

He may either say he's a " puir broken ploughman," or any other trade ; but since he has chosen that trade, some of the articles belonging to it must always be given or offered, in order to recruit him. But the article he most wants he privately tells one of the party, who is not allowed, of course, to offer him any thing, as he knows the thing, which will throw the *offerer* in a *wadd,* and must be avoided as much as possible—for to be in a *wadd,* is a very serious matter, as shall afterwards be explained. Now, the one on the left hand of the poor ploughman, makes the first offer, by way of answer to what above was said ; " I'll gie ye the *coutter* to help ye to your trade." The ploughman answers, " I don't thank ye for your *coutter,* I hae ane already." Then another offers him another article belonging to the ploughman's business, such as the *mool-bred,* but this also is refused ; another, perhaps, gives the *sock,* another the *stilts,* another the *spattle,* another the *naigs,* another the *naig-graith,* and so on; until one gives the *soam,* which was the article he most wanted; and was the thing secretly told to one, and is the thing that throws the giver into a *wadd,* out of which he is relieved in the following manner :—

The ploughman says to the one in the *wadd,* " Whether will ye hae three questions and two commands, or three commands and two questions, to answer or gang on wi', sae that ye may win out o' the *wadd ?*" For the one so fixed has always the choice which of these alternatives to take. Suppose he takes the first, two commands and three questions, then a specimen of these may run so :—

" I command ye to kiss the *crook,*" says the ploughman, which must be completely obeyed by the one in the *wadd*—his naked lips must salute the *sooty* implement.

Secondly, saith the ploughman, I command ye to stand up in that neuk, and say—

> " Here stan I, as stiff's a stake,
> " Wha 'ill kiss me for pity's sake ?"

Which must also be done; in a corner of the house must he stand and repeat that couplet, till some tender-hearted lass relieves him. Now for the questions, which are most deeply laid, or so *touching* to him, that he finds much difficulty to answer them.

Firstly, then, " Suppose ye were in a bed with *Maggie Lowden* and *Jennie Logan,* your twa great sweet-hearts, what ane o'm wad ye ding owre the bed side, and what ane wad ye turn to and *clap* and *cuddle ?*" He makes answer by choosing *Maggie Lowden,* perhaps, to the great mirth of the party.

Secondly, then, " Suppose ye were stanin stark naked on the *tap* o' *Cairnhattie,* whether wad ye cry on *Peggie Kirtle* or *Nell* o' *Killimingie* to come wi' yer *cluise ?*" He answers again in a similar manner.

Lastly, then, " Suppose ye were in a boat wi' *Tibbie Tait, Mary Kairnie, Sallie Snadrap,* and *Kate o' Minnieive,* and it was to coup wi' ye, what ane o'em wad ye *sink?* what ane wad ye *soom?* wha wad ye bring to lan'? and wha wad ye marry?" Then he answers again, to the fun of the company, perhaps in this way, " I wad sink *Mary Kairnie,* soom *Tibbie Tait,* bring *Sallie Snadrap* aneath my *oxter* to lan', and marry sweet *Kattie o' Minnieive.*"

And so ends that bout at the *wadds and the wears,* to give place to Hey Willie Wine and How Willie Wine, or the Dambrod and Legendary stories.

WAMPUZ—To make curvilinear dashes, like a large fish in the water.

WANTER—A bachelor, for why, he wants a wife.

WAPP—To wrestle; *wapping,* wrestling.

WARBLE—A short thick worm, which lodges between the skin and the *fell* of black cattle, not between the *fell* and the flesh; a little hole leads to them, and, like the West India *jeeger,* may be squeezed and picked out.

WARL O' WIG-WAG—This state of being, this world of sin and shame, good and evil. Mark the following verses :—

ON HEARING OF THE DEATH OF AN ACQUAINTANCE IN THE WEST INDIES.

And has that fatal Indian clime,
  My Willie, done for thee ;
Ere thou arrived at thy prime,
  Ere thou was twenty-three?

Determin'd ay thou wast to chace
  Shy Fortune o'er the wave ;
But she has scorn'd thy frantic race,
  And birth'd thee in the grave.

Thy parents, too, the whims did nurse,
  That thou would'st soon return
With an o'erflowing, pond'rous purse,
  But now they wretched mourn.

That thou would'st purchase an estate
　　Of acres green and wide,
And been the chief of all the great
　　On some fair country side.

Ne'er thinking fate so soon would have
　　Condemned thee to die,
Scarce rich enough to have a grave,
　　A hole wherein to lie.

O, Willie, had'st thou stay'd at home,
　　On Scotia's darling land,
And plough'd thy father's fertile loam,
　　And sow'd it with thy hand:

Perhaps ye yet in *life* had been,
　　An honest happy swain,
And many a merry *day* have seen,
　　Or many *full* of pain.

For every zone on earth below
　　Is cramm'd with various ills,
And fell disorders deadly flow
　　Thro' all in pois'nous rills.

WARROCHING —— Wallowing, struggling, like a creature *lairing* in mud.

WARSH—Fresh tasted, requiring salt; warsle, a wrestle.

WARTS—Little wens, said to be eradicated by washing with swine's blood, or *straiking* with a *dead man's* hand.

WASPET—A man is said to look *waspet*, when he is got small at the *wazban* o' the *breeks*, something like a *wasp* or *pishminnie*, when he fills not his *wast-coat* well; as after marriage, and such *serious* affairs.

WASSOCKS—A kind of turban the milkmaids carry their pails, or *stoups* on their head; also a kind of bunch put on a boring *jumper*, to hinder the water required in boring from leaping up into the *quarriers'* eyes.

WASTCOAT—Waistcoat, vest, &c. It is said that a doctor once told the wonderful Burns, that if he left not off taking whisky, he would soon be in the dust, for that the *coat* of his heart was *brunt* off with it already. " O," quoth the bard, " let *wastcoat* and a' *gang*, ay maun I prie the barly-bree." Respecting Burns, when in *Auld Reekie*, I visited *Johnnie Dowie's yill-house*, famous for being a haunt of the poet's, and for selling good *brown stout*;

scarcely had I sat down in the *Coffin Room,* before the following verses were struck off. I am no poet, as my readers well see, though I have been a rhymer from my first, and liketh by a time to try it. " What good can come from Galloway ?" saith *Hogg,* the Etterick Shepherd, in his *Queen's Wake.* Ay, his bardship damns all Galloway, because a Gallovidian ; a *Mr. Morrison parodied* him and his *Wake,* in a poem. Poor spite ! but to my work ; let that be *good* or no, it matters little to me, as I prefer putting up with injuries, rather than be *"A plague to them who'd be a plague to me."*

Verses which occurred to me in the queer tavern of *Johnnie Dowie's,* a house much haunted by Burns, while in *Auld Reekie* :—

> So this is Johnnie Dowie's cabin,
> Whare aft dear Scotia's bard got lab in,
> And then sae witty wild did gab in,
>   That roun the table,
> A' laughed to hear the mighty Rabin,
>   While they were able.

> Nae won'er that wi' right guid will,
> He aften sat and drank his fill,
> O' this delicious famous yill,
>   As pure as amber ;
> For then up the Parnassian hill
>   'Twas nought to clamber.

> I think I see him just sae now,
> Afore me, mair than middling fu',
> Keen dashing on and driving thro'
>   The inspired chiel ;
> Astonishing his social crew,
>   Ay and the de'il.

> Whiles praising up his Ayrshire lasses,
> Descanting grand on whisky glasses,
> Or damning country lairds for hashes,
>   And priests for fools ;
> Or through the rural world he brashes,
>   Despising rules.

> Whare burnies to the ocean row,
> Whare lambkins dance adown the how,
> Whare silver shakles wag their pow,
>   Upon the brae ;
> Such worthy things he rambles thro',
>   And mony mae.

The charms o' Jean, the whims o' Molly,
The joys that men hae in their folly,
The hypocrites sly grane sae holy,
            He slyer touches;
For what can stand roused melancholy
            'S giant clutches.

O, was he in reality
Aside me now, how glad I'd be,
There's nane wad mair admire his glee,
            And praise his powers;
But ah! alas! denied to me
            Are sic sweet hours.

His noble saul frae earth is fled,
Wild Genius sadly mourns him dead,
True Scotchmen may adorn his bed
            In the kirk-yard;
But wha can stem hearts that do bleed
            For the great bard?

I'll mourn his death while here below,
That death brought on by want and woe,
Ere his great strains did strongest flow,
            Or fancy fly;
Sae lofty as they mean'd to go,
            Ere he should die.

For had his country been mair kind,
And no hae slumber'd owre him blind,
We wad hae seen the strongest mind
            Displayed ere sung;
Wull Shakspeare he'd na been behind
            In pith o' tongue.

But as he is, there's few afore him,
The scowling critic maun adore him,
And every feeling man encore him,
            Wi' glorious glee;
And in Fame's glorious Temple store him,
            Nae mair to dee.

WAT—Not dry.

WATERBRASH.—An eruption in the stomach, brought on
by drinking grog.

WATERS.—Rivers; in Galloway the chief are the *Dee,*
Fleet, Urr, and *Cree.* Mine *Address to the Dee,* wrote
in *Auld Reekie,* runneth as follows, foolish enough:—

The Dee is king of all the streams,
    That roll to Scotland's southern sea,
On it I had my youthful dreams,
    Its banks are ever dear to me.

G G

For there my parents do reside,
  And worthy parents they have been,
To me, a rambler wild and wide,
  With foolish whims and fancy keen.

The Nith, the Urr, the Fleet and Cree,
  Are waters not to match with it,
No stately ship on them we see,
  For navigation they're unfit.

A seventy-four the Dee might float,
  Or any bark that scours the deep ;
But for the rest an oyster boat,
  They scarcely off the mud can keep.

What bays and havens hath the Dee,
  To shelter safe the manly tar ;
In them he tells his tale with glee,
  " Remote from where the billows jar."

Upon its banks what waving wood,
  And fertile glades for ever green ;
What salmons spouting in the flood,
  And pellocks hunting them are seen.

Around what rural swains do live,
  So honest, harmless, blythe, and free ;
With them what bonny lasses thrive,
  For ever kind and dear to me.

Oh ! when I think about the Dee,
  A thousand lovely scenes arise ;
I see the friends so sweet to me,
  I feel the charm that never dies.

When death does gore my swarthy breast,
  With his determined deadly dart,
Those charms will only sink to rest,
  Yes, with the throbbing of my heart.

The rivers in the torrid zone,
  Or those beneath the artic sky,
Do set me in another tone,
  From them that round my home do lie.

How different where the Niger flows
  Through Afric's burning dismal land ;
By it the yelling savage goes,
  With poison'd arrows in his hand.

There tygers come their thirst to slake,
  With other wild beasts of the wood ;
There's too the monstrous fanged snake,
  And crocodile intent on blood.

There grin'd the alligator's jaws,
  There tawny lions fight and growl,
There clatter tusks and darteth claws,
  Terrific to the traveller's soul.

Not like the peaceful Dee, indeed,
  Where silver fishes skip and play,
On whose sweet banks the hares do breed,
  And hop about in open day.

No frosts congeal the happy stream,
  No choaking snows its course retard,
No Rein-deer gallops there in team,
  As on the Lapland waters hard.

In it the Wallruss never snorts,
  Nor Bears prowl for the harmless Seal;
No Mallamuke there resorts,
  Tho' whiles the Widgeon and the Teal.

The Dee contains no church of ice,
  No mansion there appears so cold;
Fantastic forms are very nice,
  But I'd like better to behold

Kirkcudbright and its river fair,
  With woody sweet St. Mary's Isle;
O! for pure Gallovidian air,
  O! for to see her maidens smile.

Smoke on, old Reekie, justle on,
  Ye swagging crowds with meikle pain,
Your humble servant leaves ye soon,
  For his grand rural world again.

WAUCHLE.—To walk after a fatigued manner: *wauchling*, walking, yet almost exhausted.

WAUCK MILL.—A mill for thickening cloth.

WAUCKED.—Matted, wrought thick.

WAUCKET-LOOF.—A hand with the flesh hardened.

WAUR.—Worse.

WAUR-TIME.—The spring season, for then the farmers *waur*, or lay out; they then sow with the hope to reap.

WEATHERGAW.—A very singular object seen in a cloudy sky, when a certain kind of weather rules it. The rainbow and it seem to be of one nature, and to proceed from the same cause. The beautiful colours in the *weathergaw*, however, are stronger defined, of a deeper hue than those of the rainbow; the *back ground* of the *wea-thergaw*, as it were, is always a black cloud, and instead of being the segment of a circle, is, so far as it appears, a straight line. The whole seems to be the refraction of the sun's rays, owing to their beaming on a column of water, falling in the form of weighty rain, from one region of a dense atmosphere to another. Thus this strange appearance is termed by rustic Scottish naturalists the *weathergaw*, or the *gall* of the *weather*; and when the *gall* or gaw, bursts, woe be to the tenants of the field, down come the *sumps*, and wild foam the *spates*; however, it sometimes indicates good weather, like the *ark o' the cluds*, from its situation in the sky; thus when the *ark* runs north and south, the aftercome is not so much dreaded, as if it had stretched between any other *airts o' the lift*, and when the *weathergaw* is seen in the east, its consequences by the *weatherwise* are less dreaded, though *east rains*, when they do fall, are the *dreighest* of any :—

" The weather's taking up now,
  " For yonder is the weathergaw,
" How bonny in the east now,
  " Now the colours fade awa ;
" But turn your head tae south man,
  " Yonder it appears again,
" Let's lae the rig, and theek the stacks,
  " Or down will fa' the plumping rain.
Harrest sang.

WEE.—Small, little ; *wee, wee*, smaller than small :—

" I wuss I had a *wee, wee* house,
" A *wee, wee* cat, to catch a mouse,
" A *wee, wee* cock, to craw fu' crouse,
  " And you to rule them a'."
Popular song.

WEEL.—Well. *Weel man.* A common salutation; *weel-faurd*, well-favoured, good-looking.

WEE ROSS.—One of the best known islands belonging Galloway; it stands at the mouth of the Dee, and is about two miles in circumference; the Isle of *Heston*, in

the *Bay* of *Balcarry,* is about the same size, and swarms
with rabbits ; there are none of these animals on the *Wee
Ross,* but there are plenty of rats, which burrow amongst
the rocks, and live on *partons, pirr-eggs,* &c.; it is called
the *Wee Ross,* because the bold headland, termed the *Big
Ross,* is right beside it, and forms, from its height, a famous land-mark for sailors ; between the two lands is a
rock, termed *Janet Richardson.* This was a poor woman who belonged to *Clauchendolly,* and who went on
to the rock at ebb-tide, to gather a *powkfu' o' mussles* ;
while so employed the sea flowed round the rock, unob-
served by her, at length noticing it—she " *kilted* up her
coats, aboon the na'el," as the saying is, plunged in, but
the *buldering* waters of the sound hurried her off her
feckless shanks, but she having a *farkage o' claise* about
her, they keeped her *aboon broe,* until she was driven
ashore on the *Milton Lands* ; from such circumstance is the
rock named, and that name will likely remain as long as
if it had been given by Cook or Parry.   On the *Wee Ross*
stands two *land-marks,* erected by the wisdom of *Skipper
Skellie* ; they point out to sailors the *land's lead,* and the
Dee's Channel.   I must not pass this worthy *Skipper
Skellie,* slightly ; his honest, and feeling mind has been
exerted in behalf of the sailors, a class of men, perhaps
as much respected as any on earth, and apparently for
good cause.   Whatever the skipper sees he can do for
them, that he doth, even to hurting himself ; his daring
mind is *backed* out by that of every wise man's, and all
his plans have originality and good in them ; well may I
term him the Gallovidian marine engineer, for the same
reason that I term *Gladstone* that of the land.   After his
land marks were built, a curious *poet* fancied he addressed them thus :—

Some time ago when I was wont to cross,
   The Solway Firth, and trade in coal and lime,
Often I've found myself at no small loss,
   To know the Dee in many a stormy time ;

Deep rolling river always grand sublime,
From others stagnant, full of sludge and dross,
Which vomit round it in the sea their slime,
'Twas then methought that from these jumbling gross,
Skelly should mark it yet upon the Little Ross.

So I with you, ye brothers square and high,
Have had my wish, I glory in your birth,
Stand unscar'd beneath the sulky sky,
Let growling surfs and surges give ye mirth,
Smile at Kirkcudbright, graze across the Firth ;
The wave dash'd vessels from the tempests cry,
Do all the good ye can, remain while earth
Unsmelted will around her axle fly,
Tho' still remember, Skelly, who am I.

Whene'er a sailor from the offin hails,
Your lofty lordships boldly answer he,
" Come hither from the gale, ye tar who sails,
" Along the wild bosom of the wrathful sea,
" If for a shelter you incline to be,
" Within our arms is one which never fails,
" Through gurly hurricanes to form a lee,
" Where pitching ceases, where no anchor trails,
" Give Skellie's orders then, when ocean rails."

Whoe're can lie and snore upon the pillow,
And seamen weltring round in great distress,
Bawling for mercy, struggling with the billow,
Will surely ne'er behold the land of bliss ;
Contentment's lips thee'ill never, never kiss,
But will be scourg'd by some infernal fellow,
For such as these the devil cannot miss,
Oh, help the weather-beaten sailor, will ye,
Is ever the sincere wish of Skipper Skelly.

May commerce flutter up our lovely river,
And fright the grass from off the untrod street,
May spirit, sense, and worth, forsake us never,
Let who are foes shake hands, and friendly meet,
That pride and spleen evaporate complete,
Who brews the venom, may that venom's fever,
Retort upon themselves with furious heat ;
So we'll be look'd on borough bodies clever,
And I, an humble skipper, live for ever.

So now my *land-marks*, hear my last advice,
Let times-fell tusks scarce ere your beauty tear,
Should distant ages disregard your price,
Shake, shiver not nor stand aghast with fear
When I must sink at last, through tear and wear,
Beneath the sod in death's cold arms of ice,
And my poor soul through foreign countries steer,
Be sure ay tell the worthy and the wise,
My simple efforts, never to despise.

Beside this isle is a tolerable place for ships to anchor in, when they come from off the sea, at a wrong time of the tide, and must wait for *water* flowing of depth, to swim them up the river. However, if the storm be a hurricane, the shelter is not so great, and it requires a ship with the best holding tackle to ride secure. About two years ago, five ships were torn from their moorings there by an awful gale, and dashed to pieces on the Bar; one of these was commanded by a young man belonging to Cumberland, of the best disposition and manners; his loss was so deeply lamented both in England and Scotland, that the following *true* song was produced on the subject :—

CAPTAIN ORMONBY.

Sweet maidens fair in Cumberland, what griefs have I to tell,
The dear young Captain Ormonby, who loved ye all so well,
Is over-whelmed with the storm, is sunk beneath the wave,
In the wild deep, there he doth sleep, there is his watery grave.

He left your shores for Dublin-bay with a deep-laden bark,
The day was fine, the wind was fair, and sweetly sang the lark,
But ere the sun stood north and south, the sky was all o'ercast,
And by *Blackcoomb*, with awful boom, came roaring on the blast.

The surges o'er the head-lands rose, and buried every mool,
The Isle of Man they seem'd to sink, and break out o'er *Barool*;
What ship could stand such billows vast, she must run for a lee,
With naked masts, before the blasts, forlorn she on must flee?

So on did steer young Ormonby before the furious wind,
The tide being out along the shores, no harbour could he find;
The little *Ross* no shelter was, the anchors would not hold,
So our noble tar, upon the Bar, among the foam was roll'd.

Up high his brig was heaved whiles by the tremendous sea,
Then down again, with thundering sound, upon the sands of Dee;
But soon she stove, and soon she sunk, the sailors stood aghast,
Then, for the live did climb and strive to save't upon the mast.

As on the main-top they did cling, and gazing all around,
Four other ships, besides themselves, were on the stormy ground;
" What shall we do?" a sailor cried, " lo, yonder's one upset,
" Altho' dry land be near at hand, to it we'll never get."

" The tide will flow by six o'clock (the captain then did say),
" And down will fall our only hope, this mast here will give way;
" There's not a chance that we'll be saved, no, not a chance for one,
" No boat can live, none help can give, we're drowned every man."

" O ! let us, since we see our fate, to the Almighty pray,
" Implore him for to save our souls, and not cast them away ;
" For soon my brother sufferers dear before him they will be,
" For death doth ride upon the tide, this awful night we see."

But scarcely had good Ormonby sooth'd his desponding crew,
When down the mast with crashing fell, the surges o'er them flew ;
Their shrieks were stifled with the storm, the waters mad did roar,
And dash'd them down, to gasp and drown, and never to rise more.

Poor Bill, 'ere this an hardy tar, who had sail'd many a sea
A hunting whales among the ice, and slaves by hot Goree ;
Reach'd the fore-mast with trouble great, and saw the horrid fate
Which did befal his mess-mates all, for him but to relate.

And while poor Bill did tell the tale, with sorrow he did weep,
" My kind young captain," he did cry, " is buried in the deep ;
" 'Tis thirty years now, since a boy, I first did sail the sea,
" And I've ne'er had, such a good lad, a master over me."

Lament then for this worthy youth all who have hearts can feel,
His sweetheart's breast is wounded deep, we fear 'twill never heal ;
On Whitehaven Quay she parted that morn with her true love,
No more to see, nor with him be till she's in Heaven above.

Well mayst thou moan thou Ocean now, upon the Milton sand,
For Ormonby thou hast devoured, what can thy wrath withstand ?
The tall black rocks around thy shores, even totter with thy rage,
So how then can, the art of man, with thee in war engage ?

O ! sing this song, my sailors all, when you're in mournful mood,
And think on the distresses great your brethren whiles have stood ;
Be still prepared to meet the storm, be still prepared to drown,
So then will ye, like Ormonby, gain an eternal crown.

WEHAW !—A cry which displeases horses. Boys are frequently seen about the *clauchans* running after *auld naigs,*
and crying *wehaw!* and see how the old horses *scool,*
hang their *lugs,* and would *kick* were they able.

WHAILING—To get a lashing with a *rope's end.* This
comes from the name of a rope called a *whale-line,* used
in fishing for whales.

WHANG—Any thing of a long supple nature. A *whang o'
cheese,* as much cheese as can *wag.* A *whang o' tobacco,
whangs for steekers to shoon,* &c., are all of the same
order. *Whang,* however, is also a blow, or ratherly a
lash with a whip ; this blow is sometimes called *whack.*

WHAUKY—Whisky ; the same with *Aqua.*

WHAUP—Bird curlew; also a twist, as in a rope. Thus, *whaup i'the rape*, a doubling, a *back-spang*, a quirk, to deceive. *Wheeple*, to whistle like a *whaup*.

WHEESHT—An order for silence. *Haud your wheesht*, be silent.

WHEEZAN—The noise carriage-wheels make, when moving fast.

WHIGG—Sour cream, a pleasant acid to the taste.

WHIHE—The sound of an adder; *her fuffing noise*, when angered.

WHILLIE BILLOU—A noisy commotion, as when the *fox is up*, started for chace. French, *Whirlie Breelow*, for the same.

WHITE—To pare with a knife; also to *fleetch*, to flatter for favour. *An auld whitie*, a flatterer; the same with *white-lip*.

WHITE HAWSE—A favourite pudding, that which conducts the food to the stomach with sheep.

WHITTERING—Running about in a strange simple manner. The way a modest lover haunts his mistress; also, any thing of weak growth is a *whitter*.

WHOMMLED—Overturned. " To be *whommled* beneath a bushel," to be covered by a bushel; " to be *whommled* by a wave," to be *whelmed* in the deep.

WHOORLS—Circular backs for spindles—
 " By cank and keel we'll win our breed,
 " And *whoorles* for spinnles in time o' need."
 Gaberlunzie Man.

WHUDDING—Telling lies; also to run like a hare. We say, see " To bawdrons, how she *whudds* awa up the lee." *Whudder*, a curious kind of noise; we say, " a hare starts from her den wi' a *whudder*;" also, the wind, in a cold night, is said to *whudder*. Association must partly explain this term, bare words cannot do it.

WHUFFT—Whift. He *whufft* out the candle; he suddenly blew out the candle.

WHULT—A blow received from a fall, or the noise attending such a fall. He gat an unco *whult* from falling, and he fell with an unco *whult*; both these are said: also *whult*, any thing larger than expected; a large potatoe, like a *loltidoll*, is termed a *whulter*. *Loltidoll* is the largest species of potatoe in the three kingdoms, the British yam; Irishmen say only two grow to a stalk, and any one of these is as big as a *child's head sixteen years ould*. Our *Pinkies*, *Mack-a-ma-riches*, *Benefits*, *Blue-nurgs*, &c. are trifles to these.

WHULLILOW—The same with *Whillie-billou*.

WHUMGEES—Vexatious whisperings, trivial tricks in *truth-telling*, as it were. *Whaups in the rape*, and *whumgees*, are not widely different. *Whumper*, to whimper; to *whunge*, to whinge, to fret.

WHUNCE—A heavy blow, or the noise of such a blow, as when two *channle-stones* strike one another.

WHUNNER—A thundering sound, or the blow which causes such a sound.

WHUNS—Whins; *whun-stanes*, whin-stones; *whun blooms*, the yellow blooms of the whin. Whins, it is said, were introduced into this country from France; that the *cat-whun* is the *Scotch-whun*, the other the *French-whun*. Now, the truth is, any bad thing, as whins are, no nation will own, so we give them to the French. The French give them again to other nations; so, what belongs to all the world, and what the world detests, no nation in the world will own, and *vice versa*.

WHUPS—Whips; *whupperin*, a whipper-in amongst fox-hunters; a *loaded whup*, a whip laden in the shaft with lead; *whup*, also to run; *whup awa*, run along. Some may think that I give not all the strange words in use in the south of Scotland; this is true; but I give all those which none have noticed before me, at least the greater part. I once intended to give them all, but I found it would swell my book too much; those who wish to see the rest, may consult Jamieson's excellent Dictionary. And one of my motives for writing this book was to aid our *Scottish Dictionary* as much towards perfection as possible.

WHURLIE-BIRLIE—Any thing which whirleth round; children have little toys they spin, so termed. There is nothing so hard to make the peasantry of Scotland believe, as the truths of Astronomy; some consider the matter deeply, and instantly assent to them; but the majority are ratherly inclined to laugh at the glorious discoveries of a Pythagoras, a Copernicus, a Kepler, and a Newton. They cannot think that this earth turns round on its axis, at all; and far less that it wheels round the sun. While reasoning this matter with one of them one day, he gave out the following fancies, which I thus tagged together in rhyme—

> Quoth *Daldie*, thou's a dooms queer cheel,
> Faith thou's grown kidgie wi' the de'il,
> To tell me that this yirth doth wheel,
>   Just like a *whurlie-birlie.*

> Here hae I lived this thratty year,
> And never faun I it to steer,
> Goth, thou's a wrang man I cnd sweer,
>   Its no a *whurlie-birlie.*

> At this the astronomer did smile,
> Faith, took a laugh at Daldie's style,
> He was na grave a gye wee while,
>   About the *whurlie-birlie.*

> But Daldie reason'd still awa,
> He cudna swallie this ava,
> How he, his shiel, his wife, and a'
>   Stack on the *whurlie-birlie.*

> While heels owre gowdie every day,
> It whomel'd on the orbit way,
> And sae continued to play,
>   The meikle *whurlie-birlie.*

About some forces thou dis jaw,
I kenna how they act ava,
Centripeedel, Centrifuga',
    To trim the *whurlie-birlie.*

That famous English Isaac man,
Thou say'st did maist the hale ware plan,
And saw exactly how it ran,
    The meikle *whurlie-birlie.*

But him nor you can hardly change
What Daldie thinks wi' ought sae strange,
My mind it may be canna range,
    And seet a *whurlie-burlie.*

Let it be, tho', whate'er it is,
Frae Daldie tak na aught amiss,
There's mony a goaf wi' it maun whizz,
    Gif its a *whurlie-birlie.*

Ise gie't a thought—ay, shake my brain,
And see if aught it doth contain,
O, but wi' scholar-craft my ain,
    To see this *whurlie-birlie.*

But hech! am unco' doaf i'e horn,
A shauler gow was never born,
I sleep ate'en and start i'e morn,
    Upon this *whurlie-birlie.*

O, for the fancy that could streck,
And tow'r aboon the cluds, like reek,
Than I cud crack wi' you a week,
    About this *whurlie-birlie.*

There is another poem in my wallet respecting the peasantry, termed *Auld Wullie Birlie,* and as these poems illustrate the manners of the country people better than prose hints, I feel inclined to give it; and be it understood, when I name not the *author* of any piece, I want my readers to *guess* that, or let it alone, just as they feel:—

Auld Willie Birlie is ane laigh fiel' herd,
 And tharty years he has herded Clinkanco,'
His claes are duffle, something grey his beard,
 And healthfu' habits make him fail but slow.

He trods about wi' his bit halflin trot,
 Ane han' bears *Cloupie,* tither his *coat-tail,*
What skill has he about a *murill'd stott,*
 And croitoch'd cloots the body soon can hail.

Thro' a' the day he is amang the flocks,
 Whiles wi' the cuddochs, whiles amang the sheep,
Unless his cur smells Reynard 'mang the rocks,
 Than owre the hags and noits does Willie leap.

And sometimes gets Tod Lowrie by the tail,
   Than Willie Birlie is ane happy man,
Wi' mighty glee he hameward him doth trail,
   Tells how he *tous'd* him, how he *form'd* his plan.

Baith young and auld like Willie Birlie weel,
   Wi' him few nowt or sheep do ever traik,
And than for him they're a' sae quiet, puir chiel,
   He claws their rumps, their cheeks he'll clap and straik,

Few megrams ever enter Willie's head,
   He likes his auld wife *Meg*, and she likes him,
Their bairns are a' grown up whilk they did breed,
   In England some o'm's gane, the *pack* to trim.

And some o'm ploughs ahame, and daughter Nell
   Is married to ane honest plodding chiel,
And she lues *him*, as well's she lues *hersell*,
   Sae Willie Birlie's family's unco weel.

Quietly has Willie lived, and sae he'll dee,
   He never ken'd what were the ills of life,
He's no a melancholy wretch like me,
   Wi' mankind he had never ony strife.

He never felt the flashing passions mad,
   The burning brains which nothing can assuage,
The sorrowing soul that loveth to be sad,
   And frets for ay, like burdie in a cage,

Upon ilk sunny sabbath afternoon,
   He reads his bible on the green brae side,
And thinks about the joys in heaven aboon,
   And *sacraments* aroun' the countra wide.

The Scriptures Willie never doubt do lee,
   Believes ae passage true, anither no,
Na, na, a wiser, better man is he,
   O were a' mankind like him here below!

Nae growling then wad he 'bout this and that,
   Nae frothy, noisy, vain, translucent fools,
The shoals o' folk *alive* here, weel I wat,
   Wad be as *quiet* as them amang the mools.

O, Willie Birlie, was I but like thee,
   Wad mither nature own me for a child?
O could I ramble with a saul as free
   As you amang the hills and rocks sae wild.

Sink to my grave like thee by calm degrees,
   Hae sic grand hopes beyond that dark abode,
Resign myself to fate's most stern decrees,
   And live in peace with all mankind and God.

WHUSH-SHOW—A call made by sportsmen to start game;
they will rummage the *haunts*, and call *whush-show*, when

wood-cocks are a seeking for. *Whur-cocks* is the call,
when up flutter the birds; whiles poachers *blatter* at them,
and the shot-lead is heard rattling on the trees. *Whush*
also means a *noise* or fame; thus a marriage makes a
whush for a while on a *kintra side,* and any other great
thing. When people marry, and when they die, the character is sounded. *Whushers* and *whusherings,* mean
whispers and whisperings. This book of mine may or
may not make a *whush* for a little ; every dog has his day ;
even *Haggart* the murderer had his:—

VERSES EXTEMPORE, AFTER READING THE LIFE OF HAGGART.

Light-finger'd Davie ye hae been,
   A curious, clever chiel,
But hoch anee, its easy seen,
   Ye hae been a clever de'il.

Thy passions mad, and genius bright
   Did keep thee ay fu' thrang ;
Thou felt the pith o' inward might,
   But let that might gae wrang.

Auld Scotland now has cause to brag,
   Gif she be called upon,
That she has bred as sly a wag,
   As e'er was *Barrington.*

I wat ye war a crafty boy,
   And cud *millvader* fine,
And pump a fallow's *benjie-cloy,*
   'Twas there where ye did shine.

The poet too, I do not doubt,
   His mystic ye did ken,
Ye were like *Savage,* near about,
   And he ca'd famous *Ben.*

For baith o' thae, against the will,
   In some strange frolic wild,
By some queer blow a *man* did kill,
   Yet were not much revil'd.

And Shakspeare, too, lap owre some dykes,
   A graiping *Lucy's deer,*
Big bards are a' big blackguard tykes,
   Nor Burns nor *me* are clear.

Unless the conscience stangs awa,
   Our feelings are a' sham,
Our genius will make nought ava,
   But sangs no worth a damn.

Sae Davie, I lament your fate,
Ye might been—wha can tell?
I hope ye may be the right gate.
And thy *buik* brunt in hell.

WHUSKY PIG—The jar which holds the whisky; *whiskied*, a person is said to be so when a little tipsy.

WHUTSTANE—A whetstone; *whutting o' drink*, a little spirits, which whet the wits; *whutting*, a whispering, a quickening, &c.; *whuttle*, also a whetstone.

WHYRIPE—To mourn. to torment with mourning; thus one always railing against this world, *whyripes*, frets, &c.; a wife of this temper is past enduring: I know some who are ever *whyriping* on their poor devils of husbands. *Whyriping* and *wyringing* are one.

WICKERTON—An old cross-grained b—— of a wife; one of the *de'il's daughters* by the *third wife*.

WILD SCOTS O' GALLOWA—There is now no knowing, I believe, when this term was first applied to our ancestors, nor can the reasons be properly stated why they became honoured with such a title, for an honour of the highest nature it must have been. The word "wild," in my opinion, has something grander about it than either "brave," or "noble." Indeed, it may be said to swallow up every appellation that could possibly be given to a rare warlike race; and when it was bestowed on our forefathers through a long and eventful period of the Scottish history—when every Scotchman of pith was a bowman, a sword-player, skilled in wielding the battle-axe, and quarter-staff— the epithet truly assumes a lofty character. Doubtless many a Scotchman in those ancient days, who was no Gallovidian, enlisted himself under the banner of our "wild men," merely to get amongst glorious "untame" companions; the same as now-a-days with soldiers of "spunk," they would rather be privates in the "Forty-Twa," or "Auld Highlan' Watch," than officers in small fameless regiments.

The situation of Galloway laid it open in these days to war in every quarter; the Southrons infested them by sea and land; and when domestic broils broke out any where in Scotland (things by no means unfrequent), the Gallovidians had a share in the fray. Such work then, as fighting, beating, and plundering foes, they doubtless well understood, and much better, it seems, than any other tribe in Scotland, as ancient books affirm; and Lord Kaims, in his writings on Scotland, says, " That in all the great battles the Scotch had with the English, the *Gallwegians* led the van, led the brave Caledonians on to victory; they were a race of warriors, had no fear either of hunger or death, and were called *The Wild Scots o' Galloway."* Just as the Highlanders now-a-days do, heading the British troops, and driving the enemy before the point of the bayonet. A writer sometime ago in the public prints, made a long harangue against " *The Wild Scots o' Galloway,"* and seemed to have a hide " yeucking" for some Gallovidian to start and " clawt" with a bunch of " breers ;" but no one minded him; they let him fall asleep with the " lees" in his " gizzeron." I have seen nothing but two verses of poetry wrote against him, which are not so bad—

" THE WILD SCOTS O' GALLOWAY."

Wha's this, wha scowling shaws his tusks,
  At our famous auld forefathers?
We doubt he is a foolish gow,
  And fond o' talking blethers.
For wha but a gomerall
  Wad grasp a rung, and whap and blaw
At our worthy frien's o' auld lang syne,
  The Wild Scots o' Gallowa?

For tho' their pantries were na pang'd,
  Nor their kytes weel lin'd wi' belly timmer,
What de'il cared they 'bout Fortune's gifts,
  They damn'd the hizzy for a limmer?
Tame were the ither Scots to them,
  The Southron loons they lo'ed to claw,
Sae patriots ever will revere
  The Wild Scots o' Gallowa.

Wishie-washie—Small drink; ale without foam; whisky without *bells*.

Wizzen'd—Wilted, shrunk; *wallowed*, wasted; from the German *weest*. *Wize*, to guide, to direct. *Wizzen*, or *wyzeron*, the throat; for food is *wized* down it to the stomach.

Woo—Wool; *woo-cards*, carders for wool; *woo-creels*, wicker baskets for holding wool, spheroidal formed, like *spoon-creels*; *woo-teazing*, refining wool.

Wouch—The same with *bouch*, a dog's bark.

> " I had a wee dog, and he wouched at the moon,
> " If my sang be na lang its sooner dune."
> *Auld say.*

The which is frequently said by those unwilling to sing; they plead hoarseness, "or ill wi' the caul;" a gude singer maun ay be *fletched* wi' to sing; and whiles, in lieu of the above, is said—

> " Sing, sing, what shall I sing?
> " The cat ran away wi' my apron-string."

Wow—To wave; he *wow'd* wi his hat—*whan I wow stan fast*; there is an association starts with this phrase, which I am at a loss to explain; probably brother *James* can do it.

Wrack-boxes—Little oval-formed boxes, full of air, found made of and adhering to vegetable sea-weed; what a crackling noise they hold when exploding in a *kelp-kill*, on *Halloween night?* Country lads living by shores are sure to be provided with a stock of these boxes; and when lovers are a burning in the *greeshoch*, in the shape of nuts, some of these boxes are secretly introduced beneath a *red peat*, which in time explode, to the grievous astonishment whiles of the anxious lookers-on, who are not let into all the mysteries, and who believe the tremendous reports to proceed from the *nits*, which at once leads to the conclusion, that an awful eruption will take or has taken place between the sweethearts.

WRAITHS.—Apparitions of a certain kind. Suppose a person in London, saw his dearest friend among the crowd, whom he was sure was living with his wife and family at the *Clauchan o' Darie,* in Galloway, at that same moment, then might that person in the metropolis, say he had seen a *wraith.* Wraiths are therefore the shadows of persons alive; they differ from ghosts, which are the shadows of persons dead. But both wraiths and ghosts are suspected to have more concerning them than a mere shadow. A ghost is always thought to appear for vengeance-sake, being generally these of some wronged or murdered persons. Wraiths, on the other hand, appear as the harbingers of death, and sometimes they appear in the likeness of the person about to die, to the eye; at other times they do not appear to the sight at all, but are heard making various noises. So says superstition about these beings. For my own part, I have neither seen a ghost nor a *wraith* as yet, nor heard or seen any thing supernatural, that I could not in some way or other account for; but all men are not so. I have, in my Legendary Wallet, so frequently spoken of, scores of tales and stories about these and all other creatures of the same stamp, which have been often both seen and heard, and which I would now write down, did I not consider them as too tedious for a work of this description; for, although I be not a great believer in these things, I have my doubts about me, which have made me anxious, from the cradle till now, to preserve and horde up the smallest trifle respecting any thing of the kind. To speak a little farther, however, a young man with whom I am intimately acquainted, and who is never known to tell a lie, neither to me nor any other person; neither was he a believer in *wraiths,* nor any such beings, until the other day there. And here is the cause he gives for the alteration taking place in his belief.—" Last *vacans* (quoth he), I gaed awa to my uncle's,

or rather my granfather's, to stap a-week or twa, and
play mysell amang the Moorhills ; neive trouts, and learn
twar three tunes on the flute ; weel, I hadna been there
ony time aworth, till I saw as queer a thing as ought ever
I saw, or may see. Am out at the house-en ae morning, about aught o'clock, and a bonny harrest morning it
was, weel ye see. Am making a bit *grinwan* to mysell,
to tak down wi' me to a deep pool that was i'the burn, fu'
o' trouts, and this I was gaun to do after breakfast time,
for as yet I hadna gat my sowens ; weel ye see. I'm tying
on my grin wi' a bit o' wax'd thread, whan by the house-
en comes my auld granfather wi' his clicked staff, that
he ay had wi' him in ae han, and in the tither his auld loofie
o' a mitten, which he hadna as yet drawn on. He cam
close by me, and gaed a kinn o' a luik at what I was doing,
then wised himsell awa alang the hip o'e hill, to look how
the nowt did, and twa young foals, as was his usual wont.
Weel, awa he gaed ; I was sae thrang whan he gaed by
that I never spak to him, neither did he to me, and I
began to think about this whan I was mair at laisure, and
gaed a glent the road he tuik, just to see like how the auld
body was coming on, for he was on the borders o' four
score, yet a fearie fell auld carle, and as kine a body as
ever I saw ; sae I gaed a glent, as I was saying, alang by
the scarrow o'e hill, and did see him winglan awa by the
back-side o' the auld saugh Lochan. And in course o'
time, maybe no ten minutes after, I stepped my waes in
to see gin I could get a leap or twa o' sowens, and get
aff to the trouts ; whun wha think ye's just sitting on the
sattle-stane at the ingle-cheek taking a blaw o' the pipe—
but auld granfather—Lord preserve me, said I, and said
na mair ; I glowr'd about me awsomly." " What's wrang
wi' the boy ? (quoth my auntie) ; come out (quo' I), and I'll
tell ye, which she did. We gaed up the hill a bit, to be
sure, as she said, o' the thing I had seen ; we saw nought

ava, cam back again in an unco way. That vera night granfather grew ill, which was on a Saturday teen, and he was dead, puir body, or sax o'clock on Monday morning." The most of the tales I have, are from some who heard them at second hand, *but the tale* I have now told, was told me, as I have said, from the person who saw the wraith himself, and one whom I believe was telling the truth as nearly as any person I ever knew. Another man however, whom I give equal credit to, told me the following :—" That afore he was married, there was nae body lived wi' him i'the house ava, but twa men wha were his labourers, and helped him to work the farm ; ae night thae twa cheels gaed awa a sproagin amang the lasses, and I sat up for their hame-coming till after ten o'clock ; after that I gaed awa to my bed, for there were nae sines o' their coming; but whan I was stripped, and lay in my auld creevie, de'il a wink I coud sleep ; I kentna what was wrang wi' me either, sae I'm lying *dovering*, that's neither sleeping nor waking, but atween the twa ; whan the door gaed the awsomest brange I ever heard, as if somebody had struck it wi' a sledge-hammer ; than I thought it was catched and shooken, as it were, a' to fliners. By this time I was on my feet, and making for't full drive, wi' an auld swoople in my neive, whan I cam till't. The door that I thought was a' in smash, is hingin on its hinges, the same way as whan I gaed lie. I open'd it mair than ance, glowr'd at it wi' the light o' the moon, and gaed out into the close, the length o' the *swine-trough*, but nought saw I, every thing was quiet but my heart, I thought it wad hae jumped clean out o' my brisket; lord! what wallops it gaed. In I cam again, pat on my claise, and waited for my men wi' the greatest anxiety. Pat about half an ounce o' tobacco in my mouth at once, sat down by the fire and whistled on the dogs about me. While sae sitting, the door gets anither brange, up I started, but saw nothing again which I might say was the cause, and what astonished me as meikle as ought, the collies never gaed a single yelp, which, if they had heard the noise, or gin ony human had been about, wi' their gowls and bouchs wad hae been like to bring down the house. I ne'er gaed demented now, and whan the men cam hame about an hour after, they faun' me reeling about like a madman. Ane o' the bound men ay lay wi' me in my bed after that until I gat the wife. Mony a week after I thought about the noise o' the door, whan ae Sunday eve, about three months after, am reading a bit o' the bible, whan a bit neebour boy, cam ben wi' a letter, the seal being *black*, startled me : soon I open it, and what was in it but the doolfu' account o' my brither's death, i'that terrible Jamaica Island. He haud just deed a day or twa after I had heard the unco rumling at the door, which was his *wraith*, nae doubts, lord be wi' him !" But to finish this article : two men once told me the following :—They went into a public-house one day together, to have a bottle o' ale between them, the weather being warm ; when they had the ale decanted out of the bottle, and were just taking their private " crack" together, some invisible hand struck the upper surface of the table three distinct blows, as if with a wand. Nothing on the table was injured by the strokes ; the glasses in which was the ale, were not upset, nothing was deranged in point of situation, but their hearts, as they thought ; up they both started and made for the door, leaving the ale undrank ; in a few days afterwards they heard, to their great grief, that a dear cronie of theirs was no more ; one, when they were all met together, used to sing, " Here are we met, three merry boys." I could fill a quarto volume about *wraiths*, and after I had done, say within myself, that I was just where I started, unable positively to prove their existence, or to deny them totally. On these things as on many

others, every man ought to think for himself. There are
either something real in them, or else they are *day dreams*;
dreams, when the person is even awake. I know the
mind of man may be in this state, particularly, if a mind
of fancy, or imagination, and may even be actually surprised with its own creations; the mind at this time is
in a double state, one part of it, and perhaps its least,
is engaged with what the hands are doing, the other is
on the wild and roaming wander :—

> They see what cannot be told—told—
> The tale which none can unfold ,
> The poet's eye is a telescope,
> What singular worlds 'twill ope, ope.
>
> *English song of mine.*

WROUGHT BANES.—Sprained bones with working; how
often reapers have the *shackle-bane wrought* in the *harrest
time*; many a time my heart has bled to see a sweet young
girl oppressed with this pain, when I had it not in my power
to aid her; the best cure for it, is *working it out*, in the
way it was wrought *in*, sad method, yet the best; when
the bones begin to make a *jirging noise*, they are on the
mending hand; *eel-skins* are bound tightly round the wrists
to prevent this complaint, but I know not whether they
do much good or not.

WUDD.—Mad; *red wud*, stark mad.

WUDWISE—A yellow flower, which grows on bad land, and
has a bitter taste.

WUFF.—A person of a flighty, firey disposition.

WULL.—Will, also wild; *he's run wull*, he's run wild.

WULL NICHOLSON, THE POET.—William Nicholson, the
poet; such is the truth, and the pleasure I feel in saying
so is of the highest kind. William certainly is a rustic
bard of the first degree. Some years ago he published
a little volume, which has more delighted me than many
ten times its size, the beauty of a book is not in its bulk;
indeed, " a great book is a great evil." His bardship
wanders through the country a pedlar, and plays the bag-

pipes; every body is fond of him, his *cracks* are extremely
diverting, so humourous, yet so melancholy; as a song
writer, he may rank with any but Burns; his *Wild-wood-
side—The Braes o' Gallowa—My only hope my Harry, O,*
and some others, are truly excellent; they have all that
simplicity and genius which constitute good Scottish
songs; and as a proof of their worth, they are beginning
to be sung by all the peasantry; when this is the case,
further praise is needless; to Fame they then go, and stand
the brunts of ages unshaken. For all the songs Sir Walter
hath wrote, few or none of them do this, which is certainly much against their longevity; none but a *peasant*
can touch the feelings of the peasantry, to all others they
remain impregnable. My friend William's poems are also
substantial rustic buildings, his *Country Lass* is a dear
creature, and will live at least five hundred years; the tale
has plot, and is touched, if not by a *master's* hand, at
least by an old *journeyman's. Rural Retirement* also is
a favourite with me, particularly that verse

> This life's just like yon toddling burn,
> Tho' cross craigs whiles may stint it,
> Comes soughing by ilk thrawart turn,
> And never looks ahint it.

My wish is, that he will lay down the pack for a while,
and publish whatever other things in MS. he may have
by him; and if he feels loath to do this, let some other
one do it for him; let the world return him his cash for
the pleasure he offers; the hearts of the Scotch have never
been backward in approving genuine worth, and about
Wull Nicholson, there is a melancholy, and an independence, that will ever cause him to be admired by true
Caledonians. And should all mankind desert him, I hope
he will find me never far away; whatever I can do for
the good of that man, so shall it be. If I have a *saxpence* in the world, a part of it be his, and a *word* to
spare, let that be said in his favour.

WULLIE GRAYSON.—Those who have known a man of
original character, never forget him; death may do his
will with him, but memory keeps alive. A pleasure is
felt when speaking of such a man, even although it would
be better sometimes to padlock the tongue respecting him.
When I do so about the departed *Willie Gracie,* properly
William Grayson, I feel these sensations strong; a warmer
hearted, a more humourous and manly fellow than *Willie,*
hath seldom been known. He was a true Gallovidian,
though his father Caleb came from the sister kingdom; he
came, I believe, when very young, and being a tanner by
trade, moreover an industrious, plodding soul, he soon
amassed as much cash as enabled him to purchase the
Tannaree at Millburn, beside Kirkcudbright, where our
hero, Willie, was born. Had his father, the old Englishman, not had so much cash, probably his noble-soul'd son
would have yet been alive, and one of the best of human
beings in Galloway. Poor fellow, the worms are now his
kinsmen; yet still do we see him coming down the street
of his native village, as few are seen coming, who can give
one of his manly swings; there are many independent men,
apparently, who seem not to cringe, and all the rest of it,
at seasons. But Willie was independent always; he in-
herited the glorious gift directly from Nature. At all *balls,*
baptisms, weddings, raffles, jerkins, plys, sprees, and *rows*
of every kind, he made himself a welcome guest; and the
contents of his purse he freely flashed on all occasions,
yes, to the greatest extravagance. He had no fault, as
the *auld wives* said of him, but being *"warst for himsell."*
His mother-wit was of the first kind, none of your Irish
ginger repartee, but broad downright honest Scotch humour, similar to that possessed in such an eminent degree
by the famous Robert Burns. Of mankind, he was an
excellent judge; those whom he thought well of, " ane
might hae rade the *ford* wi' at ony time," as the saying is;

yes, these persons admired by *Willie*, would not have deceived and led those away into *deep water*, who trusted
in them, and there have left them to perish. Of books
he was as good a critic; those he delighted to read, or
those pieces of poetry he quoted; all men of a free natural
disposition do the same; yet for all, ardent spirits overcame him, and he died of apoplexy when about thirty
years of age. Though much given to debauchery, he was
greatly respected and pitied to the last; he was much too
social to do any good in this world, and the best hand at
raising the wind, that perhaps has appeared this century.
He would have started a merry meeting in a twinkling, on
nothing, or about nothing at all; and was still *Willie
Gracie*, whether among a party of the first-rate gentlemen,
or the most ignoble of mankind; for in the course of a
day, often, he would be seen with the greatest and the
meanest of the land; he was just as much at his ease with
the nobleman as the blackguard—still surrounded by that
natural halo of worth which made him always so attractive.
When in gaol for debt, as he now and then had the misfortune to be, when his father would not pay smarts and
clear him out of scrapes, young ladies of the first families in the town showed much compassion for him, and
either sent him books or bottles of spirits to pass away
the time every day, so that the *debtor's room*, where he
was in, was more like a place of good cheer, than a melancholy den in a prison. His favourite toast, when thus
carousing in durance, was, " Here's to the King and
Ma—rg—y M—l—lle, no' forgetting *Sawnie Haugh* and
Mrs. J—lly." Those who know these characters mentioned in the toast, are the only persons who know its
worth. When he was let out of gaol at one time, a gentleman met with him in the street, and after having shook
him kindly by the hand, and asked how he was, began to
wonder how he got to be so *fat* in a place of confinement,

" Wonder nothing about that, (quoth Willie) for how could
I be otherwise, seeing I have been so long *stall* fed."
Indeed, he always had on a most contented garb of flesh,
and stood more than six foot high ; sometimes he had his
whiskers in one cut, sometimes in another ; when walking
about with his majestic air, his head inclined to a side a
little, whiles he would dress like a sailor, and sport his
huge body about in jacket and trowsers, with all the
mariners in the port following in his wake. At other times
he was a horse-jockey, in wide frock coat, and boots bespattered with mud : thus would he toss through the streets
of the old Borough, amongst all the inns and public-houses
as if he was doing an immense business; indeed he was
always throng doing nothing or something less. His acquaintances were most numerous; there were some persons
who knew Willie Grayson in almost every town in Britain
and Ireland, and not a few, perhaps, in the Indies and
the United States of America. He danced and drank at
bridals with great glee, and to see his vast bulk evolving
down a country dance, it inspired the whole party with
mirth, for he was an excellent dancer ; he could not, perhaps, like a light person, " cut double quick time," as it
is called, but he was a master of " *steps*" of his own invention, which were much more amusing. Then he went
through all the ceremonies with such a manly ease, that
when he was performing them they did not seem to be
ceremonies at all. Ladies and gentlemen, young and old,
were all alike fond of the harmless humourous Willie
Gracie. Once when he was at a dancing-school ball,
where a great many young ladies were " gaun through
their steps," as it is said, before their parents, an elderly
lady who was sitting beside our hero, directed his attention
to a young lady then dancing on the floor, and wished him
to give his opinion respecting her—" Is she not just like
an *angel*, that girl there ?" said our married dame to

Wilfie; " I cannot say, (returned he, very serious) for I
have never seen an *angel* yet, wherewith I might compare
her." Indeed his mother-wit was of the first kind, and
anecdotes of his own invention just flowed on him. Great
was his humanity too; once when a hard frost had bound
the river *Dee* with ice from shore to shore, a boy happen-
ing to slide on some weak piece when the thaw had come
on, which broke from the main body, taking the poor
wretch with it furiously down the stream. Grayson being
on the shore, and observing the poor boy thus in the
greatest danger and crying out for help, plunged in
amongst the melted and melting ice, swam to him in spite
of the most chilling cold, and other obstacles, and succeeded in bringing him safe to his desponding parents;
what could exceed this in tenderness and natural sym-
pathy? He was an excellent swimmer for all his vast
bulk; quite a Dr. Franklin or a Byron in the water, and
sometimes too, like that last-mentioned poetic personage,
he would amuse himself in the water with a large New-
foundland dog. In truth, it was the largest and most
strange dog I ever saw, had it not been so, it would
not have been chosen by Willie for a fit companion, as
every article about him was always of the oddest kind;
his *staffs* were unmatched for shape, being always of
strange wood, and of stranger forms; his *snuff-box*, which
was as large as any three of the common sort, was made
after the *soap box* fashion, and always well filled
with the best *Macabaa*, or with the smartest *Irish Blackguard*; and though he snuffed but little himself, he was
not slack in presenting it to others, which he used to do
with the most laughable courtesy. When the volunteers
started, he took to the field with them at once, first in
the cavalry, but being too weighty for his horse to
carry, he left off being *aid-de-camp* to General Gordon,

and became a lieutenant in the infantry; respecting his horsemanship, he was one of the very best at it, notwithstanding his corpulency. Once when he was riding to the Dumfries rood fair, on a small horse he had of a white colour, called *Crap,* he came up with two of the sons of Erin on the road walking on foot, and, says the one to the other, while he was passing them, " Is not that, *Barney,* a damned fine horse ?" " It is, honey, (replied his comrade) but soul, it has its *load* too, I think." With that horse he would ride up and down precipices at fox hunts and other occasions, which frightened good climbers on foot to attempt, for he had very little fear always about him, and was fond of hunting, both on horse and foot ; and fonder of a badger or pole-cat hunt than of any other. He never was a good shot, but he always did *shoot,* whether the game was in reach or not; for, as he said himself, " Who knows where a *blister* may light ?" To shoot young crows he delighted in, particularly when he had a party of people with him who had not shot many guns before, then what fun he had with their blunders ; his raillery surpassed any thing for mirth, and yet was never ill taken by those whom it was pointed at. And a party always attended him of various orders, such as *Nailors* and half-bred *Lawyers*—for he generally carried with him a flask of good spirits, and plenty of cash to buy more when it began to be ebbed ; he was a great friend to the spirit dealers, and would sometimes adorn the shoulders of their wives with shawls, and their bodies with gowns, and for no adulterous motive ; for this crime, or for that of debauching young women, he never was blamed. His charity was of the most extensive nature ; he gave—God knows what he gave away for this purpose, it was so much. Some of those poor people he gave to thanked him, others not, as the charitable ever find. An old woman once rejected a *sheep's head* and *feet* he sent her, saying, " What

use were sic things to her, unless they were *sung*; had
Willie sent me sax pence to fill my cutty wi' tobacco, I
wad hae thanked him in a different way." It was past his
power to behold any being in distress and not try to ame-
liorate it. In short, he run his virtues into vices, by going
to extremes, but he always said—" he could not help
it," which was true, for he could not *" owre himsell,"* as
is said when man wants self controul.

It is needless, however, to speak of his great talents
or his great errors farther; those who knew him best,
know well, that for his abilities they cannot be praised
too much, and his vices enough execrated. Were I as
he was, in somethings I have noticed in the course of
this sketch, I might consider myself very clever indeed;
but in other things, I hope God may keep me clear of
them. Let his errors sink to oblivion though, and
his excellent feelings remain amongst us while a Gallovidian exists.

A friend of his, on hearing of his death, allowed his
soul to break forth in these verses :—

> Poor Willie Gracie, what is this of thee?
>   Art thou gone down to doze within the grave.
> Art thou forsaken every merry spree.
>   Has Death, the Tyrant, got thee made a slave?
> O! but he is a base, a bloody knave,
>   To coop thee up in a cold gloomy urn!
> But vain it is for me at him to rave,
>   For all my sayings he will only spurn,
>   And laughing shout, " thou never shalt return."
>
> But can he hinder me for thee to weep ?
>   And stem the tears that down my cheeks do flow;
> Nay, not unless he lays me down to sleep,
>   Like thee, poor Willie, in the dust below.
> For while I live and wander to and fro
>   On this strange, mystic, silent rolling ball,
> My heart for thee will often beat in woe,
>   And mourn and bleed about thy early fall;
>   For such a man again, I ne'er shall find at all.

I have matter to fill many a sheet in the way I have done about him, but prudence makes me end here with an Epitaph, some one or other composed on him.—

EPITAPH.

Here, in his cold urn
Lies the *King of the Millburn*;
Death has this monarch humbled,
And in this grave his body tumbled.
He was made up of good and ill,
Yet he was warmly loved still;
His heart was ever just and kind,
Big was the man, and big his mind;
The sun hath seldom set his face on
Such a lad as William Grayson.

WULLIE-WAGTAIL—The water-wagtail bird.

WULLSHOCH—A timid courtier; "A faint heart never gains a fair lady;" "None but the brave deserve the fair." "Mori pro patria est dulce"—"To die for one's *country* is sweet," but to die for one's *love* is sweeter. *Wullyart* and *Wullshoch* are one.

WURGILL—This and *Wurling* are one as to meaning; both signify a person of narrow mind, given to this world's care.

WURRICOW—A hobgoblin of rather an infernal order; *cow* is a kind of *de'il*, but *worri-*cow is a worrying de'il; probably some may wish to hear—

THE WAILINGS O' THE WORRICOW.

Whan the sun-light out o' Killhow had gane,
Ane worricow sat on the auld grey stane;
It seem'd to fin' a nedeum, for loud it did grano,
And gaunted out Hech-how-hum.

The neb o't was clouped, and sharp were its claws,
And they chirket on ither its lang thin jaws;
And ay now and than for some, because
It sang dolefu' Hech-how-hum.

"Weel may I, ay, may I, sae may I mourn,"
Quoth it, "for my guid friens o' Bogle Burn,
"I'the Buss o' Biel now they dinna sojourn,
"Billielu-ya-Hech-how-hum."

" Where the hnle was invented, this light o' lair,
" Whilk now to see shining, makes me ay sair,
" It has frighten'd my cronies awa for ever mair,
" Yalloch hu ya, Hech-how-hum."

" Its needless for me now to yoke to and croon
" Aneath the weak beams o' a gibbous moon ;
" For the being scared a' men hae got aboon,
" Taho-a-hu-ya, Hech-how hum."

" And as for my mighty master, the De'il,
" They look on him just like a common chiel ;
" For the power o' his glaumer they never feel,
" O ! hum, O ! yao, Hech-how-hum.

" Through a' kirk-yards now the folk can gang,
" At the mirkest hour, and sing a bit sang,
" They never trimmle, or fins ought wrang,
" Holyaalla, Hech-how-hum."

" Your *Bowrtree Ron* and the *Co' o' Kirclaugh*,
" The *Bullister Glen*, and the *Bucky Haugh*,
" Men now cares na, for, they can gang in them and laugh,
" Bemmle-whara, Hech-how-hum.'

" Curse on the dominies and colleges a',
" For they hin'er us to carry on weel now ava ;
" May knowledge some night again smoor i'the sna,
" Wullin-a-u-ya, Hech-how-hum."

WUTCH-SCORE—Anciently, witches were *scored* or cut above the eyes, to prevent their *cantrips* taking effect. The method they took to prove females having witch-craft was, by throwing them into a deep pool of water; if they *sank* they were no witches, but if they swim'd, they were, and so were taken out, and *brunt* accordingly.

WYLE—To entice, to coax, also a rope-twister.

WYTE—Blame. *Lindsay of Pitscottie,* our worthy and honest Scottish historian sayeth, that *fornication* was to *wyte,* for the Scotch losing the battle of Flodden ; and *St. John,* of Linlithgow, sayeth, that *melling with women* before a battle is what is not right. Our soldiers too had nigh *tint* the battle of Waterloo by *melling at mouth-thankless* the eve before it ; many an officer there was buried in his *dancing pumps* after that *bluidy bout* ; and many have as much cause to be *wyted* for behaviour in that affray, as ever *King Jamie* and *Mrs. Foord* had for theirs —*fy-o-hech*, verbum sat.

Y.

YABBOCK —A chattering, talkative person ; a *gabbock,* sometimes this is pronounced *abbock*. It is nearly the same with *yackuz,* a person who *yacks,* who talks thick ; who ratherly *maunts,* yet is fond of *catting.*

YALLOW-WYMED-ASK—A kind of lizard, with yellow belly and black back, seen in suspicious places, and is supposed to have poison about some of its *hinner-liths*.

YALLOW-YORLINGS—The birds yellow-hammers; sometimes termed *yoits*. These birds, like the *stane-chackers,* are disliked in the country.

YAMMER—To whine, to fret.

YANKER—The same with *Spanker,* a tall, clever girl.

YARK—A blow. *Yarking-on,* lashing away, as on horseback.

YAUD—An old mare. *Yauds,* jaded horses.

YAWP—The cry of a sickly bird ; or one in distress.

YELL—Barren ; a rock is said to be *yell* when it will not quarry but with gunpowder ; a field is said to be *yell* when nothing will grow on it ; a cow is *yell* when she gives no milk, and so on.

YELLOCH—A loud yell. *Yelloching,* yelling loudly. Some Scottish writer says, that " Jonah *yelloched* three days through the City of Niniveh, after the *whaul* spewed him out o' her wyme."

YELLPERS—Dogs which barked or yelped for some time through Galloway. They belonged to a huntsman of the name of Maxwell, who was drowned in Fleet. The people attached some supersition to these *tykes*. A verse of a song on the subject, runs thus—

> " The night was dark, the water stark,
> " And nane to help the man,
> " Sae death accost, and sae was lost
> " Brave Maxwell o' *Strawhan*."

YERL o' HELL—The *Laird o' Slagarie*; one of the wildest wretches ever known in the world. He and his sons neither dreaded hell nor the Devil; they were in the poet's eye when he wrote this strange poem—

THE BURNING O' THE BIBLE.

For a' Auld Scotlan's weel ken'd lair,
  And buiks in volumes mony,
Far a' her lads and lasses fair,
  Sweet, sensible, and bonny ;
Sad sights by orra times arise,
  Oh ! shudderin to the soul,
As that whilk did us a' surprise
  Last year at Auchenhoul
            Ae wild dark night.

There wou'd ane hallion o' a laird
  As mony a ane has seen,
Wha lo'ed to shave a tenant's beard
  Till tears stood in the e'en ;
He was a bachelor, and did hate
  To see a woman body,
And puir fowk durst na gang the gate
  O' that de'il's-scurr, Laird Wuddie,
            To bide a' night.

He was disliked far and near,
  Nane cared for him but twa ;
Twa no unlike the savage bear,
  Black Jock and *Major Gaw.*
The threesome fear'd na heaven nor hell,
  But damn'd, and drunk, and swore,
They aften gaed to the *Blue Bell*,
  And ilk ane waled his whore,
            To pass the night.

Infernal men, to be allow'd
  To live upon the earth ;
Yet it is right that whiles there should
  Big rascals here hae birth.

I I

Sae than we even frae precept, see,
  The right road frae the wrang,
And shun the pain nae saul can dree,
  The conscience that dis stang,
            By day and night.

Weel, at the laird's o' Auchenhoul
  Our wicked three did meet,
As aft they had, and owre the bowl
  Their wild lewd tales repeat.
And ane o' them, the laird himsell,
  The brocket scoolin skyble,
Which ay did rather bear the bell,
  Proposed to *burn the Bible*
            Aff han' that night.

They a' agreed, the buik's brought forth,
  And damn'd a foolish thing,
Containing neither sense nor worth,
  Then intae flames they fling
The word o' gude, our glorious light,
  And trusty guide for ever,
Then swore an aith wi' a' their might,
  " To perish vile deceiver"
            Henceforth that night.

Natur was mad, her thunner cluds
  Row'd blackly, and did battle,
The wun blew heels, owre head the wuds,
  The dawdin hail did brattle.
And cross the lift, the lightning swift,
  In forked wrath did flee,
The white faem frae the waves did drift,
  As glad to lae the sea,
            That awfu' night.

And whiles the man i'the moon wad strive
  At them to hae a peep,
He'd mirkly glowre, then seem to dive
  That moment to the deep ;
As banks o' scud drave ragged past,
  And blash'd upon his face,
For blast on blast, frae the southwast,
  Did ither raging chace,
            That horrid night.

And just ahint the infernal ha,'
  An hay-stack gaed in biaze,
The lightnin strack it, which set a'
  The household in amaze.
And right upon fair Auchenhoul
  The wun the flames did blaw,
To sloken't quick ran every soul,
  And water fast did jaw
            Frae kits that night.

But hoh anee, the waul ran dry,
  Nae mair lay near at han',
The helpers a' gat in a fry,
  And up and down they ran.
Black Jock wad to a neebor farm
  To get mair aid the hallop,
The Major he wad too alarm,
  And aff the de'il did gallop
            On naig that night.

Jock took the near cut through the mess,
  And darkly dawdg'd awa,
But fann' himsell soon at a loss,
  In the *green quakunqua.*
He warroch'd ont, tho' haflins drown'd,
  His claise about him clashin,
Then dawner'd on whar heuchs abound,
  And down dash'd to damnation
            Owre ane that night.

The Major, wi' the drink that he
  Had tooted frae the bicker,
Began to swing, and noop and jee,
  He cudna hauf sit sicker;
His cowt grew reezy, its lang tail
  'Twad swash, and lugs wad birr up,
At length it cuist him, and did trail
  Him hame, by fit i'e stirrup,
            'Thout *head,* tuat night.

The laird himsell did damn and curse,
  And stupified a' roun',
Made an attempt to save his purse,
  Containing ten-score poun'.
He scaled a winnock wi' great risk,
  What reek or lowe cud stap him;
He rave the siller frae the desk,
  But now a trap did snap him,
            Gye snell that night.

While comin through the bore outback
  A rafter down did fa',
Which catch'd a leg, then he did rack,
  And tweest himsell and dra';
But cudna freet, a' he cud rive,
  O! shockin scene to tell,
There hang he, and was fry'd alive,
  E'en or he wan to hell
            That fleysom night.

Up rump and stump did Auchen burn,
  The lairdy and his ha'
They into shuners black did turn,
  Lang or next day did daw;

I I 2

There let them lie, a warning to
Thae haters o' the light ay,
Thae frozen sinners here below
Wha fear na God Almighty,
     By day nor night.
Behold the truth, O! infidels,
It plainly lies afore ye,
Disdain *Tam Paine*, look at yersell's,
A' natur dis implore ye.
Bethink, bethink, or ye may sink,
In that black pit, wide yawnin;
O! why look at it, lae its brink,
And let the light come dawnin
    To fley the night.

YEUCK—The scab, the itch; *yeucky*, itchy. " I'll mak him claw whar he's no *yeucky*;" a phrase, meaning, " I'll strike him with the fist, so that he shall rub himself, though not itchy."

YEUL—To howl, to complain, to whinge.

YICKIE YAWKIE—A tool used by shoe-makers.

YILL-CAUPS—Cups to drink ale out of: those girls with large eyes, are said to have " e'en like *yill-cuups*," *trikle-yill* ale, made from treacle.

YIMMET—A *piece*, a lunch, several *yims* of food.

YIN—One. *Yince*, once.

YIRB-WIVES—Old females, skilled in the virtues of plants and *yirbs*. When a cow takes the *Tailill*, or is *Elfshot*, these females are sent for to cure them. The fact is, they are a species of *witch quack-doctor*.

YIRD-FASTS—Large stones sticking in the *yird*, or earth, that the plough cannot move. *Yird o' Cassle maddie*, a famous place for the fox; see the poem, *Auld Huntsman*. The *cauld yird*, the grave; various emblems of our latter end strike us. On observing an *auld tree* a blawing down by the wind—

Puir auld fallow, ye maun fa,'
And lae thy ither comrades a',
That awfu' gurl which now did bla',
    Has whurl'd ye owr;
To haud the grup with thy daz'd cla,'
    Is past thy pow'r.

Mony a roaring blast, fu' wild
Thou has't weather'd nobly sin' a child,
And at the wrath o' Boreas smil'd,
           Wi' trim'lin glee ;
Until his lordship sour, grew mild,
             But Oh! anee.

The upper han' at last he has gat,
And reel'd thee on thy hench fu' flat,
Nae mair will saucy pyets chat
           Amang thy boughs ;
Whan Bawdrons, the black gib cat,
             Sprawls up, and mews.

Nor burdies hap upon thee, trig,
And nip the green worm aff the twig,
Or sing, or seek for holes to big
           Their wee-bit nests ;
Whare they fu' coozily may lig
             Maist free o' pests.

And, o, I'm sure the craws will yarn,
Whan they in April do return,
And misses you, wha aft has borne,
           Their safest rookery ;
Indeed, there's few (but her) will mourn,
             Wha tents the cookery.

For a' wha hae thy glory seen,
Whan thou haud on thy coat o' green,
And bumbees wheeling through atween
           Thy budding leaves,
May weel lament for thee, I ween,
             Wi' bibbling heaves.

Thou art an emblem plain to me,
The day will come whan I maun be
Capsized on the yird, like thee,
           To rot awa ;
Nae mair the storms o' fate to dree,
             Which roun' me bla'.

YIRM—To chirm like a bird. *Yirms,* small-sized fruit.

YIRNS—Eagles. These birds build about the *Cairn's-moors.*

YIRTH—Earth.

YISK—To hiccup.

YOMF—A blow.

YOUNG-FOWK—People newly married; people beginning the world as it were, *young* in the wars of life.

YULE-BOYS—Boys who ramble the country during the Christmas holidays. They are dressed in *white*, all but *one* in each *gang*, the Belzebub of the corps. They have a foolish kind of a rhyme, they go through before people with, and so receive *bawbees* and *pieces*. This rhyme is now a-days so sadly mutilated, that I can make little of it as to what it means; but it evidently seems to have an ancient origin: and in old Scottish books I see some notice taken of *Quhite boys of Zule*. The plot of the rhyme seems to be, two knights dispute about a female, and fight; the one falls, and Belzebub appears and cures him. I may here give a sketch of something like the scene with the attending rhymes. Enter *Belzebub*, and proceeds—

> Here come I, auld Beelzebub,
> And over my showther I carry a club;
> And in my hand a frying-pan,
> Sae don't ye think I'm a jolly auld man.
> Christmas comes but ance in the year,
> And when it comes it brings good cheer,
> For here are two just going to fight,
> Whether I say 'tis wrong or right.
> My master loves such merry fun,
> And I the same do never shun;
> Their yarking splore with the quarter-staff,
> I almost swear will make me laugh.

The knights enter now, dressed in white robes, with sticks in their hands, and so they have a set-to at sparring, while one of them accompanies the strokes of the sticks with this rhyme—

> Strike then, strike, my boy,
> For I will strike if you are coy,
> I'm lately come frae out the west,
> Where I've made many a spirit rest;
> I've fought in my bloody wars,
> Beyond the sun, among the stars,
> With restless ghosts, and what you know
> Flock there when ere the cock doth crow;
> I've elbow'd thousands into hell,
> My ears delight to hear them yell.
> I've broke the backs of millions more
> Upon that grim infernal shore;

> So strike if your a valiant knight,
> Or I shall knock ye down with might.
> Your proud insults I'll never bear,
> To inches I'll your body tear ;
> If you, my love, can keep, can keep,
> You first must make me sleep, sleep, sleep.

The second Knight now speaks, and the sparring becomes keener:—

> Lash, dash—your staff to crash,
> My fool, have you the water brash?
> If you have not, I soon shall know,
> I soon shall cause you tumble low ;
> So thump away, and I shall fling
> Some blows on you, and make ye ring
> Like ye sounding belly bats,
> To start the music of thy guts ;
> Or clinkers on thy hairy scull,
> To fell thee like a horned bull.
> Reel away who first shall fall
> Must pardon from the other call ;
> Tho' you have fought beyond the sun,
> I find we'll have some goodly fun ;
> For I have boxed in the East,
> To solar furnace toss'd the beast.

First Knight falls, and sings out—

> A doctor ! doctor, or I die—
> " A doctor, doctor, here am I."

Wounded Knight sayeth—

> " What can you cure ?"

Belzebub answereth—

> " All disorders to be sure,
> " The gravel and the gout,
> " The rotting of the snout ;
> " If the devil be in you,
> " I can blow him out
> " Cut off legs and arms,
> " Join them too again
> " By the virtue of my *club*,
> " Up Jack, and fight a main," &c. &c.

Thus a fellow is struck out of *five senses* into *fifteen*.

To conclude the whole matter then, I console myself by singing this little song :—The *Book* personified in my *Love*.

> The wuntry sun's gane down my love,
> And cauld lies the sna ;
> But the spring may soon come roun' my love,
> And thow it a' awa ;

And thow it a' awa, my love,
  While flowers bloom out sae fair;
But the blighted root will never shoot,
  'Twill never flourish mair.

The storm delights to roar, my love,
  The faeming waters flee;
But a calm may lull the shore, my love,
  And smooth the hilly sea;
And smooth the hilly sea, my love,
  Which rows in anger sair;
But the founder'd ship will never trip
  Alang its surface mair.

Our doom is fix'd—we part, my love,
  Thy way is fu' o' wiles;
But ay, keep up thy heart, my love,
  And meet the warl wi' smiles;
And meet the warl wi' smiles, my love,
  Tho' thunders round ye rair,
In darkness sweet, we yet may meet,
  And never sinder mair.

The sun he rules the day, my love,
  The moon she rules the night
But what doth rule thy way, my love?
  What guideth thee aright;
What guideth thee aright, my love,
  On earth and sea and air,
Is *Chance*, the *Blinman*, wha can dance;
  He's wi' thee ever mair.

FINIS.

Lightning Source UK Ltd.
Milton Keynes UK
10 March 2010

151220UK00001B/197/P

9 781845 300517